I0124290

Robert Michael Ballantyne

The Young Fur-Traders

Snowflakes and Sunbeams from the Far North

Robert Michael Ballantyne

The Young Fur-Traders
Snowflakes and Sunbeams from the Far North

ISBN/EAN: 9783743423541

Manufactured in Europe, USA, Canada, Australia, Japa

Cover: Foto ©Suzi / pixelio.de

Manufactured and distributed by brebook publishing software (www.brebook.com)

Robert Michael Ballantyne

The Young Fur-Traders

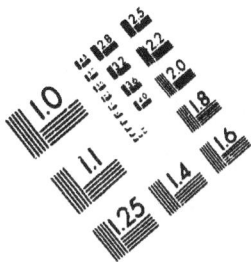

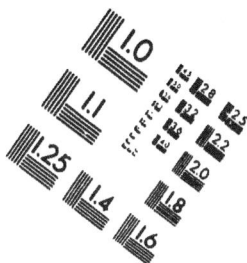

IMAGE EVALUATION
TEST TARGET (MT-3)

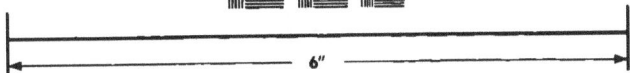

6"

Photographic
Sciences
Corporation

23 WEST MAIN STREET
WEBSTER, N.Y. 14580
(716) 872-4503

CIHM/ICMH
Microfiche
Series.

CIHM/ICMH
Collection de
microfiches.

Canadian Institute for Historical Microreproductions / Institut canadien de microreproductions historiques

© 1983

Technical and Bibliographic Notes/Notes techniques et bibliographiques

The Institute has attempted to obtain the best original copy available for filming. Features of this copy which may be bibliographically unique, which may alter any of the images in the reproduction, or which may significantly change the usual method of filming, are checked below.

L'Institut a microfilmé le meilleur exemplaire qu'il lui a été possible de se procurer. Les détails de cet exemplaire qui sont peut-être uniques du point de vue bibliographique, qui peuvent modifier une image reproduite, ou qui peuvent exiger une modification dans la méthode normale de filmage sont indiqués ci-dessous.

- [ ] Coloured covers/
  Couverture de couleur

- [ ] Covers damaged/
  Couverture endommagée

- [ ] Covers restored and/or laminated/
  Couverture restaurée et/ou pelliculée

- [ ] Cover title missing/
  La titre de couverture manque

- [ ] Coloured maps/
  Cartes géographiques en couleur

- [ ] Coloured ink (i.e. other than blue or black)/
  Encre de couleur (i.e. autre que bleue ou noire)

- [ ] Coloured plates and/or illustrations/
  Planches et/ou illustrations en couleur

- [ ] Bound with other material/
  Relié avec d'autres documents

- [ ] Tight binding may cause shadows or distortion along interior margin/
  La reliure serrée peut causer de l'ombre ou de la distortion le long de la marge intérieure

- [ ] Blank leaves added during restoration may appear within the text. Whenever possible, these have been omitted from filming/
  Il se peut que certaines pages blanches ajoutées lors d'une restauration apparaissent dans le texte, mais, lorsque cela était possible, ces pages n'ont pas été filmées.

- [ ] Additional comments:/
  Commentaires supplémentaires:

- [ ] Coloured pages/
  Pages de couleur

- [x] Pages damaged/
  Pages endommagées

- [x] Pages restored and/or laminated/
  Pages restaurées et/ou pelliculées

- [x] Pages discoloured, stained or foxed/
  Pages décolorées, tachetées ou piquées

- [ ] Pages detached/
  Pages détachées

- [x] Showthrough/
  Transparence

- [x] Quality of print varies/
  Qualité inégale de l'impression

- [ ] Includes supplementary material/
  Comprend du matériel supplémentaire

- [ ] Only edition available/
  Seule édition disponible

- [ ] Pages wholly or partially obscured by errata slips, tissues, etc., have been refilmed to ensure the best possible image/
  Les pages totalement ou partiellement obscurcies par un feuillet d'errata, une pelure, etc., ont été filmées à nouveau de façon à obtenir la meilleure image possible.

This item is filmed at the reduction ratio checked below/
Ce document est filmé au taux de réduction indiqué ci-dessous.

The copy filmed here has been reproduced thanks to the generosity of:

National Library of Canada

The images appearing here are the best quality possible considering the condition and legibility of the original copy and in keeping with the filming contract specifications.

Original copies in printed paper covers are filmed beginning with the front cover and ending on the last page with a printed or illustrated impression, or the back cover when appropriate. All other original copies are filmed beginning on the first page with a printed or illustrated impression, and ending on the last page with a printed or illustrated impression.

The last recorded frame on each microfiche shall contain the symbol → (meaning "CONTINUED"), or the symbol ▽ (meaning "END"), whichever applies.

Maps, plates, charts, etc., may be filmed at different reduction ratios. Those too large to be entirely included in one exposure are filmed beginning in the upper left hand corner, left to right and top to bottom, as many frames as required. The following diagrams illustrate the method:

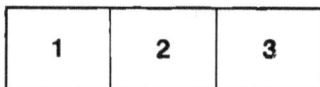

L'exemplaire filmé fut reproduit grâce à la générosité de:

Bibliothèque nationale du Canada

Les images suivantes ont été reproduites avec le plus grand soin, compte tenu de la condition et de la netteté de l'exemplaire filmé, et en conformité avec les conditions du contrat de filmage.

Les exemplaires originaux dont la couverture en papier est imprimée sont filmés en commençant par le premier plat et en terminant soit par la dernière page qui comporte une empreinte d'impression ou d'illustration, soit par le second plat, selon le cas. Tous les autres exemplaires originaux sont filmés en commençant par la première page qui comporte une empreinte d'impression ou d'illustration et en terminant par la dernière page qui comporte une telle empreinte.

Un des symboles suivants apparaîtra sur la dernière image de chaque microfiche, selon le cas: le symbole → signifie "A SUIVRE", le symbole ▽ signifie "FIN".

Les cartes, planches, tableaux, etc., peuvent être filmés à des taux de réduction différents. Lorsque le document est trop grand pour être reproduit en un seul cliché, il est filmé à partir de l'angle supérieur gauche, de gauche à droite, et de haut en bas, en prenant le nombre d'images nécessaire. Les diagrammes suivants illustrent la méthode.

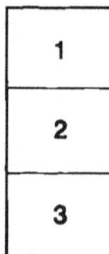

1	2	3

1
2
3

THE INDIANS LISTENING TO THE SONG.

THE
YOUNG FUR TRADERS
SNOW FLAKES

SUNBEAMS

from the

FAR NORTH

F U I

SONS

THE YOUNG
FUR-TRADERS;

OR,

SNOWFLAKES AND SUNBEAMS FROM
THE FAR NORTH.

BY

R. M. BALLANTYNE,

AUTHOR OF "HUDSON BAY," "THE CORAL ISLAND,"
"THE DOG CRUSOE," ETC.

WITH ILLUSTRATIONS.

London:

T. NELSON AND SONS, PATERNOSTER ROW.
EDINBURGH; AND NEW YORK.

1881.

PZ 7
Ball⋅⋅
⋅⋅⋅
⋅⋅⋅

135299

BALLANTYNE, M

PREFACE.

In writing this book my desire has been to draw
an exact copy of the picture which is indelibly
stamped on my own memory. I have carefully
avoided exaggeration in everything of importance.
All the chief, and most of the minor incidents are
facts. In regard to unimportant matters I have
taken the liberty of a novelist,—not to colour too
highly, or to invent improbabilities, but,—to trans-
pose time, place, and circumstance at pleasure;
while, at the same time, I have endeavoured to
convey to the reader's mind a truthful impression
of the *general effect*,—to use a painter's language,—
of the life and country of the Fur Trader.

Edinburgh, 1856

CONTENTS

SNOWFLAKES AND SUNBEAMS

FROM

THE FAR NORTH.

— ———

CHAPTER I.

Plunges the reader into the middle of an Arctic Winter; conveys him into the heart of the Wildernesses of North America; and introduces him to some of the principal personages of our Tale.

SNOWFLAKES and sunbeams, heat and cold, winter and summer, alternated with their wonted regularity for fifteen years in the wild regions of the Far North. During this space of time, the hero of our tale sprouted from babyhood to boyhood, passed through the usual amount of accidents, ailments, and vicissitudes incidental to those periods of life, and, finally, entered upon that ambiguous condition that precedes early manhood.

It was a clear cold winter's day. The sunbeams of summer were long past, and snowflakes had fallen thickly on the banks of Red River. Charley sat on a lump of

blue ice, his head drooping, and his eyes bent on the
snow at his feet, with an expression of deep disconsolation.

Kate reclined at Charley's side, looking wistfully up in
his expressive face, as if to read the thoughts that were
chasing each other through his mind, like the ever-vary-
ing clouds that floated in the winter sky above. It was
quite evident to the most careless observer, that, whatever might be the usual temperaments of the boy and
girl, their present state of mind was not joyous, but, on
the contrary, very sad.

"It won't do, sister Kate," said Charley; "I've tried
him over and over again; I've implored, begged, and
entreated him to let me go; but he won't—and I'm determined to run away, so there's an end of it!"

As Charley gave utterance to this unalterable resolution, he rose from the bit of blue ice, and, taking Kate
by the hand, led her over the frozen river, climbed up
the bank on the opposite side—an operation of some difficulty, owing to the snow, which had been drifted so deeply
during a late storm that the usual track was almost obli-
terated—and, turning into a path that lost itself among
the willows, they speedily disappeared.

As it is possible our reader may desire to know who
Charley and Kate are, and the part of the world in which
they dwell, we will interrupt the thread of our narrative
to explain.

In the very centre of the great continent of North
America, far removed from the abodes of civilised men,
and about twenty miles to the south of Lake Winipeg, ex-
ists a colony, composed of Indians, Scotchmen, and French-
Canadians, which is known by the name of Red River
Settlement. Red River differs from most colonies in

more respects than one—the chief differences being, that whereas other colonies cluster on the sea-coast, this one lies many hundreds of miles in the interior of the country, and is surrounded by a wilderness; and, while other colonies, acting on the golden rule, export their produce in return for goods imported, this of Red River imports a large quantity and exports nothing, or next to nothing. Not but that it *might* export, if it only had an outlet or a market; but, being eight hundred miles removed from the sea, and five hundred miles from the nearest market, with a series of rivers, lakes, rapids, and cataracts separating from the one, and a wide sweep of treeless prairie dividing from the other, the settlers have long since come to the conclusion that they were born to consume their own produce, and so regulate the extent of their farming operations by the strength of their appetites. Of course, there are many of the necessaries, or at least the luxuries, of life, which the colonists cannot grow—such as tea, coffee, sugar, coats, trowsers, and shirts; and which, consequently, they procure from England, by means of the Hudson's Bay Fur Company's ships, which sail once a-year from Gravesend, laden with supplies for the trade carried on with the Indians. And the bales containing these articles are conveyed in boats up the rivers, carried past the waterfalls and rapids overland on the shoulders of stalwart *royageurs*, and, finally, landed at Red River, after a rough trip of many weeks' duration. The colony was founded in 1811, by the Earl of Selkirk, previously to which it had been a trading post of the Fur Company. At the time of which we write, it contained about 5000 souls, and extended upwards of fifty miles along the Red and Assinaboine rivers, which streams sup-

plied the settlers with a variety of excellent fish.   The
banks were clothed with fine trees; and immediately behind the settlement lay the great prairies, which extend
in undulating waves—almost entirely devoid of shrub or
tree—to the base of the Rocky Mountains.

Although far removed from the civilised world, and
containing within its precincts much that is savage, and
very little that is refined, Red River is quite a popu-
lous paradise, as compared with the desolate, solitary
establishments of the Hudson's Bay Fur Company. These
lonely dwellings of the trader are scattered far and wide
over the whole continent—north, south, east, and west.
Their population generally amounts to eight or ten men
—seldom to thirty.   They are planted in the thick of
an uninhabited desert—their next neighbours being from
two to five hundred miles off—their occasional visitors,
bands of wandering Indians—and the sole object of their
existence being to trade the furry hides of foxes, martens,
beavers, badgers, bears, buffaloes, and wolves.   It will
not, then, be deemed a matter of wonder, that the gentlemen who have charge of these establishments, and who,
perchance, may have spent ten or twenty years in them,
should look upon the colony of Red River as a species of
Elysium—a sort of haven of rest, in which they may lay
their weary heads, and spend the remainder of their days
in peaceful felicity, free from the cares of a residence
among wild beasts and wild men.   Many of the retiring
traders prefer casting their lot in Canada; but not a few
of them *smoke* out the remainder of their existence in this
colony—especially those who, having left home as boys
fifty or sixty years before, cannot reasonably expect to
find the friends of their childhood where they left them,

and cannot hope to re-model tastes and habits long nurtured in the backwoods, so as to relish the manners and customs of civilised society.

Such an one was old Frank Kennedy, who, sixty years before the date of our story, ran away from school in Scotland ; got a severe thrashing from his father for so doing, and, having no mother in whose sympathising bosom he could weep out his sorrow, ran away from home, went to sea, ran away from his ship while she lay at anchor in the harbour of New York, and after leading a wandering, unsettled life for several years—during which he had been alternately a clerk, a day-labourer, a store-keeper, and a village-schoolmaster—he wound up by entering the service of the Hudson's Bay Company, in which he obtained an insight into savage life, a comfortable fortune, besides a half-breed wife and a large family.

Being a man of great energy and courage, and, moreover, possessed of a large, powerful frame, he was sent to one of the most distant posts on the Mackenzie River, as being admirably suited for the display of his powers both mental and physical. Here the small-pox broke out among the natives ; and, besides carrying off hundreds of these poor creatures, robbed Mr Kennedy of all his children save two, Charles and Kate, whom we have already introduced to the reader.

About the same time the council which is annually held at Red River in spring, for the purpose of arranging the affairs of the country for the ensuing year, thought proper to appoint Mr Kennedy to a still more outlandish part of the country—as near, in fact, to the North Pole as it was possible for mortal man to live,—and sent him

an order to proceed to his destination without loss of
time. On receiving this communication, Mr Kennedy
upset his chair, stamped his foot, ground his teeth, and
vowed, in the hearing of his wife and children, that,
sooner than obey the mandate, he would see the governors
and council of Rupert's Land hanged, quartered, and
boiled down into tallow! Ebullitions of this kind were
peculiar to Frank Kennedy, and meant *nothing*. They
were simply the safety-valves to his superabundant ire—
and, like safety-valves in general, made much noise but
did no damage. It was well, however, on such occasions
to keep out of the old fur-trader's way, for he had an
irresistible propensity to hit out at whatever stood before
him—especially if the object stood on a level with his
own eyes and wore whiskers. On second thoughts, how
ever, he sat down before his writing-table, took a sheet
of blue ruled foolscap paper, seized a quill which he had
mended six months previously, at a time when he happened to be in high good-humour, and wrote as follows :—

FORT PASKISEGUN,
June 15th, 18—.

To the Governor and Council of Rupert's Land,
    Red River Settlement.

GENTLEMEN,—I have the honour to acknowledge re-
ceipt of your favour of 26th April last, appointing me
to the charge of Peel's River, and directing me to strike
out new channels of trade in that quarter. In reply
I have to state that I shall have the honour to fulfil your
instructions by taking my departure in a light canoe
as soon as possible. At the same time I beg humbly
to submit, that the state of my health is such as to render
it expedient for me to retire from the service, and I

herewith beg to hand in my resignation. I shall hope to
be relieved early next spring.—I have the honour to be,
gentlemen, your most obedient humble servant,

F. KENNEDY.

"There!" exclaimed the old gentleman, in a tone that
would lead one to suppose he had signed the death-
warrant, and so had irrevocably fixed the certain destruction, of the entire council—"there!" said he, rising
from his chair and sticking the quill into the ink-bottle
with a *dab* that split it up to the feather, and so rendered
it *hors de combat* for all time coming.

To this letter the council gave a short reply, accepting
his resignation, and appointing a successor. On the
following spring, old Mr Kennedy embarked his wife and
children in a bark canoe, and in process of time landed
them safely in Red River Settlement. Here he purchased a house with six acres of land, in which he planted
a variety of useful vegetables, and built a summer-house,
after the fashion of a conservatory, where he was wont to
solace himself for hours together with a pipe, or, rather,
with dozens of pipes, of Canada twist tobacco.

After this he put his two children to school. The
settlement was, at this time, fortunate in having a most
excellent academy, which was conducted by a very
estimable man. Charles and Kate Kennedy, being
obedient and clever, made rapid progress under his judi-
cious management; and the only fault that he had to find
with the young people was, that Kate was a little too
quiet and fond of books, while Charley was a little too
riotous and fond of fun.

When Charles arrived at the age of fifteen and Kate

attained to fourteen years, old Mr Kennedy went into
his conservatory, locked the door, sat down on an easy
chair, filled a long clay pipe with his beloved tobacco,
smoked vigorously for ten minutes, and fell fast asleep.
In this condition he remained until the pipe fell from his
lips and broke in fragments on the floor. He then rose,
filled another pipe, and sat down to meditate on the subject that had brought him to his smoking apartment.
"There's my wife," said he, looking at the bowl of his
pipe, as if he were addressing himself to it, "she's getting
too old to be looking after everything herself (*puff*), and
Kate's getting too old to be humbugging any longer with
books; besides she ought to be at home learning to keep
house, and help her mother, and cut the baccy (*puff*), and
that young scamp Charley should be entering the service
(*puff*); he's clever enough now to trade beaver and bears
from the red-skins, besides he's (*puff*) a young rascal, and
I'll be bound does nothing but lead the other boys into (*puff*)
mischief—although, to be sure, the master *does* say he's
the cleverest fellow in the school; but he must be reined
up a bit now. I'll clap on a double curb and martingale.
I'll get him a situation in the counting-room at the fort
(*puff*), where he'll have his nose held tight to the grind-
stone. Yes, I'll fix both their flints to-morrow,"—and old
Mr Kennedy gave vent to another puff so thick and long,
that it seemed as if all the previous puffs had concealed
themselves up to this moment within his capacious chest,
and rushed out at last in one thick and long-continued
stream.

By "fixing their flints," Mr Kennedy meant to express
the fact, that he intended to place his children in an
entirely new sphere of action; and, with a view to this,

he ordered out his horse and cariole* on the following morning, went up to the school, which was about ten miles distant from his abode, and brought his children home with him the same evening. Kate was now formally installed as housekeeper and tobacco-cutter ; while Charley was told that his future destiny was to wield the quill in the service of the Hudson's Bay Company, and that he might take a week to think over it. Quiet, warm-hearted, affectionate Kate was overjoyed at the thought of being a help and comfort to her old father and mother ; but reckless, joyous, good-humoured, hare-brained Charley was cast into the depths of despair at the idea of spending the live-long day, and day after day, for years it might be, on the top of a long-legged stool. In fact, poor Charley said that he "would rather become a buffalo than do it." Now, this was very wrong of Charley, for, of course, he didn't *mean* it. Indeed, it is too much a habit among little boys, aye, and among grown-up people too, to say what they don't mean ; as, no doubt, you are aware, dear reader, if you possess half the self-knowledge we give you credit for ; and we cannot too strongly remonstrate with ourself and others against the practice—leading, as it does, to all sorts of absurd exaggerations, such as gravely asserting that we are *broiling hot*, when we are simply *rather warm*, or, more than *half dead* with fatigue, when we are merely *very tired*. However, Charley *said* that he would rather be "a buffalo than do it," and so we feel bound in honour to record the fact.

Charley and Kate were warmly attached to each other. Moreover, they had been, ever since they could walk, in the habit of mingling their little joys and sorrows in each

* A sort of sleigh.

other's bosoms ; and although, as years flew past, they gradually ceased to sob in each other's arms at every little mishap, they did not cease to interchange their inmost thoughts, and to mingle their tears when occasion called them forth. They knew the power, the inexpressible sweetness, of sympathy. They understood, experiment- ally, the comfort and joy that flow from obedience to that blessed commandment, to " rejoice with those that do re- joice, and weep with those that weep." It was natural, therefore, that on Mr Kennedy announcing his decrees, Charley and Kate should hasten to some retired spot where they could commune in solitude ; the effect of which communing was, to reduce them to a somewhat calmer and rather happy state of mind. Charley's sorrow was blunted by sympathy with Kate's joy, and Kate's joy was subdued by sympathy with Charley's sorrow ; so that, after the first effervescing burst, they settled down into a calm and comfortable state of flatness, with very red eyes and exceedingly pensive minds. We must, however, do Charley the justice to say, that the red eyes applied only to Kate ; for, although a tear or two could, without much coaxing, be induced to hop over his sun- burnt cheek, he had got beyond that period of life when boys are addicted to (we must give the word, though not pretty, because it is eminently expressive) *blubbering.*

A week later found Charley and his sister seated on the lump of blue ice where they were first introduced to the reader, and where Charley announced his unalterable resolve to run away ; following it up with the statement, that *that* was " the end of it." He was quite mistaken, however, for that was by no means the end of it. In fact it was only the beginning of it, as we shall see hereafter.

CHAPTER II.

The old fur-trader endeavours to " fix " his son's " filit," and finds the thing
more difficult to do than he expected.

NEAR the centre of the colony of Red River, the stream
from which the settlement derives its name is joined by
another, called the Assinaboine.   About five or six
hundred yards from the point where this union takes
place, and on the banks of the latter stream, stands the
Hudson's Bay Company's trading post, Fort Garry.   It is
a massive square building of stone.   Four high and thick
walls enclose a space of ground on which are built six or
eight wooden houses, some of which are used as dwellings
for the servants of the Hudson's Bay Company, and
others as stores, wherein are contained the furs, the provisions which are sent annually to various parts of the
country, and the goods (such as cloth, guns, powder and
shot, blankets, twine, axes, knives, &c., &c.) with which
the fur-trade is carried on.   Although Red River is a
peaceful colony, and not at all likely to be assaulted by
the poor Indians, it was, nevertheless, deemed prudent
by the traders to make some show of power ; and so, at
the corners of the fort, four round bastions of a very
imposing appearance were built, from the embrazures of
which several large black-muzzled guns protruded.   No
one ever conceived the idea of firing these engines of
war ; and, indeed, it is highly probable that such an

2

attempt would have been attended with consequences much more dreadful to those *behind* than to those who might chance to be in front of the guns. Nevertheless, they were imposing, and harmonised well with the flagstaff, which was the only other military symptom about the place. This latter was used on particular occasions, such as the arrival or departure of a brigade of boats, for the purpose of displaying the folds of a red flag, on which were the letters H. B. C.

The fort stood, as we have said, on the banks of the Assinaboine river, on the opposite side of which the land was somewhat wooded, though not heavily, with oak, maple, poplar, aspens, and willows, while, at the back of the fort, the great prairie rolled out like a green sea to the horizon, and far beyond that again to the base of the Rocky Mountains. The plains at this time, however, were a sheet of unbroken snow, and the river a mass of solid ice.

It was noon on the day following that on which our friend Charley had threatened rebellion, when a tall elderly man might have been seen standing at the back gate of Fort Garry, gazing wistfully out into the prairie in the direction of the lower part of the settlement. He was watching a small speck which moved rapidly over the snow in the direction of the fort.

" It's very like our friend Frank Kennedy," said he to himself (at least we presume so, for there was no one else within earshot to whom he could have said it, except the door-post, which, every one knows, is proverbially a deaf subject). " No man in the settlement drives so furiously. I shouldn't wonder if he ran against the corner of the new fence now. Ha! just so—there he goes!"

And, truly, the reckless driver did "go" just at that moment. He came up to the corner of the new fence, where the road took a rather abrupt turn, in a style that insured a capsize. In another second, the spirited horse turned sharp round, the sleigh turned sharp over, and the occupant was pitched out at full length, while a black object, that might have been mistaken for his hat, rose from his side like a rocket, and, flying over him, landed on the snow several yards beyond. A faint shout was heard to float on the breeze as this catastrophe occurred, and the driver was seen to jump up and re-adjust himself in the cariole; while the other black object proved itself not to be a hat, by getting hastily up on a pair of legs, and scrambling back to the seat from which it had been so unceremoniously ejected.

In a few minutes more the cheerful tinkling of the merry sleigh-bells was heard, and Frank Kennedy accompanied by his hopeful son Charles, dashed up to the gate, and pulled up with a jerk.

"Ha! Grant, my fine fellow, how are you?" exclaimed Mr Kennedy, senior, as he disengaged himself from the heavy folds of the buffalo robe, and shook the snow from his greatcoat. "Why on earth, man, don't you put up a sign-post and a board to warn travellers that you've been running out new fences and changing the road, eh?"

"Why, my good friend," said Mr Grant, smiling, "the fence and the road are of themselves pretty conclusive proof to most men that the road is changed; and, besides, we don't often have people driving round corners at full gallop; but ——"

"Hallo! Charley, you rascal," interrupted Mr Kennedy —"here, take the mare to the stable, and don't drive her

too fast. Mind, now, no going off upon the wrong road
for the sake of a drive, you understand."

"All right, father," exclaimed the boy, while a bright
smile lit up his features and displayed two rows of white
teeth—"I'll be particularly careful;" and he sprang into
the light vehicle, seized the reins, and with a sharp crack
of the whip dashed down the road at a hard gallop.

"He's a fine fellow that son of yours," said Mr Grant,
"and will make a first-rate fur-trader."

"Fur-trader!" exclaimed Mr Kennedy—"just look at
him! I'll be shot if he isn't thrashing the mare as if she
were made of leather." The old man's ire was rising
rapidly as he heard the whip crack every now and then,
and saw the mare bound madly over the snow.

"And see!" he continued, "I declare he *has* taken
the wrong turn after all."

"True," said Mr Grant; "he'll never reach the
stable by that road—he's much more likely to visit the
White-horse Plains. But come, friend, it's of no use
fretting. Charley will soon tire of his ride, so come with
me to my room and have a pipe before dinner."

Old Mr Kennedy gave a short groan of despair, shook
his fist at the form of his retreating son, and accompanied
his friend to the house.

It must not be supposed that Frank Kennedy was
very deeply offended with his son, although he did shower
on him a considerable amount of abuse. On the contrary,
he loved him very much. But it was the old man's nature
to give way to little bursts of passion on almost every
occasion in which his feelings were at all excited. These
bursts, however, were like the little puffs that ripple the
surface of the sea on a calm summer's day. They were

over in a second, and left his good-humoured, rough,
candid countenance in unruffled serenity. Charley knew
this well, and loved his father tenderly, so that his con
science frequently smote him for raising his anger so
often; and he over and over again promised his sister Kate
to do his best to refrain from doing anything that was
likely to annoy the old man in future. But alas! Charley's
resolves, like those of many other boys, were soon forgotten, and his father's equanimity was upset generally
two or three times a-day; but after the gust was over,
the fur-trader would kiss his son, call him a "rascal,"
and send him off to fill and fetch his pipe.

Mr Grant, who was in charge of Fort Garry, led the
way to his smoking apartment, where the two were soon
seated in front of a roaring log-fire, emulating each other
in the manufacture of smoke.

"Well, Kennedy," said Mr Grant, throwing himself
back in his chair, elevating his chin, and emitting a long,
thin stream of white vapour from his lips, through which
he gazed at his friend complacently, "Well, Kennedy, to
what fortunate chance am I indebted for this visit? It
is not often that we have the pleasure of seeing you
here."

Mr Kennedy created two large volumes of smoke,
which, by means of a vigorous puff, he sent rolling over
towards his friend, and said, "Charley."

"And what of Charley?" said Mr Grant, with a smile,
for he was well aware of the boy's propensity to fun, and
of the father's desire to curb it.

"The fact is," replied Kennedy, "that Charley must
be broke. He's the wildest colt I ever had to tame, but
I'll do it—I will—that's a fact."

If Charley's subjugation had depended on the rapidity
with which the little white clouds proceeded from his
sire's mouth, there is no doubt that it would have been a
"fact" in a very short time, for they rushed from him
with the violence of a high wind. Long habit had made
the old trader and his pipe not only inseparable companions, but part and parcel of each other—so intimately
connected that a change in the one was sure to produce
a sympathetic change in the other. In the present
instance, the little clouds rapidly increased in size and
number as the old gentleman thought on the obstinacy of
his "colt."

"Yes," he continued, after a moment's silence, "I've
made up my mind to tame him, and I want *you*, Mr
Grant, to help me."

Mr Grant looked as if he would rather not undertake
to lend his aid in a work that was evidently difficult ; but,
being a good-natured man, he said, "And how, friend,
can I assist in the operation ?"

"Well, you see, Charley's a good fellow at bottom, and a
clever fellow too—at least so says the schoolmaster—
though I must confess, that so far as my experience goes,
he's only clever at finding out excuses for not doing what
I want him to. But still, I'm told he's clever, and can
use his pen well ; and I know for certain that he can use
his tongue well. So I want to get him into the service,
and have him placed in a situation where he shall have to
stick to his desk all day. In fact, I want to have him
broken in to work ; for you've no notion, sir, how that
boy talks about bears and buffaloes and badgers, and life
in the woods among the Indians. I do believe," continued
the old gentleman, waxing warm, "that he would willingly

go into the woods to-morrow, if I would let him, and never shew his nose in the settlement again. He's quite incorrigible. But I'll tame him yet; I will!"

Mr Kennedy followed this up with an indignant grunt, and a puff of smoke, so thick, and propelled with such vigour, that it rolled and curled in fantastic evolutions towards the ceiling, as if it were unable to control itself with delight at the absolute certainty of Charley being tamed at last.

Mr Grant, however, shook his head, and remained for five minutes in profound silence, during which time the two friends puffed in concert, until they began to grow quite indistinct and ghost-like in the thick atmosphere.

At last he broke silence.

"My opinion is, that you're wrong, Mr Kennedy. No doubt, you know the disposition of your son better than I do; but even judging of it from what you have said, I'm quite sure that a sedentary life will ruin him."

"Ruin him! Humbug!" said Kennedy, who never failed to express his opinion at the shortest notice, and in the plainest language,—a fact so well known by his friends, that they had got into the habit of taking no notice of it. "Humbug!" he repeated, "perfect humbug! You don't mean to tell me, that the way to break him in, is to let him run loose and wild whenever and wherever he pleases?"

"By no means. But you may rest assured that tying him down won't do it."

"Nonsense!" said Mr Kennedy, testily; "don't tell me. Have I not broken in young colts by the score? and don't I know that the way to fix their flints, is to clap on a good strong curb?"

"If you had travelled farther south, friend," replied Mr Grant, "you would have seen the Spaniards of Mexico break in their wild horses in a very different way: for, after catching one with the lasso, a fellow gets on his back, and gives it the rein and the whip—aye, and the spur, too; and before that race is over, there is no need for a curb."

"What!" exclaimed Kennedy, "and do you mean to argue from that, that I should let Charley run—and *help* him too? Send him off to the woods with gun and blanket, canoe and tent, all complete?" The old gentleman puffed a furious puff, and broke into a loud sarcastic laugh.

"No, no," interrupted Mr Grant; "I don't exactly mean that; but I think that you might give him his way for a year or so. He's a fine, active, generous fellow; and after the novelty wore off, he would be in a much better frame of mind to listen to your proposals. Besides," (and Mr Grant smiled expressively), "Charley is somewhat like his father. He has got a will of his own; and if you do not give him his way, I very much fear that he'll ——"

"What?" inquired Mr Kennedy, abruptly.

"Take it," said Mr Grant.

The puff that burst from Mr Kennedy's lips, on hearing this, would have done credit to a thirty-six pounder.

"Take it!" said he. "He'd *better* not."

The latter part of this speech was not, in itself, of a nature calculated to convey much; but the tone of the old trader's voice, the contraction of his eyebrows, and, above all, the overwhelming flow of cloudlets that followed, imparted to it a significance that induced the belief that Charley's taking his own way would be productive of more terrific consequences than it was in the power of the most highly imaginative man to conceive.

"There's his sister Kate, now," continued the old gentleman; "she's as gentle and biddable as a lamb. I've only to say a word, and she's off like a shot to do my bidding; and she does it with such a sweet smile too." There was a touch of pathos in the old trader's voice as he said this. He was a man of strong feeling, and as impulsive in his tenderness as in his wrath. "But that rascal, Charley," he continued, "is quite different. He's obstinate as a mule. To be sure, he has a good temper; and I must say for him he never goes into the sulks, which is a comfort, for, of all things in the world, sulking is the most childish and contemptible. He *generally* does what I bid him, too. But he's *always* getting into scrapes of one kind or other. And during the last week, notwithstanding all I can say to him, he won't admit that the best thing for him is to get a place in your counting-room, with the prospect of rapid promotion in the service. Very odd. I can't understand it at all;" and Mr Kennedy heaved a deep sigh.

"Did you ever explain to him the prospects that he would have in the situation you propose for him?" inquired Mr Grant.

"Can't say I ever did."

"Did you ever point out the probable end of a life spent in the woods?"

"No."

"Nor suggest to him that the appointment to the office here would only be temporary, and to see how he got on in it?"

" Certainly not."

" Then, my dear sir, I'm not surprised that Charley
rebels. You have left him to suppose that, once placed
at the desk here, he is a prisoner for life. But see, there
he is," said Mr Grant, pointing, as he spoke, towards the
subject of their conversation, who was passing the window
at the moment, " let me call him, and I feel certain that
he will listen to reason in a few minutes."

" Humph !" ejaculated Mr Kennedy, " you may try."

In another minute Charley had been summoned, and
was seated, cap in hand, near the door.

" Charley, my boy," began Mr Grant, standing with
his back to the fire, his feet pretty wide apart, and his
coat-tails under his arms—" Charley, my boy, your father
has just been speaking of you. He is very anxious that
you should enter the service of the Hudson's Bay Company ; and as you are a clever boy and a good penman,
we think that you would be likely to get on if placed for
a year or so in our office here. I need scarcely point out
to you, my boy, that in such a position you would be sure
to obtain more rapid promotion, than if you were placed
in one of the distant outposts, where you would have
very little to do, and perhaps little to eat, and no one to
converse with, except one or two men. Of course, we
would merely place you here on trial to see how you
suited us ; and if you prove steady and diligent, there
is no saying how fast you might get on. Why, you
might even come to fill *my* place in course of time !
Come now, Charley, what think you of it ?"

Charley's eyes had been cast on the ground while Mr
Grant was speaking. He now raised them, looked at his
father, then at his interrogator, and said—

"It is very kind of you both to be so anxious about my prospects. I thank you, indeed, very much; but I—a ——"

"Don't like the desk?" said his father, in an angry tone. "Is that it, eh?"

Charley made no reply, but cast down his eyes again and smiled (Charley had a sweet smile, a peculiarly sweet, candid smile), as if he meant to say that his father had hit the nail quite on the top of the head that time, and no mistake.

"But consider," resumed Mr Grant, "although you might probably be pleased with an outpost life at first, you would be sure to grow weary of it after the novelty wore off, and then you would wish with all your heart to be back here again. Believe me, child, a trader's life is a very hard and not often a very satisfactory one ——"

"Aye," broke in the father, desirous, if possible, to help the argument, "and you'll find it a desperately wild, unsettled, roving sort of life, too, let me tell you! full of dangers both from wild beasts and wild men ——"

"Hush," interrupted Mr Grant, observing that the boy's eye kindled when his father spoke of a wild, roving life, and wild beasts, "your father does not mean that life at an outpost is wild, and *interesting*, or *exciting*. He merely means that—a—it——"

Mr Grant could not very well explain what it was that Mr Kennedy meant, if he did not mean that, so he turned to him for help.

"Exactly so," said that gentleman, taking a strong pull at the pipe for inspiration. "It's no ways interesting or exciting at all. It's slow, dull, and flat. A miserable sort of Robinson Crusoe life, with red Indians and starvation constantly staring you in the face ——"

"Besides," said Mr Grant, again interrupting the somewhat unfortunate efforts of his friend, who seemed to have a happy facility in sending a brilliant dash of romantic allusion across the dark side of his picture—"besides, you'll not have opportunity to amuse yourself, or to read, as you'll have no books, and you'll have to work hard with your hands oftentimes, like your men ——."

"In fact," broke in the impatient father, resolved, apparently, to carry the point with a grand "*coup*"—"In fact, you'll have to *rough it*, as I did, when I went up the Mackenzie River district, where I was sent to establish a new post, and had to travel for weeks and weeks through a wild country, where none of us had ever been before—where we shot our own meat, caught our own fish, and built our own house,—and were very near being murdered by the Indians—though, to be sure, afterwards they became the most civil fellows in the country, and brought us plenty of skins. Ay, lad, you'll repent of your obstinacy when you come to have to hunt your own dinner, as I've done many a day up the Saskatchewan, where I've had to fight with redskins and grizzly bears, and to chase the buffaloes over miles and miles of prairie on rough-going nags till my bones ached and I scarce knew whether I sat on——"

"Oh !" exclaimed Charley—starting to his feet, while his eyes flashed and his chest heaved with emotion—"that's the place for me, father ! Do, please, Mr Grant, send me there, and I'll work for you with all my might !"

Frank Kennedy was not a man to stand this unexpected miscarriage of his eloquence with equanimity
His first action was to throw his pipe at the head of his
enthusiastic boy, without worse effect, however, than
smashing it to atoms on the opposite wall. He then
started up and rushed towards his son, who, being near
the door, retreated precipitately and vanished.

"So," said Mr Grant, not very sure whether to laugh
or be angry at the result of their united efforts, "you've
settled the question now, at all events."

Frank Kennedy said nothing, but filled another pipe,
sat doggedly down in front of the fire, and speedily
enveloped himself, and his friend, and all that the room
contained, in thick impenetrable clouds of smoke.

Meanwhile his worthy son rushed off in a state of
great glee. He had often heard the *voyageurs* of Red
River dilate on the delights of roughing it in the woods,
and his heart had bounded as they spoke of dangers
encountered and overcome among the rapids of the Far
North, or with the bears and bison-bulls of the prairie,
but never till now had he heard his father corroborate
their testimony by a recital of his own actual experience;
and although the old gentleman's intention was undoubtedly to damp the boy's spirit, his eloquence had
exactly the opposite effect—so that it was with a hop and
a shout that he burst into the counting-room, with the
occupants of which Charley was a special favourite.

CHAPTER III.

The Counting-room.

EVERY one knows the general appearance of a counting-room. There are one or two peculiar features about such apartments that are quite unmistakable and very characteristic; and the counting-room at Fort Garry, although many hundred miles distant from other specimens of its race, and, from the peculiar circumstances of its position, not therefore likely to bear them much resemblance, possessed one or two features of similarity, in the shape of two large desks and several very tall stools, besides sundry ink-bottles, rulers, books, and sheets of blotting-paper. But there were other implements there, savouring strongly of the backwoods and savage life, which merit more particular notice.

The room itself was small, and lighted by two little windows, which opened into the court-yard. The entire apartment was made of wood. The floor was of unpainted fir boards. The walls were of the same material, painted blue from the floor upwards to about three feet, where the blue was unceremoniously stopped short by a stripe of bright red, above which the somewhat fanciful decorator had laid on a coat of pale yellow; and the ceiling, by way of variety, was of a deep ochre. As the occupants of Red River office were, however, addicted to the use of tobacco

and tallow candles, the origin   colour f the iling had
vanished entirely, and that f he wa'   had considerably
changed.

There were three doors in the room (besides the door
of entrance), each opening into another apartment, where
the three clerks were wont to court the favour of Morphe
after the labours of the day. No carpets graced the floors
of any of these rooms, and, with the exception of the
paint afore-mentioned, no ornament whatever broke the
pleasing uniformity of the scene. This was compensated,
however, to some extent, by several scarlet sashes, bright-
coloured shot-belts, and gay portions of winter costume
peculiar to the country, which depended from sundry
nails in the bedroom walls; and, as the three doors always
stood open, these objects, together with one or two
fowling-pieces and canoe-paddles, formed quite a brilliant
and highly suggestive background to the otherwise sombre
picture. A large open fireplace stood in one corner of the
room, devoid of a grate, and so constructed that large logs
of wood might be piled up on end to any extent. And
really the fires made in this manner, and in this individual
fireplace, were exquisite beyond description. A wood
fire is a particularly cheerful thing. Those who have
never seen one can form but a faint idea of its splendour;
especially on a sharp winter night in the arctic regions,
where the thermometer falls to forty degrees below zero,
without inducing the inhabitants to suppose that the
world has reached its conclusion. The billets are usually
piled up on end, so that the flames rise and twine round
them with a fierce intensity that causes them to crack
and spatter cheerfully, sending innumerable sparks of fire
into the room, and throwing out a rich glow of brilliant

light that warms a man even to look at it, and renders
candles quite unnecessary.

The clerks who inhabited this counting-room were, like
itself, peculiar. There were three—corresponding to the
bedrooms. The senior was a tall, broad-shouldered, muscular man—a Scotchman—very good-humoured, yet a
man whose under lip met the upper with that peculiar
degree of precision that indicated the presence of other
qualities besides that of good-humour. He was book-
keeper and accountant, and managed the affairs entrusted
to his care with the same dogged perseverance with which
he would have led an expedition of discovery to the
North Pole. He was thirty or thereabouts.

The second was a small man—also a Scotchman. It is
curious to note how numerous Scotchmen are in the wilds
of North America. This specimen was diminutive and
sharp. Moreover, he played the flute,—an accomplishment
of which he was so proud, that he ordered out from
England a flute of ebony, so elaborately enriched with
silver keys that one's fingers ached to behold it. This
beautiful instrument, like most other instruments of a
delicate nature, found the climate too much for its constitution, and, soon after the winter began, split from top
to bottom. Peter Mactavish, however, was a genius by
nature, and a mechanical genius by tendency; so that,
instead of giving way to despair, he laboriously bound the
flute together with waxed thread, which, although it could
not restore it to its pristine elegance, enabled him to play
with great effect sundry doleful airs, whose influence,
when performed at night, usually sent his companions to
sleep, or, failing this, drove them to distraction.

The third inhabitant of the office was a ruddy smooth

chinned youth of about fourteen, who had left home seven
months before, in the hope of gratifying a desire to lead a
wild life, which he had entertained ever since he read
"Jack the Giant Killer," and found himself most unexpectedly fastened, during the greater part of each day,
to a stool. His name was Harry Somerville, and a fine
cheerful little fellow he was,—full of spirits, and curiously
addicted to poking and arranging the fire, at least every
ten minutes—a propensity which tested the forbearance
of the senior clerk rather severely, and would have surprised any one not aware of poor Harry's incurable
antipathy to the desk, and the yearning desire with
which he longed for physical action.

Harry was busily engaged with the refractory fire,
when Charley, as stated at the conclusion of the last
chapter, burst into the room.

"Hallo!" he exclaimed, suspending his operations for
a moment, "what's up?" "Nothing," said Charley,
"but father's temper, that's all. He gave me a splendid
description of his life in the woods, and then threw his
pipe at me because I admired it too much."

"Ho!" exclaimed Harry, making a vigorous thrust at
the fire, "then you've no chance now."

"No chance! what do you mean?"

"Only that we are to have a wolf-hunt in the plains to-
morrow, and if you've aggravated your father, he'll be
taking you home to-night, that's all."

"Oh! no fear of that," said Charley, with a look that
seemed to imply that there was very great fear of "that,"
much more, in fact, than he was willing to admit even to
himself. "My dear old father never keeps his anger long
I'm sure that he'll be all right again in half-an-hour."

3

"Hope so, but doubt it I do," said Harry, making another deadly poke at the fire, and returning, with a deep sigh, to his stool.

"Would you like to go with us, Charley?" said the senior clerk, laying down his pen and turning round on his chair (the senior clerk never sat on a stool) with a benign smile.

"Oh! very, very much indeed," cried Charley; "but even should father agree to stay all night at the fort, I have no horse, and I'm sure he would not let me have the mare after what I did to-day.'

"Do you think he's not open to persuasion?" said the senior clerk.

"No, I'm sure he's not."

"Well, well, it don't much signify; perhaps we can mount you."

Charley's face brightened.

"Go," he continued, addressing Harry Somerville, "go, tell Tom Whyte I wish to speak to him."

Harry sprang from his stool with a suddenness and vigour that might have justified the belief that he had been fixed to it by means of a powerful spring, which had been set free with a sharp recoil, and shot him out at the door, for he disappeared in a trice. In a few minutes he returned, followed by the groom Tom Whyte.

"Tom," said the senior clerk, "do you think we could manage to mount Charley to-morrow?"

"Why, sir, I don't think as how we could. There aint an 'oss in the stable except them wot's required and them wot's badly."

"Couldn't he have the brown pony?" suggested the senior clerk.

Tom Whyte was a cockney, and an old soldier, and stood so bolt upright that it seemed quite a marvel how the words ever managed to climb up the steep ascent of his throat, and turn the corner so as to get out at his mouth. Perhaps this was the cause of his speaking on all occasions with great deliberation and slowness.

"Why, you see, sir," he replied, "the brown pony's got cut under the 'etlock of the right hind leg; and I 'ad 'im down to L'Esperance the smith's, sir, to look at 'im, sir; and he says to me, says he, 'That don't look well that 'oss don't,'—and he's a knowing feller, sir, is L'Esperance, though he *is* an 'alf-breed——"

"Never mind what he said, Tom," interrupted the senior clerk; "is the pony fit for use? that's the question."

"No, sir, 'e haint."

"And the black mare, can he not have that?"

"No, sir, Mr Grant is to ride 'er to-morrow."

"That's unfortunate," said the senior clerk; "I fear, Charley, that you'll need to ride behind Harry on his gray pony. It wouldn't improve his speed, to be sure, having two on his back, but then he's so like a pig in his movements at any rate, I don't think it would spoil his pace much."

"Could he not try the new horse?" he continued, turning to the groom.

"The noo 'oss, sir! he might as well try to ride a mad buffalo bull, sir. He's quite a young colt, sir, only 'alf-broke—kicks like a windmill, sir, and's got an 'ead like a steam-engine; 'e couldn't 'old 'im in no 'ow, sir. I 'ad 'im down to the smith 'tother day, sir, an' says 'e to me, says 'e, 'That's a screamer, that is.' 'Yes,' says I, 'that his a fact.' 'Well,' says 'e ——"

" Hang the smith," cried the senior clerk, losing all
patience, " can't you answer me without so much talk ?
Is the horse too wild to ride ?"

" Yes, sir, 'e is," said the groom, with a look of
slightly offended dignity, and drawing himself up—if we
may use such an expression to one who was always drawn
up to such an extent that he seemed to be just balanced
on his heels, and required only a gentle push to lay him
flat on his back.

" Oh! I have it," cried Peter Mactavish, who had been
standing, during the conversation, with his back to the
fire, and a short pipe in his mouth—"John Fowler, the
miller, has just purchased a new pony. I'm told it's an
old buffalo runner, and I'm certain he would lend it to
Charley at once."

" The very thing," said the senior clerk. " Run, Tom;
give the miller my compliments, and beg the loan of his
horse for Charley Kennedy. I think he knows you,
Charley ?"

The dinner-bell rang as the groom departed, and the
clerks prepared for their mid-day meal.

The senior clerk's order to "run" was a mere form of
speech, intended to indicate that haste was desirable.
No man imagined for a moment that Tom Whyte could,
by any possibility, run. He hadn't run since he was
dismissed from the army, twenty years before, for incurable drunkenness ; and most of Tom's friends entertained
the belief, that if he ever attempted to run, he would crack
all over, and go to pieces like a disentombed Egyptian
mummy. Tom, therefore, walked off to the row of buildings inhabited by the men, where he sat down on a bench
in front of his bed, and proceeded leisurely to fill his pipe.

 , losing all
much talk ?

h a look of
f up—if we
lways drawn
ust balanced
h to lay him

 ho had been
back to the
Fowler, the
n told it's an
ld lend it to

" Run, Tom;
e loan of his
knows you,

 ted, and he

mere form of
as desirable.
Whyte could,
since he was
re, for incur-
s entertained
would crack
ed Egyptian
row of build-
n on a bench
fill his pipe.

The room in which he sat was a fair specimen of the dwellings devoted to the *employés* of the Hudson's Bay Company throughout the country. It was large, and low in the roof, built entirely of wood, which was unpainted,—a matter, however, of no consequence, as, from long exposure to dust and tobacco-smoke, the floor, walls, and ceiling, had become one deep uniform brown. The men's beds were constructed after the fashion of berths on board ship, being wooden boxes ranged in tiers round the room. Several tables and benches were strewn miscellaneously about the floor, in the centre of which stood a large double iron stove, with the word "*Carron*" stamped on it. This served at once for cooking and warming the place. Numerous guns, axes, and canoe-paddles hung round the walls or were piled in corners, and the rafters sustained a miscellaneous mass of materials, the more conspicuous among which were snow-shoes, dog-sledges, axe-handles, and nets.

Having filled and lighted his pipe, Tom Whyte thrust his hands into his deer-skin mittens, and sauntered off to perform his errand.

CHAPTER IV.

A wolf-hunt in the prairies—Charley astonishes his father, and breaks in the "noo 'oss" effectually.

DURING the long winter that reigns in the northern regions of America, the thermometer ranges, for many months together, from zero down to 20, 30, and 40 degrees *below* it.   In different parts of the country the intensity of the frost varies a little, but not sufficiently to make any appreciable change in one's sensation of cold. At York Fort, on the shores of Hudson's Bay, where the winter is eight months long, the spirit-of-wine (mercury being useless in so cold a climate) sometimes falls so low as 50 degrees below zero ; and away in the regions of Great Bear Lake, it has been known to fall considerably lower than 60 degrees below zero of Fahrenheit.   Cold of such intensity, of course, produces many curious and interesting effects ; which, although scarcely noticed by the inhabitants, make a strong impression upon the minds of those who visit the country for the first time.   A youth goes out to walk on one of the first sharp, frosty mornings.   His locks are brown and his face ruddy.   In half-an-hour he returns with his face blue, his nose frost-bitten, and his locks *white*—the latter effect being produced by his breath congealing on his hair and breast, until both are covered with hoar-frost.   Perhaps he is of a sceptical nature, prejudiced, it may be, in favour of old

habits and customs, so that, although told, by those who
ought to know, that it is absolutely necessary to wear
moccasins in winter, he prefers the leather boots to which
he has been accustomed at home, and goes out with them
accordingly. In a few minutes the feet begin to lose sensation. First the toes, as far as feeling goes, vanish;
then the heels depart, and he feels the extraordinary, and
peculiar, and altogether disagreeable sensation of one who
has had his heels and toes amputated, and is walking
about on his insteps. Soon, however, these also fade
away, and the unhappy youth rushes frantically home
on the stumps of his ankle-bones—at least so it appears
to him—and so in reality it would turn out to be, if he
did not speedily rub the benumbed appendages into
vitality again.

The whole country, during this season, is buried in
snow, and the prairies of Red River present the appearance of a sea of the purest white, for five or six months of
the year. Impelled by hunger, troops of prairie wolves
prowl round the settlement, safe from the assault of man
in consequence of their light weight permitting them to
scamper away on the surface of the snow, into which
man or horse, from their greater weight, would sink, so
as to render pursuit either fearfully laborious, or altogether impossible. In spring, however, when the first
thaws begin to take place, and commence that delightful
process of disruption which introduces this charming
season of the year, the relative position of wolf and man
is reversed. The snow becomes suddenly soft, so that the
short legs of the wolf, sinking deep into it, fail to reach
the solid ground below, and he is obliged to drag heavily
along, while the long legs of the horse enable him to

plunge through and dash aside the snow at a rate which,
although not very fleet, is sufficient, nevertheless, to overtake the chase and give his rider a chance of shooting
it.   The inhabitants of Red River are not much addicted
to this sport, but the gentlemen of the Hudson's Bay
Service sometimes practise it; and it was to a hunt of
this description that our young friend Charley Kennedy
was now so anxious to go.

The morning was propitious. The sun blazed in
dazzling splendour in a sky of deep unclouded blue, while
the white prairie glittered as if it were a sea of diamonds
rolling out in an unbroken sheet from the walls of the
fort to the horizon, and on looking at which one experienced all the pleasurable feelings of being out on a calm
day on the wide, wide sea, without the disagreeable consequence of being very, very sick.

The thermometer stood at 39° in the shade, and
"everythink," as Tom Whyte emphatically expressed it,
"looked like a runnin' of right away into slush." That
unusual sound, the trickling of water, so inexpressibly
grateful to the ears of those who dwell in frosty climes,
was heard all around, as the heavy masses of snow on
the house-tops sent a few adventurous drops gliding down
the icicles which depended from the eves and gables ; and
there was a balmy softness in the air that told of coming
spring. Nature, in fact, seemed to have wakened from
her long nap, and was beginning to think of getting up.
Like people, however, who venture to delay so long as to
think about it, Nature frequently turns round and goes to
sleep again in her icy cradle for a few weeks after the first
awakening.

The scene in the court-yard of Fort Garry harmonised

with the cheerful spirit of the morning. Tom Whyte, with that upright solemnity which constituted one of his characteristic features, was standing in the centre of a group of horses, whose energy he endeavoured to restrain with the help of a small Indian boy, to whom, meanwhile, he imparted a variety of useful and otherwise unattainable information.

" You see, Joseph," said he to the urchin, who gazed gravely in his face with a pair of very large and dark eyes, " ponies is often skittish. Reason why one should be, an' another not, I can't comprehend. P'r'aps its nat'ral, p'r'aps not, but howsomediver so 'tis, an' if its more nor above the likes o' *me*, Joseph, you needn't be surprised that it's somethink haltogether beyond *you*."

It will not surprise the reader to be told that Joseph made no reply to this speech, having a very imperfect acquaintance with the English language, especially the peculiar dialect of that tongue in which Tom Whyte was wont to express his ideas, when he had any.

He merely gave a grunt, and continued to gaze at Tom's fishy eyes, which were about as interesting as the face to which they belonged, and *that* might have been mistaken for almost anything.

" Yes, Joseph," he continued, " that's a fact. There's the noo brown 'oss now, *it's* a skittish 'un. And there's Mr Kennedy's gray mare, wot's a standin' of beside me, she aint skittish a bit, though she's plenty of spirit, and wouldn't care hanythink for a five-barred gate. Now, wot I want to know is, wot's the reason why ?"

We fear that the reason why, however interesting it might prove to naturalists, must remain a profound secret for ever; for, just as the groom was about to entertain Joseph with one of his theories on the point, Charley Kennedy and Harry Somerville hastily approached.

"Ho, Tom!" exclaimed the former, "have you got the miller's pony for me?"

"Why, no, sir; 'e 'adn't got his shoes on, sir, last night ——"

"Oh! bother his shoes," said Charley, in a voice of great disappointment. "Why didn't you bring him up without shoes, man, eh?"

"Well, sir, the miller said 'e'd get 'em put on early this mornin', an' I 'xpect 'e'll be 'ere in 'alf a hour at farthest, sir."

"Oh, very well," replied Charley, much relieved, but still a little nettled at the bare possibility of being late. "Come along, Harry, let's go and meet him. He'll be long enough of coming if we don't go to poke him up a bit."

"You'd better wait," called out the groom, as the boys hastened away. "If you go by the river he'll p'raps come by the plains, and if you go by the plains he'll p'raps come by the river."

Charley and Harry stopped and looked at each other. Then they looked at the groom, and as their eyes surveyed his solemn, cadaverous countenance, which seemed a sort of bad caricature of the long visages of the horses that stood around him, they burst into a simultaneous and prolonged laugh.

"He's a clever old lamp-post," said Harry, at last; "we had better remain, Charley."

"You see," continued Tom Whyte, "the pony's 'oofs is in an 'orrible state. Last night w'en I see'd 'im, I said to the miller, says I, 'John, I'll take 'im down to the smith d'rectly.' 'Very good,' said John. So I 'ad him down to the smith ——"

The remainder of Tom's speech was cut short by one of those unforeseen operations of the laws of nature, which are peculiar to arctic climates. During the long winter, repeated falls of snow cover the house-tops with white mantles upwards of a foot thick, which become gradually thicker and more consolidated as winter advances. In spring, the suddenness of the thaw loosens these from the sloping roofs, and precipitates them in masses to the ground. These miniature avalanches are dangerous, people having been seriously injured and sometimes killed by them. Now, it happened that a very large mass of snow, which lay on, and partly depended from, the roof of the house near to which the horses were standing, gave way, and just at that critical point in Tom Whyte's speech when he " 'ad 'im down to the smith," fell with a stunning crash on the back of Mr Kennedy's gray mare. The mare was not " skittish "—by no means—according to Tom's idea, but it would have been more than an ordinary mare to have stood the sudden descent of half-a-ton of snow without *some* symptom of consciousness. No sooner did it feel the blow, than it sent both heels with a bang against the wooden store, by way of preliminary movement, and then, rearing up with a wild snort, it sprang over Tom Whyte's head, jerked the reins from his hand, and upset him in the snow. Poor Tom never *bent* to anything. The military despotism under which he had been reared having substituted a touch of the cap for a bow, rendered it unnecessary to bend ; prolonged drill, laziness, and rheumatism made it at last impossible.

When he stood up, he did so after the manner of a pillar ;
when he sat down, he broke across at two points, much
in the way in which a foot-rule would have done, had *it*
felt disposed to sit down, and when he fell, he came
down like an overturned lamp-post.   On the present
occasion, Tom became horizontal in a moment, and from
his unfortunate propensity to fall straight, his head,
reaching much farther than might have been expected,
came into violent contact with the small Indian boy,
who fell flat likewise, letting go the reins of the horses,
which latter no sooner felt themselves free, than they
fled, curvetting and snorting round the court, with reins
and mains flying in rare confusion.

The two boys, who could scarce stand for laughing,
ran to the gates of the fort to prevent the chargers
getting free, and in a short time they were again secured,
although evidently much elated in spirit.

A few minutes after this, Mr Grant issued from the
principal house, leaning on Mr Kennedy's arm, and followed by the senior clerk, Peter Mactavish, and one or
two friends who had come to take part in the wolf-hunt.
They were all armed with double or single barrelled
guns or pistols, according to their several fancies.   The
two elderly gentlemen alone entered upon the scene
without any more deadly weapons than their heavy
riding whips.   Young Harry Somerville, who had been
strongly advised not to take a gun lest he should shoot
himself, or his horse or his companions, was content to
take the field with a small pocket-pistol, which he
crammed to the muzzle with a compound of ball and
swan-shot.

" It won't do," said Mr Grant, in an earnest voice, to

his friend, as they walked towards the horses—"it won't do to check him too abruptly, my dear sir."

It was evident that they were recurring to the subject of conversation of the previous day, and it was also evident that the father's wrath was in that very uncertain state when a word or a look can throw it into violent agitation.

"Just permit me," continued Mr Grant, "to get him sent to the Saskatchewan or Athabasca for a couple of years. By that time he'll have had enough of a rough life, and be only too glad to get a berth at head-quarters. If you thwart him now, I feel convinced that he'll break through all restraint."

"Humph!" ejaculated Mr Kennedy, with a frown. "Come here, Charley," he said, as the boy approached with a disappointed look, to tell of his failure in getting a horse; "I've been talking with Mr Grant again about this business, and he says he can easily get you into the counting-room here for a year; so you'll make arrangements——"

The old gentleman paused: he was going to have followed his wonted course, by *commanding* instantaneous obedience; but as his eye fell upon the honest, open, though disappointed face of his son, a gush of tenderness filled his heart. Laying his hand upon Charley's head, he said, in a kind but abrupt tone, "There now, Charley, my boy, make up your mind to give in with a good grace. It'll only be hard work for a year or two, and then plain sailing after that, Charley!"

Charley's clear blue eyes fill'ed with tears as the accents of kindness fell upon his ear.

It is strange that men should frequently be so blind to

the potent influence of kindness.   Independently of **the**
Divine authority, which assures us that "a soft answer
turneth away wrath," and that "*love* is the fulfilling of
the law," who has not, in the course of his experience,
felt the overwhelming power of a truly affectionate word !
—not a word which possesses merely an affectionate sig-
nification, but a word spoken with a gush of tenderness,
where love rolls in the tone, and beams in the eye, and
revels in every wrinkle of the face !   And how much
more powerfully does such a word, or look, or tone strike
home to the heart, if uttered by one whose lips are not much
accustomed to the formation of honeyed words or sweet
sentences !   Had Mr Kennedy, senior, known more of
this power, and put it more frequently to the proof, we
venture to affirm that Mr Kennedy, junior, would have
allowed his "*flint to be fixed*" (as his father pithily expressed it) long ago.

Ere Charley could reply to the question, Mr Grant's
voice, pitched in an elevated key, interrupted them.

"Eh! what?" said that gentleman to Tom Whyte
"No horse for Charley !   How's that ?"

"No, sir," said Tom.

"Where's the brown pony ?" said Mr Grant, abruptly.

"Cut 'is fetlock, sir," said Tom, slowly.

"And the new horse ?"

"'Tant 'alf broke yet, sir."

"Ah! that's bad.   It wouldn't do to take an unbroken charger, Charley, for, although you are a pretty
good rider, you couldn't manage him, I fear.   Let me see."

"Please, sir," said the groom, touching his hat, "I've
borrowed the miller's pony for 'im, and 'e's sure to be
'ere in 'alf a hour at farthest."

"Oh, that'll do," said Mr Grant; "you can soon overtake us. We shall ride slowly out, straight into the prairie, and Harry will remain behind to keep you company."

So saying, Mr Grant mounted his horse and rode out at the back gate, followed by the whole cavalcade.

"Now, this is too bad!" said Charley, looking with a very perplexed air at his companion. "What's to be done?"

Harry evidently did not know what was to be done, and made no difficulty of saying so in a very sympathising tone. Moreover, he begged Charley very earnestly to take *his* pony, but this the other would not hear of; so they came to the conclusion that there was nothing for it but to wait as patiently as possibly for the arrival of the expected horse. In the meantime Harry proposed a saunter in the field adjoining the fort. Charley assented, and the two friends walked away, leading the gray pony along with them.

To the right of Fort Garry was a small enclosure, at the extreme end of which commences a growth of willows and underwood, which gradually increases in size till it becomes a pretty thick belt of woodland, skirting up the river for many miles. Here stood the stable belonging to the establishment; and, as the boys passed it, Charley suddenly conceived a strong desire to see the renowned "noo 'oss," which Tom Whyte had said was only "'alf broke;" so he turned the key, opened the door, and went in.

There was nothing *very* peculiar about this horse, excepting that his legs   ·ed rather long for his body, and, upon a closer examin: here was a noticeable breadth

of nostril and a latent fire in his eye, indicating a good
deal of spirit, which, like Charley's own, required taming

"Oh," said Charley, "what a splendid fellow! I say.
Harry, I'll go out with *him*."

"You'd better not."

"Why not?"

"Why? Just because if you do, Mr Grant will be
down upon you, and your father won't be very well
pleased."

"Nonsense," cried Charley. "Father didn't say I
wasn't to take him. I don't think he'd care much.
He's not afraid of my breaking my neck. And, then,
Mr Grant seemed to be only afraid of my being run off
with—not of his horse being hurt. Here goes for it!"
In another moment, Charley had him saddled and bridled,
and led him out into the yard.

"Why, I declare, he's quite quiet; just like a lamb,"
said Harry, in surprise.

"So he is," replied Charley. "He's a capital charger;
and even if he does bolt, he can't run five hundred miles
at a stretch. If I turn his head to the prairies, the
Rocky Mountains are the first things that will bring him
up. So let him run if he likes—I don't care a fig." And
springing lightly into the saddle, he cantered out of the
yard, followed by his friend.

The young horse was a well-formed, showy animal,
with a good deal of bone—perhaps too much for elegance.
He was of a beautiful dark brown, and carried a high
head and tail, with a high-stepping gait, that gave him a
noble appearance. As Charley cantered along at a steady
pace, he could discover no symptoms of the refractory
spirit which had been ascribed to him.

" Let us strike out straight for the horizon now," said
Harry, after they had galloped half-a-mile or so along the
beaten track. " See, here are the tracks of our friends."
Turning sharp round as he spoke, he leaped his pony
over the heap that lined the road, and galloped away
through the soft snow.

At this point the young horse began to shew his evil
spirit. Instead of following the other, he suddenly
halted and began to back.

" Hallo, Harry !" exclaimed Charley ; " hold on a bit.
Here's this monster begun his tricks."

" Hit him a crack with the whip," shouted Harry.

Charley acted upon the advice, which had the effect of
making the horse shake his head with a sharp snort, and
back more vigorously than ever.

" There, my fine fellow, quiet now," said Charley, in a
soothing tone, patting the horse's neck. " It's a comfort
to know you can't go far in *that* direction, anyhow !" he
added, as he glanced over his shoulder, and saw an immense drift behind.

He was right. In a few minutes the horse backed into
the snow-drift. Finding his hind-quarters imprisoned by
a power that was too much even for *his* obstinacy to overcome, he gave another snort and a heavy plunge, which
almost unseated his young rider.

" Hold on fast," cried Harry, who had now come up.

" No fear," cried Charley, as he clenched his teeth and
gathered the reins more firmly. " Now for it, you young
villain !" and, raising his whip, he brought it down with
a heavy slash on the horse's flank.

Had the snow-drift been a cannon, and the horse a
bombshell, he could scarcely have sprung from it with

4

greater velocity. One bound landed him on the road;
another cleared it; and, in a second more, he stretched
out at full speed—his ears flat on his neck, mane and tail
flying in the wind, and the bit tight between his teeth.

"Well done," cried Harry, as he passed; "you're off
now, old fellow—good-bye."

"Hurrah!" shouted Charley, in reply, leaving his cap
in the snow as a parting *souvenir*; while, seeing that it
was useless to endeavour to check his steed, he became
quite wild with excitement; gave him the rein; flourished
his whip; and flew over the white plains, casting up the
snow in clouds behind him like a hurricane!

While this little escapade was being enacted by the
boys, the hunters were riding leisurely out upon the
snowy sea in search of a wolf.

Words cannot convey to you, dear reader, an adequate
conception of the peculiar fascinatio   exhilarating
splendour of the scene by which our hunters were surrounded. Its beauty lay not in variety of feature in the
landscape, for there was none. One vast sheet of white
alone met the view, bounded all round by the blue circle
of the sky, and broken, in one or two places, by a patch
or two of willows, which, rising on the plain, appeared
like little islands in a frozen sea. It was the glittering
sparkle of the snow in the bright sunshine; the dreamy
haziness of the atmosphere, mingling earth and sky as in
a halo of gold; the first taste—the first *smell* of spring
after a long winter, bursting suddenly upon the senses,
like the unexpected visit of a long absent, much loved,
and almost forgotten friend; the soft, warm feeling of
the south wind, bearing on its wings the balmy influences
of sunny climes, and recalling vividly the scenes, the

pleasures, the bustling occupations of summer. It was this that caused the hunters' hearts to leap within them as they rode along—that induced old Mr Kennedy to forget his years, and shout as he had been wont to do in days gone by, when he used to follow the track of the elk, or hunt the wild buffalo; and it was this that made the otherwise monotonous prairies, on this particular day, so charming.

The party had wandered about without discovering anything that bore the smallest resemblance to a wolf, for upwards of an hour. Fort Garry had fallen astern (to use a nautical phrase) until it had become a mere speck on the horizon, and vanished altogether. Peter Mactavish had twice given a false alarm, in the eagerness of his spirit, and had three times plunged his horse up to the girths in a snow-drift. The senior clerk was waxing impatient, and the horses restive, when a sudden "hallo!" from Mr Grant brought the whole cavalcade to a stand.

The object which drew his attention, and to which he directed the anxious eyes of his friends, was a small speck, rather triangular in form, which overtopped a little willow-bush not more than five or six hundred yards distant.

"There he is!" exclaimed Mr Grant. "That's a fact," cried Mr Kennedy; and both gentlemen, instantaneously giving a shout, bounded towards the object; not, however, before the senior clerk, who was mounted on a fleet and strong horse, had taken the lead by six yards. A moment afterwards the speck rose up and discovered itself to be a veritable wolf. Moreover, he condescended to shew his teeth, and, then, conceiving it probable that his enemies were too numerous for him, he turned sud-

denly round and fled away. For ten minutes or so the
chase was kept up at full speed, and as the snow happened
to be shallow at the starting point, the wolf kept well
ahead of its pursuers—indeed, distanced them a little.
But soon the snow became deeper, and the wolf plunged
heavily, and the horses gained considerably. Although,
to the eye, the prairies seemed to be a uniform level,
there were numerous slight undulations, in which drifts
of some depth had collected. Into one of these the wolf
now plunged and laboured slowly through it. But so
deep was the snow that the horses almost stuck fast. A
few minutes, however, brought them out, and Mr Grant
and Mr Kennedy, who had kept close to each other
during the run, pulled up for a moment on the summit
of a ridge to breathe their panting steeds.

"What can that be?" exclaimed the former, pointing
with his whip to a distant object which was moving
rapidly over the plain.

"Eh! what! where?" said Mr Kennedy, shading his
eyes with his hand, and peering in the direction indicated.
"Why, that's another wolf, isn't it? No, it runs too fast
for that."

"Strange," said his friend, "what *can* it be?"

"If I hadn't seen every beast in the country," remarked
Mr Kennedy, "and didn't know that there are no such
animals north of the equator, I should say it was a mad
dromedary mounted by a ring-tailed roarer."

"It can't be, surely!—not possible!" exclaimed Mr
Grant. "It's not Charley on the new horse!"

Mr Grant said this with an air of vexation that annoyed his friend a little. He would not have much
minded Charley's taking a horse without leave, no matter

how wild it might be; but he did not at all relish the
idea of making an apology for his son's misconduct, and,
for the moment, did not exactly know what to say. As
usual in such a dilemma, the old man took refuge in a
towering passion, gave his steed a sharp cut with the
whip, and galloped forward to meet the delinquent.

We are not acquainted with the general appearance of
a " ring-tailed roarer;" in fact, we have grave doubts
as to whether such an animal exists at all; but if it does,
and is particularly wild, dishevelled, and fierce in deport-
ment, there is no doubt whatever, that, when Mr Kennedy applied the name to his hopeful son, the application
was singularly powerful and appropriate.

Charley had had a long run since we last saw him.
After describing a wide curve, in which his charger displayed a surprising aptitude for picking out the ground
that was least covered with snow, he headed straight for
the fort again at the same pace at which he had started.
At first, Charley tried every possible method to check
him, but in vain; so he gave it up, resolving to enjoy the
race, since he could not prevent it. The young horse
seemed to be made of lightning, with bones and muscles
of brass, for he bounded untiringly forward for miles,
tossing his head and snorting in his wild career. But
Charley was a good horseman, and did not mind *that*
much, being quite satisfied that the horse *was* a horse
and not a spirit, and that, therefore, he could not run for
ever. At last he approached the party, in search of
which he had originally set out. His eyes dilated and
his colour heightened as he beheld the wolf running di
rectly towards him. Fumbling hastily for the pistol
which he had borrowed from his friend Harry, he drew

it from his pocket, and prepared to give the animal a shot
in passing. Just at that moment the wolf caught sight
of this new enemy in advance, and diverged suddenly to
the left, plunging into a drift in his confusion ; and so
enabling the senior clerk to overtake him, and send an
ounce of heavy shot into his side, which turned him over
quite dead. The shot, however, had a double effect. At
that instant Charley swept past; and his mettlesome steed
swerved as it heard the loud report of the gun, thereby
almost unhorsing his rider, and causing him unintentionally to discharge the conglomerate of bullets and swan-shot
into the flank of Peter Mactavish's horse—fortunately at
a distance which rendered the shot equivalent to a dozen
very sharp and particularly stinging blows. On receiving
this unexpected salute, the astonished charger reared convulsively, and fell back upon his rider, who was thereby
buried deep in the snow, not a vestige of him being left,
no more than if he had never existed at all. Indeed, for
a moment it seemed to be doubtful whether poor Peter
did exist or not, until a sudden upheaving of the snow
took place, and his dishevelled head appeared, with the
eyes and mouth wide open, bearing on them an expression
of mingled horror and amazement. Meanwhile, the second
shot acted like a spur on the young horse, which flew past
Mr Kennedy like a whirlwind.

"Stop, you young scoundrel !" he shouted, shaking his
fist at Charley as he passed.

Charley was past stopping, either by inclination or
ability. This sudden and unexpected accumulation of
disasters was too much for him. As he passed his sire.
with his brown curls streaming straight out behind, and his
eyes flashing with excitement, his teeth clenched, and his

horse tearing along more like an incarnate fiend than an
animal—a spirit of combined recklessness, consternation,
indignation, and glee, took possession of him. He waved
his whip wildly over his head, brought it down with a
stinging cut on the horse's neck, and uttered a shout of
defiance that threw completely into the shade the loudest
war-whoop that was ever uttered by the brazen lungs of
the wildest savage between Hudson's Bay and Oregon.
Seeing and hearing this, old Mr Kennedy wheeled about
and dashed off in pursuit with much greater energy than
he had displayed in chase of the wolf.

The race bade fair to be a long one, for the young horse
was strong in wind and limb ; and the gray mare, though
decidedly not " the better horse," was much fresher than
the other.

The hunters, who were now joined by Harry Somerville, did not feel it incumbent on them to follow this new
chase ; so they contented themselves with watching their
flight towards the fort, while they followed at a more leisurely pace.

Meanwhile, Charley rapidly neared Fort Garry ; and
now began to wonder whether the stable door was open ;
and, if so, whether it were better for him to take his
chance of getting his neck broken, or to throw himself
into the next snow drift that presented itself.

He had not to remain long in suspense. The wooden
fence that enclosed the stable yard lay before him. It
was between four and five feet high, with a beaten track
running along the outside, and a deep snow-drift on the
other. Charley felt that the young horse had made up
his mind to leap this. As he did not, at the moment, see
that there was anything better to be done, he prepared for

it. As the horse bent on his haunches to spring, he gave
him a smart cut with the whip, went over like a rocket,
and plunged up to the neck in the snow-drift, which
brought his career to an abrupt conclusion. The sudden
stoppage of the horse was *one* thing, but the arresting of
Master Charley was *another*, and quite a different thing.
The instant his charger landed, he left the saddle like a
harlequin, described an extensive curve in the air, and
fell head foremost into the drift, above which his boots
and three inches of his legs alone remained to tell the
tale.

On witnessing this climax, Mr Kennedy, senior, pulled
up, dismounted, and ran—with an expression of some
anxiety on his countenance—to the help of his son ;
while Tom Whyte came out of the stable just in time to
receive the " noo 'oss" as he floundered out of the snow.

" I believe," said the groom, as he surveyed the trembling charger, " that your son has broke the noo 'oss, sir,
better nor I could 'ave done myself."

" I believe that my son has broken his neck," said Mr.
Kennedy, wrathfully. " Come here and help me to dig
him out."

In a few minutes Charley was dug out, in a state of in-
sensibility, and carried up to the fort, where he was laid
on a bed, and restoratives actively applied for his recovery

CHARLEY IN THE DRIFT.

CHAPTER V.

Peter Mactavish becomes an amateur doctor; Charley promulgates his views of
things in general to Kate; and Kate waxes sagacious.

SHORTLY after the catastrophe just related, Charley opened
his eyes to consciousness, and aroused himself out of a
prolonged fainting fit, under the combined influence of a
strong constitution, and the medical treatment of his
friends.

Medical treatment in the wilds of North America, by
the way, is very original in its character, and is founded
on principles so vague, that no one has ever been found
capable of stating them clearly. Owing to the stubborn
fact, that there are no doctors in the country, men have
been thrown upon their own resources; and, as a natural
consequence, *every* man is a doctor. True, there *are* two,
it may be three, real doctors in the Hudson's Bay Company's employment; but, as one of these is resident on
the shores of Hudson's Bay, another in Oregon, and a
third in Red River Settlement. they are not considered
available for every case of emergency that may chance to
occur in the hundreds of little outposts, scattered far and
wide over the whole continent of North America, with
miles and miles of primeval wilderness between each.
We do not think, therefore, that when we say there are
no doctors in the country, we use a culpable amount of
exaggeration.

If a man gets ill, he goes on till he gets better ; and, if he doesn't get better, he dies. To avert such an undesirable consummation, desperate and random efforts are made in an amateur way. The old proverb that "extremes meet," is verified. And, in a land where no doctors are to be had for love or money, doctors meet you at every turn, ready to practise on everything, with anything, and all for nothing, on the shortest possible notice. As may be supposed, the practice is novel, and, not unfrequently, extremely wild. Tooth-drawing is considered child's play — m re blacksmith's work ; bleeding is a general remedy for everything, when all else fails ; castor-oil, Epsom salts, and emetics are the three keynotes, the foundations, and the copestones of the system.

In Red River there is only one *genuine* doctor ; and, as the settlement is fully sixty miles long, he has enough to do, and cannot always be found when wanted, so that Charley had to rest content with amateur treatment in the mean time. Peter Mactavish was the first to try his powers. He was aware that laudanum had the effect of producing sleep, and, seeing that Charley looked somewhat sleepy after recovering consciousness, he thought it advisable to help out that propensity to slumber, and went to the medicine-chest, whence he extracted a small phial of tincture of rhubarb, the half of which he emptied into a wine-glass, under the impression that it was laudanum, and poured down Charley's throat ! The poor boy swallowed a little, and sputtered the remainder over the bed-clothes. It may be remarked here that Mactavish was a wild, happy, half-mad sort of fellow—wonderfully erudite in regard to some things, and profoundly ignorant in regard to others. Medicine, it need scarcely be added, was not his *forte*. Having accomplished this feat to his satisfaction, he sat down to watch by the bedside of his friend. Peter had taken this opportunity to indulge in a little private practice, just after several of the other gentlemen had left the office under the impression that Charley had better remain quiet for a short time.

"Well, Peter," whispered Mr Kennedy, senior, putting his head in at the door (it was Harry's room in which Charley lay), "how is he now?"

"Oh! doing capitally, replied Peter, in a hoarse whisper, at the same time rising and entering the office, while he gently closed the door behind him. "I gave him a small doze of physic, which I think has done him good. He's sleeping like a top now."

Mr Kennedy frowned slightly, and made one or two remarks in reference to physic, which were not calculated to gratify the ears of a physician.

"What did you give him?" he inquired, abruptly.

"Only a little laudanum."

"*Only*, indeed! it's all trash together, and that's the worst kind of trash you could have given him. Humph!" and the old gentleman jerked his shoulders testily.

"How much did you give him?" said the senior clerk, who had entered the apartment with Harry a few minutes before.

"Not quite a wineglassful," replied Peter, somewhat subdued.

"What!" cried the father, starting from his chair as if he had received an electric shock, and rushing into the adjoining room, up and down which he raved in a state of distraction, being utterly ignorant of what should be done under the circumstances.

"Oh dear!" gasped Peter, turning pale as death.

Poor Harry Somerville fell rather than leapt off his
stool, and dashed into the bedroom, where old Mr Kennedy
was occupied in alternately heaping unutterable abuse on
the head of Peter Mactavish, and imploring him to advise
what was best to be done. But Peter knew not. He could
only make one or two insane proposals to roll Charley
about the floor, and see if *that* would do him any good;
while Harry suggested in desperation that he should be
hung by the heels, and perhaps it would run out!

Meanwhile the senior clerk seized his hat, with the intention of going in search of Tom Whyte, and rushed out
at the door; which he had no sooner done, than he found
himself tightly embraced in the arms of that worthy, who
happened to be entering at the moment, and who, in
consequence of the sudden onset, was pinned up against
the wall of the porch.

"Oh, my buzzum!" exclaimed Tom, laying his hand
on his breast, "you've a'most bu'st me, sir; w'ats wrong,
sir?"

"Go for the doctor, Tom, quick! run like the wind.
Take the freshest horse; fly, Tom, Charley's poisoned;
laudanum—quick!"

"'Eavens an' 'arth!" ejaculated the groom, wheeling
round, and stalking rapidly off to the stable, like a pair of
insane compasses, while the senior clerk returned to the
bedroom, where he found Mr Kennedy still raving; Peter
Mactavish still aghast and deadly pale; and Harry Somerville staring like a maniac at his young friend, as if he
expected every moment to see him explode, although, to
all appearance, he was sleeping soundly, and comfortably,
too, notwithstanding the noise that was going on around

him. Suddenly Harry's eye rested on the label of the half-empty phial, and he uttered a loud, prolonged cheer.

"It's only tincture of ——"

"Wild cats and furies," cried Mr Kennedy, turning sharply round and seizing Harry by the collar, "why d'you kick up such a row? eh!"

"It's only tincture of rhubarb," repeated the boy, disengaging himself and holding up the phial triumphantly.

"So it is, I declare," exclaimed Mr Kennedy, in a tone that indicated intense relief of mind; while Peter Mactavish uttered a sigh so deep, that one might suppose a burden of innumerable tons' weight had just been removed from his breast.

Charley had been roused from his slumbers by this last ebullition; but, on being told what had caused it, he turned languidly round on his pillow and went to sleep again, while his friends departed and left him to repose.

Tom Whyte failed to find the doctor. The servant told him that her master had been suddenly called to set a broken leg that morning for a trapper who lived ten miles *down* the river, and, on his return, had found a man waiting with a horse and cariole, who carried him violently away to see his wife, who had been taken suddenly ill at a house twenty miles *up* the river, and so she didn't expect him back that night.

"An' where has 'e been took to?" inquired Tom.

She couldn't tell—she knew it was somewhere about the White-horse Plains, but she didn't know more than that.

"Did 'e not say w'en 'e'd be 'ome?"

"No, he didn't."

"Oh dear!" said Tom, rubbing his long nose in great

perplexity. "It's an 'orrible case o' sudden and unexpected pison."

She was sorry for it, but couldn't help that; and, thereupon, bidding him good morning, shut the door.

Tom's wits had come to that condition which just
precedes "*giving it up*" as hopeless, when it occurred to
him that he was not far from old Mr Kennedy's residence; so he stepped into the cariole again and drove
thither. On his arrival, he threw poor Mrs Kennedy and
Kate into great consternation by his exceedingly graphic,
and more than slightly exaggerated, account of what had
brought him in search of the doctor. At first Mrs Kennedy resolved to go up to Fort Garry immediately, but
Kate persuaded her to remain at home, by pointing out
that she could herself go, and if anything very serious had
occurred (which she didn't believe), Mr Kennedy could
come down for her immediately, while she (Kate) could
remain to nurse her brother.

In a few minutes Kate and Tom were seated side by
side in the little cariole, driving swiftly up the frozen river,
and two hours later the former was seated by her brother's
bedside, watching him as he slept with a look of tender
affection and solicitude.

Rousing himself from his slumbers, Charley looked
vacantly round the room.

"Have you slept well, darling?" inquired Kate, laying
her hand lightly on his forehead.

"Slept—eh! Oh, yes, I've slept. I say, Kate, what a
precious bump I came down on my head, to be sure!"

"Hush, Charley!" said Kate, perceiving that he was
becoming energetic. "Father said you were to keep

quiet—and so do I," she added, with a frown—"shut your eyes, sir, and go to sleep."

Charley complied by shutting his eyes, and opening his mouth, and uttering a succession of deep snores.

" Now, you bad boy," said Kate, " why *won't* you try to rest ? "

" Because, Kate, dear," said Charley, opening his eyes again, " because I feel as if I had slept a week at least, and not being one of the seven sleepers, I don't think it necessary to do more in that way just now. Besides, my sweet, but particularly wicked sister, I wish just at this moment to have a talk with you."

" But are you sure it won't do you harm to talk ; do you feel quite strong enough ? "

" Quite ; Samson was a mere infant compared to me."

" Oh ! don't talk nonsense, Charley dear, and keep your hands quiet, and don't lift the clothes with your knees in that way, else I'll go away and leave you."

" Very well, my pet, if you do, I'll get up and dress and follow you, that's all ! But come, Kate, tell me first of all how it was that I got pitched off that long-legged rhinoceros, and who it was that picked me up, and why wasn't I killed, and how did I come here ; for my head is sadly confused, and I scarcely recollect anything that has happened ; and, before commencing your discourse, Kate, please hand me a glass of water, for my mouth is as dry as a whistle."

Kate handed him a glass of water, smoothed his pillow, brushed the curls gently off his forehead, and sat down on the bedside.

" Thank you, Kate—now go on "

" Well, you see," she began ——

" Pardon me, dearest," interrupted Charley, " if you would please to look at me you would observe that my two eyes are tightly closed, so that I don't *see* at all."

" Well, then, you must understand ——"

" Must I ? Oh ! ——"

" That after that wicked horse leaped with you over the stable fence, you were thrown high into the air, and turning completely round, fell head foremost into the snow, and your poor head went through the top of an old cask that had been buried there all winter."

" Dear me," ejaculated Charley, " did any one see me. Kate ? "

" Oh, yes ! "

" Who ? " asked Charley, somewhat anxiously ; " not Mrs Grant, I hope, for if she did, she'd never let me hear the last of it."

" No, only our father, who was chasing you at the time," replied Kate, with a merry laugh.

" And no one else ? "

" No—oh, yes ! by the bye, Tom Whyte was there too."

" Oh, he's nobody ! Go on."

" But tell me, Charley, why do you care about Mrs Grant seeing you ? "

" Oh ! no reason at all, only she's such an abominable quiz."

We must guard the reader here against the supposition that Mrs Grant was a quiz of the ordinary kind. She was by no means a sprightly, clever woman—rather fond of a joke than otherwise—as the term might lead you to suppose. Her corporeal frame was very large, excessively

fat, and remarkably unwieldy; being an appropriate
casket in which to enshrine a mind of the heaviest and
most sluggish nature. She spoke little, ate largely, and
slept much,—the latter recreation being very frequently
enjoyed in a large arm-chair of a peculiar kind. It had
been a water-butt, which her ingenious husband had cut
half-way down the middle, then half-way across, and in
the angle thus formed fixed a bottom, which, together
with the back, he padded with tow, and covered the
whole with a mantle of glaring bed curtain chintz, whose
pattern alternated in stripes of sky-blue and china roses.
with broken fragments of the rainbow between   Notwithstanding her excessive slowness, however, Mrs Grant
was fond of taking a firm hold of anything or any circumstance in the character or affairs of her friends, and
twitting them thereupon in a grave but persevering
manner, that was exceedingly irritating. No one could
ever ascertain whether Mrs Grant did this in a sly way
or not, as her visage never expressed anything except unalterable good-humour. She was a good wife and an
affectionate mother; had a family of ten children, and
could boast of never having had more than one quarrel
with her husband. This disagreement was occasioned by a
rather awkward mischance. One day, not long after her last
baby was born, Mrs Grant waddled towards her tub with
the intention of enjoying her accustomed siesta. A few
minutes previously, her seventh child, which was just able
to walk, had scrambled up into the seat and fallen fast
asleep there. As has been already said, Mrs Grant's in-
tellect was never very bright, and at this particular time
she was rather drowsy, so that she did not observe the
child, and on reaching her chair, turned round pre-

paratory to letting herself plump into it.   She always
plumped into her chair.   Her muscles were too soft tc
lower her gently down into it.   Invariably, on reaching
a certain point, they ceased to act, and let her down with
a crash.   She had just reached this point, and her baby's
hopes and prospects were on the eve of being cruelly
crushed for ever, when Mr Grant noticed the impending
calamity.   He had no time to warn her, for she had
already passed the point at which her powers of muscular
endurance terminated; so, grasping the chair, he suddenly
withdrew it with such force that the baby rolled off upon
the floor like a hedgehog, straightened out flat, and gave
vent to an outrageous roar, while its horror-struck
mother came to the ground with a sound resembling the
fall of an enormous sack of wool.   Although the old lady
could not see exactly that there was anything very blame-
worthy in her husband's conduct upon this occasion, yet
her nerves had received so severe a shock that she refused
to be comforted for two entire days.

    But to return from this digression.   After Charley
had two or three times recommended Kate (who was a
little inclined to be quizzical) to proceed, she continued—

    "Well, then, you were carried up here by father and
Tom Whyte, and put to bed; and after a good deal of
rubbing and rough treatment, you were got round.   Then
Peter Mactavish nearly poisoned you; but fortunately he
was such a goose, that he did not think of reading the
label of the phial, and so gave you a dose of tincture of
rhubarb instead of laudanum, as he had intended; and
then father flew into a passion, and Tom Whyte was
sent to fetch the doctor, and couldn't find him; but, fortunately, he found me, which was much better, I think.

and brought me up here, and so here I am, and here I intend to remain."

"And so that's the end of it. Well, Kate, I'm very glad it was no worse."

"And I am very *thankful*," said Kate, with emphasis on the word, "that it's no worse."

"Oh, well! you know, Kate, I *meant* that, of course."

"But you did not *say* it," replied his sister, earnestly.

"To be sure not," said Charley, gaily; "it would be absurd to be always making solemn speeches, and things of that sort, every time one has a little accident."

'True, Charley; but when one has a very serious accident, and escapes unhurt, don't you think that *then* it would be ——"

"Oh, yes, to be sure!" interrupted Charley, who still strove to turn Kate from her serious frame of mind; "but, sister dear, how could I possibly *say* I was thankful, with my head crammed into an old cask and my feet pointing up to the blue sky? eh!"

Kate smiled at this, and laid her hand on his arm, while she bent over the pillow and looked tenderly into his eyes.

"Oh, my darling Charley! you are disposed to jest about it; but I cannot tell you how my heart trembled this morning, when I heard from Tom Whyte of what had happened. As we drove up to the fort, I thought how terrible it would have been if you had been killed; and then the happy days we have spent together rushed into my mind, and I thought of the willow creek where we used to fish for gold-eyes, and the spot in the woods where we have so often chased the little birds; and the lake in the prairies where we used to go in spring to

watch the waterfowl sporting in the sunshine—when I
recalled these things, Charley, and thought of you as dead,
I felt as if I should die too. And when I came here and
found that my fears were needless, that you were alive
and safe, and almost well, I felt thankful—yes, very, very
thankful—to God, for sparing your life, my dear, dear
Charley." And Kate laid her head on his bosom and
sobbed, when she thought of what might have been, as if
her very heart would break.

Charley's disposition to levity entirely vanished while
his sister spoke ; and, twining his tough little arm round
her neck, he pressed her fervently to his heart.

"Bless you, Kate," he said at length. "I am indeed
thankful to God, not only for sparing my life, but for
giving me such a darling sister to live for. But now,
Kate, tell me, what do you think of father's determination
to have me placed in the office here ?"

"Indeed, I think it's very hard. Oh, I do wish *so*
much that I could do it for you," said Kate, with a sigh

"Do *what* for me ?" asked Charley.

"Why, the office work," said Kate.

"Tuts ! fiddlesticks ! But isn't it, now, really a *very*
hard case ?"

"Indeed it is ; but, then, what can you do ?"

"Do ?" said Charley, impatiently ; "run away, to
be sure."

"Oh, don't speak of that !" said Kate, anxiously.
"You know it will kill our beloved mother ; and then
it would grieve father very much."

"Well, father don't care much about grieving me,
when he hunted me down like a wolf till I nearly broke
my neck."

" Now, Charley, you must not speak so. Father loves
you tenderly, although he *is* a little rough at times. If
you only heard how kindly he speaks of you to our mother when you are away, you could not think of giving
him so much pain. And then, the Bible says, ' Honour
thy father and thy mother, that thy days may be long in
the land which the Lord thy God giveth thee ;' and, as
God speaks in the Bible, *surely* we should pay attention
to it !"

Charley was silent for a few seconds ; then, heaving a
deep sigh, he said—

" Well, I believe you're right, Kate ; but, then, what
am I to do ? If I don't run away, I must live, like poor
Harry Somerville, on a long-legged stool ; and if I do
that, I'll—I'll ——"

As Charley spoke, the door opened, and his father
entered.

" Well, my boy," said he, seating himself on the bedside, and taking his son's hand, " how goes it now ? Head
getting all right again ? I fear that Kate has been talking too much to you. Is it so, you little chatterbox ?"

Mr Kennedy parted Kate's clustering ringlets, and
kissed her forehead.

Charley assured his father that he was almost well, and
much the better of having Kate to tend him. In fact,
he felt so much revived, that he said he would get up
and go out for a walk.

" Had I not better tell Tom Whyte to saddle the young
horse for you ?" said his father, half ironically. " No,
no, boy, lie still where you are to-day, and get up if you
feel better to-morrow. In the mean time, I've come to
say good-bye, as I intend to go home to relieve your mo-

ther's anxiety about you. I'll see you again, probably, the day after to-morrow. Hark you, boy; I've been talking your affairs over again with Mr Grant, and we've come to the conclusion to give you a run in the woods for a time. You'll have to be ready to start early in spring with the first brigades for the North. So adieu!"

Mr Kennedy patted him on the head, and hastily left the room.

A burning blush of shame arose on Charley's cheek as he recollected his late remarks about his father; and then, recalling the purport of his last words, he sent forth an exulting shout as he thought of the coming spring.

" Well, now, Charley," said Kate, with an arch smile, " let us talk seriously over your arrangements for running away."

Charley replied by seizing the pillow and throwing it at his sister's head; but, being accustomed to such eccentricities, she anticipated the movement and evaded the blow.

" Ah! Charley," cried Kate, laughing, " you mustn't let your hand get out of practice! That was a shockingly bad shot for a man thirsting to become a bear and buffalo hunter!"

" I'll make my fortune at once," cried Charley, as Kate replaced the pillow, " build a wooden castle on the shores of Great Bear Lake, take you to keep house for me, and, when I'm out hunting, you'll fish for whales in the lake, and we'll live there to a good old age; so good night, Kate, dear, and go to bed!"

Kate laughed, gave her brother a parting kiss, and left him.

CHAPTER VI

Spring and the *Voyageurs.*

WINTER, with its snow and its ice; winter, with its sharp winds and white drifts; winter, with its various characteristic occupations and employments, is past, and it is spring now.

The sun no longer glitters on fields of white; the woodman's axe is no longer heard hacking the oaken billets, to keep alive the roaring fires. That inexpressibly cheerful sound, the merry chime of sleigh-bells, that tells more of winter than all other sounds together, is no longer heard on the bosom of Red River, for the sleighs are thrown aside as useless lumber—carts and gigs have supplanted them. The old Canadian, who used to drive the ox with its water-barrel to the ice-hole for his daily supply, has substituted a small cart with wheels for the old sleigh that used to glide so smoothly over the snow, and *grit* so sharply on it in the more than usually frosty mornings in the days gone by. The trees have lost their white patches, and the clumps of willows, that used to look like islands in the prairie, have disappeared, as the carpeting that gave them prominence has dissolved. The aspect of everything in the isolated settlement has changed. The winter is gone, and spring—bright, beautiful, hilarious spring—has come again.

By those who have never known an arctic winter, the delights of an arctic spring can never, we fear, be fully appreciated or understood.   Contrast is one of its strongest elements ; indeed, we might say, *the* element which gives to all the others peculiar zest.   Life in the arctic regions is like one of Turner's pictures, in which the lights are strong, the shadows deep, and the *tout-ensemble* hazy and romantic.   So cold and prolonged is the winter, that the first mild breath of spring breaks on the senses like a zephyr from the plains of paradise. Everything bursts suddenly into vigorous life, after the long death-like sleep of Nature ; as little children burst into the romping gaieties of a new day, after the deep repose of a long and tranquil night.   The snow melts, the ice breaks up, and rushes in broken masses, heaving and tossing in the rising floods, that grind and whirl them into the ocean, or into those great fresh-water lakes that vie with ocean itself in magnitude and grandeur.   The buds come out and the leaves appear, clothing all nature with a bright refreshing green, which derives additional brilliancy from sundry patches of snow, that fill the deep creeks and hollows everywhere, and form ephemeral foun- tains whose waters continue to supply a thousand rills for many a long day, until the fierce glare of the summer sun prevails at last and melts them all away.

Red River flows on now to mix its long pent-up waters with Lake Winipeg.   Boats are seen rowing about upon its waters, as the settlers travel from place to place ; and wooden canoes, made of the hollowed-out trunks of large trees, shoot across from shore to shore,—these canoes being a substitute for bridges, of which there are none, although the settlement lies on both sides of the river.   Birds have now entered upon the scene, their wild cries and ceaseless flight adding to it a cheerful activity. Ground squirrels pop up out of their holes, to bask their round, fat, beautifully-striped little bodies in the sun, or to gaze in admiration at the farmer, as he urges a pair of *very* slow-going oxen, that drag the plough at a pace which induces one to believe that the wide field *may* possibly be ploughed up by the end of next year. Frogs whistle in the marshy grounds so loudly, that men new to the country believe they are being regaled by the songs of millions of birds. There is no mistake about their *whistle.* It is not merely *like* a whistle, but it *is* a whistle, shrill and continuous; and, as the swamps swarm with these creatures, the song never ceases for a moment, although each individual frog creates only *one* little gush of music, composed of half-a-dozen trills, and then stops a moment for breath before commencing the second bar. Bull-frogs, too, though not so numerous, help to vary the sound by croaking vociferously, as if they understood the value of bass, and were glad of having an opportunity to join in the universal hum of life and joy which rises everywhere, from the river and the swamp, the forest and the prairie, to welcome back the spring.

Such was the state of things in Red River one beautiful morning in April, when a band of *voyageurs* lounged in scattered groups about the front gate of Fort Garry. They were as fine a set of picturesque manly fellows as one could desire to see. Their mode of life rendered them healthy, hardy, and good-humoured, with a strong dash of recklessness—perhaps too much of it—in some of the younger men. Being descended, generally, from French-Canadian sires and Indian mothers, they united some of the good, and not a few of the bad, qualities of both, mentally as well as physically; combining the light, gay-hearted spirit, and full muscular frame of the Canadian, with the fierce passions and active habits of the Indian. And this wildness of disposition was n t a little fostered by the nature of their usual occupations. They were employed during a great part of the year in navigating the Hudson's Bay Company's boats, laden with furs and goods, through the labyrinth of rivers and lakes that stud and intersect the whole continent, or they were engaged in pursuit of the bisons,* which roam the prairies in vast herds.

They were dressed in the costume of the country; most of them wor light-blue cloth capotes, girded tightly round them by scarlet or crimson worsted belts. Some of them had blue, and others scarlet cloth leggins, ornamented more or less with stained porcupine quills, coloured silk, or variegated beads; while some might be seen clad in the leathern coats of winter,—deer-skin dressed like chamois leather, fringed all round with little tails, and ornamented much in the same way as those already described. The heavy winter mocassins and duffle socks, which gave to their feet the appearance of being afflicted with gout, were now replaced by mocassins of a lighter and more elegant character, having no socks below, and fitting tightly to the feet like gloves. Some wore hats similar to those made of silk or beaver, which are worn by ourselves in Britain, but so bedizened with scarlet cock-tail feathers, and silver cords and tassels, as to leave the original form of the head-dress a matter of great uncertainty. These hats, however, are only used on high

---

* These animals are always called buffaloes by American hunters and fur trade.

occasions, and chiefly by the fops. Most of the men wore
coarse blue cloth caps with peaks, and not a few discarded
head-pieces altogether, under the impression, apparently,
that nature had supplied a covering, which was in itself
sufficient. These costumes varied not only in character
but in quality, according to the circumstances of the
wearer ; some being highly ornamental and *mended*—
evincing the felicity of the owner in the possession of a
good wife—while others were soiled and torn, or but
slightly ornamented. The *voyageurs* were collected, as
we have said, in groups. Here stood a dozen of the
youngest—consequently the most noisy and showily dressed
—laughing loudly, gesticulating violently, and bragging
tremendously. Near to them were collected a number of
sterner spirits—men of middle age—with all the energy,
and muscle, and bone of youth, but without its swagger-
ing hilarity,—men whose powers and nerves had been
tried over and over again amid the stirring scenes of a
voyageur's life ; men whose heads were cool, and eyes
sharp, and hands ready and powerful, in the mad whirl of
boiling rapids, in the sudden attack of wild beast and
hostile man, or in the unexpected approach of any danger ;
men who, having been well tried, needed not to boast,
and who, having carried off triumphantly their respective
brides many years ago, needed not to decorate their persons with the absurd finery that characterized their
younger brethren. They were comparatively few in
number, but they composed a sterling band. of which
every man was a hero. Among them were those who
occupied the high positions of bowman and steersman ;
and when we tell the reader that on these two men frequently hangs the safety of a boat, with all its crew and

lading, it will be easily understood how needful it is that
they should be men of iron nerve and strength of mind.

Boat-travelling in those regions is conducted in a way
that would astonish most people who dwell in the civilised
quarters of the globe. The country being intersected in
all directions by great lakes and rivers, these have been
adopted as the most convenient highways, along which to
convey the supplies and bring back the furs from outposts. Rivers in America, however, as in other parts of
the world, are distinguished by sudden ebullitions and
turbulent points of character, in the shape of rapids, falls,
and cataracts, up and down which neither men nor boats
can by any possibility go with impunity ; consequently,
on arriving at such obstructions, the cargoes are carried
overland to navigable water above or below the falls (as
the case may be), then the boats are dragged over and
launched, again reloaded, and the travellers proceed. This
operation is called " *making a portage;* " and as these
portages vary from twelve yards to twelve miles in length,
it may be readily conceived that a *voyageur's* life is not
an easy one by any means.

This, however, is only one of his difficulties. Rapids
occur which are not so dangerous as to make a " portage "
necessary but are sufficiently turbulent to render the
descent of them perilous. In such cases, the boats, being
lightened of part of their cargo, are *run* down, and frequently they descend with full cargoes and crews. It is
then that the whole management of each boat devolves
upon its bowman and steersman. The rest of the crew,
or *middlemen* as they are called, merely sit still and look
on, or give a stroke with their oars if required ; while the
steersman, with powerful sweeps of his heavy oar, directs

the flying boat as it bounds from surge to surge like a thing of life; and the bowman stands erect in front to assist in directing his comrade at the stern, having a strong and long pole in his hands, with which, ever and anon, he violently forces the boat's-head away from sunken rocks, against which it might otherwise strike and be stove in, capsized, or seriously damaged.

Besides the groups already enumerated, there were one or two others, composed of grave, elderly men, whose wrinkled brows, gray hairs, and slow, quiet step, showed that the strength of their days was past; although their upright figures and warm brown complexions gave promise of their living to see many summers still. These were the principal steersmen and old guides—men of renown, to whom the others bowed as oracles, or looked up as fathers; men whose youth and manhood had been spent in roaming the trackless wilderness, and who were, therefore, eminently qualified to guide brigades through the length and breadth of the land; men whose power of threading their way among the perplexing intricacies of the forest had become a second nature, a kind of instinct, that was as sure of attaining its end as the instinct of the feathered tribes, which brings the swallow, after a long absence, with unerring certainty back to its former haunts again in spring

CHAPTER VII

The Store.

AT whatever establishment in the fur-trader's dominions
you may chance to alight, you will find a particular building which is surrounded by a halo of interest; towards
which there seems to be a general leaning on the part of
everybody, especially of the Indians, and with which are
connected, in the minds of all, the most stirring remi-
niscences and pleasing associations.

This is the trading store. It is always recognisable, if
natives are in the neighbourhood, by the bevy of red men
that cluster round it, awaiting the coming of the store-
keeper or the trader with that stoic patience which is
peculiar to Indians. It may be further recognised, by
a close observer, by the soiled condition of its walls,
occasioned by loungers rubbing their backs perpetually
against it, and the peculiar dinginess round the key-
hole, caused by frequent applications of the key, which
renders it conspicuous beyond all its comrades. Here is
contained that which makes the red man's life enjoyable;
that which causes his heart to leap, and induces him to
toil for months and months together in the heat of summer and amid the frost and snow of winter; that which
actually accomplishes, what music is *said* to achieve, the
" soothing of the savage breast; " in short, here are
stored up blankets, guns, powder, shot, kettles, axes, and

knives ; twine for nets, vermilion for war-paint, fish-
hooks and scalping knives, capotes, cloth, beads, needles,
and a host of miscellaneous articles, much too numerous
to mention.   Here, also, occur periodical scenes of bustle
and excitement, when bands of natives arrive from distant
hunting-grounds, laden with rich furs, which are speedily
transferred to the Hudson's Bay Company's stores in
exchange for the goods afore-mentioned.   And many a
tough wrangle has the trader on such occasions with
sharp natives, who might have graduated in Billingsgate
—so close are they at a bargain.   Here, too, *voyageurs*
are supplied with an equivalent for their wages, part in
advance, if they desire it (and they generally do desire
it), and part at the conclusion of their long and arduous
voyages.

It is to one of t' ese stores, reader, that we wish to introduce you now, that you may witness the men of the
North brigade receive their advances.

The store at Fort Garry stands on the right of the fort,
as you enter by the front gate.   Its interior resembles
that of the other stores in the country, being only a little
larger.   A counter encloses a space sufficiently wide to
admit a dozen men, and serves to keep back those who are
more eager than the rest.   Inside this counter, at the time
we write of, stood our friend Peter Mactavish, who was
the presiding genius of the scene.

"Shut the door now, and lock it," said Peter, in an
authoritative tone, after eight or ten young *voyageurs* had
crushed into the space in front of the counter.   "I'll not
supply you with so much as an ounce of tobacco if you let
in another man."

Peter needed not to repeat the command.   Three or

four stalwart shoulders were applied to the door, which
shut with a bang like a cannon-shot, and the key was
turned.

"Come, now, Antoine," began the trader, " we've lots
to do, and not much time to do it in, so pray look sharp."

Antoine, however, was not to be urged on so easily.
He had been meditating deeply all morning on what he
should purchase. Moreover, he had a sweetheart; and,
of course, he had to buy something for her, before setting
out on his travels. Besides, Antoine was six feet high,
and broad shouldered, and well made, with a dark face
and glossy black hair; and he entertained a notion that
there were one or two points in his costume which required to be carefully rectified, ere he could consider that
he had attained to perfection : so he brushed the long
hair off his forehead, crossed his arms, and gazed around
him.

"Come, now, Antoine," said Peter, throwing a green
blanket at him, "I know you want *that* to begin with.
What's the use of thinking so long about it ?—eh ? And
that, too," he added, throwing him a blue cloth capote.
" Anything else ?"

"Oui, oui, monsieur," cried Antoine, as he disengaged
himself from the folds of the coat which Peter had thrown
over his head. "Tabac, monsieur! tabac!"

"Oh, to be sure," cried Peter. "I might have guessed
that *that* was uppermost in your mind. Well, how much
will you have ?" Peter began to unwind the fragrant
weed off a coil of most appalling size and thickness, which
looked like a snake of endless length. "Will that do ?"
and he flourished about four feet of the snake before the
eyes of the *voyageur*.

Antoine accepted the quantity; and young Harry Somerville entered the articles against him in a book.

"Anything more, Antoine?" said the trader. "Ah, some beads, and silks!—eh! Oho, Antoine! By the way, Louis, have you seen Annette lately?"

Peter turned to another *voyageur* when he put this question, and the *voyageur* gave a broad grin as he replied in the affirmative; while Antoine looked a little confused. He did not care much, however, for jesting. So, after getting one or two more articles—not forgetting half-a-dozen clay pipes, and a few yards of gaudy calico, which called forth from Peter a second reference to Annette— he bundled up his goods, and made way for another comrade.

Louis Peltier, one of the principal guides, and a man of importance therefore, now stood forward. He was probably about forty-five years of age; had a plain, olive-coloured countenance, surrounded by a mass of long, jet black hair, which he inherited, along with a pair of dark piercing eyes, from his Indian mother; and a robust, heavy, yet active frame, which bore a strong resemblance to what his Canadian father's had been many years before. His arms, in particular, were of herculean mould, with large swelling veins, and strongly-marked muscles. They seemed, in fact, just formed for the purpose of pulling the heavy sweep of an inland boat among strong rapids. His face combined an expression of stern resolution with great good-humour; and, truly, his countenance did not belie him, for he was known among his comrades as the most courageous, and, at the same time, the most peaceable man in the settlement. Louis Peltier was singular in possessing the latter quality, for assuredly, the half-breeds

6

whatever other good points they boast,—cannot lay claim
to very gentle or dove-like dispositions. His gray capote
and blue leggins were decorated with no unusual orna-
ments, and the scarlet belt which encircled his massive
figure was the only bit of colour he displayed.

The younger men fell respectfully into the rear, as
Louis stepped forward, and begged pardon for coming so
early in the day. "Mais, monsieur," he said, " I have to
look after the boats to-day, and get them ready for a start
to-morrow."

Peter Mactavish gave Louis a hearty shake of t' · hand
before proceeding to supply his wants, which ·· · simple
and moderate, excepting in the article of *tobac*, in the use
of which he was *im*-moderate—being an inveterate smoker ;
so that a considerable portion of the snake had to be un-
coiled for his benefit.

" Fond as ever of smoking, Louis ?" said Peter Mactavish, as he handed him the coil.

" Oui, monsieur—very fond," answered the guide, smell-
ing the weed. " Ah, this is very good. I must take a
good supply this voyage, because I lost the half of my
roll last year ; " and the guide gave a sigh as he thought
of the overwhelming bereavement.

" Lost the half of it, Louis !" said Mactavish. " Why,
how was that ? You must have lost *more* than half your
spirits with it !"

" Ah ! oui, I lost *all* my spirits, and my comrade
François at the same time :"

" Dear me !" exclaimed the clerk, bustling about the
store while the guide continued to talk.

" Oui, monsieur—oui. I lost *him*, and my tabac,
and my spirits, and very nearly my life, all in one moment !"

" Why !—how came that about ?" said Peter, pausing in his work, and laying a handful of pipes on the counter.

" Ah ! monsieur, it was very sad (merci, monsieur, merci, thirty pipes, if you please), and I thought at the time that I should give up my *voyageur* life, and remain altogether in the settlement with my old woman. Mais, monsieur, that was not possible. When I spoke of it to my old woman, she called *me* an old woman ; and, you know, monsieur, that *two* old women never could live together in peace for twelve months under the same roof. So here I am, you see, ready again for the voyage."

The *voyageurs*, who had drawn round Louis when he alluded to an anecdote which they had often heard before, but were never weary of hearing over again, laughed loudly at this sally, and urged the guide to relate the story to " *monsieur*," who, nothing loath to suspend his operations for a little, leaned his arms on the counter, and said—

" Tell us all about it, Louis; I am anxious to know how you managed to come by so many losses all at one time."

" Bien, monsieur, I shall soon relate it, for the story is very short."

Harry Somerville, who was entering the pipes in Louis's account, had just set down the figures " 30 " when Louis cleared his throat to begin. Not having the mental fortitude to finish the line, he dropped his pen, sprang off his stool, which he upset in so doing, jumped up, sitting-ways, upon the counter, and gazed with breathless interest into the guide's face as he spoke.

" It was on a cold, wet afternoon," said Louis, " that we were descending the Hill river, at a part of the rapids

where there is a sharp bend in the stream, and two or
three great rocks that stand up in front of the water, as
it plunges over a ledge, as if they were put there a' purpose to catch it, and split it up into foam, or to stop the
boats and canoes that try to run the rapids, and cut them
up into splinters. It was an ugly place, monsieur, I can
tell you, and though I've run it again and again, I
always hold my breath tighter when we get to the top,
and breathe freer when we get to the bottom. Well,
there was a chum of mine at the bow, François by name,
and a fine fellow he was, as I ever came across. He
used to sleep with me at night under the same blanket,
although it *was* somewhat inconvenient; for, being as big
as myself and a stone heavier, it was all we could do to
make the blanket cover us. However, he and I were
great friends, and we managed it somehow. Well, he
was at the bow when we took the rapids—and a first-rate
bowman he made. His pole was twice as long and twice
as thick as any other pole in the boat, and he twisted it
about just like a fiddlestick. I remember well the night
before we came to the rapids, as he was sitting by the
fire which was blazing up among the pine branches that
overhung us, he said that he wanted a good pole for the
rapids next day, and with that he jumped up, laid hold
of an axe, and went back into the woods a bit to get one.
When he returned, he brought a young tree on his
shoulder, which he began to strip of its branches and
bark. 'Louis,' says he, 'this is hot work, give us a pipe,'
so I rummaged about for some tobacco, but found there
was none left in my bag; so I went to my kit and got
out my roll, about three fathoms or so, and cutting half
of it off, I went to the fire and twisted it round his neck

by way of a joke, and he said he'd wear it as a necklace
all night—and so he did, too, and forgot to take it off in
the morning; and when we came near the rapids I
couldn't get at my bag to stow it away, so, says I,
'François, you'll have to run with it on, for I can't stop
to stow it now.' 'All right,' says he, 'go-a-head,' and
just as he said it, we came in sight of the first run, foaming and boiling like a kettle of robiboo. 'Take care,
lads,' I cried, and the next moment we were dashing
down towards the bend in the river. As we came near
to the shoot, I saw François standing up on the gunwale
to get a better view of the rocks a-head, and every now
and then giving me a signal with his hand how to steer;
suddenly he gave a shout, and plunged his long pole into
the water, to fend off from a rock which a swirl in the
stream had concealed. For a second or two his pole bent
like a willow, and we could feel the heavy boat jerk off a
little with the tremendous strain; but all at once the pole
broke off short with a crack, François' heels made a
flourish in the air, and then he disappeared head-fo most
into the foaming water, with my tobacco coiled round his
neck! As we flew past the place, one of his arms
appeared, and I made a grab at it, and caught him by the
sleeve; but the effort upset myself, and over I went too.
Fortunately, however, one of my men caught me by the
foot and held on like a vice; but the force of the current
tore François' sleeve out of my grasp, and I was dragged
into the boat again just in time to see my comrade's legs
and arms going like the sails of a wind-mill, as he rolled
over several times and disappeared. Well, we put
ashore the moment we got into still water, and then five
or six of us started off on foot to look for François

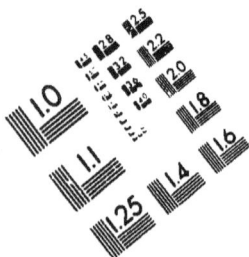

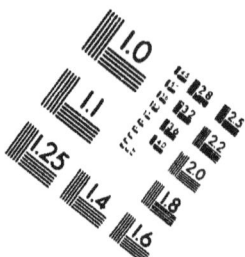

IMAGE EVALUATION
TEST TARGET (MT-3)

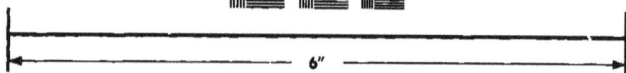

6"

Photographic
Sciences
Corporation

23 WEST MAIN STREET
WEBSTER, N.Y. 14580
(716) 872-4503

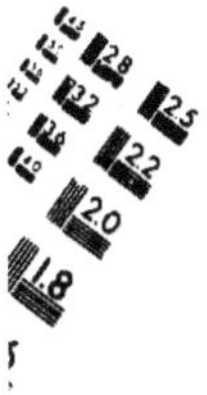
2.8
2.5
3.2
2.2
2.0
1.8

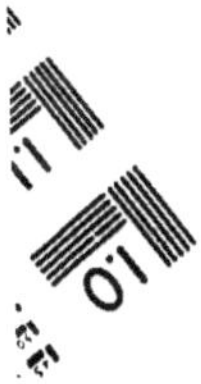
1.1
1.0

After half-an-hour's search, we found him pitched upon a
flat rock in the middle of the stream like a bit of drift-wood.
We immediately waded out to the rock and brought him
ashore, where we lighted a fire, took off all his clothes,
and rubbed him till he began to show signs of life again.
But you may judge, mes garçons, of my misery, when I
found that the coil of tobacco was gone. It had come
off his neck during his struggles, and there wasn't a
vestige of it left, except a bright red mark on the throat,
where it had nearly strangled him. When he began to
recover, he put his hand up to his neck as if feeling for
something, and muttered faintly, 'the tobac.' 'Ah,
morbleu!' said I, 'you may say that! Where is it?'
Well, we soon brought him round, but he had swallowed
so much water that it damaged his lungs, and we had to
leave him at the next post we came to, and so I lost my
friend, too."

"Did François get better?" said Charley Kennedy,
in a voice of great concern.

Charley had entered the store by another door, just as
the guide began his story, and had listened to it un-
observed with breathless interest.

"Recover! Oh, oui, monsieur, he soon got well again."

"Oh, I'm so glad," cried Charley.

"But I lost him for that voyage," added the guide;
"and I lost my tabac for ever!"

"You must take better care of it this time, Louis,"
said Peter Mactavish, as he resumed his work.

"That I shall, monsieur," replied Louis, shouldering
his goods and quitting the store, while a short, slim,
active, little Canadian took his place.

"Now, then, Baptiste," said Mactavish, "you want
a ——"

" Blanket, monsieur."

" Good.　And——"

" A capote, monsieur !'

" And——"

" An axe——"

"Stop, stop !" shouted Harry Somerville from his desk. " Here's an entry in Louis's account that I can't make out—30 something or other—what can it have been ?"

" How often," said Mactavish, going up to him with a look of annoyance—" how often have I told you, Mr Somerville not to leave an entry half-finished on any account ?"

"I didn't know that I left it so," said Harry, twisting his features, and scratching his head in great perplexity. " What *can* it have been, 30—30—not blankets, eh ?" (Harry was becoming banteringly bitter.)　" He couldn't have got thirty guns, could he ? or thirty knives, or thirty copper kettles ?"

" Perhaps it was thirty pounds of tea," suggested Charley.

" No doubt it was thirty *pipes*," said Peter Mactavish.

" Oh, that was it !" cried Harry, "that was it ! thirty pipes to be sure—what an ass I am !"

" And pray what is *that ?*" said Mactavish, pointing sarcastically to an entry in the previous account—" 5 *yards of superfine Annette ?* Really, Mr Somerville, I wish you would pay more attention to your work and less to the conversation."

" Oh dear !" cried Harry, becoming almost hysterical under the combined effects of chagrin at making so many mistakes, and suppressed merriment at the idea of selling Annettes by the yard.　" Oh, dear me !——"

Harry could say no more, but stuffed his handkerchief into his mouth and turned away.

"Well, sir," said the offended Peter, "when you have laughed to your entire satisfaction, we will go on with our work, if you please."

"All right," cried Harry, suppressing his feelings with a strong effort, "what next?"

Just then a tall, raw-boned man entered the store, and rudely thrusting Baptiste aside, asked if he could get his supplies now.

"No," said Mactavish, sharply; "you'll take your turn like the rest."

The new-comer was a native of Orkney, a country from which, and the neighbouring islands, the Fur Company almost exclusively recruits its staff of labourers. These men are steady, useful servants, although inclined to be slow and lazy *at first*; but they soon get used to the country, and rapidly improve under the example of the active Canadians and half-breeds with whom they associate; some of them are the best servants the Company possess. Hugh Mathison, however, was a very bad specimen of the race, being rough and coarse in his manners, and very lazy withal. Upon receiving the trader's answer, Hugh turned sulkily on his heel and strode towards the door. Now, it happened that Baptiste's bundle lay just behind him, and, on turning to leave the place, he tripped over it and stumbled, whereat the *voyageurs* burst into an ironical laugh (for Hugh was not a favourite).

"Confound your trash!" he cried, giving the little bundle a kick that scattered everything over the floor.

"Crapaud!" said Baptiste, between his set teeth, while

his eyes flashed angrily, and he stood up before Hugh with clenched fists, "what mean you by that? eh?"

The big Scotchman held his little opponent in contempt; so that, instead of putting himself on the defensive, he leaned his back against the door, thrust his hands into his pockets, and requested to know "what that was to him."

Baptiste was not a man of many words, and this reply, coupled with the insolent sneer with which it was uttered, caused him to plant a sudden and well-directed blow on the point of Hugh's nose, which flattened it on his face, and brought the back of his head into violent contact with the door.

"Well done!" shouted the men; "bravo, Baptiste! regardez le nez, mes enfans!"

"Hold!" cried Mactavish, vaulting the counter, and intercepting Hugh as he rushed upon his antagonist; "no fighting here, you blackguards! If you want to do *that*, go outside the fort;" and Peter, opening the door, thrust the Orkneyman out.

In the meantime, Baptiste gathered up his goods and left the store, in company with several of his friends, vowing that he would wreak his vengeance on the "gros chien" before the sun should set.

He had not long to wait, however, for, just outside the gate he found Hugh, still smarting under the pain and indignity of the blow, and ready to pounce upon him like a cat on a mouse.

Baptiste instantly threw down his bundle, and prepared for battle by discarding his coat.

Every nation has its own peculiar method of fighting, and its own ideas of what is honourable and dishonourable in combat. The English, as every one knows, have particularly stringent rules regarding the part of the body which may or may not be hit with propriety, and count it foul disgrace to strike a man when he is down; although, by some strange perversity of reasoning, they deem it right and fair to *fall* upon him while in this helpless condition, and burst him if possible. The Scotchman has less of the science, and we are half inclined to believe that he would go the length of kicking a fallen opponent; but on this point we are not quite positive. In regard to the style adopted by the half-breeds, however, we have no doubt. They fight *any* way and *every* way, without reference to rules at all; and, really, although we may bring ourselves into contempt by admitting the fact, we think they are quite right. No doubt the best course of action is *not* to fight; but, if a man does find it *necessary* to do so, surely the wisest plan is to get it over at once (as the dentist suggested to his timorous patient), and to do it in the most effectual manner.

Be this as it may, Baptiste flew at Hugh and alighted upon him, not head first, or fist first, or feet first, or *anything* first, but altogether—in a heap, as it were; fist, feet, knees, nails, and teeth, all taking effect at one and the same time, with a force so irresistible that the next moment they both rolled in the dust together.

For a minute or so they struggled and kicked like a couple of serpents, and then, bounding to their feet again, they began to perform a war-dance round each other, revolving their fists at the same time in, we presume, the most approved fashion. Owing to his bulk and natural laziness, which rendered jumping about like a jack-in-the-box impossible, Hugh Mathison preferred to

stand on the defensive ; while his lighter opponent, giving
way to the natural bent of his mercurial temperament
and corporeal predilections, comported himself in a manner
that cannot be likened to anything mortal or immortal,
human or inhuman, unless it be to an insane cat, whose
veins ran wild-fire instead of blood. Or, perhaps, we
might liken him to that ingenious piece of firework called
a zigzag cracker, which explodes with unexpected and
repeated suddenness, changing its position in a most perplexing manner at every crack. Baptiste, after the first
onset, danced backwards with surprising lightness, glaring
at his adversary the while, and rapidly revolving his fists
as before mentioned ; then, a terrific yell was heard ; his
head, arms, and legs became a sort of whirling conglomerate ; the spot on which he danced was suddenly vacant,
and, at the same moment, Mathison received a bite, a
scratch, a dab on the nose, and a kick in the stomach all
at once. Feeling that it was impossible to plant a well
directed blow on such an assailant, he waited for the next
onslaught ; and the moment he saw the explosive object
flying through the air towards him, he met it with a
crack of his heavy fist, which, happening to take effect in
the middle of the chest, drove it backwards with about as
much velocity as it had approached, and poor Baptiste
measured his length on the ground.

"Oh pauvre chien !" cried the spectators, "c'est fini !"

"Not yet," cried Baptiste, as he sprang with a scream
to his feet again, and began his dance with redoubled
energy, just as if all that had gone before was a mere
sketch—a sort of playful rehearsal, as it were, of what was
now to follow. At this moment Hugh stumbled over a
canoe-paddle and fell headlong into Baptiste's arms, as he

was in the very act of making one of his violent descents.
This unlooked-for occurrence brought them both to a
sudden pause, partly from necessity and partly from surprise. Out of this state Baptiste recovered first, and,
taking advantage of the accident, threw Mathison heavily
to the ground. He rose quickly, however, and renewed
the fight with freshened vigour.

Just at this moment a passionate growl was heard, and
old Mr Kennedy rushed out of the fort in a towering
rage.

Now, Mr Kennedy had no reason whatever for being
angry. He was only a visitor at the fort, and so had no
concern in the behaviour of those connected with it. He
was not even in the Company's service now, and could
not, therefore, lay claim, as one of its officers, to any right
to interfere with its men. But Mr Kennedy never acted
much from reason; impulse was generally his guiding
star. He had, moreover, been an absolute monarch, and
a commander of men, for many years past in his capacity
of fur-trader. Being, as we have said, a powerful, fiery
man, he had ruled very much by means of brute force,—a
species of suasion, by the way, which is too common
among many of the gentlemen (?) in the employment of
the Hudson's Bay Company. On hearing, therefore, that
the men were fighting in front of the fort, Mr Kennedy
rushed out in a towering rage.

"Oh, you precious blackguards!" he cried, running up
to the combatants, while with flashing eyes he gazed first
at one and then at the other, as if uncertain on which to
launch his ire. "Have you no place in the world to fight
but *here?* Eh! blackguards?"

"Oh, monsieur," said Baptiste, lowering his hands, and

assuming that politeness of demeanour which seems inseparable from French blood, however much mixed with
baser fluid, " I was just giving *that dog* a thrashing,
monsieur."

" Go !" cried Mr Kennedy, in a voice of thunder, turning to Hugh, who still stood in a pugilistic attitude, with
very little respect in his looks.

Hugh hesitated to obey the order, but Mr Kennedy
continued to advance, grinding his teeth and working his
fingers convulsively, as if he longed to lay violent hold
of the Orkneyman's swelled nose ; so he retreated in his
uncertainty, but still with his face to the foe. As has
been already said, the Assinaboine river flows within a
hundred yards of the gate of Fort Garry. The two men,
in their combat, had approached pretty near to the bank,
at a place where it descends somewhat precipitately into
the stream. It was towards this bank that Hugh Mathison was now retreating, crab fashion, followed by Mr
Kennedy, and both of them so taken up with each other
that neither perceived the fact until Hugh's heel struck
against a stone just at the moment that Mr Kennedy
raised his clenched fist in a threatening attitude. The
effect of this combination was to pitch the poor man head
over heels down the bank, into a row of willow bushes,
through which, as he rolled with great speed, he went
with a loud crash, and shot head first, like a startled alli-
gator, into the water, amid a roar of laughter from his
comrades and the people belonging to the fort ; most of
whom, attracted by the fight, were now assembled on the
banks of the river.

Mr Kennedy's wrath vanished immediately, and he
joined in the laughter ; but his face instantly changed

when he beheld Hugh spluttering in deep water, and heard some one say that he could not swim.

"What! can't swim?" he exclaimed, running down the bank to the edge of the water. Baptiste was before him, however. In a moment he plunged in up to the neck, stretched forth his arm, grasped Hugh by the hair, and dragged him to the land

CHAPTER VIII.

Farewell to Kate; departure of the brigade; Charley becomes a *royageur*

ON the following day at noon, the spot on which the late combat had taken place became the theatre of a stirring and animated scene.   Fort Garry, and the space between it and the river, swarmed with *royageurs*, dressed in their cleanest, newest, and most brilliant costume.   The large boats for the north, six in number, lay moored to the river's bank, laden with bales of furs, and ready to start on their long voyage.   Young men, who had never been on the route before, stood with animated looks watching the operations of the guides as they passed critical examination upon their boats, overhauled the oars to see that they were in good condition, or with crooked knives (a species of instrument in the use of which *royageurs* and natives are very expert) polished off the top of a mast, the blade of an oar, or the handle of a tiller.   Old men, who had passed their lives in similar occupations, looked on in silence ; some standing with their heads bent on their bosoms, and an expression of sadness about their faces, as if the scene recalled some mournful event of their early life ; or possibly reminded them of wild joyous scenes of other days, when the blood coursed warmly in their young veins, and the strong muscles sprang lightly to obey their will ; when the work they had to do was

hard, and the sleep that followed it was sound :—scenes
and days that were now gone by for ever. Others reclined against the wooden fence, their arms crossed, their
thin white hair waving gently in the breeze, and a kind
smile playing on their sunburnt faces, as they observed
the swagger and coxcombry of the younger men, or
watched the gambols of several dark-eyed little children
—embryo buffalo-hunters and *voyageurs*—whose mothers
had brought them to the fort to get a last kiss from *papa*,
and witness the departure of the boats.

Several tender scenes were going on, in out-of-the-way
places—in angles of the walls and bastions, or behind the
gates—between youthful couples about to be separated for
a season. Interesting scenes these of pathos and pleasantry
—a combination of soft glances and affectionate, fervent
assurances—alternate embraces (that were *apparently* received with reluctance, but *actually* with delight), and
proffers of pieces of calico and beads and other trinkets
(received both *apparently* and *actually* with extreme satisfaction), as *souvenirs* of happy days that were past, and
pledges of unalterable constancy and bright hopes in days
that were yet to come.

A little apart from the others, a youth and a girl might
be seen sauntering slowly towards the copse beyond the
stable. These were Charley Kennedy and his sister Kate.
who had retired from the bustling scene to take a last
short walk together, ere they separated, it might be, for
years, perhaps for ever ! Charley held Kate's hand, while
her sweet little head rested on his shoulder.

" Oh, Charley, Charley, my own dear, darling Charley,
I'm quite miserable, and you ought not to go away ; it's
very wrong, and I don't mind a bit what you say —I shall

die if you leave me!" And Kate pressed him tightly to her heart, and sobbed in the depth of her woe.

" Now, Kate, my darling, don't go on so! You know I can't help it ——"

"I *don't* know," cried Kate, interrupting him, and speaking vehemently. "I don't know, and I don't believe, and I don't care for anything at all; it's very hardhearted of you, and wrong, and not right, and I'm just quite wretched!"

Poor Kate was undoubtedly speaking the absolute truth; for a more disconsolate and wretched look of woebegone misery was never seen on so sweet and tender and loveable a little face before. Her blue eyes swam in two lakes of pure crystal, that overflowed continually; her mouth, which was usually round, had become an elongated oval; and her nut-brown hair fell in dishevelled masses over her soft cheeks.

"Oh, Charley," she continued, " why *won't* you stay?"

" Listen to me, dearest Kate," said Charley, in a very husky voice. " It's too late to draw back now, even if I wished to do so; and you don't consider, darling, that I'll be back again soon. Besides, I'm a man now, Kate, and I must make my own bread. Who ever heard of a man being supported by his old father?"

" Well, but you can do that here."

" Now, don't interrupt me, Kate," said Charley, kissing her forehead; "I'm quite satisfied with *two short* legs, and have no desire whatever to make my bread on the top of *three long* ones. Besides, you know I can write to you ——"

" But you won't; you'll forget."

" No, indeed, I will not. I'll write you long letters

7

about all that I see and do ; and you shall write long
letters to me about ————"

"Stop, Charley," cried Kate ; "I won't listen to you.
I hate to think of it."

And her tears burst forth again with fresh violence.
This time Charley's heart sank too. The lump in his
throat all but choked him ; so he was fain to lay his
head upon Kate's heaving bosom, and weep along with
her.

For a few minutes they remained silent, when a slight
rustling in the bushes was heard. In another moment a
tall, broad-shouldered, gentlemanly man, dressed in black,
stood before them. Charley and Kate, on seeing this
personage, arose, and, wiping the tears from their eyes,
gave a sad smile as they shook hands with their clergyman.

"My poor children," said Mr Addison, affectionately,
"I know well why your hearts are sad. May God bless
and comfort you ! I saw you enter the wood, and came
to bid you farewell, Charley, my dear boy, as I shall not
have another opportunity of doing so."

"Oh, dear Mr Addison," cried Kate, grasping his hand
in both of hers, and gazing imploringly up at him through
a perfect wilderness of ringlets and tears, "do prevail
upon Charley to stay at home ; please do."

Mr Addison could scarcely help smiling at the poor
girl's extreme earnestness.

"I fear, my sweet child, that it is too late now to attempt
to dissuade Charley. Besides, he goes with the consent
of his father ; and I am inclined to think that a change
of life for a *short* time may do him good. Come, Kate,
cheer up ! Charley will return to us again ere long,
improved, I trust, both physically and mentally."

Kate did *not* cheer up ; but she dried her eyes and endeavoured to look more composed, while Mr Addison took Charley by the hand, and, as they walked slowly through the wood, gave him much earnest advice and counsel.

The clergyman's manner was peculiar. With a large, warm, generous heart, he possessed an enthusiastic nature, a quick brusque manner, and a loud voice, which, when his spirit was influenced by the strong emotions of pity, or anxiety for the souls of his flock, sunk into a deep soft bass of the most thrilling earnestness. He belonged to the Church of England, but conducted service very much in the Presbyterian form, as being more suited to his mixed congregation. After a long conversation with Charley, he concluded by saying—

" I do not care to say much to you about being kind and obliging to all whom you may meet with during your travels, nor about the dangers to which you will be exposed, by being thrown into the company of wild and reckless, perhaps very wicked, men. There is but *one* incentive to every good, and *one* safeguard against all evil, my boy, and that is the love of God. You may, perhaps, forget much that I have said to you ; but remember this, Charley, if you would be happy in this world, and have a good hope for the next, centre your heart's affection on our blessed Lord Jesus Christ ; for believe me, boy, *his* heart's affection is centred upon you."

As Mr Addison spoke, a loud hallo from Mr Kennedy apprised them that their time was exhausted, and that the boats were ready to start. Charley sprang towards Kate, locked her in a long, passionate embrace, and then

forgetting Mr Addison altogether in his haste, ran out of
the wood, and hastened towards the scene of departure.

"Good bye, Charley!" cried Harry Somerville, running
up to his friend, and giving him a warm grasp of the hand.
"Don't forget me, Charley. I wish I were going with
you, with all my heart; but I'm an unlucky dog—good
bye." The senior clerk and Peter Mactavish had also a
kindly word and a cheerful farewell for him as he hurried
past.

"Good bye, Charley, my lad!" said old Mr Kennedy,
in an *excessively* loud voice, as if by such means he intended to crush back some unusual, but very powerful,
feelings that had a peculiar influence on a certain lump
in his throat. "Good bye, my lad; don't forget to write
to your old ——. Hang it!" said the old man, brushing
his coat-sleeve somewhat violently across his eyes, and
turning abruptly round as Charley left him and sprang
into the boat. "I say, Grant, I—I——. What are you
staring at?—eh?" The latter part of his speech was
addressed, in an angry tone, to an innocent *voyageur*, who
happened accidently to confront him at the moment.

"Come along, Kennedy," said Mr Grant, interposing;
and grasping his excited friend by the arm—"Come
with me."

"Ah, to be sure!—yes!" said he, looking over his
shoulder and waving a last adieu to Charley—"Good bye,
God bless you, my dear boy! I say, Grant, come along—
quick, man, and let's have a pipe. Yes; let's have a
pipe." Mr Kennedy, essaying once more to crush back
his rebellious feelings, strode rapidly up the bank, and,
entering the house, sought to overwhelm his sorrow in
smoke: in which attempt he failed.

CHAPTER IX.

The Voyage; the Encampment; a Surprise.

IT was a fine sight to see the boats depart for the North.
It was a thrilling heart-stirring sight to behold these picturesque athletic men, on receiving the word of command
from their guides, spring lightly into the long, heavy
boats ; to see them let the oars fall into the water with a
loud splash ; and then, taking their seats, give way with
a will, knowing that the eyes of friends and sweethearts
and rivals were bent earnestly upon them.   It was a
splendid sight to see boat after boat shoot out from the
landing-place, and cut through the calm bosom of the
river, as the men bent their sturdy backs, until the thick
oars creaked and groaned on the gunwales, and flashed in
the stream, more and more vigorously at each successive
stroke, until their friends on the bank, who were anxious
to see the last of them, had to run faster and faster, in
order to keep up with them, as the rowers warmed at their
work, and made the water gurgle at the bows—their
bright blue and scarlet and white trappings reflected in
the dark waters in broken masses of colour, streaked with
long lines of shining ripples, as if they floated on a lake
of liquid rainbows.   And it was a glorious thing to hear
the wild, plaintive song, led by one clear, sonorous voice,
that rang out, full and strong, in the still air, while, at

the close of every two lines, the whole brigade burst into
a loud enthusiastic chorus, that rolled far and wide over
the smooth waters—telling of their approach to settlers
beyond the reach of vision in advance, and floating faintly
back, a last farewell, to the listening ears of fathers, mothers,
wives, and sisters left behind.   And it was interesting to
observe how, as the rushing boats sped onwards past the
cottages on shore, groups of men and women and children
stood before the open doors, and waved adieu ; while,
ever and anon, a solitary voice rang louder than the others
in the chorus ; and a pair of dark eyes grew brighter, as
a *voyageur* swept past his home, and recognised his little
ones screaming farewell, and seeking to attract their *sire's*
attention by tossing their chubby arms, or flourishing
round their heads the bright vermilion blades of canoe-
paddles.   It was interesting, too, to hear the men shout
as they ran a small rapid which occurs about the lower
part of the settlement, and dashed in full career up to
the Lower Fort—which stands about twenty miles down
the river from Fort Garry—and then sped onward again
with unabated energy, until they passed the Indian settlement, with its scattered wooden buildings and its small
church ; passed the last cottage on the bank ; passed the
low swampy land at the river's mouth ; and emerged at
last, as evening closed, upon the wide, calm, sea-like
bosom of Lake Winipeg.

Charley saw and heard all this, during the whole of
that long, exciting afternoon ; and, as he heard and saw
it, his heart swelled as if it would burst its prison-bars ;
his voice rang out wildly in the choruses, regardless alike
of tune and time, and his spirit boiled within him as he
quaffed the first sweet draught of a rover's life—a life in

the woods—the wild, free, enchanting woods, where all
appeared in *his* eyes bright, and sunny, and green, and
beautiful!

As the sun's last rays sank in the west, and the clouds,
losing their crimson hue, began gradually to fade into
gray, the boats' heads were turned landward. In a few
seconds they grounded on a low point covered with small
trees and bushes, which stretched out into the lake.
Here Louis Peltier had resolved to bivouac for the night.
"Now then, *mes garçons*," he exclaimed, leaping ashore,
and helping to drag the boat a little way on to the beach;
"*vite! vite! à terre! à terre!* Take the kettle, Pierre, and
let's have supper."

Pierre needed no second bidding. He grasped a large
tin kettle and an axe, with which he hurried into a clump
of trees. Laying down the kettle, which he had previously filled with water from the lake, he singled out
a dead tree, and with three powerful blows of his axe
brought it to the ground. A few additional strokes cut
it up into logs, varying from three to five feet in length,
which he piled together, first placing a small bundle
of dry grass and twigs beneath them, and a few splinters
of wood which he cut from off one of the logs. Having
accomplished this, Pierre took a flint and steel out of
a gaily ornamented pouch, which depended from his
waist, and which went by the name of a *fire-bag*, in consequence of its containing the implements for procuring
that element. It might have been as appropriately named
tobacco-bag or *smoking-bag*, however, seeing that such
things had more to do with it, if possible, than fire.
Having struck a spark, which he took captive by means
of a piece of tinder, he placed it in the centre of a very

dry handful of soft grass, and whirled it rapidly round
his head, thereby producing a current of air, which blew
the spark into a flame ; which, when applied, lighted the
grass and twigs ; and so, in a few minutes, a blazing fire
roared up among the trees—spouted volumes of sparks
into the air, like a gigantic squib, which made it quite
a marvel that all the bushes in the neighbourhood were
not burnt up at once—glared out red and fierce upon the
rippling water, until it became, as it were, red-hot in the
neighbourhood of the boats ; and caused the night to
become suddenly darker by contrast ; the night re-
ciprocating the compliment, as it grew later, by causing
the space around the fire to glow brighter and brighter,
until it became a brilliant chamber, surrounded by walls
of the blackest ebony.

While Pierre was thus engaged, there were at least ten
voyageurs similarly occupied. Ten steels were made
instrumental in creating ten sparks, which were severally
captured by ten pieces of tinder, and whirled round
by ten lusty arms, until ten flames were produced, and
ten fires sprang up and flared wildly on the busy scene
that had a few hours before been so calm, so solitary, and
so peaceful, bathed in the soft beams of the setting sun.

In less than half-an-hour the several camps were completed ; the kettles boiling over the fires ; the men
smoking in every variety of attitude, and talking loudly.
It was a cheerful scene ; and so Charley thought, as he
reclined in his canvas tent, the opening of which faced
the fire, and enabled him to see all that was going on.

Pierre was standing over the great kettle, dancing
round it, and making sudden plunges with a stick into it,
in the desperate effort to stir its boiling contents—

desperate, because the fire was very fierce and large,
and the flames seemed to take a fiendish pleasure in
leaping up suddenly just under Pierre's nose, thereby
endangering his beard, or shooting out between his legs,
and licking round them at most unexpected moments,
when the light wind ought to have been blowing them
quite in the opposite direction ; and then, as he danced
round to the other side to avoid them, wheeling about
and roaring viciously in his face, until it seemed as if the
poor man would be roasted long before the supper was
boiled.   Indeed, what between the ever-changing and
violent flames, the rolling smoke, the steam from the
kettle, the showering sparks, and the man's own wild
grimaces and violent antics, Pierre seemed to Charley
like a raging demon, who danced not only round, but
above, and on, and through, and *in* the flames, as if
they were his natural element, in which he took special
delight.

Quite close to the tent, the massive form of Louis the
guide lay extended, his back supported by the stump of
a tree ; his eyes blinking sleepily at the blaze, and his
beloved pipe hanging from his lips, while wreaths of
smoke encircled his head.   Louis's day's work was done.
Few could do a better ; and, when his work was over,
Louis always acted on the belief that his position and his
years entitled him to rest, and took things very easy
in consequence.

Six of the boat's crew sat in a semicircle beside the
guide and fronting the fire, each paying particular attention to his pipe, and talking between the puffs to any
one who chose to listen.

Suddenly Pierre vanished into the smoke and flames

altogether, whence, in another moment, he issued, bear
ing in his hand the large tin kettle, which he deposited
triumphantly at the feet of his comrades.

" Now then," cried Pierre.

It was unnecessary to have said even that much by
way of invitation. *Voyageurs* do not require to have
their food pressed upon them after a hard day's work.
Indeed it was as much as they could do to refrain from
laying violent hands on the kettle long before their
worthy cook considered its contents sufficiently done.

Charley sat in company with Mr Park,—a chief factor,
on his way to Norway House. Gibault, one of the men
who acted as their servant, had placed a kettle of hot tea
before them, which, with several slices of buffalo tongue,
a lump of pemican, and some hard biscuit and butter,
formed their evening meal. Indeed, we may add that
these viands, during a great part of the voyage, constituted their every meal. In fact, they had no variety in
their fare, except a wild duck or two now and then, and
a goose when they chanced to shoot one.

Charley sipped a pannikin of tea as he reclined on his
blanket, and, being somewhat fatigued in consequence of
his exertions and excitement during the day, said nothing.
Mr Park for the same reasons, besides being naturally
taciturn, was equally mute, so they both enjoyed in
silence the spectacle of the men eating their supper.
And it *was* a sight worth seeing.

Their food consisted of *robbiboo*, a compound of flour,
pemican, and water, boiled to the consistency of very thick
soup. Though not a species of food that would satisfy
the fastidious taste of an epicure, robbiboo is, nevertheless, very wholesome, exceedingly nutritious, and, withal,

palatable. Pemican, its principal component, is made of buffalo flesh, which fully equals (some think greatly excels) beef. The recipe for making it is as follows :— First, kill your buffalo—a matter of considerable difficulty, by the way, as doing so requires you to travel to the buffalo grounds, to arm yourself with a gun, and mount a horse, on which you have to gallop, perhaps, several miles over rough ground and among badger-holes, at the imminent risk of breaking your neck. Then you have to run up alongside of a buffalo and put a ball through his heart, which, apart from the murderous nature of the action, is a difficult thing to do. But we will suppose that you have killed your buffalo. Then you must skin him; then cut him up, and slice the flesh into layers, which must be dried in the sun. At this stage of the process, you have produced a substance which, in the fur countries, goes by the name of dried-meat, and is largely used as an article of food. As its name implies, it is very dry, and it is also very tough, and very undesirable if one can manage to procure anything better. But, to proceed. Having thus prepared dried-meat, lay a quantity of it on a flat stone, and take another stone, with which pound it into shreds. You must then take the animal's hide, while it is yet new, and make bags of it about two feet and a half long, by a foot and a half broad. Into this put the pounded meat loosely. Melt the fat of your buffalo over a fire, and, when quite liquid, pour it into the bag until full ; mix the contents well together ; sew the whole up before it cools, and you have a bag of pemican of about ninety pounds' weight. This forms the chief food of the *voyageur*, in consequence of its being the largest possible quantity of sustenance

compressed into the smallest possible space, and in an extremely convenient, portable shape.   It will keep fresh
for years, and has been much used, in consequence, by the
heroes of arctic discovery, in their perilous journeys along
the shores of the frozen sea.

The *voyageurs* used no plates.   Men who travel in
these countries become independent of many things that
are supposed to be necessary *here*.   They sat in a circle
round the kettle; each man armed with a large wooden or
pewter spoon, with which he ladled the robbiboo down
his capacious throat, in a style that not only caused
Charley to laugh, but afterwards threw him into a deep
reverie on the powers of appetite in general, and the
strength of *voyageur* stomachs in particular.

At first the keen edge of appetite induced the men to
eat in silence; but, as the contents of the kettle began
to get low, their tongues loosened, and at last, when the
kettles were emptied and the pipes filled, fresh logs
thrown on the fires, and their limbs stretched out around
them, the babel of English, French, and Indian that arose
was quite overwhelming.   The middle-aged men told long
stories of what they *had* done; the young men boasted of
what they *meant* to do; while the more aged smiled,
nodded, smoked their pipes, put in a word or two as occasion offered, and listened.   While they conversed, the
quick ears of one of the men of Charley's camp detected
some unusual sound.

"Hist!" said he, turning his head aside slightly, in a
listening attitude, while his comrades suddenly ceased
their noisy laugh.

"Do ducks travel in canoes hereabouts?" said the
man, after a moment's silence; "for, if not, there's some

one about to pay us a visit. I would wager my best gun that I hear the stroke of paddles."

" If your ears had been sharper, François, you might have heard them some time ago," said the guide, shaking the ashes out of his pipe and refilling it for the third time.

" Ah, Louis, I do not pretend to such sharp ears as you possess, nor to such sharp wit either. But who do you think can be *en route* so late ?"

" That my wit does not enable me to divine," said Louis ; " but if you have any faith in the sharpness of your eyes, I would recommend you to go to the beach and see, as the best and shortest way of finding out."

By this time the men had risen and were peering out into the gloom in the direction whence the sound came, while one or two sauntered down to the margin of the lake to meet the new-comers.

" Who can it be, I wonder ?" said Charley, who had left the tent, and was now standing beside the guide.

" Difficult to say, monsieur. Perhaps Injins ; though I thought there were none here just now. But I'm not surprised that we've attracted *something* to us. Livin' creeturs always come nat'rally to the light, and there's plenty fire on the point to-night."

" Rather more than enough," replied Charley, abruptly, as a slight motion of wind sent the flames curling round his head and singed off his eye-lashes. " Why, Louis, it's my firm belief that if I ever get to the end of this journey, I'll not have a hair left on my head."

Louis smiled.

" Oh, monsieur, you will learn to *observe* things before

you have been long in the wilderness. If you *will* edge round to leeward of the fire, you can't expect it to respect you."

Just at this moment a loud hurrah rang through the copse, and Harry Somerville sprang over the fire into the arms of Charley, who received him with a hug and a look of unutterable amazement.

" Charley, my boy !"

" Harry Somerville, I declare !"

For at least five minutes Charley could not recover his composure sufficiently to *declare* anything else, but stood with open mouth and eyes, and elevated eyebrows, looking at his young friend, who capered and danced round the fire in a manner that threw the cook's performances in that line quite into the shade ; while he continued all the time to shout fragments of sentences that were quite unintelligible to any one. It was evident that Harry was in a state of immense delight at something unknown, save to himself, but which, in the course of a few minutes, was revealed to his wondering friends.

" Charley, I'm *going!* hurrah !" and he leaped about in a manner that induced Charley to say, he would not only be going but very soon *gone*, if he did not keep further away from the fire.

" Yes, Charley, I'm going with you ! I upset the stool ; tilted the ink-bottle over the invoice book ; sent the poker almost through the back of the fire-place, and smashed Tom Whyte's best whip on the back of the ' noo 'oss' as I galloped him over the plains for the last time— all for joy, because I'm going with you, Charley, my darling !"

Here Harry suddenly threw his arms round his friend's

neck meditating an embrace. As both boys were rather
fond of using their muscles violently, the embrace degenerated into a wrestle, which caused them to threaten complete destruction to the fire as they staggered in front of
it, and ended in their tumbling against the tent and
nearly breaking its poles and fastenings, to the horror
and indignation of Mr Park, who was smoking his pipe
within, quietly waiting till Harry's superabundant glee
was over, that he might get an explanation of his unexpected arrival among them.

"Ah! they will be good *voyageurs*," cried one of the
men, as he looked on at this scene.

"Oui! oui! good boys, active lads," replied the others,
laughing. The two boys rose hastily.

"Yes," cried Harry, breathless, but still excited, "I'm
going all the way, and a great deal farther. I'm going to
hunt buffaloes in the Saskatchewan, and grizzly bears in
the — the — in fact everywhere! I'm going down the
Mackenzie River—I'm going *mad*, I believe;" and Harry
gave another caper and another shout, and tossed his cap
high into the air: having been recklessly tossed, it
came down into the fire :—when it went in it was dark
blue, but when Harry dashed into the flames, in consternation, to save it, it came out of a rich brown colour.

"Now, youngster," said Mr Park, "when you've done
capering I should like to ask you one or two questions
What brought you here?"

"A canoe," said Harry, inclined to be impudent.

"Oh! and pray, for what *purpose* have you come here?"

"These are my credentials," handing him a letter.

Mr Park opened the note and read.

"Ah! oh! Saskatchewan—hum—yes—outpost—wild

boy—just so—keep him at it—ay ! fit for nothing else.
So," said Mr Park, folding the paper, "I find that Mr
Grant has sent you to take the place of a young gentleman we expected to pick up at Norway House, but who
is required elsewhere ; and that he wishes you to see a
good deal of rough life—to be made a trader of, in fact.
Is that your desire ?"

" That's the very ticket !" replied Harry, scarcely able
to restrain his delight at the prospect.

" Well, then, you had better get supper and turn in,
for you'll have to begin your new life by rising at three
o'clock to-morrow morning. Have you got a tent ?"

" Yes," said Harry, pointing to his canoe, which had
been brought to the fire and turned bottom up by the
two Indians to whom it belonged, and who were reclining
under its shelter enjoying their pipes, and watching with
looks of great gravity the doings of Harry and his friend.

" *That* will return whence it came to-morrow. Have
you no other ?"

" Oh, yes," said Harry, pointing to the overhanging
branches of a willow close at hand, " lots more."

Mr Park smiled grimly, and turning on his heel re-
entered the tent and continued his pipe, while Harry
flung himself down beside Charley under the bark canoe.

This species of " tent" is, however, by no means a perfect one. An Indian canoe is seldom three feet broad—
frequently much narrower—so that it only affords shelter
for the body as far down as the waist, leaving the
extremities exposed. True, one *may* double up as nearly
as possible into half one's length, but this is not a desirable
position to maintain throughout an entire night Sometimes, when the weather is *very* bad, an additional pro-

tection is procured by leaning several poles against the bottom of the canoe, on the weath side, in such a way as to slope considerably over the front ; and over these are spread pieces of birch bark or branches and moss, so as to form a screen, which is an admirable shelter. But this involves too much time and labour to be adopted during a voyage, and is only done when the travellers are under the necessity of remaining for some time in one place.

The canoe in which Harry arrived was a pretty large one, and looked so comfortable when arranged for the night, that Charley resolved to abandon his own tent and Mr Park's society, and sleep with his friend.

"I'll sleep with you, Harry, my boy," said he, after Harry had explained to him in detail the cause of his being sent away from Red River; which was no other than that a young gentleman, as Mr Park said, who *was* to have gone, had been ordered elsewhere.

"That's right, Charley, spread out our blankets, while I get some supper, like a good fellow." Harry went in search of the kettle while his friend prepared their bed. First, he examined the ground on which the canoe lay, and found that the two Indians had already taken possession of the only level places under it. "Humph!" he ejaculated, half inclined to rouse them up, but immediately dismissed the idea as unworthy of a *voyageur*. Besides, Charley was an amiable, unselfish fellow, and would rather have lain on the top of a dozen stumps than have made himself comfortable at the expense of any one else.

He paused a moment to consider. On one side was a hollow, "that," (as he soliloquized to himself) "would break the back of a buffalo." On the other side

8

were a dozen little stumps surrounding three very prominent ones, that threatened destruction to the ribs of
any one who should venture to lie there. But Charley
did not pause to consider long. Seizing his axe, he laid
about him vigorously with the head of it, and in a few
seconds destroyed all the stumps, which he carefully collected, and, along with some loose moss and twigs, put into
the hollow, and so filled it up. Having improved things
thus far, he rose and strode out of the circle of light into
the wood. In a few minutes he re-appeared, bearing a
young spruce-fir tree on his shoulder, which, with the axe,
he stripped of its branches. These branches were flat in
form, and elastic—admirably adapted for making a bed
on ; and when Charley spread them out under the canoe
in a pile of about four inches in depth, by four feet broad,
and six feet long, the stumps and the hollow were overwhelmed altogether. He then ran to Mr Park's tent,
and fetched thence a small flat bundle, covered with oil-
cloth, and tied with a rope. Opening this, he tossed out
its contents, which were two large and very thick blankets
—one green, the other white ; a particularly minute
feather pillow, a pair of moccasins, a broken comb, and a
bit of soap. Then he opened a similar bundle, containing
Harry's bed, which he likewise tossed out ; and then
kneeling down, he spread the two white blankets on the
top of the branches, the two green blankets above these,
and the two pillows at the top, as far under the shelter of
the canoe as he could push them. Having completed the
whole in a manner that would have done credit to a
chambermaid, he continued to sit on his knees, with his
hands in his pockets, smiling complacently, and saying,
" capital — first-rate !"

· Here we are, Charley.   Have a second supper—do!"

Harry placed the smoking kettle by the head of the
bed; and squatting down beside it, began to eat, as only
a boy *can* eat who has had nothing since breakfast.

Charley attacked the kettle too—as he said, "out of
sympathy," although he "wasn't hungry a bit."   And
really, for a man who was not hungry, and had supped
half-an-hour before, the appetite of *sympathy* was wonderfully strong.

But Harry's powers of endurance were now exhausted.
He had spent a long day of excessive fatigue and excitement, and, having wound it up with a heavy supper,
sleep began to assail him with a full ferocity that nothing
could resist.   He yawned once or twice, and sat on the
bed blinking unmeaningly at the fire, as if he had something to say to it, which he could not recollect just then.
He nodded violently, much to his own surprise, once or
twice, and began to address remarks to the kettle instead
of to his friend.   "I say, Charley, this won't do.   I'm off
to bed!" and, suiting the action to the word, he took off
his coat and placed it on his pillow.   He then removed
his moccasins, which were wet, and put on a dry pair;
and this being all that is ever done in the way of preparation before going to bed in the woods, he lay down and
pulled the green blankets over him.

Before doing so, however, Harry leant his head on his
hands and prayed.   This was the one link left of the
chain of habit with which he had left home.   Until the
period of his departure for the wild scenes of the North-
west, Harry had lived in a quiet, happy home in the West
Highlands of Scotland, where he had been surrounded by
the benign influences of a family, the members of which

were united by the sweet bonds of Christian love—bonds
which were strengthened by the additional tie of amiability of disposition.   From childhood he had been accustomed to the routine of a pious and well-regulated household, where the Bible was perused and spoken of with an
interest that indicated a genuine hungering and thirsting
after righteousness, and where the name of JESUS sounded
often and sweetly on the ear.   Under such training, Harry,
though naturally of a wild, volatile disposition, was deeply
and irresistibly impressed with a reverence for sacred
things, which, now that he was thousands of miles away
from his peaceful home, clung to him with the force of
old habit and association, despite the jeers of comrades,
and the evil influences and ungodliness by which he was
surrounded.   It is true that he was not altogether unhurt
by the withering indifference to God that he beheld on all
sides.   Deep impression is not renewal of heart.   But
early training in the path of Christian love saved him
many a deadly fall.   It guarded him from many of the
grosser sins into which other boys, who had merely broken
away from the *restraints* of home, too easily fell.   It twined
round him—as the ivy encircles the oak—with a soft,
tender, but powerful grasp, that held him back when he
was tempted to dash aside all restraint—and held him up,
when, in the weakness of his human nature, he was about
to fall.   It exerted its benign sway over him in the silence
of night, when his thoughts reverted to home, and during
his waking hours, when he wandered from scene to scene
in the wide wilderness; and in after years, when sin prevailed, and intercourse with rough men had worn off much
of at least the superficial amiability of his character, and
to some extent blunted the finer feelings of his nature,

it clung faintly to him still, in the memory of his mother's gentle look and tender voice, and never forsook him altogether. Home had a blessed and powerful influence on Harry. May God bless such homes, where the ruling power is *love!* God bless and multiply such homes in the earth! Were there more of them, there would be fewer heart-broken mothers, to weep over the memory of the blooming, manly boys they sent away to foreign climes—with trembling hearts, but high hopes—and never saw them more. They were vessels launched upon the troubled sea of time, with stout timbers, firm masts, and gallant sails--with all that was necessary above and below, from stem to stern, for battling with the billows of adverse fortune, for stemming the tide of opposition, for riding the storms of persecution, or bounding with a press of canvas before the gales of prosperity; but without the rudder—without the guiding principle that renders the great power of plank and sail and mast available; *with* which the vessel moves obedient to the owner's will; *without* which, it drifts about with every current, and sails along with every shifting wind that blows. Yes; may the best blessings of prosperity and peace rest on such families, whose bread, cast continually on the waters, returns to them after many days!

After Harry had lain down, Charley, who did not feel inclined for repose, sauntered to the margin of the lake, and sat down upon a rock.

It was a beautiful calm evening. The moon shone faintly through a mass of heavy clouds, casting a pale light on the waters of Lake Winipeg, which stretched, without a ripple, out to the distant horizon. The great fresh-water lakes of America bear a strong resemblance to the sea. In storms the waves rise mountains high, and break with heavy sullen roar upon a beach, com posed, in many places, of sand and pebbles; while they are so large that one not only looks out to a straight horizon, but may even sail *out of sight of land* altogether.

As Charley sat resting his head on his hand, and listening to the soft hiss that the ripples made upon the beach, he felt all the solemnising influence that steals irresistibly over the mind as we sit on a still night gazing out upon the moonlit sea. His thoughts were sad; for he thought of Kate, and his mother and father, and the home he was now leaving. He remembered all that he had ever done to injure or annoy the dear ones he was leaving; and it is strange how much alive our consciences become, when we are unexpectedly or sud denly removed from those with whom we have lived and held daily intercourse. How bitterly we reproach our selves for harsh words, unkind actions; and how intensely we long for one word more with them, one fervent embrace, to prove at once that all we have ever said or done was not *meant* ill; and, at any rate, is deeply, sincerely repented of now! As Charley looked up into the starry sky, his mind recurred to the parting words of Mr Addison. With uplifted hands and a full heart, he prayed that God would bless, for Jesus' sake, the beloved ones in Red River, but especially Kate; for, whether he prayed or meditated, Charley's thoughts *always* ended with Kate.

A black cloud passed across the moon, and reminded him that but a few hours of the night remained; so, hastening up to the camp again, he lay gently down beside his friend, and drew the green blanket over him.

In the camp all was silent. The men had chosen their several beds according to fancy, under the shadow of a bush or tree. The fires had burnt low—so low, that it was with difficulty Charley as he lay could discern the recumbent forms of the men, whose presence was indicated by the deep, soft, regular breathing of tired, but healthy constitutions. Sometimes a stray moonbeam shot through the leaves and branches, and cast a ghost-like, flickering light over the scene, which ever and anon was rendered more mysterious by a red flare of the fire as an ember fell, blazed up for an instant, and left all shrouded in greater darkness than before.

At first, Charley continued his sad thoughts, staring all the while at the red embers of the expiring fire ; but soon his eyes began to blink, and the stumps of trees began to assume the form of *voyageurs*, and *voyageurs* to look like stumps of trees. Then a moonbeam darted in, and Mr Addison stood on the other side of the fire. At this sight Charley started, and Mr Addison disappeared, while the boy smiled to think how he had been dreaming while only half-asleep. Then Kate appeared. and seemed to smile on him ; but another ember fell, and another red flame sprang up, and put her to flight too. Then a low sigh of wind rustled through the branches, and Charley felt sure that he saw Kate again coming through the woods, singing the low, soft tune that she was so fond of singing, because it was his own favourite air. But soon the air ceased ; the fire faded away ; so did the trees, and the sleeping *voyageurs* ; Kate last of all dissolved, and Charley sank into a deep, untroubled slumber.

CHAPTER X.

Varieties, Vexations, and Vicissitudes

LIFE is chequered—there is no doubt about that; whatever doubts a man may entertain upon other subjects, he can have none upon this, we feel quite certain. In fact, so true is it, that we would not for a moment have drawn the reader's attention to it here, were it not that our experience of life in the backwoods corroborates the truth—and truth, however well corroborated, is none the worse of getting a little additional testimony now and then, in this sceptical generation.

Life is chequered, then, undoubtedly. And life in the backwoods strengthens the proverb, for it is a peculiarly striking and remarkable specimen of life's variegated character.

There is a difference between sailing smoothly along the shores of Lake Winipeg with favouring breezes, and being tossed on its surging billows by the howling of a nor'-west wind, that threatens destruction to the boat, or forces it to seek shelter on the shore. This difference is one of the chequered scenes of which we write, and one that was experienced by the brigade more than once, during its passage across the lake.

Since we are dealing in truisms, it may not, perhaps, be out of place here to say, that going to bed at night is not by any means getting up in the morning—at least so several of our friends found to be the case when the deep

sonorous voice of Louis Peltier sounded through the camp
on the following morning, just as a very faint, scarcely
perceptible, light tinged the eastern sky.

"Lève! lève! lève!" **he cried,** "lève! lève! mes
enfans!"

Some of Louis' *infants* replied to the summons in a way
that would have done credit to a harlequin. One or two
active little Canadians, on hearing the cry of the awful
word, *lève,* rose to their feet with a quick bound, as if
they had been keeping up an appearance of sleep as a
sort of practical joke all night, on purpose to be ready to
leap as the first sound fell from the guide's lips. Others
lay still, in the same attitude in which they had fallen
asleep, having made up their minds, apparently, to lie
there in spite of all the guides in the world. Not a few
got slowly into the sitting position, their hair dishevelled,
their caps awry, their eyes alternately winking very hard
and staring awfully in the vain effort to keep open, and
their whole physiognomy wearing an expression of blank
stupidity that is peculiar to man when engaged in that
struggle which occurs each morning as he endeavours to
disconnect and shake off the entanglement of nightly
dreams, and the realities of the breaking day. Throughout the whole camp there was a low muffled sound, as of
men moving lazily, with broken whispers and disjointed
sentences uttered in very deep hoarse tones, mingled with
confused, unearthly noises, which, upon consideration,
sounded like prolonged yawns. Gradually these sounds
increased, for the guide's "*lève*" is inexorable, and the
voyageur's fate inevitable.

"Oh, dear!—yei a—a——ow" (*yawning*); "hang your
lève!"

" Oui, vraiment—yei a—a——ow—morbleu !

" Eh, what's that ?   Oh, misère !"

" Tare an' ages !" (from an Irishman), " an' I had only
got to shape yit ! but—yei a—a——ow !"

French and Irish yawns are very similar, the only
difference being, that whereas the Frenchman finishes the
yawn resignedly, and springs to his legs, the Irishman
finishes it with an energetic gasp, as if he were hurling it
remonstratively into the face of Fate, turns round again
and shuts his eyes doggedly—a piece of bravado which he
knows is useless and of very short duration.

" Lève ! lève !! lève !!!"   There was no mistake this
time in the tones of Louis's voice.   " Embark, embark,
vite ! vite !"

The subdued sounds of rousing broke into a loud
buzz of active preparation, as the men busied themselves
in bundling up blankets, carrying down camp-kettles to
the lake, launching the boats, kicking up lazy comrades,
stumbling over and swearing at fallen trees which were
not visible in the cold uncertain light of the early dawn,
searching hopelessly, among a tangled conglomeration of
leaves and broken branches and crushed herbage, for lost
pipes and missing tobacco-pouches.

" Hallo !" exclaimed Harry Somerville, starting suddenly from his sleeping posture, and unintentionally
cramming his elbow into Charley's mouth, " I declare
they're all up and nearly ready to start "

" That's no reason," replied Charley, " why you should
knock out all my front teeth, is it ?"

Just then Mr Park issued from his tent, dressed and
ready to step into his boat.   He first gave a glance round
the camp to see that all the men were moving, then he

looked up through the trees to ascertain the present state,
and, if possible, the future prospects of the weather.
Having come to a satisfactory conclusion on that head, he
drew forth his pipe and began to fill it, when his eye fell
on the two boys, who were still sitting up in their lairs,
and staring idiotically at the place where the fire had
been, as if the white ashes, half-burnt logs, and bits of
charcoal, were a sight of the most novel and interesting
character, that filled them with intense amazement.

Mr Park could scarce forbear smiling.

" Hallo, youngsters, precious *voyageurs you'll* make, to
be sure, if this is the way you're going to begin. Don't
you see that the things are all aboard, and we'll be ready
to start in five minutes, and you sitting there with your
neckcloths off ? "

Mr Park gave a slight sneer when he spoke of *neckcloths*,
as if he thought, in the first place, that they were quite
superfluous portions of attire, and, in the second place,
that, having once put them on, the taking of them off at
night was a piece of effeminacy altogether unworthy of a
Nor'wester.

Charley and Harry needed no second rebuke. It
flashed instantly upon them that, sleeping comfortably
under their blankets when the men were bustling about
the camp, was extremely inconsistent with the hero c
resolves of the previous day. They sprang up, rolled
their blankets in the oil-cloths, which they fastened
tightly with ropes ; tied the neckcloths, held in such contempt by Mr Park, in a twinkling ; threw on their coats,
and in *less* than five minutes were ready to embark.
They then found that they might have done things more
leisurely, as the crews had not yet got all their traps on

board, so they began to look around them, and discovered
that each had omitted to pack up a blanket.

Very much crestfallen at their stupidity, they proceeded to untie the bundles again, when it became
apparent to the eyes of Charley that his friend had put
on his capote inside out, which had a peculiarly ragged
and grotesque effect. These mistakes were soon rectified,
and shouldering their beds, they carried them down to
the boat, and tossed them in. Meanwhile Mr Park, who
had been watching the movements of the boys with a
peculiar smile, that filled them with confusion, went
round the different camps to see that nothing was left behind. The men were all in their places with oars ready,
and the boats floating on the calm water, a yard or two
from shore, with the exception of the guide's boat, the
stern of which still rested on the sand awaiting Mr Park.

"Who does this belong to?" shouted that gentleman,
holding up a cloth cap, part of which was of a mottled
brown and part deep blue.

Harry instantly tore the covering from his head, and
discovered that among his numerous mistakes he had put
on the head-dress of one of the Indians who had brought
him to the camp. To do him justice, the cap was not
unlike his own, excepting that it was a little more mottled
and dirty in colour, besides being decorated with a gaudy
but very much crushed and broken feather.

"You had better change with our friend here, I think,"
said Mr Park, grinning from ear to ear, as he tossed the
cap to its owner, while Harry handed the other to the
Indian, amid the laughter of the crew.

"Never mind, boy," added Mr Park, in an encouraging
tone, "you'll make a *voyageur* yet. Now then, lads,

give way," and, with a nod to the Indians, who stood on
the shore watching their departure, the trader sprang into
the boat and took his place beside the two boys.

"Ho! sing, mes garçons," cried the guide, seizing the
massive sweep and directing the boat out to sea.

At this part of the lake there occurs a deep bay or
inlet, to save rounding which travellers usually strike
straight across from point to point, making what is called
in *voyageur* parlance a *traverse*. These *traverses* are subjects of considerable anxiety, and frequently of delay to
travellers, being sometimes of considerable extent, varying
from four and five,—and, in such immense seas as Lake
Superior,—to fourteen miles. With boats, indeed, there
is little to fear, as the inland craft of the fur-traders can
stand a heavy sea, and often ride out a pretty severe
storm ; but it is far otherwise with the bark canoes that
are often used in travelling. These frail craft can stand
very little sea,—their frames being made of thin flat slips
of wood and sheets of bark, not more than a quarter of an
inch thick, which are sewed together with the fibrous
roots of the pine (called by the natives *wattape*), and
rendered watertight by means of melted gum. Although
light and buoyant, therefore, and extremely useful in a
country where *portages* are numerous, they require very
tender usage ; and when a *traverse* has to be made, the
guides have always a grave consultation with some of the
most sagacious among the men, as to the probability of
the wind rising or falling ;—consultations which are more
or less marked by anxiety and tediousness in proportion
to the length of the *traverse*, the state of the weather, and
the courage or timidity of the guides.

On the present occasion there was no consultation, as

has been already seen. The *traverse* was a short one, the
morning fine, and the boats good. A warm glow began
to overspread the horizon, giving promise of a splendid
day, as the numerous oars dipped with a plash and a loud
hiss into the water, and sent the boats leaping forth upon
the white wave.

"Sing, sing!" cried the guide again, and clearing his
throat, he began the beautiful quick-tuned canoe song,
"Rose Blanche," to which the men chorused with such
power of lungs, that a family of plovers which, up to that
time, had stood in mute astonishment on a sandy point,
tumbled precipitately into the water, from which they
rose with a shrill, inexpressibly wild, plaintive cry, and
fled screaming away to a more secure refuge among the
reeds and sedges of a swamp. A number of ducks too,
awakened by the unwonted sound, shot suddenly out from
the concealment of their night's bivouac with erect heads
and startled looks, spluttered heavily over the surface of
their liquid bed, and rising into the air, flew in a wide
circuit, with whistling wings, away from the scene of so
much uproar and confusion.

The rough voices of the men grew softer and softer, as
the two Indians listened to the song of their departing
friends, mellowing down and becoming more harmonious
and more plaintive as the distance increased, and the
boats grew smaller and smaller, until they were lost in
the blaze of light that now bathed both water and sky
in the eastern horizon, and began rapidly to climb the
zenith, while the sweet tones became less and less audible
as they floated faintly across the still water, and melted
at last into the deep silence of the wilderness.

The two Indians still stood, with downcast heads and

listening ears, as if they loved the last echo of the dying
music, while their grave, statue-like forms, added to,
rather than detracted from, the solitude of the deserted
scene.

CHAPTER XI.

Charley and Harry begin their sporting career, without much success.
Whisky-John catching.

THE place in the boats usually allotted to gentlemen
in the Company's service while travelling is the stern.
Here the lading is so arranged as to form a pretty level
hollow, where the flat bundles containing their blankets
are placed, and a couch is thus formed that rivals Eastern
effeminacy in luxuriance.   There are occasions, however,
when this couch is converted into a bed, not of thorns
exactly, but of corners ; and, really, it would be hard
to say which of the two is the more disagreeable.   Should
the men be careless in arranging the cargo, the inevitable
consequence is, that "monsieur" will find the leg of an
iron stove, the sharp edge of a keg, or the corner of a
wooden box, occupying the place where his ribs should be.
So common, however, is this occurrence that the clerks
usually superintend the arrangements themselves, and
so secure comfort.

On a couch, then, of this kind, Charley and Harry
now found themselves constrained to sit all morning ;
sometimes asleep, occasionally awake, and always earnestly
desiring that it was time to put ashore for breakfast,
as they had now travelled for four hours without halt.
except twice for about five minutes, to let the men light
their pipes.

"Charley," said Harry Somerville to his friend, who sat beside him, "it strikes me that we are to have no breakfast at all to-day. Here have I been holding my breath and tightening my belt, until I feel much more like a spider or a wasp, than a—a ——"

"*Man*, Harry; out with it at once, don't be afraid," said Charley.

"Well, no, I wasn't going to have said *that* exactly, but I was going to have said, a *voyageur*, only I recollected our doings this morning, and hesitated to take the name until I had won it."

"It's well that you entertain so modest an opinion of yourself," said Mr Park, who still smoked his pipe as if he were impressed with the idea that to stop for a moment would produce instant death. "I may tell you for your comfort, youngsters, that we shan't breakfast till we reach yonder point."

The shores of Lake Winipeg are flat and low, and the point indicated by Mr Park lay directly in the light of the sun, which now shone with such splendour in the cloudless sky, and flashed on the polished water, that it was with difficulty they could look towards the point of land.

"Where is it?" asked Charley, shading his eyes with his hand; "I cannot make out anything at all."

"Try again, my boy, there's nothing like practice."

"Ah! yes, I make it out now, a faint shadow just under the sun. Is that it?"

"Ay, and we'll break our fast there."

"I would like very much to break your head *here*," thought Charley, but he did not say it; as, besides being likely to produce unpleasant consequences, he felt that

9

such a speech to an elderly gentleman would be highly
improper; and Charley had *some* respect for gray hairs,
for their own sake, whether the owner of them was a
good man or a goose.

"What shall we do, Harry? If I had only thought of
keeping out a book."

"I know what *I* shall do," said Harry, with a resolute
air, "I'll go and shoot!"

"Shoot!" cried Charley, "you don't mean to say that
you're going to waste your powder and shot by firing
at the clouds; for, unless you take *them*, I see nothing
else here."

"That's because you don't use your eyes," retorted
Harry. "Will you just look at yonder rock ahead of us,
and tell me what you see."

Charley looked earnestly at the rock, which, to a cursory
glance, seemed as if composed of whiter stone on the top.
"Gulls! I declare!" shouted Charley; at the same time
jumping up in haste.

Just then one of the gulls, probably a scout sent out to
watch the approaching enemy, wheeled in a circle overhead. The two youths dragged their guns from beneath
the thwarts of the boat, and rummaged about in great
anxiety for shot-belts and powder-horns. At last they
were found, and, having loaded, they sat on the edge of
the boat looking out for game with as much,—ay, with
more intense, interest than a Blackfoot Indian would have
watched for a fat buffalo cow.

"There he goes," said Harry; "take the first shot,
Charley."

"Where? where is it?"

"Right ahead. Look out!"

As Harry spoke, a small white gull, with bright red legs and beak, flew over the boat so close to them that, as the guide remarked, " he could see it wink!" Charley's equanimity, already pretty well disturbed, was entirely upset at the suddenness of the bird's appearance, for he had been gazing intently at the rock when his friend's exclamation drew his attention in time to see the gull within about four feet of his head. With a sudden " Oh!" Charley threw forward his gun, took a short, wavering aim, and blew the cocktail feather out of Baptiste's hat, while the gull sailed tranquilly away, as much as to say, " If *that's* all you can do, there's no need for me to hurry!"

" Confound the boy!" cried Mr Park ; " you'll be the death of some one yet. I'm convinced of that."

" Parbleu! you may say that, c'est vrai," remarked the *voyageur*, with a rueful gaze at his hat, which, besides having its ornamental feather shattered, was sadly cut up about the crown.

The poor lad's face became much redder than the legs or beak of the gull as he sat down in confusion, which he sought to hide by busily reloading his gun ; while the men indulged in a somewhat witty and sarcastic criticism of his powers of shooting, remarking, in flattering terms, on the precision of the shot that blew Baptiste's feather into atoms, and declaring that if every shot he fired was as truly aimed, he would certainly be the best in the country.

Baptiste also came in for a share of their repartee. " It serves you right," said the guide, laughing, " for wearing such things on the voyage. You should put away such foppery till you return to the settlement. where there are *girls* to admire you." (Baptiste had con-

tinued to wear the tall hat, ornamented with gold cords
and tassels, with which he had left Red River.)

"Ah!" cried another, pulling vigorously at his oar, "I
fear that Marie won't look at you, now that all your
beauty's gone."

" 'Tis not quite gone," said a third; "there's all the
brim and half a tassel left, besides the wreck of the
remainder."

"Oh! I can lend you a few fragments," retorted Baptiste, endeavouring to parry some of the thrusts. "They
would improve *you* vastly."

"No, no, friend, gather them up and replace them;
they will look more picturesque and becoming now. I
believe if you had worn them much longer all the men in
the boat would have fallen in love with you."

"By St Patrick," said Mike Brady—an Irishman who
sat at the oar immediately behind the unfortunate Canadian—"there's more than enough o' rubbish scattered
over myself nor would do to stuff a fither bed with."

As Mike spoke, he collected the fragments of feathers
and ribbons with which the unlucky shot had strewn
him, and placed them slyly on the top of the dilapidated
hat, which Baptiste, after clearing away the wreck, had
replaced on his head.

"It's very purty," said Mike, as the action was received
by the crew with a shout of merriment.

Baptiste was waxing wrathful under this fire, when the
general attention was drawn again towards Charley and
his friend, who, having now got close to the rock, had
quite forgotten their mishap in the excitement of expectation.

This excitement in the shooting of such small game

might perhaps surprise our readers, did we not acquaint
them with the fact that neither of the boys had, up to
that time, enjoyed much opportunity of shooting. It is
true that Harry had once or twice borrowed the fowling-
piece of the senior clerk, and had sallied forth with a
beating heart to pursue the grouse which are found in the
belt of woodland skirting the Assinaboine river, near
to Fort Garry. But these expeditions were of rare occurrence, and they had not sufficed to rub off much of the
bounding excitement with which he loaded and fired at
anything and everything that came within range of his
gun. Charley, on the other hand, had never fired a shot
before, except out of an old horse-pistol ; having, up to
this period, been busily engaged at school, except during
the holidays, which he always spent in the society of his
sister Kate, whose tastes were not such as were likely to
induce him to take up the gun, even if he had possessed
such a weapon. Just before leaving Red River his father
presented him with his own gun, remarking, as he did so,
with a sigh, that *his* day was past now ; and adding, that
the gun was a good one for shot or ball, and if he (Charley)
brought down *half* as much game with it as he (Mr Kennedy) had brought down in the course of his life, he
might consider himself a crack shot, undoubtedly.

It was not surprising, therefore, that the two friends
went nearly mad with excitation when the whole flock of
gulls rose into the air like a white cloud, and sailed in
endless circles and gyrations above and around their
heads ;—flying so close at times that they might almost
have been caught by the hand. Neither was it surprising
that innumerable shots were fired, by both sportsmen,
without a single bird being a whit the worse for it, nor

themselves much the better; the energetic efforts made
to hit being rendered abortive by the very eagerness
which caused them to miss. And this was the less extraordinary, too, when it is remembered that Harry in his
haste loaded several times without shot, and Charley
rendered the right barrel of his gun *hors de combat* at last,
by ramming down a charge of shot and omitting powder
altogether, whereby he snapped and primed, and snapped
and primed again, till he grew desperate, and then sus-
picions of the true cause, which he finally rectified with
much difficulty.

Frequently the gulls flew straight over the heads of
the youths, which produced peculiar consequences—as, in
such cases, they took aim while the birds were approaching, but being somewhat slow at taking aim, the gulls
were almost perpendicularly above them ere they were
ready to shoot, so that they were obliged to fire hastily in
hope, feeling that they were losing their balance, or give
up the chance altogether.

Mr Park sat grimly in his place all the while, enjoying
the scene, and smoking.

" Now then, Charley," said he ; " take that fellow."

" Which ? Where ? Oh ! if I could only get *one*,"
said Charley, looking up eagerly at the screaming birds,
at which he had been staring so long, in their varying
and crossing flight, that his sight had become hopelessly
unsteady.

" There ! Look sharp ; fire away ! "

Bang went Charley's piece, as he spoke, at a gull
which flew straight towards him, but so rapidly that it
was directly above his head ; indeed, he was leaning a
little backwards at the moment, which caused him to

miss again, while the recoil of the gun brought matters to
a climax, by toppling him over into Mr Park's lap, thereby
smashing that gentleman's pipe to atoms.   The fall
accidently exploded the second barrel, causing the butt to
strike Charley in the pit of his stomach,—as if to ram him
well home into Mr Park's open arms,—and hitting, with a
stray shot, a gull that was sailing high up in the sky in
fancied security.   It fell with a fluttering crash into the
boat, while the men were laughing at the accident.

"Didn't 1 say so?" cried Mr Park, wrathfully, as he
pitched Charley out of his lap, and spat out the remnants
of his broken pipe.

Fortunately for all parties, at this moment, the boat
approached a spot on which the guide had resolved to
land for breakfast ; and, seeing the unpleasant predicament into which poor Charley had fallen, he assumed the
strong tones of command with which guides are frequently
gifted, and called out—

"Ho ! ho ! à terre ! à terre ! to land ! to land ! Breakfast, my boys ; breakfast !" at the same time sweeping
the boat's head shoreward, and running into a rocky bay,
whose margin was fringed by a growth of small trees.
Here, in a few minutes, they were joined by the other
boats of the brigade, which had kept within sight of each
other nearly the whole morning.

While travelling through the wilds of North America
in boats, *voyageurs* always make a point of landing to
breakfast.   Dinner is a meal with which they are unacquainted, at least on the voyage, and luncheon is likewise
unknown.   If a man feels hungry during the day, the
pemican bag and its contents are there ; he may pause in
his work at any time, for a minute, to seize the axe and

cut off a lump, which he may devour as he best can ; but
there is no going ashore—no resting for dinner.   Two
great meals are recognised, and the time allotted to their
preparation and consumption held inviolable—breakfast
and supper ;—the first varying between the hours of
seven and nine in the morning ; the second about sunset,
at which time travellers usually encamp for the night.
Of the two meals, it would be difficult to say which is
more agreeable.   For our own part, we prefer the former.
It is the meal to which a man addresses himself with
peculiar gusto, especially if he has been astir three or four
hours previously in the open air.   It is the time of day,
too, when the spirits are freshest and highest, animated
by the prospect of the work, the difficulties, the pleasures, or the adventures of the day that has begun ; and
cheered by that cool, clear *buoyancy* of Nature, which
belongs exclusively to the happy morning hours, and has
led poets in all ages to compare these hours to the first
sweet months of spring, or the early years of childhood.

Voyageurs, not less than poets, have felt the exhilarating
influence of the young day, although they have lacked the
power to tell it in sounding numbers ; but, where words
were wanting, the sparkling eye, the beaming countenance, the light step, and hearty laugh, were more
powerful exponents of the feelings within.   Poet, and
painter too, might have spent a profitable hour on the
shores of that great sequestered lake ; and, as they
watched the picturesque groups—clustering round the
blazing fires, preparing their morning meal, smoking
their pipes, examining and repairing the boats, or sun-
ning their stalwart limbs in wild, careless attitudes upon
the green sward,—might have found a subject worthy the

most brilliant effusions of the pen, or the most graphic touches of the pencil.

An hour sufficed for breakfast. While it was preparing, the two friends sauntered into the forest in search of game, in which they were unsuccessful ; in fact, with the exception of the gulls before mentioned, there was not a feather to be seen,—save, always, one or two whisky-johns.

Whisky-johns are the most impudent, puffy, conceited, little birds that exist. Not much larger in reality than sparrows, they nevertheless manage to swell out their feathers to such an extent that they appear to be as large as magpies, which they farther resemble in their plumage. Go where you will in the woods of Rupert's Land, the instant that you light a fire, two or three whisky-johns come down and sit beside you, on a branch, it may be, or on the ground, and generally so near that you cannot but wonder at their recklessness. There is a species of impudence which seems to be specially attached to little birds. In them it reaches the highest pitch of perfection. A bold, swelling, arrogant effrontery ; a sort of stark, staring, self-complacent, comfortable, and yet innocent impertinence, which is at once irritating and amusing, aggravating and attractive, and which is exhibited in the greatest intensity in the whisky-john. He will jump down almost under your nose, and seize a fragment of biscuit or pemican. He will go right into the pemican bag, when you are but a few paces off, and pilfer, as it were, at the fountain-head. Or, if these resources are closed against him, he will sit on a twig, within an inch of your head, and look at you as only a whisky-john can look.

" I'll catch one of these rascals," said Harry, as he saw them jump unceremoniously into and out of the pemican bag.

Going down to the boat, Harry hid himself under the tarpaulin, leaving a hole open near to the mouth of the bag. He had not remained more than a few minutes in this concealment, when one of the birds flew down, and alighted on the edge of the boat. After a glance round to see that all was right, it jumped into the bag. A moment after, Harry, darting his hand through the aperture, grasped him round the neck, and secured him. Poor whisky-john screamed and pecked ferociously, while Harry brought him in triumph to his friend ; but so unremittingly did the bird scream, that its captor was fain at last to let him off, the more especially as the cook came up at the moment and announced that breakfast was ready.

CHAPTER XII

The Storm.

Two days after the events of the last chapter, the brigade was making one of the *traverses* which have already been noticed as of frequent occurrence in the great lakes. The morning was calm and sultry. A deep stillness pervaded nature, which tended to produce a corresponding quiescence in the mind, and to fill it with those indescribably solemn feelings that frequently arise before a thunderstorm. Dark, lurid clouds hung overhead in gigantic masses, piled above each other like the battlements of a dark fortress, from whose ragged embrasures the artillery of heaven was about to play.

"Shall we get over in time, Louis?" asked Mr Park, as he turned to the guide, who sat holding the tiller with a firm grasp; while the men, aware of the necessity of reaching shelter ere the storm burst upon them, were bending to the oars with steady and sustained energy.

"Perhaps," replied Louis, laconically. "Pull, lads, pull! else you'll have to sleep in wet skins to-night."

A low growl of distant thunder followed the guide's words, and the men pulled with additional energy; while the slow, measured hiss of the water, and clank of oars, as they cut swiftly through the lake's clear surface, alone interrupted the dead silence that ensued.

Charley and his friend conversed in low whispers; for

there is a strange power in a thunder-storm, whether raging or about to break, that overawes the heart of man—
as if Nature's God were nearer then than at other times;
as if He—whose voice, indeed, if listened to, speaks even
in the slightest evolution of natural phenomena—were
about to tread the visible earth with more than usual
majesty, in the vivid glare of the lightning flash, and in
the awful crash of thunder.

" I don't know how it is, but I feel more like a coward,"
said Charley, "just before a thunder-storm, than I think
I should do in the arms of a polar bear. Do you fee.
queer, Harry?"

" A little," replied Harry, in a low whisper; "and yet
I'm not frightened. I can scarcely tell what I feel; but
I'm certain it's not fear."

" Well, I don't know," said Charley. " When father's
black bull chased Kate and me in the prairies, and almost
overtook us, as we ran for the fence of the big field, I felt
my heart leap to my mouth, and the blood rush to my
cheeks, as I turned about and faced him, while Kate
climbed the fence; but after she was over, I felt a wild
sort of wickedness in me, as if I should like to tantalise
and torment him; and I felt altogether different from
what I feel now while I look up at these black clouds.
Isn't there something quite awful in them, Harry?"

Ere Harry replied, a bright flash of lightning shot
athwart the sky, followed by a loud roll of thunder, and
in a moment the wind rushed—like a fiend set suddenly
free—down upon the boats, tearing up the smooth surface
of the water as it flew, and cutting it into gleaming white
streaks. Fortunately the storm came down behind the
boats, so that, after the first wild burst was over, they

hoisted a small portion of their lug sails, and scudded rapidly before it.

There was still a considerable portion of the *traverse* to cross, and the guide cast an anxious glance over his shoulder occasionally, as the dark waves began to rise, and their crests were cut into white foam by the increasing gale. Thunder roared in continued, successive peals, as if the heavens were breaking up ; while rain descended in sheets. For a time the crews continued to ply their oars ; but, as the wind increased, these were rendered superfluous. They were taken in, therefore, and the men sought partial shelter under the tarpaulin ; while Mr Park and the two boys were covered, excepting their heads, by an oil-cloth, which was always kept at hand in rainy weather.

"What think you now, Louis ?" said Mr Park, resuming the pipe which the sudden outburst of the storm had caused him to forget. "Have we seen the worst of it ?"

Louis replied abruptly in the negative ; and, in a few seconds, shouted loudly—" Look out, lads ; here comes a squall. Stand by to let go the sheet there !"

Mike Brady, happening to be near the sheet, seized hold of the rope, and prepared to let go ; while the men rose, as if by instinct, and gazed anxiously at the approaching squall, which could be seen in the distance, extending along the horizon, like a bar of blackest ink, spotted with flakes of white. The guide sat with compressed lips and motionless as a statue, guiding the boat as it bounded madly towards the land, which was now not more than half-a-mile distant.

"Let go !" shouted the guide, in a voice that was heard loud and clear above the roar of the elements.

" Ay, ay," replied the Irishman, untwisting the rope instantly, as, with a sharp hiss, the squall descended on the boat.

At that moment the rope became entangled round one of the oars, and the gale burst with all its fury on the distended sail, burying the prow in the waves, which rushed in-board in a black volume, and in an instant half filled the boat.

" Let go!" roared the guide again, in a voice of thunder ; while Mike struggled with awkward energy to disentangle the rope.

As he spoke, an Indian, who during the storm had been sitting beside the mast, gazing at the boiling water with a grave contemplative aspect, sprang quickly forward, drew his knife, and, with two blows (so rapidly delivered that they seemed but one) cut asunder, first the sheet and then the halyards, which let the sail blow out and fall flat upon the boat. He was just in time. Another moment and the gushing water, which curled over the bow, would have filled them to the gunwale. As it was, the little vessel was so full of water that she lay like a log, while every toss of the waves sent an additional torrent into her.

" Bail for your lives, lads," cried Mr Park, as he sprang forward, and, seizing a tin dish, began energetically to bail out the water. Following his example, the whole crew seized whatever came first to hand in the shape of dish or kettle, and began to bail. Charley and Harry Somerville acted a vigorous part on this occasion, the one with a bark dish, (which had been originally made by the natives for the purpose of holding maple sugar,) the other with his cap.

For a time, it seemed doubtful whether the curling waves should send most water *into* the boat, or the crew should bail most *out* of it. But the latter soon prevailed, and in a few minutes it was so far got under, that three of the men were enabled to leave off bailing and re-set the sail, while Louis Peltier returned to his post at the helm. At first the boat moved but slowly, owing to the weight of water in her; but, as this grew gradually less, she increased her speed and neared the land.

"Well done, Redfeather," said Mr Park, addressing the Indian as he resumed his seat; "your knife did us good service that time, my fine fellow."

Redfeather, who was the only pure native in the brigade, acknowledged the compliment with a smile.

"*Ah! oui,*" said the guide, whose features had now lost their stern expression. "Them Injins are always 'eady enough with their knives. It's not the first time my life has been saved by the knife of a redskin."

"Humph! bad luck to them," muttered Mike Brady; "it's not the first time that my windpipe has been pretty near spiflicated by the knives o' the redskins, the murtherin' varmints!"

As Mike gave vent to this malediction, the boat ran swiftly past a low rocky point, over which the surf was breaking wildly.

"Down with the sail, Mike," cried the guide, at the same time putting the helm hard up. The boat flew round obedient to the ruling power, made one last plunge as it left the rolling surf behind, and slid gently and smoothly into still water under the lee of the point.

Here, in the snug shelter of a little bay, two of the other boats were found, with their prows already on the

beach, and their crews actively employed in landing
their goods, opening bales that had received damage from
the water, and preparing the encampment; while ever
and anon they paused a moment, to watch the various
boats as they flew before the gale, and one by one doubled
the friendly promontory.

If there is one thing that provokes a *voyageur* more
than another, it is being wind-bound on the shores of
a large lake. Rain or sleet, heat or cold, icicles forming
on the oars, or a broiling sun glaring in a cloudless sky,
the stings of sand-flies, or the sharp probes of a million
mosquitoes, he will bear with comparative indifference;
but being detained by high wind for two, three, or four
days together—lying inactively on shore, when everything
else, it may be, is favourable—the sun bright, the sky
blue, the air invigorating, and all but the wind propitious—
is more than his philosophy can carry him through with
equanimity. He grumbles at it; sometimes makes believe
to laugh at it; very often, we are sorry to say, swears
at it; does his best to sleep through it, but, whatever he
does, he does with a bad grace, because he's in a bad
humour and can't stand it.

For the next three days this was the fate of our friends.
Part of the time it rained, when the whole party slept as
much as was possible, and then *endeavoured* to sleep *more*
than was possible, under the shelter afforded by the
spreading branches of the trees. Part of the time was
fair, with occasional gleams of sunshine, when the men
turned out to eat, and smoke, and gamble round the fires;
and the two friends sauntered down to a sheltered place
on the shore, sunned themselves in a warm nook among
the rocks, while they gazed ruefully at the foaming

billows, told endless stories of what they had done in time past, and equally endless *prospective* adventures that they earnestly hoped should befall them in time to come.

While they were thus engaged, Redfeather, the Indian who had cut the ropes so opportunely during the storm, walked down to the shore, and sitting down on a rock not far distant, fell apparently into a reverie.

"I like that fellow," said Harry, pointing to the Indian.

"So do I. He's a sharp, active man. Had it not been for him we should have had to swim for it."

"Indeed, had it not been for him, I should have had to sink for it," said Harry, with a smile, "for I can't swim."

"Ah, true, I forgot that. I wonder what the redskin, as the guide calls him, is thinking about," added Charley, in a musing tone.

"Of home, perhaps, 'sweet home,'" said Harry, with a sigh. "Do you think much of home, Charley, now that you have left it?"

Charley did not reply for a few seconds. He seemed to muse over the question.

At last he said, slowly—

"Think of home? I think of little else when I am not talking with you, Harry. My dear mother is always in my thoughts, and my poor old father. Home, ay, and darling Kate, too, is at my elbow night and day, with the tears streaming from her eyes, and her ringlets scattered over my shoulder, as I saw her the day we parted, beckoning me back again, or reproaching me for having gone away—God bless her! Yes, I often, very often, think of home, Harry."

10

Harry made no reply. His friend's words had directed
his thoughts to a very different and far distant scene—to
another Kate, and another father and mother, who lived
in a glen far away over the waters of the broad Atlantic.
He thought of them as they used to be when he was one
of the number, a unit in the beloved circle, whose absence
would have caused a blank there. He thought of the
kind voice that used to read the Word of God, and the
tender kiss of his mother as they parted for the night.
He thought of the dreary day when he left them all
behind, and sailed away, in the midst of strangers, across
the wide ocean to a strange land. He thought of them
now—*without* him—accustomed to his absence, and forget-
ful, perhaps, at times, that he had once been there. As
he thought of all this, a tear rolled down his cheek, and
when Charley looked up in his face, that tear-drop told
plainly that he too thought sometimes of home.

"Let us ask Redfeather to tell us something about the
Indians," he said, at length, rousing himself. "I have no
doubt he has had many adventures in his life; shall we,
Charley?"

"By all means. Ho, Redfeather! are you trying to
stop the wind by looking it out of countenance?"

The Indian rose and walked towards the spot where
the boys lay.

"What was Redfeather thinking about," said Charley,
adopting the somewhat pompous style of speech occasionally used by Indians. "Was he thinking of the white
swan and his little ones in the prairie; or did he dream of
giving his enemies a good licking the next time he meets
them?"

"Redfeather has no enemies," replied the Indian

" He was thinking of the great Manito,* who made the wild winds, and the great lakes, and the forest."

" And, pray, good Redfeather, what did your thoughts tell you ?"

" They told me that men are very weak, and very foolish, and wicked ; and that Manito is very good and patient to let them live."

" That is to say," cried Harry, who was surprised and a little nettled to hear what he called the heads of a sermon from a redskin, " that *you*, being a man, are very weak, and very foolish, and wicked, and that Manito is very good and patient to let *you* live ?"

" Good," said the Indian, calmly ; " that is what I mean."

" Come, Redfeather," said Charley, laying his hand on the Indian's arm, " sit down beside us, and tell us some of your adventures. I know that you must have had plenty, and it's quite clear that we're not to get away from this place all day, so you've nothing better to do."

The Indian readily assented, and began his story in English.

Redfeather was one of the very few Indians who had acquired the power of speaking the English language. Having been, while a youth, brought much into contact with the fur-traders ; and, having been induced by them to enter their service for a time, he had picked up enough of English to make himself easily understood. Being engaged at a later period of life as guide to one of the exploring parties sent out by the British Government to discover the famous North-west Passage, he had learned to read and write, and had become so much accustomed

* God.

to the habits and occupations of the " pale-faces," that he
spent more of his time, in one way or another, with
them than in the society of his tribe, which dwelt in the
thick woods bordering on one of the great prairies of the
interior.   He was about thirty years of age ; had a tall,
thin, but wiry and powerful frame, and was of a mild,
retiring disposition.   His face wore a habitually grave
expression, verging towards melancholy ; induced, probably, by the vicissitudes of a wild life (in which he had
seen much of the rugged side of nature in men and
things), acting upon a sensitive heart and a naturally warm
temperament.   Redfeather, however, was by no means
morose ; and when seated along with his Canadian comrades round the camp fire, he listened with evidently
genuine interest to their stories, and entered into the
spirit of their jests.   But he was always an auditor, and
rarely took part in their conversations.   He was frequently consulted by the guide in matters of difficulty,
and it was observed that the " redskin's " opinion always
carried much weight with it, although it was seldom
given unless asked for.   The men respected him much
because he was a hard worker, obliging, and modest,—
three qualities that insure respect, whether found under a
red skin or a white one.

"I shall tell you," he began, in a soft musing tone, as if
he were wandering in memories of the past ; "I shall tell
you how it was that I came by the name of Redfeather."

"Ah !" interrupted Charley, "I intended to ask you
about that ; you don't wear one."

"I did once.   My father was a great warrior in his
tribe," continued the Indian ; "and I was but a youth
when I got the name."

" My tribe was at war at the time with the Chipewyans, and one of our scouts having come in with the intelligence that a party of our enemies was in the neighbourhood, our warriors armed themselves to go in pursuit of them. I had been out once before with a war-party, but had not been successful, as the enemy's scouts gave notice of our approach in time to enable them to escape. At the time the information was brought to us, the young men of our village were amusing themselves with athletic games, and loud challenges were being given and accepted to wrestle, or race, or swim in the deep water of the river, which flowed calmly past the green bank on which our wigwams stood. On a bank near to us sat about a dozen of our women,—some employed in ornamenting moccasins with coloured porcupine-quills ; others making rogans of bark for maple sugar, or nursing their young infants ; while a few, chiefly the old women, grouped themselves together and kept up an incessant chattering, chiefly with reference to the doings of the young men.

" Apart from these stood three or four of the principal men of our tribe, smoking their pipes, and although apparently engrossed in conversation, still evidently interested in what was going forward on the bank of the river.

" Among the young men assembled, there was one of about my own age, who had taken a violent dislike to me, because the most beautiful girl in all the village preferred me before him. His name was Misconna. He was a hot-tempered, cruel youth ; and although I endeavoured as much as possible to keep out of his way, he sought every opportunity of picking a quarrel with me. I had just been running a race along with several other youths, and, although not the winner, I had kept ahead of

Misconna all the distance. He now stood leaning against
a tree, burning with rage and disappointment. I was sorry
for this, because I bore him no-ill will, and, if it had
occurred to me at the time, I would have allowed him to
pass me, since I was unable to gain the race at any rate.

" 'Dog!' he said, at length, stepping forward and confronting me, 'will you wrestle?'

" Just as he approached, I had turned round to leave
the place. Not wishing to have more to do with him, I
pretended not to hear, and made a step or two towards
the lodges. 'Dog!' he cried again, while his eyes
flashed fiercely, and he grasped me by the arm, 'will
you wrestle, or are you afraid? Has the brave boy's
heart changed into that of a girl?'

" 'No, Misconna,' said I. 'You *know* that I am not
afraid; but I have no desire to quarrel with you.'

" 'You lie!' cried he, with a cold sneer; 'you are
afraid—and see,' he added, pointing towards the women
with a triumphant smile, 'the dark-eyed girl sees it and
believes it, too!'

" I turned to look, and there I saw Wabisca gazing on
me with a look of blank amazement. I could see, also, that
several of the other women, and some of my companions,
shared in her surprise.

" With a burst of anger I turned round. 'No, Misconna,' said I, 'I am *not* afraid, as you shall find;' and,
springing upon him, I grasped him round the body. He
was nearly, if not quite, as strong a youth as myself; but
I was burning with indignation at the insolence of his
conduct before so many of the women, which gave me
more than usual energy. For several minutes we swayed
to and fro, each endeavouring in vain to bend the other's

back; but we were too well matched for this, and sought to accomplish our purpose by taking advantage of an unguarded movement. At last such a movement occurred. My adversary made a sudden and violent attempt to throw me to the left, hoping that an inequality in the ground would favour his effort. But he was mistaken. I had seen the danger, and was prepared for it, so that the instant he attempted it, I threw forward my right leg, and thrust him backwards with all my might. Misconna was quick in his motions. He saw my intention,—too late, indeed, to prevent it altogether, but in time to throw back his left foot and stiffen his body till it felt like a block of stone. The effort was now entirely one of endurance. We stood, each with his muscles strained to the utmost, without the slightest motion. At length I felt my adversary give way a little. Slight though the motion was, it instantly removed all doubt as to who should go down. My heart gave a bound of exultation, and, with the energy which such a feeling always inspires, I put forth all my strength, threw him heavily over on his back, and fell upon him.

"A shout of applause from my comrades greeted me as I rose and left the ground; but at the same moment the attention of all was taken from myself and the baffled Misconna, by the arrival of the scout, bringing us information that a party of Chipewyans were in the neighbourhood. In a moment all was bustle and preparation. An Indian war-party is soon got ready. Forty of our braves threw off the principal parts of their clothing; painted their faces with stripes of vermilion and charcoal; armed themselves with guns, bows, tomahawks, and scalping-knives, and in a few minutes left the camp in silence and at a quick pace.

"One or two of the youths who had been playing on the river's bank were permitted to accompany the party, and among these were Misconna and myself. As we passed a group of women, assembled to see us depart, I observed the girl who had caused so much jealousy between us She cast down her eyes as we came up, and as we advanced close to the group she dropt a white feather, as if by accident. Stooping hastily down, I picked it up in passing, and stuck it in an ornamented band that bound my hair. As we hurried on, I heard two or three old hags laugh, and say, with a sneer, 'His hand is as white as the feather: it has never seen blood.' The next moment we were hid in the forest, and pursued our rapid course in dead silence.

"The country through which we passed was varied,— extending in broken bits of open prairie, and partly covered with thick wood; yet not so thick as to offer any hindrance to our march. We walked in single file, each treading in his comrade's footsteps, while the band was headed by the scout who had brought the information. The principal chief of our tribe came next, and he was followed by the braves according to their age or influence. Misconna and I brought up the rear. The sun was just sinking as we left the belt of woodland in which our village stood, crossed over a short plain, descended a dark hollow, at the bottom of which the river flowed, and, following its course for a considerable distance, turned off to the right and emerged upon a sweep of prairie land. Here the scout halted, and taking the chief and two or three braves aside, entered into earnest consultation with them.

"What they said we could not hear; but as we stood

leaning on our guns in the deep shade of the forest, we
could observe by their animated gestures that they dif-
fered in opinion. We saw that the scout pointed
several times to the moon, which was just rising above the
tree-tops, and then to the distant horizon, but the chief
shook his head, pointed to the woods, and seemed to be
much in doubt, while the whole band watched his motions in deep silence, but evident interest. At length
they appeared to agree. The scout took his place at the
head of the line, and we resumed our march, keeping
close to the margin of the wood. It was perhaps three
hours after this ere we again halted to hold another consultation. This time their deliberations were shorter.
In a few seconds, our chief himself took the lead and
turned into the woods, through which he guided us to a
small fountain, which bubbled up at the root of a birch-
tree, where there was a smooth green spot of level ground.
Here we halted, and prepared to rest for an hour, at the
end of which time, the moon, which now shone bright and
full in the clear sky, would be nearly down, and we could
resume our march. We now sat down in a circle, and,
taking a hasty mouthful of dried meat, stretched ourselves on the ground with our arms beside us, while our
chief kept watch, leaning against the birch-tree. It
seemed as if I had scarcely been asleep five minutes
when I felt a light touch on my shoulder. Springing up,
I found the whole party already astir, and, in a few
minutes more, we were again hurrying onwards.

"We travelled thus until a faint light in the east told
us that the day was at hand, when the scout's steps
became more cautious, and he paused to examine the
ground frequently. At last we came to a place where

the ground sank slightly, and, at the distance of a hundred yards, rose again, forming a low ridge which was crowned with small bushes. Here we came to a halt, and were told that our enemies were on the other side of that ridge, that they were about twenty in number, all Chipewyan warriors, with the exception of one pale-face, —a trapper, and his Indian wife. The scout had learned, while lying like a snake in the grass around their camp, that this man was merely travelling with them on his way to the Rocky Mountains, and that, as they were a war-party, he intended to leave them soon. On hearing this the warriors gave a grim smile, and our chief, directing the scout to fall behind, cautiously led the way to the top of the ridge. On reaching it we saw a valley of great extent, dotted with trees and shrubs, and watered by one of the many rivers that flow into the great Saskatchewan. It was nearly dark, however, and we could only get an indistinct view of the land. Far ahead of us, on the right bank of the stream, and close to its margin, we saw the faint red light of watch-fires, which caused us some surprise, for watch-fires are never lighted by a war-party so near to an enemy's country. So we could only conjecture that they were quite ignorant of our being in that part of the country—which was, indeed, not unlikely, seeing that we had shifted our camp during the summer.

"Our chief now made arrangements for the attack. We were directed to separate and approach individually as near to the camp as was possible without risk of discovery, and then, taking up an advantageous position, to await our chief's signal—which was to be the hooting of an owl. We immediately separated. My course lay

along the banks of the stream, and, as I strode rapidly
along, listening to its low solemn murmur, which sounded
clear and distinct in the stillness of a calm summer night,
I could not help feeling as if it were reproaching me for
the bloody work I was hastening to perform. Then the
recollection of what the old women said of me, raised a
desperate spirit in my heart. Remembering the white
feather in my head, I grasped my gun and quickened my
pace. As I neared the camp, I went into the woods and
climbed a low hillock to look out. I found that it still
lay about five hundred yards distant, and that the greater
part of the ground between it and the place where I
stood, was quite flat, and without cover of any kind. I
therefore prepared to creep towards it, although the
attempt was likely to be attended with great danger, for
Chipewyans have quick ears and sharp eyes. Observing,
however, that the river ran close past the camp, I determined to follow its course as before. In a few seconds
more, I came to a dark narrow gap where the river flowed
between broken rocks, overhung by branches, and from
which I could obtain a clear view of the camp within
fifty yards of me. Examining the priming of my gun, I
sat down on a rock to await the chief's signal.

"It was evident, from the careless manner in which the
fires were placed, that no enemy was supposed to be near.
From my concealment I could plainly distinguish ten or
fifteen of the sleeping forms of our enemies, among which
the trapper was conspicuous, from his superior bulk, and
the reckless way in which his brawny arms were flung on
the turf, while his right hand clutched his rifle. I could
not but smile as I thought of the proud boldness of the
pale-face—lying all exposed to view in the gray light of

dawn, while an Indian's rifle was so close at hand.   One
Indian kept watch, but he seemed more than half asleep.
I had not sat more than a minute, when my observations
were interrupted by the cracking of a branch in the
bushes near me.   Starting up, I was about to bound into
the underwood, when a figure sprang down the bank and
rapidly approached me.   My first impulse was to throw
forward my gun, but a glance sufficed to shew me that it
was a woman.

" ' Wah !' I exclaimed, in surprise, as she hurried forward and laid her hand on my shoulder.   She was dressed
partly in the costume of the Indians, but wore a shawl
on her shoulders, and a handkerchief on her head, that
shewed she had been in the settlements ; and, from the
lightness of her skin and hair, I judged at once that she
was the trapper's wife of whom I had heard the scout
speak.

" ' Has the light-hair got a medicine bag, or does she
speak with spirits, that she has found me so easily ?'

" The girl looked anxiously up in my face as if to read
my thoughts, and then said, in a low voice—

" ' No, I neither carry the medicine bag nor hold palaver
with spirits ; but I do think the good Manito must have
led me here.   I wandered into the woods because I could
not sleep, and I saw you pass.   But tell me,' she added
with still deeper anxiety, ' does the white feather come
alone ?   Does he approach *friends* during the dark hours
with a soft step like a fox ?'

" Feeling the necessity of detaining her until my comrades should have time to surround the camp, I said—
' The white feather hunts far from his lands.   He sees

FEERATHER PREPARING THE CAMP

of
gl
de
a
to
an
th
kn
to

th
yo
he
de
y

m
lo
th
ru
',,

b
Y
h
l

g

Indians whom he does not know, and must approach with
a light step. Perhaps they are enemies.'

"'Do Knisteneux hunt at night, prowling in the bed
of a stream?' said the girl, still regarding me with a keen
glance. 'Speak truth, stranger' (and she started suddenly back); 'in a moment I can alarm the camp with
a cry, and if your tongue is forked!—but I do not wish
to bring enemies upon you, if they are indeed such. I
am not one of them. My husband and I travel with
them for a time. We do not desire to see blood. God
knows,' she added, in French, which seemed her native
tongue, 'I have seen enough of that already.'

"As her earnest eyes looked into my face, a sudden
thought occurred to me. 'Go,' said I, hastily, 'tell
your husband to leave the camp instantly, and meet me
here; and see that the Chipewyans do not observe your
departure. Quick! his life and yours may depend on
your speed.'

"The girl instantly comprehended my meaning. In a
moment she sprang up the bank; but as she did so, the
loud report of a gun was heard, followed by a yell, and
the war-whoop of the Knisteneux rent the air as they
rushed upon the devoted camp, sending arrows and bullets
into the camp.

"On the instant, I sprang after the girl and grasped her
by the arm. 'Stay, white-cheek, it is too late now.
You cannot save your husband, but I think he'll save
himself. I saw him dive into the bushes like a carriboo.
Hide yourself here, perhaps you may escape.'

"The half-breed girl sank on a fallen tree with a deep
groan, and clasped her hands convulsively before her eyes.

while I bounded over the tree, intending to join my comrades in pursuing the enemy.

"As I did so a shrill cry arose behind me, and, looking
back, I beheld the trapper's wife prostrate on the ground,
and Misconna standing over her, his spear uplifted, and a
fierce frown on his dark face.

"'Hold,' I cried, rushing back and seizing his arm.
'Misconna did not come to kill *women*. She is not our
enemy.'

"'Does the young wrestler want *another* wife?' he said
with a wild laugh, at the same time wrenching his arm
from my gripe, and driving his spear through the fleshy
part of the woman's breast and deep into the ground. A
shriek rent the air as he drew it out again to repeat the
thrust; but, before he could do so, I struck him with the
butt of my gun on the head. Staggering backwards, he
fell heavily among the bushes. At this moment a second
whoop rang out, and another of our band sprang from the
thicket that surrounded us. Seeing no one but myself
and the bleeding girl, he gave me a short glance of surprise, as if he wondered why I did not finish the work
which he evidently supposed I had begun.

"'Wah!' he exclaimed; and uttering another yell
plunged his spear into the woman's breast, despite my
efforts to prevent him—this time with more deadly effect,
as the blood spouted from the wound, while she uttered a
piercing scream, and twined her arms round my legs as I
stood beside her, as if imploring for mercy. Poor girl! I
saw that she was past my help. The wound was evidently
mortal. Already the signs of death overspread her features, and I felt that a second blow would be one of mercy,
so that when the Indian stooped and passed his long knife

through her heart, I made but a feeble effort to prevent
it. Just as the man rose, with the warm blood dripping
from his keen blade, the sharp crack of a rifle was heard,
and the Indian fell dead at my feet, shot through the
forehead, while the trapper bounded into the open space,
his massive frame quivering, and his sunburnt face distorted with rage and horror. From the other side of the
brake, six of our band rushed forward and levelled their
guns at him. For one moment the trapper paused to
cast a glance at the mangled corpse of his wife, as if to
make quite sure that she was dead ; and then uttering a
howl of despair, he hurled his axe with a giant's force at
the Knisteneux, and disappeared over the precipitous
bank of the stream.

"So rapid was the action, that the volley which imme-
ately succeeded passed harmlessly over his head, while
the Indians dashed forward in pursuit. At the same
instant I myself was felled to the earth. The axe which
the trapper had flung struck a tree in its flight, and, as it
glanced off, the handle gave me a violent blow in passing.
I fell stunned. As I did so, my head alighted on the
shoulder of the woman, and the last thing I felt, as my
wandering senses forsook me, was her still warm blood
flowing over my face and neck.

"While this scene was going on, the yells and screams
of the warriors in the camp became fainter and fainter as
they pursued and fled through the woods. The whole
band of Chipewyans was entirely routed, with the exception of four who escaped, and the trapper whose flight I
have described ; all the rest were slain, and their scalps
hung at the belts of the victorious Knisteneux warriors,
while only one of our party was killed.

" Not more than a few minutes after receiving the blow
that stunned me, I recovered, and rising as hastily as my
scattered faculties would permit me, I staggered towards
the camp, where I heard the shouts of our men as they
collected the arms of their enemies. As I rose, the
feather which Wabisca had dropped fell from my brow,
and, as I picked it up to replace it, I perceived that it
was *red;* being entirely covered with the blood of the half-
breed girl.

" The place where Misconna had fallen was vacant as I
passed, and I found him standing among his comrades
round the camp fires, examining the guns and other
articles which they had collected. He gave me a short
glance of deep hatred as I passed, and turned his head
hastily away. A few minutes sufficed to collect the
spoils, and so rapidly had everything been done, that the
light of day was still faint as we silently returned on our
track. We marched in the same order as before,
Misconna and I bringing up the rear. As we passed
near the place where the poor woman had been murdered, I felt a strong desire to return to the spot. I
could not very well understand the feeling, but it lay so
strong upon me, that when we reached the ridge where
we first came in sight of the Chipewyan camp, I fell
behind until my companions disappeared in the woods,
and then ran swiftly back. Just as I was about to step
beyond the circle of bushes that surrounded the spot, I saw
that some one was there before me. It was a man, and,
as he advanced into the open space and the light fell on his
face, I saw that it was the trapper. No doubt, he had
watched us off the ground, and then, when all was safe,
returned to bury his wife. I crouched to watch him.

Stepping slowly up to the body of his murdered wife, he stood beside it with his arms folded on his breast and quite motionless. His head hung down, for the heart of the white man was heavy, and I could see, as the light increased, that his brows were dark as the thunder cloud, and the corners of his mouth twitched from a feeling that the Indian scorns to shew. My heart is full of sorrow for him now ;" (Redfeather's voice sank as he spoke), "it was full of sorrow for him even *then*, when I was taught to think that pity for an enemy was unworthy of a brave. The trapper stood gazing very long. His wife was young ; he could not leave her yet. At length a deep groan burst from his heart, as the waters of a great river, long held down, swell up in spring, and burst the ice at last. Groan followed groan as the trapper still stood and pressed his arms on his broad breast, as if to crush the heart within. At last he slowly knelt beside her, bending more and more over the lifeless form, until he lay extended on the ground beside it, and, twining his arms round the neck, he drew the cold cheek close to his and pressed the blood-covered bosom tighter and tighter, while his form quivered with agony as he gave her a last, long embrace. Oh !" continued Redfeather, while his brow darkened, and his black eye flashed with an expression of fierceness that his young listeners had never seen before, " may the curse ——" (he paused). " God forgive them ! how could they know better !

" At length the trapper rose hastily. The expression of his brow was still the same, but his mouth was altered. The lips were pressed tightly like those of a brave when led to torture, and there was a fierce activity in his motions as he sprang down the bank and proceeded to

11

dig a hole in the soft earth. For half an hour he laboured, shovelling away the earth with a large flat stone, and carrying down the body, he buried it there, under the shadow of a willow. The trapper then shouldered his rifle and hurried away. On reaching the turn of the stream which shuts the little hollow out from view, he halted suddenly, gave one look into the prairie he was henceforth to tread alone, one short glance back, and then, raising both arms in the air, looked up into the sky, while he stretched himself to his full height. Even at that distance, I could see the wild glare of his eye and the heaving of his breast. A moment after, and he was gone."

" And did you never see him again ?" inquired Harry Somerville, eagerly.

" No, I never saw him more. Immediately afterwards I turned to rejoin my companions, whom I soon overtook, and entered our village along with them. I was regarded as a poor warrior, because I brought home no scalps, and ever afterwards I went by the name of *Red-feather* in our tribe."

" But are you still thought a poor warrior ?" asked Charley, in some concern, as if he were jealous of the reputation of his new friend.

The Indian smiled. " No," he said ; " our village was twice attacked afterwards, and, in defending it, Red-feather took many scalps. He was made a chief !"

" Ah !" cried Charley, " I'm glad of that. And Wabisca, what came of her ? Did Misconna get her ?"

" She is my wife," replied Redfeather.

" Your wife ! Why, I thought I heard the *voyageurs* call your wife the white swan."

" *Wabisca* is *white* in the language of the Knisteneux. She is beautiful in form, and my comrades call her the white swan."

Redfeather said this with an air of gratified pride. He did not, perhaps, love his wife with more fervour than he would have done, had he remained with his tribe ; but Redfeather had associated a great deal with the traders, and he had imbibed much of that spirit which prompts " *white men* " to treat their females with deference and respect, a feeling which is very foreign to an Indian's bosom. To do so was, besides, more congenial to his naturally unselfish and affectionate disposition, so that any flattering allusion to his partner was always received by him with immense gratification.

" I'll pay you a visit some day, Redfeather, if I'm sent to any place within fifty miles of your tribe," said Charley, with the air of one who had fully made up his mind.

" And Misconna ?" asked Harry.

" Misconna is with his tribe," replied the Indian, and a frown overspread his features as he spoke ; " but Red-feather has been following in the track of his white friends · he has not seen his nation for many moons."

CHAPTER XIII.

The Canoe.   Ascending the Rapids.   The Portage.   Deer Shooting and Life in
the Woods.

WE must now beg the patient reader to take a leap with
us, not only through space, but also through time.   We
must pass over the events of the remainder of the journey
along the shore of Lake Winipeg.   Unwilling though
we are to omit anything in the history of our friends that
would be likely to prove interesting, we think it wise not
to run the risk of being tedious, or of dwelling too minutely
on the details of scenes which recall powerfully the feelings
and memories of bygone days to the writer, but may,
nevertheless, appear somewhat flat to the reader.

We shall not, therefore, enlarge at present on the arrival of the boats at Norway House, which lies at the
north end of the lake, nor of what was said and done by
our friends and by several other young comrades whom
they found there.   We shall not speak of the horror of
Harry Somerville, and the extreme disappointment of his
friend Charley Kennedy, when the former was told that
instead of hunting grizzly bears up the Saskatchewan, he
was condemned to the desk again, at York Fort, the depôt on Hudson's Bay, a low swampy place near the sea-
shore, where the goods for the interior are annually landed
and the furs shipped for England, where the greater part
of the summer and much of the winter is occupied by the

clerks, who may be doomed to vegetate there, in making
up the accounts of what is termed the Northern De-
partment, and where the brigades converge from all the
wide-scattered and far distant outposts, and the *ship* from
England—that great event of the year—arrives, keeping
the place in a state of constant bustle and effervescence
until autumn, when ship and brigades finally depart,
leaving the residents (about 30 in number) shut up for
eight long, dreary months of winter—with a tenantless
wilderness around and behind them, and the wide, cold,
frozen sea before. This was among the first of Harry's
disappointments. He suffered many afterwards, poor
fellow i

Neither shall we accompany Charley up the south
branch of the Saskatchewan, where his utmost expectations
in the way of hunting were more than realised, and where
he became so accustomed to shooting ducks and geese, and
bears and buffaloes, that he could not forbear smiling when
he chanced to meet with a red-legged gull, and remembered how he and his friend Harry had comported themselves when they first met with these birds on the shores
of Lake Winipeg! We shall pass over all this, and the
summer, autumn, and winter too, and leap at once into
the spring of the following year.

On a very bright, cheery morning of that spring, a canoe
might have been seen slowly ascending one of the numerous streams which meander through a richly-wooded,
fertile country, and mingle their waters with those of the
Athabasca river, terminating their united career in a
large lake of the same name. The canoe was small—one
of the kind used by the natives while engaged in hunting,
and capable of holding only two persons conveniently, with

their baggage.   To any one unacquainted with the nature
or capabilities of a Northern Indian canoe, the fragile,
bright orange-coloured machine that was battling with
the strong current of a rapid, must indeed have appeared
an unsafe and insignificant craft; but a more careful study
of its performances in the rapid, and of the immense quantity of miscellaneous goods and chattels which were, at a
later period of the day, disgorged from its interior, would
have convinced the beholder that it was in truth the most
convenient and serviceable craft that could be devised for
the exigencies of such a country.

True, it could hold only two men (it *might* have taken
three at a pinch), because men, and women too, are awkward, unyielding baggage, very difficult to stow com-
pactly, but it is otherwise with tractable goods.   The
canoe is exceedingly thin, so that no space is taken up or
rendered useless by its own structure, and there is no end
to the amount of blankets, and furs, and coats, and
paddles, and tent-covers, and dogs, and babies, that can
be stowed away in its capacious interior.   The canoe of
which we are now writing contained two persons, whose
active figures were thrown alternately into every graceful
attitude of manly vigour, as, with poles in hand, they
struggled to force their light craft against the boiling
stream.   One was a man apparently of about forty-five
years of age.   He was a square-shouldered, muscular
man, and from the ruggedness of his general appearance,
the soiled hunting-shirt that was strapped round his
waist with a parti-coloured worsted belt, the leather leg
gins, a good deal the worse for wear, together with the
quiet self-possessed glance of his gray eye, the compressed
lip and the sunburnt brow, it was evident that he was a

hunter, and one who had seen rough work in his day.
The expression of his face was pleasing, despite a look of
habitual severity which sat upon it, and a deep scar
which traversed his brow from the right temple to the top
of his nose. It was difficult to tell to what country he
belonged. His father was a Canadian, his mother a
Scotchwoman. He was born in Canada, brought up in
one of the Yankee settlements on the Missouri, and had,
from a mere youth, spent his life as a hunter in the wilderness. He could speak English, French, or Indian
with equal ease and fluency, but it would have been hard
for any one to say which of the three was his native
tongue. The younger man, who occupied the stern of the
canoe, acting the part of steersman, was quite a youth,
apparently about seventeen, but tall and stout beyond his
years, and deeply sunburnt. Indeed, were it not for this
fact, the unusual quantity of hair that hung in massive
curls down his neck, and the *voyageur* costume, we should
have recognised our young friend Charley Kennedy again
more easily. Had any doubts remained in our mind, the
shout of his merry voice would have scattered them at
once.

"Hold hard, Jacques," he cried, as the canoe trembled in the current, "one moment, till I get my pole
fixed behind this rock. Now, then, shove ahead. Ah!"
he exclaimed, with chagrin, as the pole slipt on the treach-
erous bottom, and the canoe whirled round.

"Mind the rock," cried the bowsman, giving an energetic thrust with his pole, that sent the light bark into an
eddy formed by a large rock, which rose above the turbulent waters. Here it rested while Jacques and Charley
raised themselves on their knees (travellers in small

canoes always sit in a kneeling position) to survey the rapid.

" It's too much for us, I fear, Mr Charles," said Jacques, shading his brow with his horny hand. " I've paddled up it many a time alone, but never saw the water so big as now."

" Humph ! we shall have to make a portage, then, I presume. Could we not give it one trial more ? I think we might make a dash for the tail of that eddy, and then the stream above seems not quite so strong. Do you think so, Jacques ? "

Jacques was not the man to check a daring young spirit. His motto through life had ever been " Never venture, never win,"—a sentiment which his intercourse among fur-traders had taught him to embody in the pithy expression, " Never say die ;" so that, although quite satisfied that the thing was impossible, he merely replied to his companion's speech by an assenting " Ho," and pushed out again into the stream. An energetic effort enabled them to gain the tail of the eddy spoken of, when Charley's pole snapt across, and, falling heavily on the gunwale, he would have upset the little craft, had not Jacques, whose wits were habitually on the *qui vive*, thrown his own weight at the same moment on the opposite side, and counterbalanced Charley's slip. The action saved them a ducking ; but the canoe, being left to its own devices for an instant, whirled off again into the stream, and before Charley could seize a paddle to prevent it, they were floating in the still water at the foot of the rapids.

" Now, isn't that a bore?" said Charley, with a comical look of disappointment at his companion.

Jacques laughed.

" It was well to *try*, master. I mind a young clerk who came into these parts the same year as I did, and *he* seldom *tried* anything. He couldn't abide canoes. He didn't want for courage neither; but he had a nat'ral dislike to them, I suppose, that he couldn't help, and never entered one except when he was obliged to do so. Well, one day he wounded a grizzly bear on the banks o' the Saskatchewan (mind the tail o' that rapid, Mr Charles; we'll land 'tother side o' yon rock.) Well, the bear made after him, and he cut stick right away for the river, where there was a canoe hauled up on the bank. He didn't take time to put his rifle aboard, but dropt it on the gravel, crammed the canoe into the water and jumped in, almost driving his feet through its bottom as he did so, and then plumped down so suddenly to prevent its capsizing, that he split it right across. By this time the bear was at his heels, and took the water like a duck. The poor clerk, in his hurry, swayed from side to side tryin' to prevent the canoe goin' over. But when he went to one side, he was so unused to it that he went too far, and had to jerk over to the other pretty sharp; and so he got worse and worse, until he heard the bear give a great snort beside him. Then he grabbed the paddle in desperation, but at the first dash he missed his stroke and over he went. The current was pretty strong at the place, which was lucky for him, for it kept him down a bit, so that the bear didn't observe him for a little; and while it was pokin' away at the canoe, he was carried down stream like a log and stranded on a shallow. Jumping up, he made tracks for the wood, and the bear (which had found out its mistake) after him, so he was obliged

at last to take to a tree, where the beast watched him for
a day and a night, till his friends, thinking that something must be wrong, sent out to look for him. (Steady,
now, Mr Charles. A little more to the right—that's it.)
Now, if that young man had only ventured boldly into
small canoes when he got the chance, he might have
laughed at the grizzly and killed him too."

As Jacques finished, the canoe glided into a quiet bay
formed by an eddy of the rapid, where the still water was
overhung by dense foliage.

" Is the portage a long one ?" asked Charley, as he
stepped out on the bank, and helped to unload the canoe.

" About half a mile," replied his companion. " We
might make it shorter by poling up the last rapid ; but
it's still work, Mr Charles, and we'll do the thing quicker
and easier at one lift."

The two travellers now proceeded to make a portage.
They prepared to carry their canoe and baggage overland,
so as to avoid a succession of rapids and waterfalls which
intercepted their further progress.

" Now, Jacques, up with it," said Charley, after the
loading had been taken out and placed on the grassy
bank.

The hunter stooped, and, seizing the canoe by its
centre bar, lifted it out of the water, placed it on his
shoulders, and walked off with it into the woods. This
was not accomplished by the man's superior strength.
Charley could have done it quite as well ; and, indeed,
the strong hunter could have carried a canoe of twice the
size with perfect ease. Immediately afterwards Charley
followed with as much of the lading as he could carry,
leaving enough on the bank to form another load

The banks of the river were steep; in some places so much so that Jacques found it a matter of no small difficulty to climb over the broken rocks with the unwieldy canoe on his back : the more so that the branches interlaced overhead so thickly as to present a strong barrier, through which the canoe had to be forced, at the risk of damaging its delicate bark covering. On reaching the comparatively level land above, however, there was more open space, and the hunter threaded his way among the tree stems more rapidly, making a detour occasionally to avoid a swamp or piece of broken ground ; sometimes descending a deep gorge formed by a small tributary of the stream they were ascending, and which, to an unpractised eye, would have appeared almost impassable, even without the incumbrance of a canoe. But the said canoe never bore Jacques more gallantly or safely over the surges of lake or stream than did he bear it through the intricate mazes of the forest ; now diving down and disappearing altogether in the umbrageous foliage of a dell ; anon reappearing on the other side and scrambling up the bank on all-fours, he and the canoe together looking like some frightful yellow reptile of antediluvian proportions ; and then speeding rapidly forward over a level plain until he reached a sheet of still water above the rapids. Here he deposited his burden on the grass ; and halting only for a few seconds to carry a few drops of the clear water to his lips, retraced his steps to bring over the remainder of the baggage. Soon afterwards Charley made his appearance on the spot where the canoe was left, and, throwing down his load, seated himself on it and surveyed the prospect. Before him lay a reach of the stream, which spread out so widely as to resemble a small lake, in whose clear, still

bosom wer reflected the overhanging foliage of graceful
willows, and here and there the bright stem of a silver
birch, whose light green leaves contrasted well with scattered groups and solitary specimens of the spruce fir.
Reeds and sedges grew in the water along the banks,
rendering the junction of the land and the stream uncertain and confused. All this and a great deal more
Charley noted at a glance; for the hundreds of beautiful
and interesting objects in nature that take so long to describe, even partially, and are feebly set forth after all,
even by the most graphic language, flash upon the *eye* in
all their force and beauty, and are drunk in at once in a
single glance.

But Charley noted several objects floating on the water
which we have not yet mentioned. These were five gray
geese feeding among the reeds at a considerable distance
off, and all unconscious of the presence of a human foe in
their remote domains. The travellers had trusted very
much to their guns and nets for food, having only a small
quantity of pemican in reserve, lest these should fail—an
event which was not at all likely, as the country through
which they passed was teeming with wildfowl of all kinds,
besides deer. These latter, however, were only shot
when they came inadvertently within rifle range, as our
voyageurs had a definite object in view, and could not
afford to devote much of their time to the chase.

During the day previous to that on which we have
introduced them to our readers, Charley and his companion had been so much occupied in navigating their
frail bark among a succession of rapids, that they had not
attended to the replenishing of their larder, so that the
geese which now shewed themselves were looked upon by

SHIRLEY FED FINISHING THE LADDER

Charley with a longing eye. Unfortunately they were
feeding on the opposite side of the river, and out of shot.
But Charley was a hunter now, and knew how to overcome slight difficulties. He first cut down a pretty large
and leafy branch of a tree, and placed it in the bow of
the canoe in such a way as to hang down before it and
form a perfect screen, through the interstices of which he
could see the geese, while they could only see, what was
to them no novelty, the branch of a tree floating down
the stream. Having gently launched the canoe, Charley
was soon close to the unsuspecting birds, from among
which he selected one that appeared to be unusually
complacent and self-satisfied, concluding at once, with an
amount of wisdom that bespoke him a true philosopher,
that such *must* as a matter of course be the fattest.

"Bang" went the gun, and immediately the sleek
goose turned round upon its back and stretched out its
feet towards the sky, waving them once or twice as if
bidding adieu to its friends. The others thereupon took
to flight, with such a deal of splutter and noise as made
it quite apparent that their astonishment was unfeigned.
Bang went the gun again, and down fell a second goose.

"Ha!" exclaimed Jacques, throwing down the remainder of the cargo as Charley landed with his booty,
"that's well. I was just thinking as I comed across that
we should have to take to pemican to-night."

"Well, Jacques, and if we had, I'm sure an old hunter
like you, who have roughed it so often, need not com-
plain," said Charley, smiling.

"As to that, master," replied Jacques, "I've roughed
it often enough; and when it does come to a clear fix, I
can eat my shoes without grumblin' as well as any man.

But, you see, fresh meat is better than dried meat when it's to be had ; and so I'm glad to see that you've been lucky, Mr Charles."

" To say truth, so am I ; and these fellows are delightfully plump. But you spoke of eating your shoes, Jacques ; when were you reduced to that direful extremity ?"

Jacques finished reloading the canoe while they conversed, and the two were seated in their places, and quietly but swiftly ascending the stream again, ere the hunter replied.

" You've heerd of Sir John Franklin, I s'pose ?" he inquired, after a minute's consideration.

" Yes, often."

" An' p'raps you've heerd tell of his first trip of discovery along the shores of the Polar Sea ?"

" Do you refer to the time when he was nearly starved to death, and when poor Hood was shot by the Indian ?"

" The same," said Jacques.

" Oh, yes—I know all about that. Were you with them ?" inquired Charley, in great surprise.

" Why, no—not exactly on the trip; but i was sent in winter with provisions to them,—and much need they had of them, poor fellows ! I found them tearing away at some old parchment skins that had lain under the snow all winter, and that an Injin's dog would ha' turned up his nose at,—and they don't turn up their snouts at many things, I can tell ye. Well, after we had left all our provisions with them, we started for the fort again, just keepin' as much as would drive off starvation ; for, you see, we thought that surely we would git something on the road. But neither hoof nor feather did we see all the way (I was travellin' with an Injin), and our grub was soon done, though we saved it up, and only took a mouthful or two the last three days. At last it was done, and we was pretty well used up, and the fort two days ahead of us. So says I to my comrade —who had been looking at me for some time as if he thought that a cut off my shoulder wouldn't be a bad thing—says I, 'Nipitabo, I'm afeer'd the shoes must go for it now;' so with that I pulls out a pair o' deerskin moccasins. 'They looks tender,' said I, trying to be cheerful. 'Wah,' said the Injin; and then I held them over the fire till they was done black, and Nipitabo ate one, and I ate the 'tother, with a lump o' snow to wash it down !"

"It must have been rather dry eating," said Charley, laughing.

"Rayther; but it was better than the Injin's leather breeches which we took in hand next day. They was *uncommon* tough, and very dirty, havin' been worn about a year and a half. Hows'ever, they kept us up; an', as we only ate the legs, he had the benefit o' the stump to arrive with at the fort next day."

"What's yon ahead?" exclaimed Charley, pausing as he spoke, and shading his eyes with his hand.

"It's uncommon like trees," said Jacques. "It's likely a tree that's been tumbled across the river; and, from its appearance, I think we'll have to cut through it."

"Cut through it !" exclaimed Charley; "if my sight is worth a gunflint, we'll have to cut through a dozen trees."

Charley was right. The river ahead of them became rapidly narrower; and, either from the looseness of the surrounding soil, or the passing of a whirlwind, dozens of trees had been upset, and lay right across the narrow stream

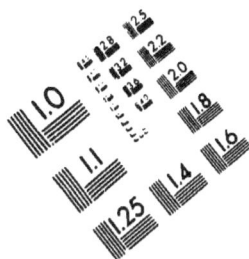

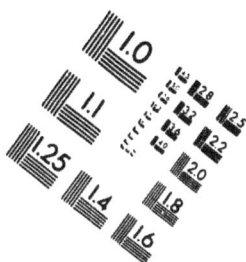

**IMAGE EVALUATION
TEST TARGET (MT-3)**

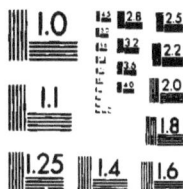

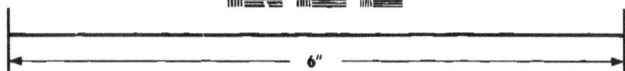

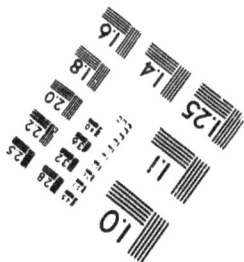

|← 6" →|

Photographic
Sciences
Corporation

23 WEST MAIN STREET
WEBSTER, N.Y. 14580
(716) 872-4503

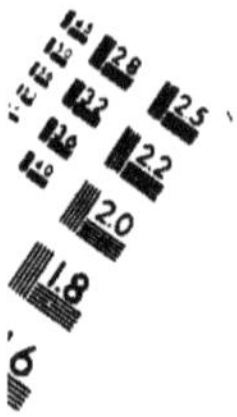

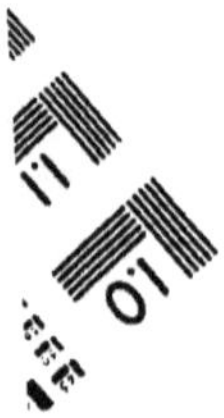

in terrible confusion. What made the thing worse was
that the banks on either side, which were low and flat,
were covered with such a dense thicket down to the
water's edge, that the idea of making a portage to overcome the barrier seemed altogether hopeless.

"Here's a pretty business, to be sure!" cried Charley,
in great disgust.

"Never say die, Mister Charles," replied Jacques,
taking up the axe from the bottom of the canoe; "it's
quite clear that cuttin' through the trees is easier than
cuttin' through the bushes, so here goes."

For fully three hours the travellers were engaged in
cutting their way up the encumbered stream, during
which time they did not advance three miles; and it was
evening ere they broke down the last barrier, and paddled
out into a sheet of clear water again.

"That'll prepare us for the geese, Jacques," said Charley,
as he wiped the perspiration from his brow; "there's
nothing like warm work for whetting the appetite, and
making one sleep soundly."

"That's true," replied the hunter, resuming his paddle.
"I often wonder how them white-faced fellows in the
settlements manage to keep body and soul together—a'
sittin', as they do, all day in the house, and a' lyin' all
night in a feather bed. For my part, rather than live as
they do, I would cut my way up streams like them we've
just passed every day and all day, and sleep on top of a flat
rock o' nights, under the blue sky, all my life through."

With this decided expression of his sentiments, the
stout hunter steered the canoe up alongside of a huge flat
rock, as if he were bent on giving a practical illustration
of the latter part of his speech then and there.

" We'd better camp now, Mister Charles, there's a portage o' two miles here, and it'll take us till sun-down to get the canoe and things over."

" Be it so," said Charley, landing ; " is there a good place at the other end to camp on ? "

" First-rate. It's smooth as a blanket on the turf, and a clear spring bubbling at the root of a wide tree that would keep off the rain if it was to come down like water-spouts."

The spot on which the travellers encamped that evening overlooked one of those scenes in which vast extent, and rich, soft variety of natural objects, were united with much that was grand and savage. It filled the mind with the calm satisfaction that is experienced when one gazes on the wide lawns, studded with noble trees ; the spreading fields of waving grain that mingle with stream and copse, rock and dell, vineyard and garden, of the cultivated lands oi civilised men ; while it produced that exulting throb of freedom which stirs man's heart to its centre, when he casts a first glance over miles and miles of broad lands that are yet unowned, unclaimed ; that yet lie in the unmutilated beauty with which the beneficent Creator originally clothed them — far away from the well-known scenes of man's chequered history ; entirely devoid of those ancient monuments of man's power and skill, that carry the mind back with feelings of awe to bygone ages ; yet stamped with evidences of an antiquity more ancient still, in the wild primeval forests, and the noble trees that have sprouted and spread and towered in their strength for centuries— trees that have fallen at their posts, while others took their place, and rose and fell as they did, like long-lived sentinels, whose duty it was to keep perpetual guard over the **vast** solitudes of the great American Wilderness.

12

The fire was lighted and the canoe turned bottom up in front of it, under the branches of a spreading tree which stood on an eminence, whence was obtained a bird's-eye view of the noble scene.   It was a flat valley, on either side of which rose two ranges of hills, which were clothed to the top with trees of various kinds, the plain of the valley itself being dotted with clumps of wood, among which the fresh green foliage of the plane-tree and the silver-stemmed birch were conspicuous, giving an airy lightness to the scene and enhancing the picturesque effect of the dark pines.   A small stream could be traced winding out and in among clumps of willows, reflecting their drooping boughs and the more sombre branches of the spruce-fir and the straight larch with which, in many places, its banks were shaded.   Here and there were stretches of clearer ground, where the green herbage of spring gave to it a lawn-like appearance, and the whole magnificent scene was bounded by blue hills that became fainter as they receded from the eye and mingled at last with the horizon. The sun had just set, and a rich glow of red bathed the whole scene, which was further enlivened by flocks of wild-fowls and herds of reindeer.

These last soon drew Charley's attention from the contemplation of the scenery, and, observing a deer feeding in an open space, towards which he could approach without coming between it and the wind, he ran for his gun and hurried into the woods, while Jacques busied himself in arranging their blankets under the upturned canoe, and in preparing supper.

Charley discovered, soon after starting, what all hunters discover sooner or later, namely, that appearances are deceitful, for he no sooner reached the foot of the hill than

FROM THE FAR NORTH.173

he found, between him and the lawn-like country, an
almost impenetrable thicket of underwood.   Our young
hero, however, was of that disposition which sticks at
nothing, and instead of taking time to search for an opening, he took a race and sprang into the middle of it, in
hopes of forcing his way through.   His hopes were not
disappointed.   He got through — quite through — and
alighted up to the armpits in a swamp, to the infinite consternation of a flock of teal-ducks that were slumbering
peacefully there with their heads under their wings, and
had evidently gone to bed for the night.   Fortunately he
held his gun above the water and kept his balance, so
that he was able to proceed with a dry charge, though
with an uncommonly wet skin.   Half an hour brought
Charley within range, and, watching patiently until the
animal presented his side towards the place of his concealment, he fired and shot it through the heart.

  "Well done, Mister Charles," exclaimed Jacques, as
the former staggered into camp with the reindeer on his
shoulders,—"a fat doe too."

  "Ay," said Charley, "but she hast cost me a wet skin ;
so pray, Jacques, rouse up the fire, and let's have supper
as soon as you can."

  Jacques speedily skinned the deer, cut a couple of
steaks from its flank, and, placing them on wooden spikes,
stuck them up to roast, while his young friend put on a
dry shirt, and hung his coat before the blaze.   The goose
which had been shot earlier in the day was also plucked,
split open, impaled in the same manner as the steaks, and
set up to roast.   By this time the shadows of night had
deepened, and ere long all was shrouded in gloom, except
the circle of ruddy light around the camp fire, in the

centre of which Jacques and Charley sat, with the canoe
at their backs, knives in their hands, and the two spits,
on the top of which smoked their ample supper, planted
in the ground before them.

One by one the stars went out, until none were visible
except the bright, beautiful morning star, as it rose
higher and higher in the eastern sky.   One by one the
owls and the wolves, ill-omened birds and beasts of night,
retired to rest in the dark recesses of the forest.   Little
by little the gray dawn overspread the sky, and paled the
lustre of the morning star, until it faded away altogether,
and then Jacques awoke with a start, and throwing out
his arm, brought it accidently into violent contact with
Charley's nose.

This caused Charley to awake, not only with a start,
but also with a roar, which brought them both suddenly
into a sitting posture, in which they continued for some
time in a state between sleeping and waking, their faces
meanwhile expressive of mingled imbecility and extreme
surprise.   Bursting into a simultaneous laugh, which
degenerated into a loud yawn, they sprang up, launched
and reloaded their canoe, and resumed their journey.

CHAPTER XIV

The Indian Camp; the new Outpost; Charley sent on a Mission to the
Indians.

In the councils of the fur-traders, on the spring previous
to that about which we are now writing, it had been
decided to extend their operations a little in the lands
that lie in central America, to the north of the Saskatchewan river; and, in furtherance of that object, it had
been intimated to the chief trader in charge of the district, that an expedition should be set on foot, having for
its object the examination of a territory into which they
had not yet penetrated, and the establishment of an outpost therein. It was furthermore ordered that operations
should be commenced at once, and that the choice of men
to carry out the end in view was graciously left to the
chief trader's well-known sagacity.

Upon receiving this communication, the chief trader
selected a gentleman, named Mr Whyte, to lead the party;
gave him a clerk and five men; provided him with a boat
and a large supply of goods necessary for trade, implements requisite for building an establishment, and sent
him off with a hearty shake of the hand, and a recommendation to "go and prosper."

Charles Kennedy spent part of the previous year at
Rocky Mountain House, where he had shewn so much
energy in conducting the trade — especially what he

called the " rough and tumble " part of it, that he was
selected as the clerk to accompany Mr Whyte to his new
ground.   After proceeding up many rivers, whose waters
had seldom borne the craft of white men, and across innumerable lakes, the party reached a spot that presented so
inviting an aspect, that it was resolved to pitch their tent
there for a time, and, if things in the way of trade and
provision looked favourable, establish themselves altogether.   The place was situated on the margin of a large
lake, whose shores were covered with the most luxuriant
verdure, and whose waters teemed with the finest fish,
while the air was alive with wildfowl, and the woods
swarming with game.   Here Mr Whyte rested awhile ;
and, having found everything to his satisfaction, he took
his axe, selected a green lawn that commanded an extensive view of the lake, and going up to a tall larch, struck
the steel into it, and thus put the first touch to an establishment which afterwards went by the name of Stoney
Creek.

A solitary Indian, whom they had met with on the
way to their new home, had informed them that a large
band of Knisteneux had lately migrated to a river about
four days' journey beyond the lake, at which they halted ;
and when the new fort was just beginning to spring up
our friend Charley and the interpreter, Jacques Caradoc,
were ordered by Mr Whyte to make a canoe, and then,
embarking in it, to proceed to the Indian camp, to inform
the natives of their rare good luck in having a band of
white men come to settle near their lands to trade
with them.   The interpreter and Charley soon found
birch bark, pine roots for sewing it, and gum for plaster-
ing the seams, wherewith they constructed the light

machine whose progress we have partly traced in the last chapter, and which on the following day at sunset, carried them to their journey's end.

From some remarks made by the Indian who gave them information of the camp, Charley gathered that it was the tribe to which Redfeather belonged, and furthermore, that Redfeather himself was there at that time; so that it was with feelings of no little interest that he saw the tops of the yellow tents embedded among the green trees, and soon afterwards beheld them and their picturesque owners reflected in the clear river, on whose banks the natives crowded to witness the arrival of the white men.

Upon the green sward, and under the umbrageous shade of the forest trees, the tents were pitched to the number of perhaps eighteen or twenty, and the whole population, of whom very few were absent on the present occasion, might number a hundred—men, women, and children. They were dressed in habiliments formed chiefly of materials procured by themselves in the chase, but ornamented with cloth, beads, and silk thread, which shewed that they had had intercourse with the fur-traders before now. The men wore leggins of deer-skin, which reached more than half way up the thigh, and were fastened to a leathern girdle, strapped round the waist. A loose tunic or hunting-shirt, of the same material, covered the figure from the shoulders almost to the knees, and was confined round the middle by a belt—in some cases of worsted, in others, of leather gaily ornamented with quills. Caps of various indescribable shapes, and made chiefly of skin, with the animal's tail left on by way of ornament, covered their heads, and moccasins for the feet completed their costume. These last may be

simply described as leather mittens for the feet without
fingers, or rather toes.   They were gaudily ornamented,
as was almost every portion of costume, with porcu-
pines' quills dyed with brilliant colours, and worked
into fanciful, and in many cases, extremely elegant figures
and designs; for North American Indians oftentimes
display an amount of taste in the harmonious arrangement
of colour, that would astonish those who fancy that *education* is absolutely necessary to the just appreciation of the
beautiful.

The women attired themselves in leggins and coats
differing little from those of the men, except that the
latter were longer, the sleeves detached from the body,
and fastened on separately — while on their heads they
wore caps, which hung down and covered their backs
to the waist.   These caps were of the simplest construc-
tion, being pieces of cloth cut into an oblong shape, and
sewed together at one end.   They were, however, richly
ornamented with silk-work and beads.

On landing, Charley and Jacques walked up to a tall
good-looking Indian, whom they judged from his demeanour, and the somewhat deferential regard paid to him by
the others, to be one of the chief men of the little community.

"Ho! what cheer?" said Jacques, taking him by the
hand after the manner of Europeans, and accosting him
with the phrase used by the fur-traders to the natives.
The Indian returned the compliment in kind, and led
the visitors to his tent, where he spread a buffalo robe for
them on the ground, and begged them to be seated.   A
repast of dried meat and reindeer-tongues was then
served, to which our friends did ample justice ; while the

women and children satisfied their curiosity by peering at them through chinks and holes in the tent. When they had finished, several of the principal men assembled, and the chief who had entertained them made a speech, to the effect that he was much gratified by the honour done to his people by the visit of his white brothers; that he hoped they would continue long at the camp to enjoy their hospitality; and that he would be glad to know what had brought them so far into the country of the red men.

During the course of this speech, the chief made eloquent allusion to all the good qualities supposed to belong to white men in general, and (he had no doubt) to the two white men before him in particular. He also boasted considerably of the prowess and bravery of himself and his tribe; launched a few sarcastic hits at his enemies; and wound up with a poetical hope that his guests might live for ever in these beautiful plains of bliss, where the sun never sets, and nothing goes wrong anywhere, and everything goes right at all times, and where, especially, the deer are outrageously fat, and always come out on purpose to be shot! During the course of these remarks, his comrades signified their hearty concurrence in his sentiments, by giving vent to sundry low-toned "hums!" and "has!" and "wahs!" and "hos!" according to circumstances. After it was over, Jacques rose, and, addressing them in their own language, said—

"My Indian brethren are great. They are brave, and their fame has travelled far. Their deeds are known even so far as where the Great Salt Lake beats on the shore where the sun rises. They are not women, and when their enemies hear the sound of their name, they grow

pale ; their hearts become like those of the reindeer
My brethren are famous, too, in the use of the snow-shoe,
the snare, and the gun.   The fur-traders know that they
must build large stores when they come into their lands.
They bring up much goods, because the young men are
active, and require much.   The silver fox and the marten
are no longer safe when their traps and snares are set.
Yes, they are good hunters, and we have now come to
live among you (Jacques changed his style as he came
nearer to the point), to trade with you, and to save you
the trouble of making long journeys with your skins.   A
few days' distance from your wigwams we have pitched
our tents.   Our young men are even now felling the trees
to build a house.   Our nets are set, our hunters are
prowling in the woods, our goods are ready, and my
young master and I have come to smoke the pipe of
friendship with you, and to invite you to come to trade
with us."

Having delivered this oration, Jacques sat down amid
deep silence.   Other speeches, of a highly satisfactory
character, were then made, after which "the house
adjourned," and the visitors, opening one of their pack-
ages, distributed a variety of presents to the delighted
natives.

Several times during the course of these proceedings,
Charley's eyes wandered among the faces of his enter-
tainers, in the hope of seeing Redfeather among them,
but without success ; and he began to fear that his friend
was not with the tribe.

"I say, Jacques," he said, as they left the tent, "ask
whether a chief called Redfeather is here.   I knew him
of old, and half-expected to find him at this place."

The Indian to whom Jacques put the question, replied that Redfeather was with them, but that he had gone out on a hunting expedition that morning, and might be absent a day or two.

" Ah !" exclaimed Charley, " I'm glad he's here. Come, now, let us take a walk in the wood; these good people stare at us as if we were ghosts." And, taking Jacques' arm, he led him beyond the circuit of the camp, turned into a path, which, winding among the thick underwood, speedily screened them from view, and led them into a sequestered glade, through which a rivulet trickled along its course, almost hid from view by the dense foliage and long grasses that overhung it.

" What a delightful place to live in !" said Charley. " Do you ever think of building a hut in such a spot as this, Jacques, and settling down altogether ?"

Charley's thoughts reverted to his sister Kate when he said this.

" Why, no," replied Jacques, in a pensive tone, as if the question had aroused some sorrowful recollections ; " I can't say that I'd like to settle here *now*. There *was* a time when I thought nothin' could be better than to squat in the woods with one or two jolly comrades, and——(*Jacques sighed*) ; but times is changed now, master, and so is my mind. My chums are most of them dead or gone, one way or other. No ; I shouldn't care to squat alone."

Charley thought of the hut *without* Kate; and it seemed so desolate and dreary a dwelling, notwithstanding its beautiful situation, that he agreed with his companion that to "squat" *alone* would never do at all.

" No, man was not made to live alone," continued

Jacques, pursuing the subject; "even the Injins draw
together. I never knew but one as didn't like his fellows,
and he's gone now, poor fellow. He cut his foot with an
axe one day, while fellin' a tree. It was a bad cut; and
havin' nobody to look after him, he half-bled and half-
starved to death."

"By the way, Jacques," said Charley, stepping over
the clear brook, and following the track which led
up the opposite bank, "what did you say to these redskins? You made them a most eloquent speech apparently."

"Why, as to that, I can't boast much of its eloquence,
but I think it was clear enough. I told them that they
were a great nation; for, you see, Mr Charles, the
red men are just like the white in their fondness for
butter; so I gave them some to begin with, though, for
the matter o' that, I'm not overly fond o' givin' butter to
any man, red or white. But I holds that it's as well
always to fall in with the ways and customs o' the people
a man happens to be among, so long as them ways and
customs a'n't contrary to what's right. It makes them
feel more kindly to you, an' don't raise any onnecessary
ill-will. However, the Knisteneux *are* a brave race;
and, when I told them that the hearts of their enemies
trembled when they heard of them, I told nothing but
the truth, for the Chipewyans are a miserable set and not
much given to fighting."

"Your principles on that point won't stand much
sifting, I fear," replied Charley; "according to your own
shewing you would fall into the Chipewyan's way of glo-
rifying themselves on account of their bravery, if you
chanced to be dwelling among them, and yet you say they

are not brave. That would not be sticking to truth, Jacques, would it?"

"Well," replied Jacques, with a smile, "perhaps not exactly, but I'm sure there could be small harm in helping the miserable objects to boast sometimes, for they've little else than boasting to comfort them."

"And yet, Jacques, I cannot help feeling that truth is a grand, a glorious thing, that should not be trifled with even in small matters."

Jacques opened his eyes a little. "Then do you think, master, that a man should *never* tell a lie, no matter what fix he may be in?"

"I think not, Jacques."

The hunter paused a few minutes, and looked as if an unusual train of ideas had been raised in his mind by the turn their conversation had taken. Jacques was a man of no religion, and little morality, beyond what flowed from a naturally kind, candid disposition, and entertained the belief that the *end*, if a good one, always justifies the *means*,—a doctrine which, had it been clearly exposed to him in all its bearings and results, would have been spurned by his straightforward nature with the indignant contempt that it merits.

"Mr Charles," he said, at length, "I once travelled across the plains to the head waters of the Missouri with a party of six trappers. One night we came to a part of the plains which was very much broken up with wood here and there, and bein' a good place for water we camped. While the other lads were gettin' ready the supper, I started off to look for a deer, as we had been unlucky that day—we had shot nothin'. Well, about three miles from the camp, I came upon a band o' somewhere about thirty Sieux (ill-looking, sneaking dogs they are, too !) and before I could whistle, they rushed upon me, took away my rifle and hunting knife, and were dancing round me like so many devils. At last, a big black-lookin' thief stepped forward, and said in the Cree language—'White men seldom travel through this country alone ; where are your comrades ?' Now, thought I, here's a nice fix ! If I pretend not to understand, they'll send out parties in all directions, and as sure as fate they'll find my companions in half an hour, and butcher them in cold blood ; for, you see, we did not expect to find Sieux, or, indeed, any Injins in them parts ; so I made believe to be very narvous, and tried to tremble all over and look pale. Did you ever try to look pale and fright-ened, Mr Charles ?"

"I can't say that I ever did," said Charley, laughing.

"You can't think how troublesome it is," continued Jacques, with a look of earnest simplicity; "I shook and trembled pretty well, but the more I tried to grow pale, the more I grew red in the face, and when I thought of the six broad-shouldered, raw-boned lads in the camp, and how easy they would have made these jumping villains fly like chaff, if they only knew the fix I was in, I gave a frown that had well-nigh shewed I was shamming. Hows'ever, what with shakin' a little more, and givin' one or two most awful groans, I managed to deceive them. Then I said I was hunter to a party of white men that were travellin' from Red River to St Louis, with all their goods, and wives, and children, and that they were away in the plains about a league off.

"'The big chap looked very hard into my face when I said this, to see if I was telling the truth ; and I tried to make my teeth chatter, but it wouldn't do, so I took to groanin' very bad instead. But them Sioux are such awful liars nat'rally, that they couldn't understand the signs of truth, even if they saw them. 'Whitefaced coward,' says he to me, 'tell me in what direction your people are.' At this I made believe not to understand; but the big chap flourished his knife before my face, called me a dog, and told me to point out the direction. I looked as simple as I could, and said I would rather not. At this they laughed loudly, and then gave a yell, and said if I didn't shew them the direction they would roast me alive. So I pointed towards a part of the plains pretty wide o' the spot where our camp was. 'Now, lead us to them,' said the big chap, givin' me a shove with the butt of his gun; 'an' if you have told lies —— he gave the handle of his scalpin' knife a slap, as much as to say he'd tickle up my liver with it. Well, away we went in silence, me thinkin' all the time how I was to get out o' the scrape. I led them pretty close past our camp, hopin' that the lads would hear us. I didn't dare to yell out, as that would have shewed them there was somebody within hearin', and they would have made short work of me. Just as we came near the place where my companions lay, a prairie wolf sprang out from under a bush where it had been sleepin,' so I gave a loud hurrah, and shied my cap at it. Giving a loud growl, the big Injin hit me over the head with his fist, and told me to keep silence. In a few minutes I heard the low distant howl of a wolf. I recognised the voice of one of my comrades, and knew that they had seen us, and would be on our track soon. Watchin' my opportunity, and walkin' for a good bit as if I was awful tired—all but done up—

to throw them off their guard, I suddenly tripped up the big chap as he was stepping over a small brook, and dived in among the bushes. In a moment a dozen bullets tore up the bark on the trees about me, and an arrow passed through my hair. The clump of wood into which I had dived was about half a mile long; and as I could run well (I've found in my experience that white men are more than a match for redskins at their own work), I was almost out of range by the time I was forced to quit the cover and take to the plain. When the blackguards got out of the cover, too, and saw me cuttin' ahead like a deer, they gave a yell of disappointment, and sent another shower of arrows and bullets after me, some of which came nearer than was pleasant. I then headed for our camp with the whole pack screechin' at my heels. 'Yell away, you stupid sinners,' thought I; 'some of you shall pay for your music.' At that moment an arrow grazed my shoulder; and, looking over it, I saw that the black fellow I had pitched into the water was far ahead of the rest, strainin' after me like mad, and every now and then stopping to try an arrow on me; so I kept a look out, and when I saw him stop to draw, I stopped too, and dodged, so the arrows passed me, and then we took to our heels again. In this way I ran for dear life, till I came up to the cover. As I came close up I saw our six fellows crouchin' in the bushes, and one o' them takin' aim almost straight for my face. 'Your day's come at last,' thought I, looking over my shoulder at the big Injin, who was drawing his bow again. Just then there was a sharp crack heard—a bullet whistled past my ear, and the big fellow fell like a stone, while my comrade stood coolly up to reload his rifle. The Injins, on seein' this, pulled up in a moment; and our lads stepping forward, delivered a volley that made three more o' them bite the dust. There would have been six in that fix, but, somehow or other, three of us pitched upon the same man, who was afterwards found with a bullet in each eye and one through his heart. They didn't wait for more, but turned about and bolted like the wind. Now, Mr Charles, if I had told the truth that time, we would have been all killed; and if I had simply said nothin' to their questions, they would have sent out to scour the country, and have found out the camp for sartin, so that the only way to escape was by tellin' them a heap o' downright lies."

Charley looked very much perplexed at this.

" You have indeed placed me in a difficulty. I know not what I would have done. I don't know even what I *ought to do* under these circumstances. Difficulties may perplex me, and the force of circumstances might tempt me to do what I believed to be wrong. I am a sinner, Jacques, like other mortals, I know; but one thing I am quite sure of, namely, that, when men speak, it should *always* be truth and *never* falsehood."

Jacques looked perplexed too. He was strongly impressed with the necessity of telling falsehood in the circumstances in which he had been placed, as just related, while at the same time he felt deeply the grandeur and the power of Charley's last remark.

" I should have been under the sod *now*," said he, " if I had not told a lie *then*. Is it better to die than to speak falsehood ?"

" Some men have thought so," replied Charley. " I acknowledge the difficulty of *your* case, and of all similar

13

cases. I don't know what should be done; but I have
read of a minister of the gospel whose people were very
wicked and would not attend to his instructions, although
they could not but respect himself, he was so consistent
and Christianlike in his conduct. Persecution arose in
the country where he lived, and men and women were
cruelly murdered because of their religious belief. For
a long time he was left unmolested; but one day a band
of soldiers came to his house, and asked him whether he
was a Papist or a Protestant—(Papist, Jacques, being a
man who has sold his liberty in religious matters to the
Pope, and a Protestant being one who protests against
such an ineffably silly and unmanly state of slavery.) Well,
his people urged the good old man to say he was a Papist,
telling him that he would then be spared to live among
them, and preach the true faith for many years perhaps.
Now, if there was one thing that this old man would have
toiled for and *died* for, it was, that his people should become true Christians,—and he told them so, 'but,' headded,
'I will not tell a lie to accomplish that end, my children;
no, not even to save my life.' So he told the soldiers
that he was a Protestant, and immediately they carried
him away, and he was soon afterwards burned to death."

"Well," said Jacques, "*he* didn't gain much by sticking to the truth, I think."

"I'm not so sure of *that*. The story goes on to say,
that he *rejoiced* that he had done so, and wouldn't draw
back even when he was in the flames. But the point lies
here, Jacques : so deep an impression did the old man's
conduct make on his people, that from that day forward
they were noted for their Christian life and conduct.
They brought up their children with a deeper reverence

for the truth than they would otherwise have done, always
bearing in affectionate remembrance, and holding up to
them as an example, the unflinching truthfulness of the
good old man who was burned in the year of the terrible
persecutions ; and at last their influence and example had
such an effect that the Protestant religion spread like wild-
fire, far and wide around them, so that the very thing
was accomplished for which the old pastor said he would
have died : accomplished, too, very much in consequence
of his death, and in a way, and to an extent that very
likely would not have been the case, had he lived and
preached among them for a hundred years."

"I don't understand it, nohow," said Jacques, "it seems
to me right both ways and wrong both ways, and all up-
side down everyhow."

Charley smiled. "Your remark is about as clear as my
head on the subject, Jacques, but I still remain convinced
that truth is *right* and that falsehood is *wrong*, and that
we should stick to the first through thick and thin."

"I s'pose," remarked the hunter, who had walked along
in deep cogitation for the last five minutes, and had apparently come to some conclusion of profound depth and
sagacity, "I s'pose that it's all human natur' ; that some
men takes to preachin' as Injins take to huntin', and that
to understand sich things requires them to begin young,
and risk their lives in it, as I would in followin' up a
grizzly she-bear with cubs."

"Yonder is an illustration of one part of your remark.
They begin *young* enough, anyhow," said Charley, pointing
as he spoke to an opening in the bushes, where a particularly small Indian boy stood in the act of discharging
an arrow.

The two men halted to watch his movements. According to a common custom among juvenile Indians during
the warm months of the year, he was dressed in *nothing*
save a mere rag tied round his waist.   His body was
very brown, extremely round, fat, and wonderfully
diminutive, while his little legs and arms were dis-
proportionately small.   He was so young as to be barely
able to walk, and yet there he stood, his black eyes glittering with excitement, his tiny bow bent to its utmost,
and a blunt-headed arrow about to be discharged at a
squirrel, whose flight had been suddenly arrested by the
unexpected apparition of Charley and Jacques.   As he
stood there for a single instant, perfectly motionless, he
might have been mistaken for a grotesque statue of an
Indian cupid.   Taking advantage of the squirrel's pause,
the child let fly the arrow, hit it exactly on the point of
the nose, and turned it over, dead,—a consummation
which he greeted with a rapid succession of frightful
yells.

   " Cleverly done, my lad ; you're a chip of the old block,
I see," said Jacques, patting the child's head as he passed,
and retraced his steps, with Charley, to the Indian camp.

CHAPTER XV.

SAVAGES, not less than civilised men, arc fond of a good dinner. In saying this, we do not expect our reader to be overwhelmed with astonishment. He might have guessed as much; but when we state that savages, upon particular occasions, eat six dinners in one, and make it a point of honour to do so, we apprehend that we have thrown a slightly new light on an old subject. Doubtless, there are men in civilised society who would do likewise if they could; but they cannot, fortunately, as great gastronomic powers are dependent on severe, healthful, and prolonged physical exertion. Therefore it is that in England we find men capable only of eating about two dinners at once, and suffering a good deal for it afterwards, while in the backwoods we see men consume a week's dinners in one, without any evil consequences following the act.

The feast which was given by the Knisteneux in honour of the visit of our two friends was provided on a more moderate scale than usual, in order to accommodate the capacities of the " white men ; " three days' allowance being cooked for each man. (Women are never admitted to the public feasts.) On the day preceding the ceremony. Charley and Jacques had received cards of invitation

from the principal chief, in the shape of two quills;
similar invites being issued at the same time to all the
braves. Jacques, being accustomed to the doings of
Indians, and aware of the fact, that whatever was pro
vided for each man, *must* be eaten before he quitted the
scene of operations, advised Charley to eat no breakfast,
and to take a good walk as a preparative. Charley had
strong faith, however, in his digestive powers, and felt
much inclined, when morning came, to satisfy the
cravings of his appetite as usual ; but Jacques drew such
a graphic picture of the work that lay before him, that he
forbore to urge the matter, and went off to walk with a
light step, and an uncomfortable feeling of vacuity about
the region of the stomach.

About noon, the chiefs and braves assembled in an
open enclosure situated in an exposed place on the banks
of the river, where the proceedings were watched by the
women, children, and dogs. The oldest chief sat himself
down on the turf at one end of the enclosure, with
Jacques Caradoc on his right hand, and next to him
Charley Kennedy, who had ornamented himself with a
blue stripe painted down the middle of his nose, and a
red bar across his chin. Charley's propensity for fun
had led him thus to decorate his face, in spite of his
companion's remonstrances, urging, by way of excuse,
that worthy's former argument, " that it was well to fall
in with the ways o' the people a man happened to be
among, so long as these ways and customs were not contrary to what was right." Now, Charley was sure there
was nothing wrong in his painting his nose skyblue, if he
thought fit.

Jacques thought it was absurd, and entertained the

opinion that it would be more dignified to leave his face
" its nat'ral colour."

Charley didn't agree with him at all. He thought it
would be paying the Indians a high compliment to follow
their customs as far as possible, and said, that, after all,
his blue nose would not be very conspicuous, as he
(Jacques) had told him that he would " look blue" at any
rate, when he saw the quantity of deer's meat he should
have to devour.

Jacques laughed at this, but suggested that the bar
across his chin was *red*. Whereupon Charley said that
he could easily neutralise that by putting a green star
under each eye. And then uttered a fervent wish that his
friend Harry Somerville could only see him in that guise.
Finding him incorrigible, Jacques, who, notwithstanding
his remonstrances, was more than half-imbued with
Charley's spirit, gave in, and accompanied him to the
feast, himself decorated with the additional ornament of a
red night-cap, to whose crown was attached a tuft of
white feathers.

A fire burned in the centre of the enclosure, round
which the Indians seated themselves according to seni-
ority, and with deep solemnity; for it is a trait in the
Indian's character that all his ceremonies are performed
with extreme gravity. Each man brought a dish or
platter, and a wooden spoon.

The old chief, whose hair was very gray, and his face
covered with old wounds and scars, received either in war
or in hunting, having seated himself, allowed a few
minutes to elapse in silence, during which the company
sat motionless; gazing at their plates as if they half
expected them to become converted into beefsteaks

While they were seated thus, another party of Indians, who had been absent on a hunting expedition, strode rapidly but noiselessly into the enclosure, and seated themselves in the circle. One of these passed close to Charley, and in doing so stooped, took his hand, and pressed it. Charley looked up in surprise, and beheld the face of his old friend Redfeather, gazing at him with an expression in which was mingled affection, surprise, and amusement at the peculiar alteration in his visage.

"Redfeather!" exclaimed Charley, in delight, half rising; but the Indian pressed him down.

"You must not rise," he whispered, and, giving his hand another squeeze, passed round the circle, and took his place directly opposite.

Having continued motionless for five minutes with becoming gravity, the company began operations by proceeding to smoke out of the sacred stem, a ceremony which precedes all occasions of importance; and is conducted as follows :—The sacred stem is placed on two forked sticks to prevent its touching the ground, as that would be considered a great evil. A stone pipe is then filled with tobacco, by an attendant appointed specially to that office, and affixed to the stem, which is presented to the principal chief. That individual, with a gravity and *hauteur* that is unsurpassed in the annals of pomposity, receives the pipe in both hands, blows a puff to the east (probably in consequence of its being the quarter whence the sun rises) and thereafter pays a similar mark of attention to the other three points. He then raises the pipe above his head, points and balances it in various directions (for what reason and with what end in view is best known to himself), and replaces it again on the forks. The company meanwhile observe his proceedings with sedate interest, evidently imbued with the idea that they are deriving from the ceremony a vast amount of edification ; an idea which is helped out, doubtless, by the appearance of the women and children, who surround the enclosure, and gaze at the proceedings with looks of awe-struck seriousness that is quite solemnising to behold.

The chief then makes a speech relative to the circumstance which has called them together ; and which is always more or less interlarded with boastful reference to his own deeds, past, present, and prospective, eulogistic remarks on those of his forefathers, and a general condemnation of all other Indian tribes whatever. These speeches are usually delivered with great animation, and contain much poetic allusion to the objects of nature that surround the homes of the savage. The speech being finished, the chief sits down amid a universal " Ho ! " uttered by the company with an emphatic prolongation of the last letter—this syllable being the Indian substitute, we presume, for " rapturous applause."

The chief who officiated on the present occasion, having accomplished the opening ceremonies thus far, sat down, while the pipe-bearer presented the sacred stem to the members of the company in succession, each of whom drew a few whiffs and mumbled a few words.

" Do as you see the redskins do, Mr Charles," whispered Jacques, while the pipe was going round.

" That's impossible," replied Charley, in a tone that could not be heard except by his friend. " I couldn't make a face of hideous solemnity like that black thief opposite. if I was to try ever so hard."

"Don't let them think you're laughing at them," returned the hunter; "they would be ill-pleased if they thought so."

"I'll try," said Charley, "but it is hard work, Jacques, to keep from laughing; I feel like a high pressure steam-engine already. There's a woman standing out there with a little brown baby on her back; she has quite fascinated me; I can't keep my eyes off her, and if she goes on contorting her visage much longer, I feel that I shall give way."

"Hush!"

At this moment the pipe was presented to Charley, who put it to his lips, drew three whiffs, and returned it with a bland smile to the bearer.

The smile was a very sweet one, for that was a peculiar trait in the native urbanity of Charley's disposition, and it would have gone far in civilised society to prepossess strangers in his favour; but it lowered him considerably in the estimation of his red friends, who entertained a wholesome feeling of contempt for any appearance of levity on high occasions. But Charley's face was of that agreeable stamp, that, though gentle and bland when lighted up with a smile, is particularly masculine and manly in expression when in repose, and the frown that knit his brows when he observed the bad impression he had given, almost reinstated him in their esteem. But his popularity became great, and the admiration of his swarthy friends greater, when he rose and made an eloquent speech in English, which Jacques translated into the Indian language.

He told them, in reply to the chief's oration (wherein that warrior had complimented his pale-faced brothers on their numerous good qualities) that he was delighted and

proud to meet with his Indian friends; that the object of
his mission was to acquaint them with the fact that a new
trading fort was established not far off, by himself and his
comrades, for their special benefit and behoof; that the
stores were full of goods which he hoped they would soon
obtain possession of, in exchange for furs; that he had
travelled a great distance on purpose to see their land and
ascertain its capabilities in the way of fur bearing animals
and game; that he had not been disappointed in his expectations, as he had found the animals to be as numerous
as bees, the fish plentiful in the rivers and lakes, and
the country at large a perfect paradise. He proceeded to
tell them further that he expected they would justify the
report he had heard of them, that they were a brave nation
and good hunters, by bringing in large quantities of furs.

Being strongly urged by Jacques to compliment them
on their various good qualities, Charley launched out into
an extravagantly poetic vein, said that he had *heard* (but
he hoped to have many opportunities of seeing it proved)
that there was no nation under the sun equal to them in
bravery, activity, and perseverance; that he had heard of
men in olden times who made it their profession to fight
with wild bulls for the amusement of their friends, but
he had no doubt whatever their courage would be made
conspicuous in the way of fighting wild bears and buffaloes,
not for the amusement, but the benefit of their wives and
children (he might have added of the Hudson's Bay Company, but he didn't, supposing that that was self-evident,
probably.) He complimented them on the way in which
they had conducted themselves in war in times past, com-
paring their stealthy approach to enemies' camps, to the
insidious snake that glides among the bushes and darts

unexpectedly on its prey ; said that their eyes were sharp
to follow the war-trail through the forest or over the dry
sward of the prairie ; their aim with gun or bow true and
sure as the flight of the goose when it leaves the lands of
the sun, and points its beak to the icy regions of the
north ; their war-whoops loud as the thunders of the
cataract ; and their sudden onset like the lightning flash
that darts from the sky and scatters the stout oak in
splinters on the plain.

At this point Jacques expressed his satisfaction at the
style in which his young friend was progressing.

" That's your sort, Mr Charles.   Don't spare the
butter.   Lay it on thick.   You've not said too much
yet, for they *are* a brave race, that's a fact, as I've good
reason to know."

Jacques, however, did not feel quite so well satisfied
when Charley went on to tell them that, although bravery
in war was an admirable thing, war itself was a thing not at
all to be desired, and should only be undertaken in case of
necessity.   He especially pointed out that there was not
much glory to be earned in fighting against the Chipewyans, who, everybody knew, were a poor, timid set of
people, whom they ought rather to pity than to destroy ;
and recommended them to devote themselves more to the
chase than they had done in times past, and less to the
prosecution of war in time to come.

All this, and a great deal more, did Charley say, in a
manner, and with a rapidity of utterance, that surprised
himself, when he considered the fact that he had never
adventured into the field of public speaking before.   All
this, and a great deal more—a *very* great deal more—did
Jacques Caradoc interpret to the admiring Indians, who

listened with the utmost gravity and profound attention, greeting the close with a very emphatic " Ho ! "

Jacques' translation was by no means perfect. Many of the flights into which Charley ventured, especially in regard to the manners and customs of the *savages* of ancient Greece and Rome, were quite incomprehensible to the worthy backwoodsman—but he invariably proceeded, when Charley halted, giving a flight of his own when at a loss, varying and modifying when he thought it advisable, and altering, adding, or cutting off as he pleased.

Several other chiefs addressed the assembly, and then dinner, if we may so call it, was served. In Charley's case, it was breakfast. To the Indians, it was breakfast, dinner, and supper in one. It consisted of a large platter of dried meat, reindeer tongues (considered a great delicacy), and marrow-bones.

Notwithstanding the graphic power with which Jacques had prepared his young companion for this meal, Charley's heart sank when he beheld the mountain of boiled meat that was placed before him. He was ravenously hungry, it is true, but it was patent to his perception at a glance, that no powers of gormandising of which he was capable could enable him to consume the mass in the course of one day.

Jacques observed his consternation, and was not a little entertained by it, although his face wore an expression of profound gravity, while he proceeded to attack his own dish, which was equal to that of his friend.

Before commencing, a small portion of meat was thrown into the fire, as a sacrifice to the Great Master of Life.

" How they do eat, to be sure ! " whispered Charley to Jacques, after he had glanced in wonder at the circle of

men who were devouring their food with the most extraordinary rapidity.

" Why, you must know," replied Jacques, " that it's
considered a point of honour to get it over soon, and the
man that is done first gets most credit. But it's hard
work " (he sighed and paused a little to breathe), "and I've
not got half through yet."

" It's quite plain that I must lose credit with them, then,
if it depends on my eating that. Tell me, Jacques, is there
no way of escape? Must I sit here till it is all consumed ? "

" No doubt of it. Every bit that has been cooked
must be crammed down our throats somehow or other."

Charley heaved a deep sigh, and made another desperate attack on a large steak, while the Indians around
him made considerable progress in reducing their respective mountains.

Several times Charley and Redfeather exchanged
glances as they paused in their labours.

" I say, Jacques." said Charley, pulling up once more
" how do you get on ? Pretty well stuffed by this time,
I should imagine ? "

" Oh, no ! I've a good deal o' room yet."

" I give in.   Credit or disgrace, it's all one. I'll not
make a pig of myself for any redskin in the land."

Jacques smiled.

" See," continued Charley, " there's a fellow opposite
who has devoured as much as would have served me for
three days. I don't know whether it's imagination or
not, but I do verily believe that he's *blacker* in the face
than when he sat down !"

" Very likely," replied Jacques, wiping his lips : " now
I've done."

" Done ? you have left at least a third of your supply."

" True, and I may as well tell you for your comfort, that there is one way of escape open to you. It is a custom among these fellows, that when any one cannot gulp his share o' the prog, he may get help from any of his friends who can cram it down their throats ; and as there are always such fellows among these Injins, they seldom have any difficulty."

" A most convenient practice," replied Charley ; " I'll adopt it at once."

Charley turned to his next neighbour with the intent to beg of him to eat his remnant of the feast.

" Bless my heart, Jacques, I've no chance with the fellow on my left hand; he's stuffed quite full already, and is not quite done with his own share."

" Never fear," replied his friend, looking at the individual in question, who was languidly lifting a marrow-bone to his lips, " he'll do it easy, I knows the gauge o' them chaps, and, for all his sleepy look just now, he's game for a lot more."

" Impossible," replied Charley, looking in despair at his unfinished viands and then at the Indian. A glance round the circle seemed further to convince him that if he did not eat it himself, there were none of the party likely to do so.

" You'll have to give him a good lump o' tobacco to do it, though ; he won't undertake so much for a trifle, I can tell you." Jacques chuckled as he said this, and handed his own portion over to another Indian, who readily undertook to finish it for him.

" He'll burst ; I feel certain of that," said Charley, with a deep sigh, as he surveyed his friend on the left.

At last he took courage to propose the thing to him
and, just as the man finished the last morsel of his own
repast, Charley placed his own plate before him, with a
look that seemed to say, " Eat it, my friend, *if you can.*"

The Indian, much to his surprise, immediately commenced to it, and in less than half-an-hour the whole
was disposed of.

During this scene of gluttony, one of the chiefs entertained the assembly with a wild and most unmusical chaunt,
to which he beat time on a sort of tambourine, while the women outside of the enclosure beat a similar accompaniment.

" I say, master," whispered Jacques, " it seems to my
observation that the fellow you called Redfeather eats less
than any Injin I ever saw. He has got a comrade to eat
more than half of his share ; now that's strange."

" It won't appear strange, Jacques, when I tell you
that Redfeather has lived much more among white men
than Indians during the last ten years, and although
voyageurs eat an enormous quantity of food, they don't
make it a point of honour, as these fellows seem to do, to
eat much more than enough. Besides, Redfeather is a
very different man from those around him ; he has been
partially educated by the missionaries on Playgreen Lake,
and I think has a strong leaning towards them."

While they were thus conversing in whispers, Redfeather rose, and, holding forth his hand, delivered himself
of the following oration :—

" The time has come for Redfeather to speak. He has
kept silence for many moons now ; but his heart has been
full of words. It is too full. He must speak now.
Redfeather has fought with his tribe and has been ac-
counted a brave, and one who loves his people. This

is true. He *does* love, even more than they can understand.   His friends know that he has never feared to
face danger or death in their defence, and that, if it were
necessary, he would do so still.   But Redfeather is going
to leave his people now.   His heart is heavy at the thought.
Perhaps many moons will come and go, many snows may
fall and melt away before he sees his people again; and it is
this that makes him full of sorrow, it is this that makes
his head to droop like the branches of the weeping willow."

Redfeather paused at this point, but not a sound escaped
from the listening circle : the Indians were evidently taken
by surprise at this abrupt announcement.   He proceeded :—

"When Redfeather travelled not long since with the
white men, he met with a pale-face, who came from the
other side of the Great Salt Lake towards the rising sun.
This man was called by some of the people a missionary.
He spoke wonderful words in the ears of Redfeather.
He told him of things about the Great Spirit which he
did not know before, and he asked Redfeather to go and
help him to speak to the Indians about these strange
things.   Redfeather would not go.   He loved his people
too much, and he thought that the words of the missionary seemed foolishness.   But he has thought much about
it since.   He does not understand the strange things that
were told to him, and he has tried to forget them, but he
cannot.   He can get no rest.   He hears strange sounds
in the breeze that shakes the pine.   He thinks that there
are voices in the waterfall; the rivers seem to speak.
Redfeather's spirit is vexed.   The Great Spirit, perhaps,
is talking to him.   He has resolved to go to the dwelling
of the missionary and stay with him."

14

The Indian paused again, but still no sound escaped from his comrades. Dropping his voice to a soft plaintive tone, he continued—

"But Redfeather loves his kindred. He desires very much that they should hear the things that the missionary said. He spoke of the happy hunting grounds to which the spirits of our fathers have gone, and said that we required a *guide* to lead us there ; that there was but one guide, whose name, he said, was Jesus. Redfeather would stay and hunt with his people, but his spirit is troubled ; he cannot rest ; he must go !"

Redfeather sat down, and a long silence ensued. His words had evidently taken the whole party by surprise, although not a countenance there shewed the smallest symptom of astonishment, except that of Charley Kennedy, whose intercourse with Indians had not yet been so great as to have taught him to conceal his feelings.

At length the old chief rose, and, after complimenting Redfeather on his bravery in general, and admitting that he had shewn much love to his people on all occasions, went into the subject of his quitting them at some length. He reminded him that there were evil spirits as well as good ; that it was not for him to say which kind had been troubling him, but that he ought to consider well before he went to live altogether with pale-faces. Several other speeches were made, some to the same effect, and others applauding his resolve. These latter had, perhaps, some idea that his bringing the pale-faced missionary among them would gratify their taste for the marvellous— a taste that is pretty strong in all uneducated minds.

One man, however, was particularly urgent in endavouring to dissuade him from his purpose. He was a tall, low-browed man ; muscular and well built, but possessed of a most villanous expression of countenance. From a remark that fell from one of the company, Charley discovered that his name was Misconna, and so learned, to his surprise, that he was the very Indian mentioned by Redfeather as the man who had been his rival for the hand of Wabisca, and who had so cruelly killed the wife of the poor trapper the night on which the Chipewyan camp was attacked, and the people slaughtered.

What reason Misconna had for objecting so strongly to Redfeather's leaving the community no one could tell, although some of those who knew his unforgiving nature suspected that he still entertained the hope of being able, some day or other, to wreak his vengeance on his old rival. But, whatever was his object, he failed in moving Redfeather's resolution ; and it was at last admitted by the whole party that Redfeather was a " wise chief ;" that he knew best what ought to be done under the circumstances, and it was hoped that his promised visit, in company with the missionary, would not be delayed many moons.

That night, in the deep shadow of the trees, by the brook that murmured near the Indian camp, while the stars twinkled through the branches overhead, Charley introduced Redfeather to his friend Jacques Caradoc, and a friendship was struck up between the bold hunter and the red-man, that grew and strengthened as each successive day made them acquainted with their respective good qualities. In the same place, and with the same stars looking down upon them, it was further agreed that Redfeather should accompany his new friends, taking his

wife along with him in another canoe, as far as their
several routes led them in the same direction, which was
about four or five days' journey; and that while the one
party diverged towards the fort at Stoney Creek, the
other should pursue its course to the missionary station
on the shores of Lake Winipeg.

But there was a snake in the grass there that they
little suspected. Misconna had crept through the bushes
after them, with a degree of caution that might have
baffled their vigilance, even had they suspected treason in
a friendly camp. He lay listening intently to all their
plans, and when they returned to their camp, he rose out
from among the bushes, like a dark spirit of evil, clutched
the handle of his scalping-knife, and gave utterance to a
malicious growl; then, walking hastily after them, his
dusky figure was soon concealed among the trees.

CHAPTER XVI.

The return ; narrow escape ; a murderous attempt, which fails;
and a discovery.

ALL nature was joyous and brilliant, and bright and beautiful. Morning was still very young—about an hour old.
Sounds of the most cheerful light-hearted character floated
over the waters and echoed through the woods, as birds
and beasts hurried to and fro with all the bustling energy
that betokened preparation and search for breakfast.
Fish leaped in the pools with a rapidity that brought forcibly to mind that wise saying, "The more hurry, the
less speed," for they appeared constantly to miss their
mark, although they jumped twice their own length out
of the water in the effort.

Ducks and geese sprang from their liquid beds with an
amazing amount of unnecessary splutter, as if they had
awakened to the sudden consciousness of being late for
breakfast, then alighted in the water again with a *squash*,
on finding (probably) that it was too early for that meal,
but, observing other flocks passing and re-passing on noisy
wing, took to flight again, unable apparently to restrain
their feelings of delight at the freshness of the morning
air, the brightness of the rising sun, and the sweet perfume
of the dewy verdure, as the mists cleared away over the
tree-tops and lost themselves in the blue sky.   Everything
seemed instinct not only with life, but with a large amount

of superabundant energy.   Earth, air, sky, animal, vegetable and mineral, solid and liquid, all were either actually in a state of lively exulting motion, or had a peculiarly sprightly look about them, as if nature had just
burst out of prison *en masse*, and gone raving mad with
joy.

Such was the delectable state of things the morning on
which two canoes darted from the camp of the Knisteneux, amid many expressions of good-will.   One canoe
contained our two friends, Charley and Jacques ; the other
Redfeather and his wife Wabisca.

A few strokes of the paddle shot them out into the
stream, which carried them rapidly away from the scene
of their late festivities.   In five minutes they swept
round a point, which shut them out from view, and they
were swiftly descending those rapid rivers that had cost
Charley and Jacques so much labour to ascend.

"Look out for rocks ahead, Mr Charles," cried Jacques,
as he steered the light bark into the middle of a rapid,
which they had avoided when ascending, by making a
portage.   "Keep well to the left o' yon swirl.   *Parbleu*,
if we touch the rock *there*, it'll be all over with us."

"All right," was Charley's laconic reply.   And so it
proved, for their canoe, after getting fairly into the run
of the rapid, was evidently under the complete command
of its expert crew, and darted forward amid the foaming
waters, like a thing instinct with life.   Now it careered
and plunged over the waves, where the rough bed of the
stream made them more than usually turbulent.   Anon
it flew with increased rapidity through a narrow gap
where the compressed water was smooth and black, but
deep and powerful, rendering great care necessary to

prevent the canoe's frail sides from being dashed on the rocks. Then it met a curling wave, into which it plunged like an impetuous charger, and was checked for a moment by its own violence. Presently an eddy threw the canoe a little out of its course, disconcerting Charley's intention of *shaving* a rock which lay in their track, so that he slightly grazed it in passing.

"Ah, Mr Charles," said Jacques, shaking his head, "that was not well done; an inch more would have sent us down the rapids like drowned cats."

"True," replied Charley, somewhat crestfallen, "but you see the other inch was not lost, so we're not much the worse for it."

"Well, after all, it was a ticklish bit, and I should have guessed that your experience was not up to it quite. I've seen many a man in my day who wouldn't ha' done it *half* so slick, an' yet ha' thought no small beer of himself: so you needn't be ashamed, Mr Charles. But Wabisca beats you for all that," continued the hunter, glancing hastily over his shoulder at Redfeather, who followed closely in their wake, he and his modest-looking wife guiding their little craft through the dangerous passage with the utmost *sangfroid* and precision.

"We've about run them all now," said Jacques, as they paddled over a sheet of still water which intervened between the rapid they had just descended and another which thundered about a hundred yards in advance.

"I was so engrossed with the one we have just come down," said Charley, "that I quite forgot this one."

"Quite right, Mr Charles," said Jacques, in an approving tone; "quite right. I holds that a man should

always attend to what he's at, an' to nothin' else. I've
lived long in the woods now, and that fact becomes more
and more sartin every day. I've know'd chaps, now, as
timersome as settlement girls, that were always in such
a mortal funk about what *was* to happen, or *might*
happen, that they were never fit for anything that *did*
happen ; always lookin' ahead, and never around them.
Of coorse, I don't mean that a man shouldn't look ahead
at all, but their great mistake was, that they looked out too
far ahead, and always kep' their eyes nailed there, just as
if they had the fixin' o' everything, an' Providence had
nothin' to do with it at all. I mind a Canadian o' that
sort, that travelled in company with me once. We were
goin' just as we are now, Mr Charles, two canoes of us ;
him and a comrade in one, and me and a comrade in
t'other. One night we got to a lot o' rapids, that came
one after another for the matter o' three miles or thereabouts. They were all easy ones, however, except the
last, but it *was* a tickler, with a sharp turn o' the land
that hid it from sight till ye were right into it, with a
foamin' current, and a range o' ragged rocks that stood
straight in front o' ye, like the teeth of a cross-cut saw.
It was easy enough, however, if a man *knew* it, and was
a cool hand. Well, the *pauvre* Canadian was in a terrible
takin' about this shoot, long afore he came to it. He
had run it often enough in boats where he was one of a
half-dozen men, and had nothin' to do but look on ; but
he had never *steered* down it before. When he came to
the top o' the rapids, his mind was so filled with this
shoot, that he couldn't attend to nothin' ; and scraped
agin' a dozen rocks in almost smooth water, so that when
he got little more than half way down, the canoe was as

ricketty as if it had just come off a six months' cruise. At
last we came to the big rapid, and after we'd run down
our canoe, I climbed the bank to see them do it. Down
they came, the poor Canadian white as a sheet, and his
comrade, who was brave enough, but knew nothin' about
light craft, not very comfortable. At first he could see
nothin' for the point, but, in another moment, round they
went, end on, for the big rocks. The Canadian gave a
great yell when he saw them, and plunged at the paddle
till I thought he'd have capsized altogether. They ran it
well enough, straight between the rocks (more by good
luck than good guidance), and sloped down to the smooth
water below, but the canoe had got such a battering in
the rapids above, where an Injin baby could have steered
it in safety, that the last plunge shook it all to pieces.
It opened up, and lay down flat on the water, while
the two men fell right through the bottom, screechin'
like mad, and rolling about among shreds o' birch-bark!"

While Jacques was thus descanting philosophically on
his experiences in time past, they had approached the
head of the second rapid, and, in accordance with the
principles just enunciated, the stout backwoodsman
gave his undivided attention to the work before him.
The rapid was short and deep, so that little care was
required in descending it, excepting at one point, where
the stream rushed impetuously between two rocks about
six yards asunder. Here it was requisite to keep the
canoe as much in the middle of the stream as possible.

Just as they began to feel the drag of the water, Redfeather was heard to shout in a loud warning tone,
which caused Jacques and Charley to back their paddles
hurriedly.

" What can the Injin mean, I wonder?" said Jacques,
in a perplexed tone. " He don't look like a man that
would stop us at the top of a strong rapid for nothin'."

" It's too late to do that now, whatever is his reason,"
said Charley, as he and his companion struggled in vain
to paddle up stream.

" It's o' no use, Mr Charles, we must run it now ; the
current's too strong to make head against ; besides, I do
think the man has only seen a bear, or somethin' o' that
sort, for I see he's ashore, and jumpin' among the bushes
like a cariboo."

Saying this, they turned the canoe's head down stream
again, and allowed it to drift, merely retarding its progress a little with the paddles.

Suddenly Jacques uttered a sharp exclamation. " *Mon
Dieu!*" said he, " it's plain enough now. Look there !"

Jacques pointed as he spoke to the narrows to which
they were now approaching with tremendous speed, which
increased every instant. A heavy tree lay directly across
the stream, reaching from rock to rock, and placed in
such a way that it was impossible for a canoe to descend
without being dashed in pieces against it. This was the
more curious, that no trees grew in the immediate
vicinity, so that this one must have been designedly
conveyed there.

" There has been foul work here," said Jacques in a
deep tone. " We must dive, Mr Charles; there's no chance
any way else, and *that's* but a poor one."

This was true. The rocks on each side rose almost
perpendicularly out of the water, so that it was utterly
impossible to run ashore, and the only way of escape, as
Jacques said, was by diving under the tree, a thing in-

volving great risk, as the stream immediately below was broken by rocks, against which it dashed in foam, and through which the chances of steering one's way in safety by means of swimming, were very slender indeed.

Charley made no reply, but, with tightly compressed lips, and a look of stern resolution on his brow, threw off his coat, and hastily tied his belt tightly round his waist The canoe was now sweeping forward with lightning speed In a few minutes it would be dashed to pieces.

At that moment a shout was heard in the woods, and Redfeather darting out, rushed over the ledge of rock, on which one end of the tree rested, seized the trunk in his arms, and exerting all his strength, hurled it over into the river. In doing so he stumbled, and, ere he could recover himself, a branch caught him under the arm as the tree fell over, and dragged him into the boiling stream. This accident was probably the means of saving his life, for, just as he fell, the loud report of a gun rang through the woods, and a bullet passed through his cap. For a second or two both man and tree were lost in the foam, while the canoe dashed past in safety. The next instant Wabisca passed the narrows in her small craft, and steered for the tree. Redfeather, who had risen and sank several times, saw her as she passed, and, making a violent effort, he caught hold of the gunwale, and was carried down in safety.

" I'll tell you what it is," said Jacques, as the party stood on a rock promontory after the events just narrated, " I would give a dollar to have that fellow's nose and the sights o' my rifle in a line at any distance short of two hundred yards."

" It was Misconna," said Redfeather. " I did not see

him, but there's not another man in the tribe that could
do that."

"I'm thankful we escaped, Jacques. I never felt so
near death before, and had it not been for the timely aid
of our friend here, it strikes me that our wild life would
have come to an abrupt close. God bless you, Redfeather," said Charley, taking the Indian's hand in both
of his and kissing it.

Charley's ebullition of feeling was natural. He had
not yet become used to the dangers of the wilderness so
as to treat them with indifference. Jacques, on the other
hand, had risked his life so often, that escape from danger
was treated very much as a matter of course, and called
forth little expression of feeling. Still, it must not be
inferred from this that his nature had become callous.
The backwoodsman's frame was hard and unyielding as
iron, but his heart was as soft still as it was on the day
on which he first donned the hunting-shirt; and there
was much more of tenderness than met the eye in the
squeeze that he gave Redfeather's hand on landing.

As the four travellers encircled the fire that night,
under the leafy branches of the forest, and smoked
their pipes in concert, while Wabisca busied herself in
clearing away the remnants of their evening meal, they
waxed communicative, and stories, pathetic, comic, and
tragic, followed each other in rapid succession.

"Now, Redfeather," said Charley, while Jacques rose
and went down to the luggage to get more tobacco, "tell
Jacques about the way in which you got your name. I
am sure he will feel deeply interested in that story,—at
least I am certain that Harry Somerville and I did when
you told it to us the day we were wind-bound on Lake
Winipeg."

Redfeather made no reply for a few seconds. "Will Mr Charles speak for me ?" he said, at length ; "his tongue is smooth and quick."

"A doubtful kind of compliment," said Charley, laughing ; "but I will, if you don't wish to tell it yourself."

"And don't mention names. Do not let him know that you speak of me or my friends," said the Indian, in a low whisper, as Jacques returned and sat down by the fire again.

Charley gave him a glance of surprise ; but, being prevented from asking questions, he nodded in reply, and proceeded to relate to his friend the story that has been recounted in a previous chapter. Redfeather leaned back against a tree, and appeared to listen intently.

Charley's powers of description were by no means inconsiderable, and the backwoodsman's face assumed a look of good-humoured attention as the story proceeded. But when the narrator went on to tell of the meditated attack, and the midnight march, his interest was aroused, the pipe which he had been smoking was allowed to go out, and he gazed at his young friend with the most earnest attention. It was evident that the hunter's spirit entered with deep sympathy into such scenes ; and, when Charley described the attack, and the death of the trapper's wife, Jacques seemed unable to restrain his feelings. He leaned his elbows on his knees, buried his face in his hands, and groaned aloud.

"Mr Charles," he said, in a deep voice, when the story was ended, "there are two men I would like to meet with in this world before I die. One is the young Injin who tried to save that girl's life, the other is the

cowardly villain that took it. I don't mean the one who
finished the bloody work,—my rifle sent his accursed
spirit to its own place ——"

"*Your* rifle!" cried Charley, in amazement.

"Ay, mine! It was *my* wife who was butchered by
these savage dogs on that dark night. Oh! what avails
the strength o' that right arm!" said Jacques, bitterly,
as he lifted up his clenched fist; "it was powerless to
save *her*—the sweet girl who left her home and people to
follow me, a rough hunter, through the lonesome wilderness!"

He covered his face again, and groaned in agony
of spirit, while his whole frame quivered with emotion.

Jacques remained silent; and his sympathising friends
refrained from intruding on a sorrow which they felt
they had no power to relieve.

At length he spoke. "Yes," said he; "I would give
much to meet with the man who tried to save her. I
saw him do it twice; but the devils about him were too
eager to be baulked of their prey."

Charley and the Indian exchanged glances. "That
Indian's name," said the former, "was *Redfeather!*"

"What!" exclaimed the trapper, jumping to his feet,
and, grasping Redfeather, who had also risen, by the two
shoulders, stared wildly into his face, "was it *you* that
did it?"

Redfeather smiled, and held out his hand, which the
other took and wrung with an energy that would have
extorted a cry of pain from any one but an Indian.
Then, dropping it suddenly, and clenching his hands, he
exclaimed—

"I said that I would like to meet the villain who

killed her—-yes, I said it in passion, when your words
had roused all my old feelings again ; but I am .hankful
—I bless God, that I did not know this sooner—that
you did not tell me of it when I was at the camp, for I
verily believe that I would not only have fixed *him*, but
half the warriors o' your tribe too, before they had settled
me !"

It need scarcely be added, that the friendship which
already subsisted between Jacques and Redfeather was
now doubly cemented ; nor will it create surprise when
we say that the former, in the fulness of his heart, and
from sheer inability to find adequate outlets for the expression of his feelings, offered Redfeather in succession
all the articles of value he possessed, even to his much-
loved rifle, and was seriously annoyed at their not being
accepted.   At last he finished off by assuring the Indian
that he might look out for him soon at the missionary
settlement, where he meant to stay with him evermore
in the capacity of hunter, fisherman, and jack-of-all-trades
to the whole clan.

CHAPTER XVII.

The scene changes : Bachelor's Hall; a practical joke and its consequences ; a snow-shoe walk at night in the forest.

LEAVING Charley to pursue his adventurous career among the Indians, we will introduce our reader to a new scene, and follow, for a time, the fortunes of our friend Harry Somerville.   It will be remembered that we left him labouring under severe disappointment, at the idea of having to spend a year, it might be many years, at the depôt ; and being condemned to the desk, instead of realising his fond dreams of bear-hunting and deer-stalking in the woods and prairies.

It was now the autumn of Harry's second year at York Fort.   This period of the year happens to be the busiest at the depôt, in consequence of the preparation of the annual accounts for transmission to England, in the solitary ship which visits this lonely spot once a year ; so that Harry was tied to his desk all day and the greater part of the night too, till his spirits fell infinitely below zero, and he began to look on himself as the most miserable of mortals.   His spirits rose, however, with amazing rapidity, after the ship went away, and the "young gentlemen," as the clerks were styled *en masse*, were permitted to run wild in the swamps and woods for the three weeks succeeding that event.   During this glimpse of

sunshine they recruited their exhausted frames, by paddling about all day in Indian canoes, or wandering
through the marshes, sleeping at nights in tents or under
the pine-trees, and spreading dismay among the feathered
tribes, of which there were immense numbers of all kinds.
After this they returned to their regular work at the
desk, but, as this was not so severe as in summer, and was
farther lightened by Wednesdays and Saturdays being
devoted entirely to recreation, Harry began to look on
things in a less gloomy aspect, and at length regained his
wonted cheerful spirits.

Autumn passed away. The ducks and geese took their
departure to more genial climes. The swamps froze up
and became solid. Snow fell in great abundance, covering
every vestige of vegetable nature, except the dark fir-
trees that only helped to render the scenery more dreary,
and winter settled down upon the land. Within the
pickets of York Fort, the thirty or forty souls who lived
there were actively employed in cutting their firewood ;
putting in double window-frames, to keep out the severe
cold ; cutting tracks in the snow from one house to
another ; and otherwise preparing for a winter of eight
months' duration, as cold as that of Nova Zembla, and
in the course of which the only new faces they had any
chance of seeing were those of the two men who conveyed
the annual winter packet of letters from the next station.
Outside of the fort all was a wide, waste wilderness for
thousands of miles around. Death-like stillness and solitude reigned everywhere, except when a covey of ptarmigan
whirred like large snowflakes athwart the sky, or an arctic
fox prowled stealthily through the woods in search of prey.

As if in opposition to the gloom, and stillness, and soli

15

tude outside, the interior of the clerks' house presented a
striking contrast of ruddy warmth, cheerful sounds, and
bustling activity.

It was evening, but, although the sun had set, there
was still sufficient daylight to render candles unnecessary,
though not enough to prevent a bright glare from the
stove in the centre of the hall taking full effect in the
darkening chamber, and making it glow with fiery red.
Harry Somerville sat in front, and full in the blaze of
this stove, resting after the labours of the day; his
arms crossed on his breast; his head a little to one side,
as if in deep contemplation, as he gazed earnestly into
the fire, and his chair tilted on its hind legs so as to
balance with such nicety that a feather's weight additional,
outside its centre of gravity, would have upset it.   He
had divested himself of his coat—a practice that prevailed
among the young gentlemen when *at home*, as being free-
and-easy as well as convenient.   The doctor, a tall,
broad-shouldered man, with red hair and whiskers, paced
the room sedately, with a long pipe depending from his
lips, which he removed occasionally to address a few
remarks to the accountant, a stout heavy man of about
thirty, with a voice like a Stentor, eyes sharp and active
as those of a ferret, and a tongue that moved with twice
the ordinary amount of lingual rapidity.   The doctor's
remarks seemed to be particularly humorous, if one
might judge from the peals of laughter with which they
were received by the accountant, who stood with his
back to the stove in such a position that, while it warmed
him from his heels to his waist, he enjoyed the additional
benefit of the pipe or chimney, which rose upwards,
parallel with his spine, and, taking a sudden bend near

the roof, passed over his head—thus producing a genial and equable warmth from top to toe.

"Yes," said the doctor, "I left him hotly following up a rabbit-track, in the firm belief that it was that of a silver fox."

"And did you not undeceive the greenhorn?" cried the accountant, with another shout of laughter.

"Not I," replied the doctor, "I merely recommended him to keep his eye on the sun, lest he should lose his way, and hastened home; for it just occurred to me that I had forgotten to visit Louis Blanc, who cut his foot with an axe yesterday, and whose wound required redressing, so I left the poor youth to learn from experience."

"Pray, who did you leave to that delightful fate?" asked Mr Wilson, issuing from his bedroom and approaching the stove.

Mr Wilson was a middle-aged, good-humoured, active man, who filled the onerous offices of superintendent of the men, trader of furs, seller of goods to the Indians, and general factotum.

"Our friend Hamilton," answered the doctor, in reply to his question. "I think he is, without exception, the most egregious nincompoop I ever saw. Just as I passed the long swamp on my way home, I met him crashing through the bushes in hot pursuit of a rabbit, the track of which he mistook for a fox. Poor fellow, he had been out since breakfast, and only shot a brace of ptarmigan, although they are as thick as bees and quite tame. 'But then, do you see,' said he, in excuse, 'I'm so very short-sighted! Would you believe it, I've blown fifteen lumps of snow to atoms, in the belief that they were ptarmigan!' and then he rushed off again."

"No doubt," said Mr Wilson, smiling, "the lad is very green—but he's a good fellow for all that."

"I'll answer for that," said the accountant; "I found him over at the men's houses this morning doing *your* work for you, doctor."

"How so?" inquired the disciple of Æsculapius.

"Attending to your wounded man, Louis Blanc, to be sure; and he seemed to speak to him as wisely as if he had walked the hospitals, and regularly passed for an M.D."

"Indeed!" said the doctor with a mischievous grin. "Then I must pay him off for interfering with my patients."

"Ah, doctor, you're too fond of practical jokes. You never let slip an opportunity of 'paying off' your friends for something or other. It's a bad habit. Practical jokes are very bad things—shockingly bad," said Mr Wilson, as he put on his fur cap, and wound a thick shawl round his throat, preparatory to leaving the room.

As Mr Wilson gave utterance to this opinion, he passed Harry Somerville, who was still staring at the fire in deep mental abstraction, and, as he did so, gave his tilted chair a very slight push backwards with his finger,—an action which caused Harry to toss up his legs, grasp convulsively with both hands at empty air, and fall with a loud noise and an angry yell to the ground, while his persecutor vanished from the scene.

"O you outrageous villain!" cried Harry, shaking his fist at the door, as he slowly gathered himself up : "I might have expected that."

"Quite so," said the doctor, "you might. It was very neatly done, undoubtedly. Wilson deserves credit for the way in which it was executed."

"He deserves to be executed for doing it at all," replied Harry, rubbing his elbow as he resumed his seat.

"Any bark knocked off?" inquired the accountant, as he took a piece of glowing charcoal from the stove, wherewith to light his pipe. "Try a whiff, Harry. It's good for such things; bruises, sores, contusions, sprains, rheumatic affections of the back and loins, carbuncles and earache— there's nothing that smoking won't cure—eh, doctor?"

"Certainly. If applied inwardly, there's nothing so good for digestion when one doesn't require tonics. Try it, Harry, it will do you good, I assure you."

"No, thank you," replied Harry, "I'll leave that to you and the chimney. I don't wish to make a soot-bag of my mouth. But tell me, doctor, what do you mean to do with that lump of snow there?"

Harry pointed to a mass of snow, of about two feet square, which lay on the floor beside the door. It had been placed there by the doctor sometime previously.

"Do with it? Have patience, my friend, and you shall see. It is a little surprise I have in store for Hamilton."

As he spoke, the door opened, and a short, square-built man rushed into the room, with a pistol in one hand, and a bright little bullet in the other.

"Hallo, skipper!" cried Harry, "what's the row?"

"All right," cried the skipper, "here it is at last, solid as the fluke of an anchor. Toss me the powder-flask, Harry; look sharp, else it'll melt."

A powder-flask was immediately produced, from which the skipper hastily charged the pistol, and rammed down the shining bullet.

" Now then," said he, " look out for squalls. Clear the
decks there."

And, rushing to the door, he flung it open, took a
steady aim at something outside, and fired.

" Is the man mad?" said the accountant, as, with a
look of amazement, he beheld the skipper spring through
the doorway, and immediately return bearing in his arms
a large piece of fir plank.

" Not quite mad yet," he said, in reply, " but I've sent
a ball of quicksilver through an inch plank, and that's
not a thing to be done every day—even *here*, although it
is cold enough sometimes to freeze up one's very ideas."

" Dear me," interrupted Harry Somerville, looking
as if a new thought had struck him, " that must be it!
I've no doubt that poor Hamilton's ideas are *frozen*,
which accounts for the total absence of any indication of
his possessing such things."

" I observed," continued the skipper, not noticing the
interruption, " that the glass was down at 45 degrees
below zero this morning, and put out a bullet-mould full
of mercury, and you see the result ; " as he spoke, he held
up the perforated plank in triumph.

The skipper was a strange mixture of qualities. To a
wild, off-hand, sailor-like hilarity of disposition, in hours
of leisure, he united a grave, stern energy of character
while employed in the performance of his duties. Duty
was always paramount with him. A smile could scarcely
be extracted from him, while it was in the course of performance. But, the instant his work was done, a new
spirit seemed to take possession of the man. Fun, mischief of any kind, no matter how childish, he entered into
with the greatest delight and enthusiasm. Among othe:

peculiarities, he had become deeply imbued with a thirst
for scientific knowledge, ever since he had acquired, with
infinite labour, the small modicum of science necessary to
navigation ; and his doings in pursuit of statistical information relative to the weather, and the phenomena of
nature generally, were very peculiar, and in some cases
outrageous. His transaction with the quicksilver was in
consequence of an eager desire to see that metal frozen,
(an effect which takes place when the spirit-of-wine thermometer falls to 39 degrees below zero of Fahrenheit,) and
a wish to be able to boast of having actually fired a mercurial bullet through an inch plank. Having made a
careful note of the fact, with all the relative circumstances attending it, in a very much blotted book, which
he denominated his scientific log, the worthy skipper
threw off his coat, drew a chair to the stove, and prepared to regale himself with a pipe. As he glanced
slowly round the room, while thus engaged, his eye fell
on the mass of snow before alluded to. On being informed by the doctor for what it was intended, he laid
down his pipe and rose hastily from his chair.

" You've not a moment to lose," said he. " As I came
in at the gate just now, I saw Hamilton coming down
the river on the ice, and he must be almost arrived now."

" Up with it then," cried the doctor, seizing the snow,
and lifting it to the top of the door ; "hand me those
bits of stick, Harry ; quick, man, stir your stumps. Now
then, skipper, fix them in so, while I hold this up."

The skipper lent willing and effective aid, so that in a
few minutes the snow was placed in such a position,
that, upon the opening of the door, it must inevitably fall
on the head of the first person who should enter the room

"So," said the skipper, "that's rigged up in what I call a ship-shape fashion."

"True," remarked the doctor, eying the arrangement with a look of approval; "it will do, I think, admirably."

"Don't you think, skipper," said Harry Somerville, gravely, as he resumed his seat in front of the fire, "that it would be worth while to make a careful and minute entry in your private log of the manner in which it was put up, to be afterwards followed by an account of its effect? You might write an essay on it, now; and call it the extraordinary effects of a fall of snow in latitude so and so; eh? What think you of it?"

The skipper vouchsafed no reply, but made a significant gesture with his fist, which caused Harry to put himself in a posture of defence.

At this moment, footsteps were heard on the wooden platform in front of the building.

Instantly all became silence and expectation in the hall, as the result of the practical joke was about to be realised. Just then another step was heard on the platform, and it became evident that two persons were approaching the door.

"Hope it'll be the right man," said the skipper, with a look savouring slightly of anxiety.

As he spoke, the door opened, and a foot crossed the threshold; the next instant, the miniature avalanche descended on the head and shoulders of a man, who reeled forward from the weight of the blow, and, covered from head to foot with snow, fell to the ground amid shouts of laughter.

With a convulsive stamp and shake, the prostrate figure sprang up and confronted the party. Had the cast-iron stove suddenly burst into atoms, and blown the roof off the house, it could scarcely have created greater consternation than that which filled the merry jesters when they beheld the visage of Mr Rogan, the superintendent of the fort, red with passion, and fringed with snow.

"So," said he, stamping violently with his foot, partly from anger, and partly with the view of shaking off the unexpected covering, which stuck all over his dress in little patches, producing a somewhat piebald effect, "so you are pleased to jest, gentlemen. Pray, who placed that piece of snow over the door?" Mr Rogan glared fiercely round upon the culprits, who stood speechless before him.

For a moment he stood silent, as if uncertain how to act; then, turning short on his heel, he strode quickly out of the room, nearly overturning Mr Hamilton, who at the same instant entered it, carrying his gun and snow-shoes under his arm.

"Dear me, what has happened?" he exclaimed, in a peculiarly gentle tone of voice, at the same time regarding the snow and the horror-stricken circle with a look of intense surprise.

"You see what has happened," replied Harry Somerville, who was the first to recover his composure; "I presume you intended to ask, 'What has caused it to happen?' Perhaps the skipper will explain. It's beyond me, quite."

Thus appealed to, that worthy cleared his throat, and said—

"Why, you see, Mr Hamilton, a great phenomenon of meteorology has happened. We were all standing, you

must know, at the open door, taking a squint at the
weather, when our attention was attracted by a curious
object that appeared in the sky, and seemed to be coming
down at the rate of ten knots an hour, right end-on for
the house. I had just time to cry, ' Clear out, lads,' when
it came slap in through the doorway, and smashed to
shivers there, where you see the fragments. In fact, it's
a wonderful aërolite, and Mr Rogan has just gone out
with a lot of the bits in his pocket, to make a careful
examination of them, and draw up a report for the Geo-
logical Society in London. I shouldn't wonder if he
were to send off an express to-night; and maybe you
will have to convey the news to head-quarters ; so you'd
better go and see him about it soon."

Soft although Mr Hamilton was supposed to be, he
was not quite prepared to give credit to this explanation ;
but, being of a peaceful disposition, and altogether unaccustomed to retort, he merely smiled his disbelief, as he
proceeded to lay aside his fowling-piece, and divest himself of the voluminous out-of-door trappings with which
he was clad. Mr Hamilton was a tall, slender youth, of
about nineteen. He had come out by the ship in autumn,
and was spending his first winter at York Fort. Up to
the period of his entering the Hudson's Bay Company's
service, he had never been more than twenty miles from
home ; and, having mingled little with the world, was
somewhat unsophisticated, besides being by nature gentle
and unassuming.

Soon after this, the man who acted as cook, waiter,
and butler to the mess, entered, and said that Mr Rogan
desired to see the accountant immediately.

" Who am I to say did it ?" inquired that gentleman, as he rose to obey the summons.

" Wouldn't it be a disinterested piece of kindness if you were to say it was yourself ?" suggested the doctor.

" Perhaps it would, but I won't," replied the accountant, as he made his exit.

In about half-an-hour, Mr Rogan and the accountant re-entered the apartment.   The former had quite regained his composure.   He was naturally amiable ; which happy disposition was indicated by a habitually cheerful look and smile.

" Now, gentlemen," said he, " I find that this practical joke was not intended for me, and therefore look upon it as an unlucky accident; but I cannot too strongly express my dislike to practical jokes of all kinds.   I have seen great evil, and some bloodshed, result from practical jokes ; and I think that, being a sufferer in consequence of your fondness for them, I have a right to beg that you will abstain from such doings in future,—at least from such jokes as involve risk to those who do not choose to enter into them."

Having given vent to this speech, Mr Rogan left his volatile friends to digest it at their leisure.

" Serves us right," said the skipper, pacing up and down the room in a repentant frame of mind, with his thumbs hooked into the arm-holes of his vest.

The doctor said nothing, but breathed hard, and smoked vigorously.

While we admit most thoroughly with Mr Rogan that practical jokes are exceedingly bad, and productive, fre-quently, of far more evil than fun, we feel it our duty,

as a faithful delineator of manners, customs, and character in these regions, to urge in palliation of the offence
committed by the young gentlemen at York Fort, that
they had really about as few amusements, and sources
of excitement, as fall to the lot of any class of men.
They were entirely dependent on their own unaided
exertions, during eight or nine months of the year, for
amusement or recreation of any kind.   Their books
were few in number, and soon read through.   The desolate wilderness around afforded no incidents to form
subjects of conversation, further than the events of a
day's shooting, which, being nearly similar every day,
soon lost all interest.   No newspapers came to tell of the
doings of the busy world from which they were shut out,
and nothing occurred to vary the dull routine of their
life; so that it is not matter for wonder that they were
driven to seek for relaxation and excitement, occasionally, in most outrageous and unnatural ways, and to
indulge, now and then, in the perpetration of a practical
joke.

For some time after the rebuke administered by Mr
Rogan, silence reigned in *Bachelor's Hall*, as the clerks'
house was termed.   But at length symptoms of *ennui*
began to be displayed.   The doctor yawned, and lay down
on his bed to enjoy an American newspaper about twelve
months old.   Harry Somerville sat down to re-read a
volume of Franklin's travels in the Polar Regions, which
he had perused twice already.   Mr Hamilton busied
himself in cleaning his fowling-piece; while the skipper
conversed with Mr Wilson, who was engaged in his room
in adjusting an ivory head to a walking-stick.   Mr Wilson
was a jack-of-all-trades, who could make shift, one way

or other, to do *anything*. The accountant paced the
uncarpeted floor in deep contemplation.

At length he paused, and looked at Harry Somerville
for some time.

"What say you to a walk through the woods to North
River, Harry?"

"Ready," cried Harry, tossing down the book with a
look of contempt,—"ready for anything."

"Will *you* come, Hamilton?" added the accountant.
Hamilton looked up in surprise.

"You don't mean, surely, to take so long a walk in the
dark, do you? It is snowing, too, very heavily, and I think
you said that North River was five miles off, did you not?"

"Of course I mean to walk in the dark," replied the
accountant, "unless you can extemporise an artificial
light for the occasion, or prevail on the moon to come out
for my special benefit. As to snowing, and a short tramp
of five miles, why, the sooner you get to think of such
things as *trifles* the better, if you hope to be fit for anything in this country."

"I *don't* think much of them," replied Hamilton,
softly, and with a slight smile; "I only meant that such
a walk was not very *attractive* so late in the evening."

"Attractive!" shouted Harry Somerville, from his
bedroom, where he was equipping himself for the walk,
"what can be more attractive than a sharp run of ten
miles through the woods on a cool night, to visit your
traps, with the prospect of a silver fox, or a wolf, at the
end of it, and an extra sound sleep as the result? Come,
man, don't be soft; get ready, and go along with us."

"Besides," added the accountant, "I don't mean to
come back to-night. To-morrow, you know, is a holi-

day, so we can camp out in the snow, after visiting the
traps,—have our supper, and start early in the morning
to search for ptarmigan."

"Well, I will go," said Hamilton, after this account
of the pleasures that were to be expected; "I am exceedingly anxious to learn to shoot birds on the wing."

"Bless me! have you not learned that yet?" asked the
doctor, in affected surprise, as he sauntered out of his
bedroom to relight his pipe.

The various bedrooms in the clerks' house were ranged
round the hall, having doors that opened directly into it,
so that conversation carried on in a loud voice was heard
in all the rooms at once, and was not unfrequently sustained in elevated tones from different apartments, when
the occupants were lounging, as they often did of an
evening, in their beds.

"No," said Hamilton, in reply to the doctor's question,
"I have not learned yet, although there were a great
many grouse in the part of Scotland where I was brought
up. But my aunt, with whom I lived, was so fearful
of my shooting either myself or some one else, and had
such an aversion to firearms, that I determined to make
her mind easy, by promising that I would never use
them, so long as I remained under her roof."

"Quite right; very dutiful and proper," said the doctor,
with a grave patronising air.

"Perhaps you'll fall in with more *fox* tracks of the same
sort as the one you gave chase to this morning," shouted
the skipper, from Wilson's room.

"Oh! there's hundreds of them out there," said the
accountant; "so let's off at once."

The trio now proceeded to equip themselves for the

walk. Their costumes were peculiar, and merit description. As they were similar in the chief points, it will suffice to describe that of our friend Harry.

On his head he wore a fur cap made of otter-skin, with a flap on each side to cover the ears, the frost being so intense in these climates that, without some such protection, they would inevitably freeze and fall off.

As the nose is constantly in use for the purposes of respiration, it is always left uncovered to fight with the cold as it best can; but it is a hard battle, and there is no doubt that, if it were possible, a nasal covering would be extremely pleasant. Indeed, several desperate efforts *have* been made to construct some sort of nose-bag, but hitherto without success, owing to the uncomfortable fact that the breath issuing from that organ immediately freezes, and converts the covering into a bag of snow or ice, which is not agreeable. Round his neck, Harry wound a thick shawl of such portentous dimensions, that it entirely enveloped the neck and lower part of the face; thus the entire head was, as it were, eclipsed, the eyes, the nose, and the cheek-bones alone being visible. He then threw on a coat made of deer-skin, so prepared that it bore a slight resemblance to excessively coarse chamois leather. It was somewhat in the form of a long, wide surtout, overlapping very much in front, and confined closely to the figure by means of a scarlet worsted belt instead of buttons, and was ornamented round the foot by a number of cuts, which produced a fringe of little tails. Being lined with thick flannel, this portion of attire was rather heavy, but extremely necessary. A pair of blue cloth leggins, having a loose flap on the outside, were next drawn on over the trousers, as an additional protection to the knees. The feet, besides being portions of the body that are peculiarly susceptible of cold, had further to contend against the chafing of the lines which attach them to the snow-shoes, so that special care in their preparation for duty was necessary. First were put on a pair of blanketing or duffle socks, which were merely oblong in form, without sewing or making up of any kind. These were wrapped round the feet, which were next thrust into a pair of made-up socks, of the same material, having ankle pieces; above these were put *another* pair, *without* flaps for the ankles. Over all was drawn a pair of moccasins made of stout deer-skin, similar to that of the coat. Of course, the elegance of Harry's feet was entirely destroyed, and had he been met in this guise by any of his friends in the "old country," they would infallibly have come to the conclusion that he was afflicted with gout. Over his shoulders he slung a powder-horn and shot-pouch, the latter tastefully embroidered with dyed quill work. A pair of deer-skin mittens, having a little bag for the thumb, and a large bag for the fingers, completed his costume.

While the three were making ready, with a running accompaniment of grunts and groans at refractory pieces of apparel, the night without became darker, and the snow fell thicker, so that, when they issued suddenly out of their warm abode, and emerged into the sharp frosty air, which blew the snowdrift into their eyes, they felt a momentary desire to give up the project and return to their comfortable quarters.

"What a dismal-looking night it is!" said the accountant, as he led the way along the wooden platform towards the gate of the fort.

"Very!" replied Hamilton, with an involuntary shudder.

"Keep up your heart," said Harry, in a cheerful voice, "you've no notion how your mind will change on that point when you have walked a mile or so and got into a comfortable heat. I must confess, however, that a little moonshine would be an improvement," he added, on stumbling, for the third time, off the platform into the deep snow.

"It is full moon just now," said the accountant, "and I think the clouds look as if they would break soon. At any rate, I've been at North River so often that I believe I could walk out there blindfold."

As he spoke they passed the gate, and diverging to the right, proceeded, as well as the imperfect light permitted, along the footpath that led to the forest.

CHAPTER XVIII.

The walk continued; frozen toes; an encampment in the snow.

AFTER quitting York Fort, the three friends followed the track leading to the spot where the winter's firewood was cut. Snow was still falling thickly, and it was with some difficulty that the accountant kept in the right direction. The night was excessively dark, while the dense fir forest, through which the narrow road ran, rendered the gloom if possible more intense.

When they had proceeded about a mile, their leader suddenly came to a stand.

"We must quit the track now," said he, "so get on your snow-shoes as fast as you can."

Hitherto they had carried their snow-shoes under their arms, as the beaten track along which they travelled rendered them unnecessary; but now, having to leave the path and pursue the remainder of their journey through deep snow, they availed themselves of those useful machines, by means of which the inhabitants of this part of North America are enabled to journey over many miles of trackless wilderness, with nearly as much ease as a sportsman can traverse the moors in autumn, and that over snow so deep that one hour's walk through it *without* such aids would completely exhaust the stoutest trapper, and advance him only a mile or so on his journey. In other words, to walk without snow-shoes would be utterly impossible, while to walk with them is easy and agreeable. They are not used after the manner of skates, with a *sliding*, but a *stepping* action, and their sole use is to support the wearer on the top of snow, into which, without them, he would sink up to the waist. When we say that they support the wearer on the *top* of the snow, of course we do not mean that they literally do not break the surface at all. But the depth to which they sink is comparatively trifling, and varies according to the state of the snow and the season of the year. In the woods they sink frequently about six inches, sometimes more, sometimes less, while on frozen rivers, where the snow is packed solid by the action of the wind, they sink only two or three inches and sometimes so little as to render it preferable to walk without them altogether. Snow-shoes are made of light strong framework of wood, varying from three to six feet long by eighteen and twenty inches broad, tapering to a point before and behind, and turning up in front. Different tribes of Indians modify the form a little, but in all essential points they are the same. The framework is filled up with a netting of deer-skin threads, which unites lightness with great strength, and permits any snow that may chance to fall upon the netting to pass through it like a sieve.

On the present occasion, the snow, having recently fallen, was soft, and the walking, consequently, what is called heavy.

"Come on," shouted the accountant, as he came to a stand for the third time within half an hour, to await the coming up of poor Hamilton, who, being rather awkward in snow-shoe walking, even in daylight, found it nearly impossible in the dark.

"Wait a little, please," replied a faint voice in the distance, "I've got among a quantity of willows, and find it very difficult to get on. I've been down twice at ——"

The sudden cessation of the voice, and a loud crash as of breaking branches, proved too clearly that our friend had accomplished his third fall.

"There he goes again," exclaimed Harry Somerville, who came up at the moment. "I've helped him up once already. We'll never get to North River at this rate. What *is* to be done?"

"Let's see what has become of him this time, however," said the accountant, as he began to retrace his steps. "If I mistake not, he made rather a heavy plunge that time, judging from the sound."

At that moment the clouds overhead broke, and a moonbeam shot down into the forest, throwing a pale light over the cold scene. A few steps brought Harry and the accountant to the spot whence the sound had proceeded, and a loud startling laugh rang through the night air, as the latter suddenly beheld poor Hamilton struggling with his arms, head, and shoulders stuck into the snow, his snow-shoes twisted and sticking with the heels up and awry, in a sort of rampant confusion, and his gun buried to the locks beside him. Regaining one's perpendicular after a fall in deep snow, when the feet are encumbered by a pair of long snow-shoes, is by no means an easy thing to accomplish, in consequence of the impossibility of getting hold of anything solid, on which to rest the hands. The depth is so great that the outstretched arms cannot find bottom, and every successive struggle only sinks the unhappy victim deeper down. Should no assistance be near, he will soon beat the snow to a solidity that will enable

THE THIRD FALL ACCOMPLISHED

him to rise, but not in a very enviable or comfortable condition.

"Give me a hand, Harry," gasped Hamilton, as he managed to twist his head upwards for a moment.

"Here you are," cried Harry, holding out his hand and endeavouring to suppress his desire to laugh, "up with you," and in another moment the poor youth was upon his legs, with every fold and crevice about his person stuffed to repletion with snow.

"Come, cheer up," cried the accountant, giving the youth a slap on the back, "there's nothing like experience —the proverb says that it even teaches fools, so you need not despair."

Hamilton smiled as he endeavoured to shake off some of his white coating

"We'll be all right immediately," added Harry, "I see that the country ahead is more open, so the walking will be easier."

"Oh! I wish that I had not come," said Hamilton, sorrowfully, "because I am only detaining you. But perhaps I shall do better as we get on. At any rate I cannot go back now, as I could never find the way."

"Go back! of course not," said the accountant, "in a short time we shall get into the old woodcutters' track of last year, and although it's not beaten at all, yet it is pretty level and open, so that we shall get on famously."

"Go on, then," sighed Hamilton.

"Drive ahead," laughed Harry, and without farther delay they resumed their march, which was soon rendered more cheerful as the clouds rolled away, the snow ceased to fall, and the bright, full moon poured its rays down upon their path.

For a long time they proceeded in silence; the muffled sound of the snow, as it sank beneath their regular footsteps, being the only interruption to the universal stillness around. There is something very solemnising in a scene such as we are now describing. The calm tranquillity of the arctic night; the pure whiteness of the snowy carpet, which rendered the dark firs inky black by contrast; the clear, cold, starry sky, that glimmered behind the dark clouds, whose heavy masses, now rolling across the moon, partially obscured the landscape, and anon, passing slowly away, let a flood of light down upon the forest, which, penetrating between the thick branches, scattered the surface of the snow, as it were, with flakes of silver. Sleep has often been applied as a simile to nature in repose, but in this case death seemed more appropriate. So silent, so cold, so still was the scene, that it filled the mind with an indefinable feeling of dread, as if there was some mysterious danger near. Once or twice during their walk the three travellers paused to rest, but they spoke little, and in subdued voices, as if they feared to break the silence of the night.

"It is strange," said Harry, in a low tone, as he walked beside Hamilton, "that such a scene as this always makes me think more than usual of home."

"And yet it is natural," replied the other, "because it reminds us more forcibly than any other that we are in a foreign land—in the lonely wilderness—far away from home."

Both Harry and Hamilton had been trained in families where the Almighty was feared and loved; and where their minds had been early led to reflect upon the Creator when regarding the works of his hand; their thoughts, therefore, naturally reverted to another home, compared with which, this world is indeed a cold, lonely wilderness; but on such subjects they feared to converse, partly from a dread of the ridicule of reckless companions, partly from ignorance of each other's feelings on religious matters, and, although their minds were busy, their tongues were silent.

The ground over which the greater part of their path lay was a swamp, which, being now frozen, was a beautiful white plain, so that their advance was more rapid, until they approached the belt of woodland that skirts North River. Here they again encountered the heavy snow, which had been such a source of difficulty to Hamilton at setting out. He had profited by his former experience, however, and, by the exercise of an excessive degree of caution, managed to scramble through the woods tolerably well, emerging at last, along with his companions, on the bleak margin of what appeared to be the frozen sea.

North River, at this place, is several miles broad, and the opposite shore is so low, that the snow causes it to appear but a slight undulation of the frozen bed of the river. Indeed, it would not be distinguishable at all, were it not for the willow bushes and dwarf pines, whose tops, rising above the white garb of winter, indicate that *terra firma* lies below.

" What a cold, desolate-looking place ! " said Hamilton, as the party stood still to recover breath before taking their way over the plain to the spot where the accountant's traps were set. " It looks much more like the frozen sea than a river."

" It can scarcely be called a river at this place," re

marked the accountant, "seeing that the water hereabouts is brackish, and the tides ebb and flow a good way up. In fact, this is the extreme mouth of North River, and if you turn your eyes a little to the right, towards yonder ice-hummock in the plain, you behold the frozen sea itself."

"Where are your traps set?" inquired Harry.

"Down in the hollow behind yon point covered with brushwood."

"Oh, we shall soon get to them, then; come along," cried Harry.

Harry was mistaken, however. He had not yet learned by experience the extreme difficulty of judging of distance in the uncertain light of night; a difficulty that was increased by his ignorance of the locality, and by the gleams of moonshine that shot through the driving clouds, and threw confused, fantastic shadows over the plain. The point which he had at first supposed was covered with low bushes, and about a hundred yards off, proved to be clad in reality with large bushes and small trees, and lay at a distance of two miles.

"I think you have been mistaken in supposing the point so near, Harry," said Hamilton, as he trudged on beside his friend.

"A fact, evident to the naked eye," replied Harry "How do your feet stand it, eh? Beginning to lose bark yet?"

Hamilton did not feel quite sure. "I think," said he, softly, "that there is a blister under the big toe of my left foot. It feels very painful."

"If you feel at all *uncertain* about it, you may rest assured that there *is* a blister. These things don't give much pain at first. I'm sorry to tell you, my dear fellow, that you'll be painfully aware of the fact to-morrow. However, don't distress yourself. It's a part of the experience that every one goes through in this country. Besides," said Harry, smiling, " we can send to the fort for medical advice."

" Don't bother the poor fellow, and hold your tongue, Harry," said the accountant, who now began to tread more cautiously as he approached the place where the traps were set.

" How many traps have you ?" inquired Harry, in a low tone.

" Three," replied the accountant.

" Do you know I have a very strange feeling about my heels—or, rather, a want of feeling," said Hamilton, smiling dubiously.

" A want of feeling! what do you mean ?" cried the accountant, stopping suddenly and confronting his young friend.

" Oh! I daresay it's nothing," he exclaimed, looking as if ashamed of having spoken of it, "only I feel exactly as if both my heels were cut off, and I were walking on tip-toe ! "

" Say you so ? then right-about wheel. Your heels are frozen, man, and you'll lose them if you don't look sharp."

" Frozen !" cried Hamilton, with a look of incredulity.

" Ay, frozen ; and it's lucky you told me. I've a place up in the woods here, which I call my winter camp, where we can get you put to rights ; but step out ; the longer we are about it, the worse for you."

Harry Somerville was at first disposed to think that

the accountant jested, but seeing that he turned his back
towards his traps, and made for the nearest point of the
thick woods, with a stride that betokened thorough sincerity, he became anxious too, and followed as fast as
possible.

The place to which the accountant led his young
friends was a group of fir trees which grew on a little
knoll, that rose a few feet above the surrounding level
country. At the foot of this hillock, a small rivulet or
burn ran in summer, but the only evidence of its presence
now was the absence of willow bushes all along its
covered narrow bed. A level track was thus formed by
nature, free from all underwood, and running inland
about the distance of a mile, where it was lost in the
swamp whence the stream issued. The wooded knoll, or
hillock, lay at the mouth of this brook, and, being the
only elevated spot in the neighbourhood, besides having
the largest trees growing on it, had been selected by the
accountant as a convenient place for " camping out " on,
when he visited his traps in winter, and happened to be
either too late, or disinclined, to return home. Moreover,
the spreading fir branches afforded an excellent shelter
alike from wind and snow in the centre of the clump ;
while from the margin was obtained a partial view of the
river and the sea beyond. Indeed, from this look-out
there was a very fine prospect on clear winter nights of
the white landscape, enlivened occasionally by groups of
arctic foxes, which might be seen scampering about in
sport, and gambolling among the hummocks of ice like
young kittens.

"Now we shall turn up here," said the accountant, as
he walked a short way up the brook before-mentioned.

and halted in front of what appeared to be an impenetrable mass of bushes.

"We shall have to cut our way, then," said Harry, looking to the right and left, in the vain hope of discovering a place where, the bushes being less dense, they might effect an entrance into the knoll or grove.

"Not so. I have taken care to make a passage into my winter camp, although it was only a whim after all to make a concealed entrance ; seeing that no one ever passes this way, except wolves and foxes, whose noses render the use of their eyes in most cases unnecessary."

So saying, the accountant turned aside a thick branch, and disclosed a narrow track, into which he entered, followed by his two companions.

A few minutes brought them to the centre of the knoll. Here they found a clear space of about twenty feet in diameter, around which the trees circled so thickly, that in daylight nothing could be seen but tree stems as far as the eye could penetrate, while overhead the broad flat branches of the firs, with their evergreen verdure, spread out and interlaced so thickly, that very little light penetrated into the space below. Of course at night, even in moonlight, the place was pitch dark. Into this retreat the accountant led his companions, and, bidding them stand still for a minute lest they should tumble into the fireplace, he proceeded to strike a light.

Those who have never travelled in the wild parts of this world can form but a faint conception of the extraordinary and sudden change that is produced, not only in the scene, but in the mind of the beholder, when a blazing fire is lighted in a dark night. Before the fire is kindled, and you stand, perhaps, (as Harry and his friend did on the present occasion) shivering in the cold, the heart sinks, and sad gloomy thoughts arise, while your eye endeavours to pierce the thick darkness, which, if it succeed in doing so, only adds to the effect by disclosing the pallid snow, the cold, chilling beams of the moon, the wide vistas of savage scenery, the awe-inspiring solitudes that tell of your isolated condition, or stir up sad memories of other and far distant scenes. But the moment the first spark of fire sends a fitful gleam of light upwards, these thoughts and feelings take wing and vanish. The indistinct scenery is rendered utterly invisible by the red light, which attracts and rivets the eye as if by a species of fascination. The deep shadows of the woods immediately around you grow deeper and blacker as the flames leap and sparkle upwards, causing the stems of the surrounding trees, and the foliage of the overhanging branches, to stand out in bold relief, bathed in a ruddy glow, which converts the forest chamber into a snug *home-like* place, and fills the mind with agreeable, *home-like* feelings and meditations. It seems as if the spirit, in the one case, were set loose and etherealised to enable it to spread itself over the plains of cold, cheerless, illimitable space, and left to dwell upon objects too wide to grasp, too indistinct to comprehend ;— while, in the other, it is recalled and concentrated upon matters circumscribed and congenial, things of which it has long been cognisant, and which it can appreciate and enjoy without the effort of a thought.

Some such thoughts and feelings passed rapidly through the minds of Harry and Hamilton, while the accountant struck a light and kindled a roaring fire of logs, which he had cut and arranged there on a previous occasion. In the middle of the space thus brilliantly illuminated,

the snow had been cleared away till the moss was uncovered, thus leaving a hole of about ten feet in diameter.
As the snow was quite four feet deep, the hole was surrounded with a pure white wall, whose height was further
increased by the masses, thrown out in the process
of digging, to a height of nearly six feet. At one end
of this space was the large fire which had just been
kindled, and which, owing to the intense cold, only melted
a very little of the snow in its immediate neighbourhood.
At the other end lay a mass of flat pine branches, which
were piled up so thickly as to form a pleasant elastic couch,
the upper end being slightly raised so as to form a kind
of bolster, while the lower extended almost into the fire.
Indeed, the branches at the extremity were burnt quite
brown, and some of them charred. Beside the bolster lay
a small wooden box, a round tin kettle, an iron tea-kettle,
two tin mugs, a hatchet, and a large bundle tied up in a
green blanket. There were thus, as it were, two apartments, one within the other ; namely the outer one, whose
walls were formed of tree-stems and thick darkness, and the
ceiling of green boughs ; and then the inner one with walls
of snow, that sparkled in the firelight as if set with precious stones, and a carpet of evergreen branches.

Within this latter our three friends were soon actively
employed. Poor Hamilton's moccasins were speedily removed, and his friends, going down on their knees, began
to rub his feet with a degree of energy that induced him
to beg for mercy.

"Mercy !" exclaimed the accountant, without pausing
for an instant, "faith, it's little mercy there would be in
stopping just now. Rub away, Harry. Don't give in.
They're coming right at last.

After a very severe rubbing, the heels began to shew symptoms of returning vitality. They were then wrapped up in the folds of a thick blanket, and held sufficiently near to the fire to prevent any chance of the frost getting at them again.

"Now, my boy," said the accountant, as he sat down to enjoy a pipe and rest himself on a blanket, which, along with the one wrapped round Hamilton's feet, had been extracted from the green bundle before mentioned—"Now, my boy, you'll have to enjoy yourself here as you best can for an hour or two, while Harry and I visit the traps. Would you like supper before we go, or shall we have it on our return?"

"Oh, I'll wait for it by all means till you return. I don't feel a bit hungry just now, and it will be much more cheerful to have it after all your work is over. Besides, I feel my feet too painful to enjoy it just now."

"My poor fellow," said Harry, whose heart smote him for having been disposed at first to treat the thing lightly, "I'm really sorry for you. Would you not like me to stay with you?"

"By no means," replied Hamilton, quickly. "You can do nothing more for me, Harry; and I should be very sorry if you missed seeing the traps."

"Oh, never mind the traps. I've seen traps, and set them too, fifty times before now. I'll stop with you, old boy, I will;" said Harry, doggedly, while he made arrangements to settle down for the evening.

"Well, if *you* won't go, I will," said Hamilton, coolly, as he unwound the blanket from his feet and began to pull on his socks.

"Bravo, my lad!" exclaimed the accountant, patting

him approvingly on the back ; " I didn't think you had half so much pluck in you. But it won't do, old fellow You're in *my* castle just now, and must obey orders. You couldn't walk half a mile for your life ; so just be pleased to pull off your socks again. Besides, I want Harry to help me to carry up my foxes, if there are any ; so get ready, sirrah !"

" Ay, ay, captain," cried Harry, with a laugh, while he sprang up and put on his snow-shoes.

" You needn't bring your gun," said the accountant, shaking the ashes from his pipe as he prepared to depart; " but you may as well shove that axe into your belt ; you may want it. Now, mind, don't roast your feet," he added, turning to Hamilton.

" Adieu !" cried Harry, with a nod and a smile, as he turned to go. " Take care the bears don't find you out."

" No fear ; good bye, Harry," replied Hamilton, as his two friends disappeared in the wood and left him to his solitary meditations.

CHAPTER XIX.

Shows how the accountant and Harry set their traps, and what came of it.

THE moon was still up, and the sky less overcast, when our amateur trappers quitted the encampment, and, descending to the mouth of the little brook, took their way over North River in the direction of the accountant's traps. Being somewhat fatigued both in mind and body by the unusual exertions of the night, neither of them spoke for some time, but continued to walk in silence, contemplatively gazing at their long shadows.

" Did you ever trap a fox, Harry ?" said the accountant, at length.

" Yes, I used to set traps at Red River ; but the foxes there are not numerous, and are so closely watched by the dogs, that they have become suspicious. I caught but few."

" Then you know how to *set* a trap ?"

" Oh, yes ! I've set both steel and snow traps often. You've heard of old Labonté, who used to carry one of the winter packets from Red River until within a few years back ?"

" Yes, I've heard of him : his name is in my ledger, at least if you mean Pierre Labonté, who came down last fall with the brigade."

" The same. Well, he was a great friend of mine. His little cabin lay about two miles from Fort Garry, and after work was over in the office, I used to go down to sit and chat with him by the fire; and many a time I have sat up half the night listening to him as he recounted his adventures. The old man never tired of relating them, and of smoking twist tobacco. Among other things, he set my mind upon trapping, by giving me an account of an expedition he made, when quite a youth, to the Rocky Mountains; so I got him to go into the woods and teach me how to set traps and snares, and I flatter myself he found me an apt pupil."

"Humph!" ejaculated the accountant; "I have no doubt you do *flatter* yourself. But here we are. The traps are just beyond that mound; so look out, and don't stick your feet into them."

"Hist!" exclaimed Harry, laying his hand suddenly on his companion's arm. "Do you see *that?*" pointing towards the place where the traps were said to be.

"You have sharp eyes, younker; I *do* see it, now that you point it out. It's a fox, and caught, too, as I'm a scrivener."

"You're in luck, to-night," exclaimed Harry, eagerly. "It's a *silver* fox. I see the white tip on its tail."

"Nonsense," cried the accountant, hastening forward; "but we'll soon settle the point."

Harry proved to be right. On reaching the spot they found a beautiful black fox, caught by the fore leg in a steel trap, and gazing at them with a look of terror.

The skin of the silver fox—so called from a slight sprinkling of pure white hairs covering its otherwise jet black body—is the most valuable fur obtained by the fur-traders, and fetches an enormous price in the British market—so much as thirty pounds sterling being frr

17

quently obtained for a single skin. The foxes vary in
colour from jet black, which is the most valuable, to a
light silvery hue, and are hailed as great prizes by the
Indians and trappers when they are so fortunate as to
catch them. They are not numerous, however, and being
exceedingly wary and suspicious, are difficult to catch. It
may be supposed, therefore, that our friend the accountant
ran to secure his prize with some eagerness.

"Now then, my beauty, don't shrink," he said, as the
poor fox backed, at his approach, as far as the chain
which fastened the trap to a log of wood would permit;
and then, standing at bay, shewed a formidable row of
teeth. That grin was its last; another moment, and the
handle of the accountant's axe stretched it lifeless on the
snow.

"Isn't it a beauty?" cried he, surveying the animal with
a look of triumphant pleasure: and then feeling as if he
had compromised his dignity a little by betraying so much
glee, he added, "But come now, Harry, we must see to the
other traps. It's getting late."

The others were soon visited; but no more foxes were
caught. However, the accountant set them both off to see
that all was right; and then re-adjusting one himself, told
Harry to set the other, in order to clear himself of the
charge of boasting.

Harry, nothing loath, went down on his knees to do
so.

The steel trap used for catching foxes is of exactly the
same form as the ordinary rat-trap, with this difference
that it has two springs instead of one, is considerably
larger, and has no teeth, as these latter would only tend
to spoil the skin. Owing to the strength of the springs

a pretty strong effort is required to set the trap, and clumsy fellows frequently catch the tails of their coats or the ends of their belts, and, not unfrequently, the ends of their fingers, in their awkward attempts. Having set it without any of the above untoward accidents occurring, Harry placed it gently on a hole which he had previously scraped; placing it in such a manner that the jaws and plate, or trigger, were a hairsbreadth below the level of the snow. After this he spread over it a very thin sheet of paper, observing as he did so that hay or grass was preferable; but, as there was none at hand, paper would do. Over this he sprinkled snow very lightly, until every vestige of the trap was concealed from view, and the whole was made quite level with the surrounding plain, so that even the accountant himself, after he had once removed his eyes from it, could not tell where it lay. Some chips of a frozen ptarmigan were then scattered around the spot, and a piece of wood left to mark its whereabouts. The bait is always scattered *round* and not *on* the trap, as the fox, in running from one piece to another, is almost certain to set his foot on it, and so get caught by the leg; whereas, were the bait placed *upon* the trap, the fox would be apt to get caught while in the act of eating, by the snout, which, being wedge-like in form, is easily dragged out of its gripe.

" Now then, what say you to going farther out on the river, and making a snow trap for white foxes?" said the accountant. " We shall still have time to do so before the moon sets."

" Agreed," cried Harry. " Come along."

Without further parley, they left the spot and stretched out towards the sea.

The snow on the river was quite hard on its surface, so that snow-shoes being unnecessary, they carried them over their shoulders, and advanced much more rapidly. It is true that their road was a good deal broken, and jagged pieces of ice protruded their sharp corners so as to render a little attention necessary in walking; but one or two severe bumps on their toes made our friends sensitively alive to these minor dangers of the way.

"There goes a pack of them!" exclaimed Harry, as a troop of white foxes scampered past, gambolling as they went, and, coming suddenly to a halt at a short distance, wheeled about and sat down on their haunches, apparently resolved to have a good look at the strangers who dared to venture into their wild domain.

"Oh! they are the most stupid brutes alive," said the accountant, as he regarded the pack with a look of contempt. "I've seen one of them sit down and look at me while I set a trap right before his eyes; and I had not got a hundred yards from the spot when a yell informed me that the gentleman's curiosity had led him to put his foot right into it."

"Indeed!" exclaimed Harry. "I had no idea that they were so tame. Certainly no other kind of fox would do that."

"No, that's certain. But these fellows have done it to me again and again. I shouldn't wonder if we got one to-night in the very same way. I'm sure, by the look of these rascals, that they would do anything of a reckless, stupid nature just now."

"Had we not better make our trap here, then? There is a point, not fifty yards off, with trees on it large enough for our purpose."

"Yes, it will do very well here; now, then, to work. Go to the wood, Harry, and fetch a log or two, while I cut out the slabs." So saying, the accountant drew the axe which he always carried in his belt; and, while Harry entered the wood and began to hew off the branch of a tree, he proceeded, as he had said, to "cut out the slabs." With the point of his knife he first of all marked out an oblong in the snow, then cut down three or four inches with the axe, and, putting the handle under the cut, after the manner of a lever, detached a thick solid slab of about three inches thick, which, although not so hard as ice, was quite hard enough for the purpose for which it was intended. He then cut two similar slabs, and a smaller one, the same in thickness and breadth, but only half the length. Having accomplished this, he raised himself to rest a little, and observed that Harry approached, staggering under a load of wood, and that the foxes were still sitting on their haunches, gazing at him with a look of deep interest.

"If I only had my gun here!" thought he. But not having it, he merely shook his fist at them, stooped down again and resumed his work. With Harry's assistance the slabs were placed in such a way as to form a sort of box or house, having one end of it open. This was further plastered with soft snow at the joinings, and banked up in such a way that no animal could break into it easily,—at least such an attempt would be so difficult as to make an entrance into the interior by the open side much more probable. When this was finished, they took the logs that Harry had cut and carried with so much difficulty from the wood, and began to lop off the smaller branches and twigs. One large log was placed across the

opening of the trap, while the others were piled on one
end of it so as to press it down with their weight.
Three small pieces of stick were now prepared; two of
them being about half a foot long, and the other about a
foot.   On the long piece of stick the breast of a ptarmigan was fixed as a bait, and two notches cut, the one at
the end of it, the other about four or five inches further
down.   All was now ready to set the trap.

"Raise the log now while I place the trigger," said
Harry, kneeling down in front of the door, while the
accountant, as directed, lifted up the log on which the
others lay so as to allow his companion to introduce the
bait-stick, in such a manner as to support it, while the
slightest pull on the bait would set the stick with the
notches free, and thus permit the log to fall on the back
of the fox, whose effort to reach the bait would necessarily
place him under it.

While Harry was thus engaged, the accountant stood
up and looked towards the foxes.   They had approached
so near in their curiosity, that he was induced to throw
his axe frantically at the foremost of the pack.   This set
them galloping off, but they soon halted and sat down as
before.

"What aggravating brutes they are, to be sure!" said
Harry, with a laugh, as his companion returned with the
hatchet.

"Humph! yes, but we'll be upsides with them yet.
Come along into the wood, and I wager that in ten
minutes we shall have one."

They immediately hurried towards the wood, but had
not walked fifty paces, when they were startled by a loud
yell behind them.

" Dear me!" exclaimed the accountant, while he and
Harry turned round with a start.   " It cannot surely be
possible that they have gone in already." A loud howl followed the remark, and the whole pack fled over the plain
like snowdrift and disappeared.

" Ah! that's a pity, something must have scared them,
to make them take wing like that. However, we'll get
one to-morrow for certain; so come along, lad, let us make
for the camp."

" Not so fast," replied the other; "if you hadn't pored
over the big ledger till you were blind, you would see that
there is *one* prisoner already."

This proved to be the case. On returning to the spot
they found an arctic fox in his last gasp, lying flat on the
snow, with the heavy log across his back, which seemed to
be broken. A slight tap on the snout with the accountant's deadly axe-handle completed his destruction.

" We're in luck to-night," cried Harry, as he kneeled
again to re-set the trap. " But after all, these white
brutes are worth very little; I fancy a hundred of
their skins would not be worth the black one you got
first."

" Be quick, Harry. The moon is almost down, and
poor Hamilton will think that the polar bears have got
hold of us."

" All right! now then, step out," and, glancing once
more at the trap to see that all was properly arranged,
the two friends once more turned their faces homewards,
and travelled over the snow with rapid strides.

The moon had just set, leaving the desolate scene in
deep gloom, so that they could scarcely find their way to
the forest; and, when they did at last reach its shelter,

the night became so intensely dark that they had almost
to grope their way, and would certainly have lost it altogether were it not for the accountant's thorough knowledge of the locality.   To add to their discomfort, as they
stumbled on, snow began to fall; and, ere long, a pretty
steady breeze of wind drove it sharply in their faces.
However, this mattered but little, as they penetrated
deeper in among the trees, which proved a complete shelter both from wind and snow.   An hour's march brought
them to the mouth of the brook, although half that time
would have been sufficient had it been daylight, and, a
few minutes later, they had the satisfaction of hearing
Hamilton's voice hailing them as they pushed aside the
bushes, and sprang into the cheerful light of their encampment.

"Hurrah!" shouted Harry, as he leapt into the space
before the fire, and flung the two foxes at Hamilton's feet.
"What do you think of *that*, old fellow?   How are the
heels? Rather sore? eh! Now for the kettle. 'Polly, put
the kettle on, we'll all have ——' My eye! where's the
kettle, Hamilton?   Have you eaten it?"

"If you compose yourself a little, Harry, and look at
the fire, you'll see it boiling there."

"Man, what a chap you are for making unnecessary
speeches.   Couldn't you tell me to look at the fire, without
the preliminary piece of advice to *compose* myself?   Besides, you talk nonsense, for I'm composed already, of
blood, bones, flesh, sinews, fat, and ——"

"Humbug," interrupted the accountant.   "Lend a hand
to get supper, you young goose!"

"And so," continued Harry, not noticing the interruption, "I cannot be expected, nor is it necessary, to *com-*

pose myself over again. But, to be serious." he added, " it was very kind and considerate of you, Hammy, to put on the kettle, when your heels were in a manner uppermost."

" Oh! it was nothing at all; my heels are much better, thank you, and it kept me from wearying."

" Poor fellow," said the accountant, while he busied himself in preparing their evening meal, " you must be quite ravenous by this time, at least *I* am, which is the same thing."

Supper was soon ready. It consisted of a large kettle of tea, a lump of pemican, a handful of broken biscuit and three ptarmigan; all of which were produced from the small wooden box which the accountant was wont to call his camp-larder. The ptarmigan had been shot two weeks before, and carefully laid up for future use, the intense frost being a sufficient guarantee for their preservation for many months, had that been desired.

It would have done you good, reader, (supposing you to be possessed of sympathetic feelings) to have witnessed those three nor'westers enjoying their supper in the snowy camp. The fire had been replenished with logs, till it roared and crackled again, as if it were endued with a vicious spirit, and wished to set the very snow in flames. The walls shone like alabaster studded with diamonds, while the green boughs overhead and the stems around were of a deep red colour in the light of the fierce blaze. The tea-kettle hissed, fumed, and boiled over into the fire. A mass of pemican simmered in the lid in front of it. Three pannikins of tea reposed on the green branches, their refreshing contents sending up little clouds of steam, while the ptarmigan, now split up, skewered, and roasted

were being heartily devoured by our three hungry
friends.

The pleasures that fall to the lot of man are transient.
Doubtless they are numerous and oft recurring,—still they
are transient, and so—supper came to an end.

"Now for a pipe," said the accountant, disposing his limbs
at full length on a green blanket. "O thou precious
weed, what should we do without thee!"

"Smoke *tea*, to be sure," answered Harry.

"Ah! true, it *is* possible to exist on a pipe of tea-
leaves for a time, but *only* for a time. I tried it myself
once, in desperation, when I ran short of tobacco on a
journey, and found it execrable, but better than nothing."

"Pity we can't join you in that," remarked Harry.

"True, but perhaps since you cannot pipe, it might prove
an agreeable diversification to dance."

"Thank you, I'd rather not," said Harry; "and as for
Hamilton, I'm convinced that *his* mind is made up on the
subject. How go the heels now?"

"Thank you, pretty well," he replied, reclining his
head on the pine branches, and extending his smitten
members towards the fire. "I think they will be quite
well in the morning."

"It is a curious thing," remarked the accountant, in a
soliloquising tone, "that *soft* fellows *never* smoke!"

"I beg your pardon," said Harry; "I've often seen hot
leaves smoke, and they're soft enough fellows, in all
conscience!"

"Ah!" sighed the accountant, "that reminds me of
poor Peterkin, who was *so* soft that he went by the name
of 'Butter.' Did you ever hear of what he did the summer before last with an Indian's head?"

" No, never ; what was it ? "

" I'll tell you the story," replied the accountant, drawing a few vigorous whiffs of smoke, to prevent his pipe going out while he spoke.

As the story in question, however, depicts a new phase of society in the woods, it deserves a chapter to itself.

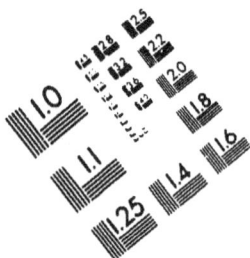

IMAGE EVALUATION
TEST TARGET (MT-3)

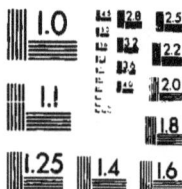

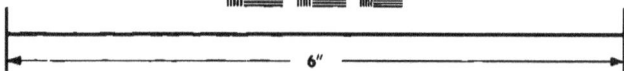

|← —————————— 6" —————————— →|

Photographic
Sciences
Corporation

23 WEST MAIN STREET
WEBSTER, N.Y. 14580
(716) 872-4503

CHAPTER XX.

The accountant's story.

Spring had passed away; and York Fort was filled with all the bustle and activity of summer. Brigades came pouring in upon us with furs from the interior, and as every boat brought a C. T. or a clerk, our mess-table began to overflow.

"You've not seen the summer mess-room filled yet, Hamilton. That's a treat in store for you."

"It was pretty full last autumn, I think," suggested Hamilton, "at the time I arrived from England."

"Full! why, man, it was getting to feel quite lonely at that time. I've seen more than fifty sit down to table there, and it was worth going fifty miles to hear the row they kicked up. Telling stories without end (and sometimes without foundation) about their wild doings in the interior, where every man-jack of them having spent at least eight months almost in perfect solitude, they hadn't had a chance of letting their tongues go till they came down here. But to proceed. When the ship came out in the fall, she brought a batch of new clerks, and among them was this miserable chap Peterkin, whom we soon nicknamed *Butter*. He was the softest fellow I ever knew, (far worse than you, Hamilton), and he hadn't been here a week before the wild blades from the interior, who

were bursting with fun and mischief, began to play off all
kinds of practical jokes upon him. The very first day he
sat down at the mess-table, our worthy governor (who,
you are aware, detests practical jokes) played him a trick,
quite unintentionally, which raised a laugh against him
for many a day. You know that old Mr Rogan is rather
absent at times ; well, the first day that Peterkin came to
mess (it was breakfast), the old governor asked him, in a
patronising sort of way, to sit at his right hand. Accordingly, down he sat, and having never, I fancy, been away
from his mother's apron-string before, he seemed to feel
very uncomfortable, especially as he was regarded as a
sort of novelty. The first thing he did was to capsize his
plate into his lap, which set the youngsters at the lower
end of the table into suppressed fits of laughter. However, he was eating the leg of a dry grouse at the time, so
it didn't make much of a mess.

"'Try some fish, Peterkin,' said Mr Rogan, kindly,
seeing that the youth was ill at ease. 'That old grouse
is tough enough to break your knife.'

"' A very rough passage,' replied the youngster, whose
mind was quite confused by hearing the captain of the
ship, who sat next to him, giving to his next neighbour a
graphic account of the voyage in a very loud key—'I
mean, if you please, no, thank you,' he stammered, endeavouring to correct himself.

"'Ah! a cup of tea, perhaps. Here, Anderson,'(turning
to the butler) 'a cup of tea to Mr Peterkin.'

"The butler obeyed the order.

"' And, here, fill my cup,' said old Rogan, interrupting himself in an earnest conversation, into which he had
plunged with the gentleman on his left hand. As he

said this, he lifted his cup to empty the slops, but without paying attention to what he was doing. As luck
would have it, the slop-basin was not at hand, and
Peterkin's cup *was*, so he emptied it innocently into that.
Peterkin hadn't courage to arrest his hand ; and when
the deed was done, he looked timidly round to see if the
action had been observed. Nearly half the table had
seen it, but they pretended ignorance of the thing so
well, that he thought no one had observed, and so went
quietly on with his breakfast, and drank the tea ! But
I am wandering from my story. Well, about this time
there was a young Indian who shot himself accidentally
in the woods, and was brought to the fort to see if anything could be done for him. The doctor examined his
wound, and found that the ball had passed through the
upper part of his right arm, and the middle of his right
thigh, breaking the bone of the latter in its passage. It
was an extraordinary shot for a man to put into himself,
for it would have been next to impossible even for
another man to have done it, unless the Indian had been
creeping on all fours. When he was able to speak, however, he explained the mystery. While running through
a rough part of the wood after a wounded bird, he
stumbled, and fell on all fours. The gun, which he was
carrying over his shoulder, holding it, as the Indians
usually do, by the muzzle, flew forward, and turned
right round as he fell, so that the mouth of it was presented towards him. Striking against the stem of a tree,
it exploded, and shot him through the arm and leg, as
described, ere he had time to rise. A comrade carried
him to his lodge, and his wife brought him in a canoe to
the fort. For three or four days the doctor had hopes of

him, but at last he began to sink, and died on the sixth day after his arrival. His wife, and one or two friends, buried him in our graveyard, which lies, as you know, on that lonely-looking point just below the powder magazine. For several months previous to this, our worthy doctor had been making strenuous efforts to get an Indian skull to send home to one of his medical friends, but without success. The Indians could not be prevailed upon to cut off the head of one of their dead countrymen for love or money, and the doctor had a dislike to the idea (I suppose) of killing one for himself; but now, here was a golden opportunity. The Indian was buried near to the fort, and his relatives had gone away to their tents again. What was to prevent his being dug up? The doctor brooded over the thing for one hour and a half (being exactly the length of time required to smoke out his large Turkey pipe), and then sauntered into Wilson's room. Wilson was busy, as usual, at some of his mechanical contrivances.

"Thrusting his hands deep into his breeches-pockets, and seating himself on an old sea-chest, he began—

"'I say, Wilson, will you do me a favour?'

"'That depends entirely on what the favour is,' he replied, without raising his head from his work.

"'I want you to help me to cut off an Indian's head!'

"'Then I *won't* do you the favour; but, pray, don't humbug me just now, I'm busy.'

"'No; but I'm serious, and I can't get it done without help, and I know you're an obliging fellow. Besides, the savage is dead, and has no manner of use for his head now.'

"Wilson turned round with a look of intelligence on hearing this.

"'Ha!' he exclaimed, 'I see what you're up to; but I don't half like it. In the first place, his friends would be terribly cut up if they heard of it; and then, I've no sort of aptitude for the work of a resurrectionist; and then, if it got wind, we should never hear the last of it; and then ——'

"'And then,' interrupted the doctor, 'it would be adding to the light of medical science, you unaspiring monster.'

"'A light,' retorted Wilson, 'which, in passing through *some* members of the medical profession, is totally absorbed, and reproduced in the shape of impenetrable darkness.'

"'Now, don't object, my dear fellow; you *know* you're going to do it, so don't coquette with me, but agree at once.'

"'Well, I consent, upon one condition.'

"'And what is that?'

"'That you do not play any practical jokes on *me* with the head when you have got it.'

"'Agreed!' cried the doctor, laughing; 'I give you my word of honour. Now, he has been buried three days already, so we must set about it at once. Fortunately the graveyard is composed of a sandy soil, so he'll keep for some time yet.'

"The two worthies then entered into a deep consultation as to how they were to set about this deed of darkness. It was arranged that Wilson should take his gun, and sally forth a little before dark, as if he were bent on an hour's sport, and, not forgetting his game-bag, proceed to the graveyard, where the doctor engaged to meet him with a couple of spades and a dark lantern. Accordingly, next evening, Mr Wilson, true to his promise, shouldered his gun, and sallied forth.

" It soon become an intensely dark night. Not a single star shone forth to illumine the track along which he stumbled. Everything around was silent and dark, and congenial with the work on which he was bent. But Wilson's heart beat a little more rapidly than usual. He is a bold enough man, as you know, but boldness goes for nothing when superstition comes into play. However, he trudged along fearlessly enough till he came to the thick woods just below the fort, into which he entered with something of a qualm. Scarcely had he set foot on the narrow track that leads to the graveyard, when he ran slap against the post that stands there, but which, in his trepidation, he had entirely forgotten. This quite upset the small amount of courage that remained, and he has since confessed that if he had not had the hope of meeting with the doctor in a few minutes, he would have turned round and fled at *that* moment.

" Recovering a little from this accident, he hurried forward, but with more caution, for, although the night seemed as dark as could possibly be while he was crossing the open country, it became speedily evident that there were several shades of darkness which he had not yet conceived. In a few minutes he came to the creek that runs past the graveyard, and here again his nerves got another shake, for, slipping his foot while in the act of commencing the descent, he fell and rolled heavily to the bottom, making noise enough in his fall to scare away all the ghosts in the country. With a palpitating heart, poor Wilson gathered himself up, and searched for his gun, which fortunately had not been injured, and then

18

commenced to climb the opposite bank, starting at every
twig that snapped under his feet.   On reaching the level
ground again, he breathed a little more freely, and hurried
forward with more speed than caution.   Suddenly he came
into violent contact with a figure, which uttered a loud
growl as Wilson reeled backwards.

" ' Back, you monster,' he cried, with a hysterical yell,
' or I'll blow your brains out.'

" ' It's little good *that* would do ye,' cried the doctor, as
he came forward; 'why, you stupid, what did you take me
for ?   You've nearly knocked out my brains as it is,' and
the doctor rubbed his forehead ruefully.

" ' Oh ! it's *you,* doctor,' said Wilson, feeling as if a ton
weight had been lifted off his heart ; ' I verily thought it
was the ghost of the poor fellow we're going to disturb.
I do think you had better give it up.   Mischief will come
of it, you'll see.'

" ' Nonsense,' cried the doctor, ' don't be a goose, but
let's to work at once.   Why, I've got half the thing dug
up already.'   So saying, he led the way to the grave, in
which there was a large opening.   Setting the lantern
down by the side of it, the two seized their spades and
began to dig as if in earnest.

" The fact is that the doctor was nearly as frightened as
Wilson, and he afterwards confessed to me that it was
an immense relief to him when he heard him fall down the
bank of the creek, and knew by the growl he gave that
it was he.

" In about half an hour the doctor's spade struck upon
the coffin lid, which gave forth a hollow sound.

" ' Now then, we're about done with it,' said he, standing up to wipe away the perspiration that trickled down

his face. 'Take the axe and force up the lid, it's only
fixed with common nails, while I ——' He did not finish
the sentence, but drew a large scalping-knife from a sheath
which hung at his belt.

"Wilson shuddered and obeyed. A good wrench
caused the lid to start, and while he held it partially open,
the doctor inserted the knife. For five minutes he continued to twist and work his arms, muttering between
his teeth, every now and then, that he was a 'tough
subject,' while the crackling of bones and other disagreeable sounds struck upon the horrified ears of his companion.

"'All right,' he exclaimed at last, as he dragged a
round object from the coffin and let down the lid with a
bang, at the same time placing the savage's head with its
ghastly features full in the blaze of the lantern.

"'Now, then, close up,' said he, jumping out of the
hole, and shovelling in the earth.

"In a few minutes they had filled the grave up and
smoothed it down on the surface, and then, throwing the
head into the game-bag, retraced their steps to the fort.
Their nerves were by this time worked up to such a pitch
of excitement, and their minds filled with such a degree
of supernatural horror, that they tripped and stumbled
over stumps and branches innumerable in their double-
quick march. Neither would confess to the other, however, that he was afraid. They even attempted to pass a
few facetious remarks as they hurried along, but it would
not do, so they relapsed into silence till they came to the
hollow beside the powder-magazine. Here the doctor's
foot happening to slip, he suddenly grasped Wilson by the
shoulder, to support himself,—a movement which, being

unexpected, made his friend leap, as he afterwards expressed
it, nearly out of his skin. This was almost too much for
them. For a moment they looked at each other as well
as the darkness would permit, when all at once a large
stone, which the doctor's slip had overbalanced, fell down
the bank and through the bushes with a loud crash. Nothing more was wanting. All further effort to disguise
their feelings was dropped. Leaping the rail of the open
field in a twinkling, they gave a simultaneous yell of consternation and fled to the fort like autumn leaves before
the wind, never drawing breath till they were safe within
the pickets."

"But what has all this to do with Peterkin?" asked
Harry, as the accountant paused to re-light his pipe and
toss a fresh log on the fire.

"Have patience, lad; you shall hear."

The accountant stirred the logs with his toe, drew a few
whiffs to see that the pipe was properly ignited, and proceeded.

"For a day or two after this, the doctor was observed
to be often mysteriously engaged in an outhouse, of which
he kept the key. By some means or other, the skipper,
who is always up to mischief, managed to discover the
secret. Watching where the doctor hid the key, he possessed himself of it one day, and sallied forth, bent on a
lark of some kind or other, but without very well knowing
what. Passing the kitchen, he observed Anderson, the
butler, raking the fire out of the large oven which stands
in the back-yard.

"'Baking again, Anderson?' said he in passing. 'You
get soon through with a heavy cargo of bread, just
now.'

" ' Yes, sir ; many mouths to feed, sir,' replied the butler, proceeding with his work.

" The skipper sauntered on, and took the track which leads to the boat-house, where he stood for some time in meditation. Casting up his eyes, he saw Peterkin in the distance, looking as if he didn't very well know what to do.

" A sudden thought struck him. Pulling off his coat, he seized a mallet and a caulking-chisel, and began to belabour the side of a boat, as if his life depended on it. All at once he stopped and stood up, blowing with the exertion.

" ' Hallo, Peterkin !' he shouted, and waved his hand.

" Peterkin hastened towards him.

" ' Well, sir,' said he, ' do you wish to speak to me ?

" ' Yes,' replied the skipper, scratching his head, as if in great perplexity. ' I wish you to do me a favour, Peterkin, but I don't know very well how to ask you.'

" ' Oh, I shall be most happy,' said poor Butter, eagerly, ' if I can be of any use to you.'

" ' I don't doubt your willingness,' replied the other ; ' but then—the doctor, you see—the fact is, Peterkin, the doctor being called away to see a sick Indian, has intrusted me with a delicate piece of business—rather a nasty piece of business, I may say—which I promised to do for him. You must know that the Surgical Society of London has written to him, begging, as a great favour, that he would, if possible, procure them the skull of a native. After much trouble he has succeeded in getting one, but is obliged to keep it a great secret, even from his fellow-clerks, lest it should get wind ; for if the Indians heard of it, they would be sure to kill him, and perhaps burn the fort too. Now, I suppose you are aware that it is necessary to boil an Indian's head, in order to get the flesh clean off the skull?'

"' Yes, I have heard something of that sort from the students at college, who say that boiling brings flesh more easily away from the bone; but I don't know much about it,' replied Peterkin.

"' Well,' continued the skipper, ' the doctor, who is fond of experiments, wishes to try whether *baking* won't do better than *boiling*, and ordered the oven to be heated for that purpose this morning; but being called suddenly away, as I have said, he begged me to put the head into it as soon as it was ready. I agreed, quite forgetting at the time that I had to get this precious boat ready for sea this very afternoon. Now, the oven is prepared and I dare not leave my work; indeed, I doubt whether I shall have it quite ready and taut after all, and there's the oven cooling; so, if you don't help me, I'm a lost man.'

" Having said this, the skipper looked as miserable as his jolly visage would permit, and rubbed his nose.

"' Oh, I'll be happy to do it for you, although it is not an agreeable job,' replied Butter.

"' That's right—that's friendly now!' exclaimed the skipper, as if greatly relieved. ' Give us your flipper, my lad;' and seizing Peterkin's hand, he wrung it affectionately. ' Now, here is the key of the outhouse; do it as quickly as you can, and don't let any one see you. It's in a good cause, you know; but the results might be terrible, if discovered.'

" So saying, the skipper fell to hammering the boat again with surprising vigour till Butter was out of sight, and then, resuming his coat, returned to the house.

" An hour after this, Anderson went to take his loaves out of the oven; but he had no sooner taken down the door than a rich odour of cooked meat greeted his nostrils. Uttering a deep growl, the butler shouted out—' Sprat !'

" Upon this, a very thin boy, with arms and legs like pipe stems, issued from the kitchen, and came timidly towards his master.

" ' Didn't I tell you, you young blackguard, that the grouse-pie was to be kept for Sunday, and there you've gone and put it to fire to-day.'

" ' The grouse-pie !' said the boy, in amazement.

" ' Yes, the grouse-pie,' retorted the indignant butler ; and seizing the urchin by the neck, he held his head down to the mouth of the oven.

" ' Smell *that*, you villain ! What did you mean by it ? eh ?'

" ' Oh, murder !' shouted the boy, as, with a violent effort, he freed himself, and ran shrieking into the house.

" ' Murder !' repeated Anderson, in astonishment, while he stooped to look into the oven, where the first thing that met his gaze was a human head, whose ghastly visage, and staring eyeballs, worked and moved about under the influence of the heat as if it were alive.

" With a yell that rung through the whole fort, the horrified butler rushed through the kitchen, and out at the front door, where, as ill-luck would have it, Mr Rogan happened to be standing at the moment. Pitching head first into the small of the old gentleman's back, he threw him off the platform, and fell into his arms. Starting up in a moment, the governor dealt Anderson a cuff that sent him reeling towards the kitchen door again, on the

steps of which he sat down, and began to sing out, 'Oh!
murder, murder! the oven, the oven!' and not another
word, bad, good, or indifferent, could be got out of him
for the next half-hour, as he swayed himself to and fro,
and wrung his hands.

"To make a long story short, Mr Rogan went himself
to the oven, and fished out the head, along with the
loaves, which were, of course, all spoiled."

"And what was the result?" inquired Harry.

"Oh! there was a long investigation, and the skipper
got a blowing-up, and the doctor a warning to let Indian's
skulls lie at peace in their graves for the future, and poor
Butter was sent to M'Kenzie's River as a punishment,
for old Rogan could never be brought to believe that he
hadn't been a willing tool in the skipper's hands; and
Anderson lost his batch of bread and his oven, for it had
to be pulled down, and a new one built."

"Humph! and I've no doubt the governor read you a
pretty stiff lecture on practical joking."

"He did," replied the accountant, laying aside his
pipe, and drawing the green blanket over him, while
Harry piled several large logs on the fire.

"Good night," said the accountant.

"Good night," replied his companions; and in a few
minutes more they were sound asleep in their snowy
camp, while the huge fire continued, during the greater
part of the night, to cast its light on their slumbering
forms.

CHAPTER XXI.

Ptarmigan hunting; Hamilton's shooting powers severely tested;
a snow-storm.

AT about four o'clock on the following morning, the
sleepers were awakened by the cold, which had become
very intense. The fire had burned down to a few embers,
which merely emitted enough light to make darkness
visible. Harry, being the most active of the party, was
the first to bestir himself. Raising himself on his
elbow, while his teeth chattered, and his limbs trembled
with cold, he cast a wobegone and excessively sleepy
glance towards the place where the fire had been;
then he scratched his head slowly; then he stared at the
fire again; then he languidly glanced at Hamilton's
sleeping visage; and then he yawned. The accountant
observed all this; for although he appeared to be buried
in the depths of slumber, he was wide awake in reality,
and, moreover, intensely cold. The accountant, however,
was sly—deep—as he would have said himself, and knew
that Harry's active habits would induce him to rise, on
awaking, and re-kindle the fire,—an event which the accountant earnestly desired to see accomplished, but which
he as earnestly resolved should not be performed by *him*.
Indeed, it was with this end in view that he had given
vent to the terrific snore which had aroused his young

companion a little sooner than would have otherwise been the case.

"My eye," exclaimed Harry, in an undertone, "how precious cold it is!"

His eye making no reply to this remark, he arose, and, going down on his hands and knees, began to coax the charcoal into a flame. By dint of severe blowing, he soon succeeded, and, heaping on a quantity of small twigs, the fitful flame sprang up into a steady blaze. He then threw several heavy logs on the fire, and in a very short space of time restored it almost to its original vigour.

"What an abominable row you are kicking up," growled the accountant; "why, you would waken the seven sleepers. Oh! mending the fire," he added, in an altered tone; "ah! I'll excuse you my boy, since that's what you're at."

The accountant hereupon got up, along with Hamilton, who was now also awake, and the three spread their hands over the bright fire, and revolved their bodies before it, until they imbibed a satisfactory amount of heat. They were much too sleepy to converse, however, and contented themselves with a very brief inquiry as to the state of Hamilton's heels, which elicited the sleepy reply, "They feel quite well, thank you." In a short time, having become agreeably warm, they gave a simultaneous yawn, and, lying down again, fell into a sleep, from which they did not awaken until the red winter sun shot its early rays over the arctic scenery.

Once more Harry sprang up, and let his hand fall heavily on Hamilton's shoulder. Thus rudely assailed, that youth also sprang up, giving a shout, at the same time, that brought the accountant to his feet in an instant; and so, as if by an electric spark, the sleepers were simultaneously roused into a state of wide-awake activity.

"How excessively hungry I feel; isn't it strange?" said Hamilton, as he assisted in re-kindling the fire, while the accountant filled his pipe, and Harry stuffed the tea-kettle full of snow.

"Strange!" cried Harry, as he placed the kettle on the fire—"strange! to be hungry after a five miles' walk, and a night in the snow? I would rather say it was strange if you were *not* hungry. Throw on that billet, like a good fellow, and spit those grouse, while I cut some pemican and prepare the tea."

"How are the heels now, Hamilton?" asked the accountant, who divided his attention between his pipe and his snow-shoes, the lines of which required to be re-adjusted.

"They appear to be as well as if nothing had happened to them," replied Hamilton; "I've been looking at them, and there is no mark whatever. They do not even feel tender."

"Lucky for you. old boy, that they were taken in time, else you'd have had another story to tell."

"Do you mean to say that people's heels really freeze and fall off?" inquired the other, with a look of incredulity.

"Soft, very soft, and green," murmured Harry, in a low voice, while he continued his work of adding fresh snow to the kettle, as the process of melting reduced its bulk.

"I mean to say," replied the accountant, tapping the ashes out of his pipe, "that not only heels, but hands,

feet, noses, and ears, frequently freeze, and often fall off
in this country, as you will find by sad experience, if you
don't look after yourself a little better than you have
done hitherto."

One of the evil effects of the perpetual jesting that prevailed at York Fort was, that "soft" (in other words,
straightforward, unsuspecting) youths had to undergo a
long process of learning-by-experience : first, *believing*
everything, and then *doubting* everything, ere they arrived
at that degree of sophistication which enabled them to
distinguish between truth and falsehood.

Having reached the *doubting* period in his training,
Hamilton looked down and said nothing, at least with
his mouth, though his eyes evidently remarked, " I don't
believe you." In future years, however, the evidence of
these same eyes convinced him that what the accountant
said upon this occasion was but too true.

Breakfast was a repetition of the supper of the previous
evening. During its discussion they planned proceedings
for the day.

" My notion is," said the accountant, interrupting the
flow of words ever and anon to chew the morsel with
which his mouth was filled, " my notion is, that, as it's
a fine clear day, we should travel five miles through the
country parallel with North River. I know the ground,
and can guide you easily to the spots where there are lots
of willows, and, therefore, plenty of ptarmigan, seeing
that they feed on willow tops; and the snow that fell last
night will help us a little."

" How will the snow help us ?" inquired Hamilton.

" By covering up all the old tracks, to be sure, and shewing only the new ones."

"Well, captain," said Harry, as he raised a can of tea to his lips, and nodded to Hamilton, as if drinking his health, "go on with your proposals for the day. Five miles up the river to begin with then———."

"Then, we'll pull up," continued the accountant; "make a fire, rest a bit, and eat a mouthful of pemican: after which we'll strike across country for the southern woodcutters' track, and so home."

"And how much will that be?"

"About fifteen miles."

"Ha!" exclaimed Harry; "pass the kettle, please. Thanks. Do you think you're up to that, Hammy?"

"I will try what I can do," replied Hamilton. "If the snow-shoes don't cause me to fall often, I think I shall stand the fatigue very well."

"That's right," said the accountant; "faint heart, &c., you know. If you go on as you've begun, you'll be chosen to head the next expedition to the north pole."

"Well," replied Hamilton, good-humouredly, "pray head the present expedition, and let us be gone."

"Right!" ejaculated the accountant, rising. "I'll just put my odds and ends out of the reach of the foxes and then we shall be off."

In a few minutes everything was placed in security, guns loaded, snow-shoes put on, and the winter camp deserted. At first the walking was fatiguing, and poor Hamilton more than once took a sudden and eccentric plunge; but, after getting beyond the wooded country, they found the snow much more compact, and their march, therefore, much more agreeable. On coming to the place where it was probable that they might fall in with ptarmigan, Hamilton became rather excited, and

apt to imagine that little lumps of snow, which hung
upon the bushes here and there, were birds.

"There now," he cried, in an energetic and slightly
positive tone, as another of these masses of snow suddenly
met his eager eye—"that's one, I'm *quite* sure."

The accountant and Harry both stopped short on hearing this, and looked in the direction indicated.

"Fire away, then, Hammy," said the former, endeavouring to suppress a smile.

"But do you think it *really* is one?" asked Hamilton,
anxiously.

"Well, I don't *see* it exactly, but then, you know, I'm
near-sighted."

"Don't give him a chance of escape," cried Harry,
seeing that his friend was undecided. "If you really do
see a bird, you'd better shoot it, for they've got a strong
propensity to take wing when disturbed."

Thus admonished, Hamilton raised his gun and took
aim. Suddenly he lowered his piece again, and looking
round at Harry, said in a low whisper—

"Oh! I should like *so* much to shoot it while flying.
Would it not be better to set it up first?"

"By no means," answered the accountant. "'A bird in
the hand,' &c. Take him as you find him—look sharp; he'll
be off in a second."

Again the gun was pointed, and, after some difficulty
in taking aim, fired.

"Ah! what a pity you've missed him," shouted Harry;
"but see, he's not off yet; how tame he is, to be sure;
give him the other barrel, Hammy."

This piece of advice proved to be unnecessary. In his
anxiety to get the bird, Hamilton had cocked both barrels

and while gazing, half in disappointment, half in surprise,
at the supposed bird, his finger unintentionally pressed
the second trigger. In a moment the piece exploded.
Being accidentally aimed in the right direction, it blew
the lump of snow to atoms, and at the same time hitting
its owner on the chest with the butt, knocked him over
flat upon his back.

"What a gun it is, to be sure!" said Harry, with a
roguish laugh, as he assisted the discomfited sportsman to
rise ; " it knocks over game with butt and muzzle at once."

"Quite a rare instance of one butt knocking another
down," added the accountant.

At this moment a large flock of ptarmigan, startled by
the double report, rose with a loud whirring noise about
a hundred yards in advance, and after flying a short distance, alighted.

"There's real game at last, though," cried the accountant, as he hurried after the birds, followed closely by his
young friends.

They soon reached the spot where the flock had alighted,
and after following up the tracks for a few yards further,
set them up again. As the birds rose, the accountant
fired and brought down two ; Harry shot one and missed
another, Hamilton being so nervously interested in the
success of his comrades that he forgot to fire at all.

"How stupid of me !" he exclaimed, while the others
loaded their guns.

"Never mind ; better luck next time," said Harry, as
they resumed their walk. " I saw the flock settle down
about half a mile in advance of us ; so step out."

Another short walk brought the sportsmen again within
range.

"Go to the front, Hammy," said the accountant, "and take the first shot this time."

Hamilton obeyed. He had scarcely made ten steps in advance, when a single bird, that seemed to have been separated from the others, ran suddenly out from under a bush, and stood stock still, at a distance of a few yards, with its neck stretched out and its black eye wide open, as if in astonishment.

"Now, then, you can't miss *that*."

Hamilton was quite taken aback by the suddenness of this necessity for instantaneous action. Instead, therefore, of taking aim leisurely, (seeing that he had abundant time to do so,) he flew entirely to the opposite extreme, took no aim at all, and fired off both barrels at once, without putting the gun to his shoulder. The result of this was that the affrighted bird flew away unharmed, while Harry and the accountant burst spontaneously into fits of laughter.

"How very provoking!" said the poor youth, with a dejected look.

"Never mind—never say die—try again," said the accountant, on recovering his gravity. Having re-loaded, they continued the pursuit.

"Dear me!" exclaimed Harry, suddenly, "here are three dead birds ; I verily believe, Hamilton, that you have killed them all at one shot by accident."

"Can it be possible?" exclaimed his friend, as, with a look of amazement, he regarded the birds.

There was no doubt about the fact. There they lay, plump and still warm, with one or two drops of bright red blood upon their white plumage. Ptarmigan are almost pure white, so that it requires a practised eye to detect them, even at the distance of a few yards; and it would be almost impossible to hunt them without dogs, but for the tell-tale snow, in which their tracks are distinctly marked, enabling the sportsman to follow them up with unerring certainty. When Hamilton made his bad shot, neither he nor his companions observed a group of ptarmigan not more than fifty yards before them, their attention being rivetted at the time on the solitary bird, and the gun happening to be directed towards them when it was fired, three were instantly and unwittingly placed *hors de combat*, while the others ran away. This the survivors frequently do when very tame, instead of taking wing. Thus it was that Hamilton, to his immense delight, made such a successful shot without being aware of it.

Having bagged their game, the party proceeded on their way. Several large flocks of birds were raised, and the game-bags nearly filled, before reaching the spot where they intended to turn, and bend their steps homewards. This induced them to give up the idea of going further; and it was fortunate they came to this resolution, for a storm was brewing, which, in the eagerness of pursuit after game, they had not noticed. Dark masses of leaden-coloured clouds were gathering in the sky overhead, and faint sighs of wind came, ever and anon, in fitful gusts from the north-west.

Hurrying forward as quickly as possible, they now pursued their course in a direction which would enable them to cross the wood-cutters' track. This they soon reached, and finding it pretty well beaten, were enabled to make more rapid progress. Fortunately the wind was blowing on their backs, otherwise they would have had to

19

contend not only with its violence, but also with the snow-
drift, which now whirled in bitter fury among the trees,
or scoured like driving clouds over the plain.   Under this
aspect, the flat country over which they travelled seemed
the perfection of bleak desolation.   Their way, however,
did not lie in a direct line.   The track was somewhat
tortuous, and gradually edged towards the north, until
the wind blew nearly in their teeth.   At this point, too,
they came to the stretch of open ground, which they had
crossed at a point some miles further to the northward,
in their night march.   Here the storm raged in all its
fury, and as they looked out upon the plain, before quitting the shelter of the wood, they paused to tighten their
belts and re-adjust their snow-shoe lines.   The gale was
so violent that the whole plain seemed tossed about like
billows of the sea, as the drift rose and fell, curled, eddied,
and dashed along, so that it was impossible to see more
than half a dozen yards in advance.

"Heaven preserve us from ever being caught in an
exposed place on such a night as this," said the accountant, as he surveyed the prospect before him.   "Luckily
the open country here is not more than a quarter of a
mile broad, and even that little bit will try our wind
somewhat."

Hamilton and Harry seemed by their looks to say,
"We could easily face even a stiffer breeze than that, if
need be."

"What should we do," inquired the former, "if the
plain were five or six miles broad?"

"Do? why, we should have to camp in the woods till
it blew over, that's all," replied the accountant; "but,
seeing that we are not reduced to such a necessity just now,

and that the day is drawing to a close, let us face it at once. I'll lead the way, and see that you follow close at my heels. Don't lose sight of me for a moment, and if you do, by chance, give a shout ; d'ye hear ?"

The two lads replied in the affirmative; and then bracing themselves up as if for a great effort, stepped vigorously out upon the plain, and were instantly swallowed up in clouds of snow. For half an hour or more, they battled slowly against the howling storm ; pressing forward, for some minutes, with heads down, as if *boring* through it,— then turning their backs to the blast for a few seconds' relief,—but always keeping as close to each other as possible. At length the woods were gained ; on entering which it was discovered that Hamilton was missing.

"Hallo ! where's Hamilton ?" exclaimed Harry ; " I saw him beside me not five minutes ago."

The accountant gave a loud shout, but there was no reply. Indeed, nothing short of his own stentorian voice could have been heard at all amid the storm.

" There's nothing for it," said Harry, " but to search at once, else he'll wander about and get lost." Saying this, he began to retrace his steps, just as a brief lull in the gale took place.

" Hallo ! don't you hear a cry, Harry ?"

At this moment, there was another lull ; the drift fell, and, for an instant, cleared away, revealing the bewildered Hamilton, not twenty yards off, standing, like a pillar of snow, in mute despair.

Profiting by the glimpse, Harry rushed forward, caught him by the arm, and led him into the partial shelter of the forest.

Nothing further befel them after this. Their route

lay in shelter all the way to the fort. Poor Hamilton, it is true, took one or two of his occasional plunges by the way, but without any serious result,—not even to the extent of stuffing his nose, ears, neck, mittens, pockets, gun-barrels, and everything else with snow, because, these being quite full and hard packed already, there was no room left for the addition of another particle.

CHAPTER XXII.

The winter packet; Harry hears from old friends, and wishes that
he was with them.

LETTERS from home!   What a burst of sudden emotion—
what a riot of conflicting feelings, of dread and joy,
expectation and anxiety—what a flood of old memories—
what stirring up of almost forgotten associations, these
three words create in the hearts of those who dwell
in distant regions of this earth, far, far away from
kith and kin—from friends and acquaintances—from
the much-loved scenes of childhood, and from *home!*
Letters from home!   How gratefully the sound falls
upon ears that have been long unaccustomed to
sounds and things connected with home, and so long
accustomed to wild, savage sounds, that these have
at length lost their novelty, and become everyday and
commonplace, while the first have gradually grown
strange and unwonted.   For many long months, home and
all connected with it has become a dream of other days,
and savage-land a present reality.   The mind has by degrees become absorbed by surrounding objects—objects so
utterly unassociated with, or unsuggestive of any other
land, that it involuntarily ceases to think of the scenes of
childhood with the same feelings that it once did.   As
time rolls on, home assumes a misty, undefined character, as
if it were not only distant in reality, but were also slowly

retreating further and further away—growing gradually
faint and dream-like, though not less dear, to the mental view.

"Letters from home!" shouted Mr Wilson, and the
doctor, and the skipper, simultaneously, as the sportsmen,
after dashing through the wild storm, at last reached the
fort, and stumbled tumultuously into Bachelors' Hall.

"What!— Where!— How!— You don't mean it!"
they exclaimed, coming to a sudden stand, like three pil-
lars of snow-clad astonishment.

"Ay," replied the doctor—who affected to be quite
cool upon all occasions, and rather cooler than usual if
the occasion was more than ordinarily exciting—"ay, we
do mean it. Old Rogan has got the packet, and is even
now disembowelling it."

"More than that," interrupted the skipper, who sat
smoking as usual by the stove, with his hands in his
breeches-pockets—"more than that, I saw him dissect-
ing into the very marrow of the thing; so, if we don't
storm the old admiral in his cabin, he'll go to sleep over
these prosy yarns that the governor-in-chief writes to
him, and we'll have to whistle for our letters till midnight."

The skipper's remark was interrupted by the opening
of the outer door and the entrance of the butler. "Mr
Rogan wishes to see you, sir," said that worthy to the
accountant.

"I'll be with him in a minute," he replied, as he threw
off his capote and proceeded to unwind himself as quickly
as his multitudinous haps would permit.

By this time Harry Somerville and Hamilton were
busily occupied in a similar manner, while a running fire
of question and answer, jesting remark and bantering

reply, was kept up between the young men, from their various apartments and the hall. The doctor was cool, as usual, and impudent. He had a habit of walking up and down while he smoked, and was thus enabled to look in upon the inmates of the several sleeping rooms, and make his remarks in a quiet, sarcastic manner, the galling effect of which was heightened by his habit of pausing at the end of every two or three words, to emit a few puffs of smoke. Having exhausted a good deal of small talk in this way, and having, moreover, finished his pipe, the doctor went to the stove to re-fill and re-light.

" What a deal of trouble you do take to make yourself comfortable," said he to the skipper, who sat with his chair tilted on its hind legs, and a pillow at his back.

" No harm in that, doctor," replied the skipper, with a smile.

" No harm, certainly ; but it looks uncommonly lazy-like."

" What does ?"

" Why, putting a pillow at your back, to be sure."

The doctor was a full-fleshed, muscular man, and, owing to this fact, it mattered little to him whether his chair happened to be an easy one or not. As the skipper sometimes remarked, he carried padding always about with him ; he was, therefore, a little apt to sneer at the attempts of his brethren to render the ill-shaped, wooden-bottomed chairs, with which the hall was ornamented, bearable.

" Well, doctor," said the skipper, " I cannot see how you make me out lazy. Surely it is not an evidence of laziness my endeavouring to render these instruments of torture less tormenting ? Seeking to be comfortable, if

it does not inconvenience any one else, is not laziness
Why, what *is* comfort ?" The skipper began to wax
philosophical at this point, and took the pipe from his
mouth as he gravely propounded the momentous question. " What *is* comfort ? If I go out to camp in the
woods, and, after turning in, find a sharp stump sticking
into my ribs on one side, and a pine root driving in the
small of my back on the other side, is *that* comfort ?
Certainly not. And if I get up, seize a hatchet, level
the stump, cut away the root, and spread pine brush
over the place, am I to be called lazy for doing so ? Or
if I sit down on a chair, and, on trying to lean back to
rest myself, find that the stupid lubber who made it, has
so constructed it, that four small hard points alone touch
my person,—two being at the hip-joints, and two at the
shoulder-blades ; and if, to relieve such physical agony, I
jump up and clap a pillow at my back, am *I* to be called
lazy for doing *that ?*"

" What a glorious entry that would make in the log !"
said the doctor, in a low tone, soliloquisingly, as if he
made the remark merely for his own satisfaction, while
he tapped the ashes out of his pipe.

The skipper looked as if he meditated a sharp reply ;
but his intentions, whatever they might have been, were
interrupted by the opening of the door, and the entrance
of the accountant, bearing under his arm a packet of
letters.

A general rush was made upon him, and in a few
minutes a dead silence reigned in the hall, broken only
at intervals by an exclamation of surprise or pathos, as
the inmates, in the retirement of their separate apartments, perused letters from friends in the interior of the

country, and friends at home,—letters that were old—
some of them bearing dates many months b... k—and
travel-stained, but new, and fresh, and cheering, nevertheless, to their owners, as the clear bright sun in winter,
or the verdant leaves in spring.

Harry Somerville's letters were numerous and long.
He had several from friends in Red River, besides one or
two from other parts of the Indian country, and one—it
was very thick and heavy--that bore the post-marks of
Britain.   It was late that night ere the last candle was
extinguished in the hall, and it was late too before
Harry Somerville ceased to peruse and re-peruse the
long letter from home, and found time or inclination to
devote to his other correspondents.   Among the rest was
a letter from his old friend and companion, Charley
Kennedy, which ran as follows :—

MY DEAR HARRY,—It really seems more than an age
since I saw you.   Your last epistle, written in the perturbation of mind consequent upon being doomed to spend
another winter at York Fort, reached me only a few days
ago, and filled me with pleasant recollections of other
days.   Oh ! man, how much I wish that you were with me
in this beautiful country !   You are aware that I have
been what they call " roughing it" since you and I parted
on the shores of Lake Winipeg ; but, my dear fellow, the
idea that most people have of what that phrase means, is
a very erroneous one indeed.   " Roughing it " I certainly
have been, inasmuch as I have been living on rough
fare, associating with rough men, and sleeping on rough
beds under the starry sky ; but I assure you, that all this
is not half so rough upon the constitution as what they

call leading an *easy life;* which is simply a life that makes a poor fellow stagnate, body and spirit, till the one comes to be unable to digest its food, and the other incompetent to jump at so much as half an idea. Anything but an easy life, to my mind. Ah! there's nothing like roughing it, Harry, my boy. Why, I am thriving on it; growing like a young walrus; eating like a Canadian *voyageur,* and sleeping like a top. This is a splendid country for sport, and, as our *Bourgeois* [*] has taken it into his head that I am a good hand at making friends with the Indians, he has sent me out on several expeditions, and afforded me some famous opportunities of seeing life among the redskins. There is a talk just now of establishing a new outpost in this district, so, if I succeed in persuading the governor to let me accompany the party, I shall have something interesting to write about in my next letter. By the way, I wrote to you a month ago, by two Indians who said they were going to the missionary station at Norway House. Did you ever get it? There is a hunter here just now, who goes by the name of Jacques Caradoc. He is a first-rater—can do anything, in a wild way, that lies within the power of mortal man, and is an inexhaustible anecdote-teller, in a quiet way. He and I have been out buffalo-hunting two or three times, and it would have done your heart good, Harry, my dear boy, to have seen us scouring over the prairie together on two big-boned Indian horses;—regular trained buffalo-runners, that didn't need the spur to urge, nor the rein to guide them, when once they caught sight of the black cattle, and kept a sharp look-out for badger

---

[*] The gentleman in charge of an establishment is always designated the Bourgeois.

holes, just as if they had been reasonable creatures. The
first time I went out I had several rather ugly falls,
owing to my inexperience. The fact is, that if a man
has never run buffaloes before, he's sure to get one or two
upsets, no matter how good a horseman he may be.
And that monster, Jacques, although he's the best fellow
I ever met with for a hunting companion, always took
occasion to grin at my mishaps, and gravely to read me a
lecture to the effect that they were all owing to my own
clumsiness or stupidity; which, you will acknowledge,
was not calculated to restore my equanimity.

The very first run we had cost me the entire skin of
my nose, and converted that feature into a superb Roman
for the next three weeks. It happened thus. Jacques
and I were riding over the prairie in search of buffaloes.
The place was interspersed with sundry knolls covered
with trees, slips and belts of woodland, with ponds
scattered among them, and open sweeps of the plain here
and there; altogether a delightful country to ride
through. It was a clear early morning, so that our
horses were fresh and full of spirit. They knew, as well
as we ourselves did, what we were out for, and it was no
easy matter to restrain them. The one I rode was a great
long-legged beast, as like as possible to that abominable
kangaroo that nearly killed me at Red River; as for
Jacques, he was mounted on a first-rate charger. I don't
know how it is, but, somehow or other, everything about
Jacques, or belonging to him, or in the remotest degree
connected with him, is always first-rate! He generally
owns a first-rate horse, and if he happens by any unlucky
chance to be compelled to mount a bad one, it immediately
becomes another animal. He seems to infuse some of his

own wonderful spirit into it! Well, as Jacques and I
curvetted along, skirting the low bushes at the edge of a
wood, out burst a whole herd of buffaloes. Bang went
Jacques' gun, almost before I had winked to make sure
that I saw rightly, and down fell the fattest of them all,
while the rest tossed up their tails, heels, and heads, in one
grand whirl of indignant amazement, and scoured away
like the wind. In a moment our horses were at full
stretch after them, on their *own* account entirely, and
without any reference to *us*. When I recovered my self-
possession a little, I threw forward my gun and fired,
but, owing to my endeavouring to hold the reins at the
same time, I nearly blew off one of my horse's ears, and
only knocked up the dust about six yards ahead of us!
Of course Jacques could not let this pass unnoticed. He
was sitting quietly loading his gun, as cool as a cucumber,
while his horse was dashing forward at full stretch, with
the reins hanging loosely on his neck.

"Ah! Mister Charles," said he, with the least possible
grin on his leathern visage, "that was not well done.
You should never hold the reins when you fire, nor try
to put the gun to your shoulder. It a'nt needful. The
beast'll look arter itself, if it's a riglar buffalo runner;
anyways holdin' the reins is of no manner of use. I once
know'd a gentleman that came out here to see the buffalo
huntin'. He was a good enough shot in his way, an' a
first-rate rider. But he was full o' queer notions, he
would load his gun with the ramrod in the riglar way,
instead o' doin' as we do, tumblin' in a drop powder,
spittin' a ball out your mouth down the muzzle, and
hittin' the stock on the pommell of the saddle to send it
home. And he had them miserable things—the *somethin'*

'cussion-caps, and used to fiddle away with them, while
we were knockin' over the cattle in all directions.
Moreover he had a notion that it was altogether wrong
to let go his reins even for a moment, and so, what
between the ramrod, and the 'cussion-caps, and the reins,
he was worse than the greenest clerk that ever came to
the country. He gave it up in despair at last, after
lamin' two horses, and finished off by runnin' after a big
bull, that turned on him all of a sudden, crammed its
head and horns into the side of his horse, and sent the
poor fellow head over heels on the green grass. He
wasn't much the worse for it, but his fine double-barrelled
gun was twisted into a shape that would almost have
puzzled an Injin to tell what it was." Well, Harry, all
the time that Jacques was telling me this we were gaining
on the buffaloes, and at last we got quite close to them,
and as luck would have it, the very thing that happened
to the amateur sportsman happened to me. I went madly
after a big bull in spite of Jacques' remonstrances, and,
just as I got alongside of him, up went his tail, (a sure
sign that his anger was roused) and round he came, head
to the front, stiff as a rock, my poor charger's chest went
right between his horns, and, as a matter of course, I
continued the race upon *nothing*, head first, for a distance
of about thirty yards, and brought up on the bridge of
my nose. My poor dear father used to say I was a bull-
headed rascal, and, upon my word, I believe he was more
literally correct than he imagined, for, although I fell
with a fearful crash, head first, on the hard plain, I rose
up immediately, and in a few minutes was able to resume
the chase again. My horse was equally fortunate, for, although thus brought to a sudden stand while at full gallop,

he wheeled about, gave a contemptuous flourish with his
heels, and cantered after Jacques, who soon caught him
again. My head bothered me a good deal for some time
after this accident, and swelled up till my eyes became
almost undistinguishable; but a few weeks put me all
right again. And who do you think this man Jacques
is? You'd never guess. He's the trapper whom Redfeather told us of long ago, and whose wife was killed by
the Indians. He and Redfeather have met and are very
fond of each other. How often in the midst of these
wild excursions have my thoughts wandered to you,
Harry! The fellows I meet with here are all kind-
hearted, merry companions, but none like yourself. I
sometimes say to Jacques, when we become communicative to each other beside the camp-fire, that my earthly
felicity would be perfect if I had Harry Somerville here,
and then I think of Kate, my sweet, loving sister Kate,
and feel that, even although I had you with me, there
would still be something wanting to make things perfect.
Talking of Kate, by the way, I have received a letter
from her, the first sheet of which, as it speaks of mutual
Red River friends, I herewith enclose. Pray keep it safe,
and return per first opportunity. We've loads of furs
here and plenty of deer-stalking—not to mention galloping on horseback on the plains in summer, and dog-sledg-
ing in winter. Alas! my poor friend, I fear that it is
rather selfish in me to write so feelingly about my agreeable circumstances, when I know you are slowly dragging
out your existence at that melancholy place, York Fort;
but, believe me, I sympathise with you, and I hope earnestly that you will soon be appointed to more genial
scenes. I have much very much to tell you yet, but am

compelled to reserve it for a future epistle, as the packet
which is to convey this is on the point of being closed.

Adieu, my dear Harry, and wherever you may happen
to pitch your tent, always bear in kindly remembrance
your old friend,   CHARLES KENNEDY.

The letter was finished, but Harry did not cease to
hold intercourse with his friend. With his head resting
on his two hands and his elbows on the table, he sat long,
silently gazing on the signature, while his mind revelled
in the past, the present, and the future. He bounded
over the wilderness that lay between him and the beautiful plains of the Saskatchewan. He seized Charley round
the neck, and hugged and wrestled with him as in days of
yore. He mounted an imaginary charger and swept across
the plains along with him ; — listened to anecdotes
innumerable from Jacques, attacked thousands of buffaloes, singled out scores of wild bulls, pitched over horses'
heads and alighted precisely on the bridge of his nose,
always in close proximity to his old friend. Gradually his
mind returned to its prison-house, and his eye fell on
Kate's letter, which he picked up and began to read. It
ran thus :—

MY DEAR, DEAR, DARLING CHARLEY,—I cannot tell you
how much my heart has yearned to see you, or hear from
you, for many long, long months past. Your last delightful letter, which I treasure up as the most precious object
I possess, has indeed explained to me how utterly impossible it was to have written a day sooner than you did ;
but that does not comfort me a bit, or make those weary
packets more rapid and frequent in their movements, or

the time that passes between the periods of hearing from
you less dreary and anxious. God bless and protect you, my
darling, in the midst of all the dangers that surround you.
But I did not intend to begin this letter by murmuring,
so pray forgive me, and I shall try to atone for it by
giving you a minute account of everybody here, about
whom you are interested. Our beloved father and mother,
I am thankful to say, are quite well. Papa has taken
more than ever to smoking since you went away. He is
seldom out of the summer-house in the garden now, where
I very frequently go, and spend hours together in reading
to and talking with him. He very often speaks of you,
and I am certain that he misses you far more than we
expected, although I think he cannot miss you nearly so
much as I do. For some weeks past, indeed ever since
we got your last letter, papa was engaged all the forenoon
in some mysterious work, for he used to lock himself up
in the summer-house,—a thing he never did before. One
day I went there at my usual time, and instead of having
to wait till he should unlock the door, I found it already
open and entered the room, which was so full of smoke
that I could hardly see. I found papa writing at a small
table, and the moment he heard my footstep, he jumped
up with a fierce frown, and shouted, "Who's there?" in
that terrible voice that he used to speak in long ago when
angry with his men, but which he has almost quite given
up for some time past. He never speaks to me, as you
know very well, but in the kindest tones, so you may
imagine what a dreadful fright I got for a moment, but
it was only for a moment, because the instant he saw that
it was me, his dear face changed, and he folded me in his
arms, saying, "Ah! Kate, forgive me, my darling! I did

not know it was you, and I thought I had locked the door
and was angry at being so unceremoniously interrupted.
He then told me he was just finishing a letter of advice
to you, and, going up to the table, pushed the papers
hurriedly into a drawer. As he did so, I guessed what
had been his mysterious occupation, for he seemed to
have covered *quires* of paper with the closest writing.
Ah! Charley, you're a lucky fellow to be able to extort
such long letters from our dear father. You know how
difficult he finds it to write even the shortest note, and
you remember his old favourite expression, " I would
rather skin a wild buffalo bull alive than write a long
letter." He deserves long ones in return, Charley; but
I need not urge you on that score—you are an excellent
correspondent. Mamma is able to go out every day now
for a drive in the prairie. She was confined to the house
for nearly three weeks last month, with some sort of illness
that the doctor did not seem to understand, and at one
time I was much frightened, and very, very anxious
about her, she became so weak. It would have made
your heart glad to have seen the tender way in which
papa nursed her through the illness. I had fancied that
he was the very last man in the world to make a sick-
nurse, so bold and quick in his movements, and with such
a loud gruff voice—for it *is* gruff, although very sweet at
the same time. But the moment he began to tend mamma
he spoke more softly even than dear Mr Addison does,
and he began to walk about the house on tiptoe, and per-
severed so long in this latter that all his moccasins began
to be worn out at the toes, while the heels remained quite
strong. I begged of him often not to take so much
trouble, as *I* was naturally the proper nurse for mamma,

but he wouldn't hear of it, and insisted on carrying
breakfast, dinner, and tea to her, besides giving her all
her medicine. He was for ever making mistakes, however, much to his own sorrow, the darling man; and I
had to watch him pretty closely, for more than once he
has been on the point of giving mamma a glass of laudanum
in mistake for a glass of port wine. I was a good deal
frightened for him at first, as, before he became accustomed to the work, he tumbled over the chairs and tripped
on the carpets while carrying trays with dinners and
breakfasts, till I thought he would really injure himself
at last, and then he was so terribly angry with himself
at making such a noise and breaking the dishes—I think
he has broken nearly an entire dinner and tea set of
crockery. Poor George, the cook, has suffered most from
these mishaps, for you know that dear papa cannot get
angry without letting a *little* of it out upon somebody; and
whenever he broke a dish or let a tray fall, he used to rush
into the kitchen, shake his fist in George's face, and ask
him, in a fierce voice, what he meant by it. But he
always got better in a few seconds, and finished off by
telling him never to mind, that he was a good servant on
the whole, and he wouldn't say any more about it
just now, but he had better look sharp out and not do it
again. I must say, in praise of George, that on such
occasions, he looked very sorry indeed, and said he hoped
that he would always do his best to give him satisfaction.
This was only proper in him, for he ought to be very
thankful that our father restrains his anger so much; for
you know he was rather violent *once*, and you've no idea,
Charley, how great a restraint he now lays on himself.
He seems to me quite like a lamb, and I am beginning to

feel somehow as if we had been mistaken, and that he never was a passionate man at all. I think it is partly owing to dear Mr Addison, who visits us very frequently now, and papa and he are often shut up together for many hours in the smoking-house. I was sure that papa would soon come to like him, for his religion is so free from everything like severity or affected solemnity. The cook, and Rosa, and my dog that you named Twist, are all quite well. The last has grown into a very large and beautiful animal, something like the stag-hound in the picture-book we used to study together long ago. He is exceedingly fond of me, and I feel him to be quite a protector. The cocks and hens, the cow and the old mare, are also in perfect health ; so now, having told you a good deal about ourselves, I will give you a short account of the doings in the colony.

First of all, your old friend Mr Kipples is still alive and well, and so are all our old companions in the school. One or two of the latter have left, and young Naysmith has joined the Company's service. Betty Peters comes very often to see us, and she always asks for you with great earnestness. I think you have stolen the old woman's heart, Charley, for she speaks of you with great affection. Old Mr Seaforth is still as vigorous as ever, dashing about the settlement on a high-mettled steed, just as if he were one of the youngest men in the colony. He nearly poisoned himself, poor man, a month ago, by taking a dose of some kind of medicine by mistake. I did not hear what it was, but I am told that the treatment was rather severe. Fortunately the doctor happened to be at home when he was sent for, else our old friend would, I fear, have died. As it was, the doctor cured him

with great difficulty.   He first gave him an emetic, then
put mustard blisters to the soles of his feet, and afterwards
lifted him into one of his own carts, without springs, in
which he drove him for a long time over all the ploughed
fields in the neighbourhood.   If this is not an exaggerated
account, Mr Seaforth is certainly made of sterner stuff
than most men.   I was told a funny anecdote of him a
few days ago, which I am sure you have never heard, otherwise you would have told it to me, for there used to be no
secrets between us, Charley,—alas ! I have no one to con-
fide in, or advise with, now that you are gone.   You
have often heard of the great flood—not Noah's one—but
the flood that nearly swept away our settlement, and did
so much damage before you and I were born.   Well, you
recollect that people used to tell of the way in which the
river rose after the breaking up of the ice, and how it soon
overflowed all the low points, sweeping off everything in
its course.   Old Mr Seaforth's house stood at that time on
the little point, just beyond the curve of the river, at the
foot of which our own house stands, and as the river continued to rise, Mr Seaforth went about actively securing
his property.   At first he only thought of his boat and
canoes, which, with the help of his son Peter and a Canadian, who happened at the time to be employed about the
place, he dragged up and secured to an iron staple in the
side of his house.   Soon, however, he found that the danger was greater than at first he imagined.   The point
became completely covered with water, which brought
down great numbers of *half*-drowned and *quite*-drowned
cattle, pigs, and poultry; and stranded them at the garden fence, so that in a short time poor Mr Seaforth could
scarcely move about his overcrowded domains.   On seeing

this, he drove his own cattle to the highest land in his
neighbourhood and hastened back to the house, intending
to carry as much of the furniture as possible to the same
place.   But during his short absence, the river had risen
so rapidly, that he was obliged to give up all thoughts of
this, and think only of securing a few of his valuables.
The bit of land round his dwelling was so thickly covered
with the poor cows, sheep, and oth r animals, that he
could scarcely make his way to the house, and you may
fancy his consternation on reaching it, to find that the
water was more than knee-deep round the walls, while a
few of the cows and a whole herd of pigs had burst open
the door (no doubt accidentally) and coolly entered the
dining-room, where they stood with drooping heads, very
wet, and apparently very miserable.   The Canadian was
busy at the back of the house, loading the boat and canoe
with everything he could lay hands on, and was not aware
of the foreign invasion in front.   Mr Seaforth cared little
for this, however, and began to collect all the things he
held most valuable, and threw them to the man, who
stowed them away in the boat.   Peter had been left in
charge of the cattle, so they had to work hard.   While
thus employed the water continued to rise with fearful
rapidity, and rushed against the house like a mill-race, so
that it soon became evident that the whole would, ere
long, be swept away.   Just as they finished loading the
boat and canoes, the staple which held them gave way ;
in a moment they were swept into the middle of the river,
and carried out of sight.   The Canadian was in the boat
at the time the staple broke, so that Mr Seaforth was
now left in a dwelling that bid fair to emulate Noah's ark
in an hour or two, without a chance of escape, and with

no better company than five black oxen, in the dining-room,
besides three sheep that were now scarcely able to keep their
heads above water, and three little pigs that were already
drowned. The poor old man did his best to push out the
intruders, but only succeeded in ejecting two sheep and
an ox. All the others positively refused to go, so he was
fain to let them stay. By shutting the outer door, he succeeded in keeping out a great deal of water. Then he
waded into the parlour, where he found some more little
pigs floating about and quite dead. Two, however, more
adventurous than their comrades, had saved their lives by
mounting first on a chair and then upon the table, where
they were comfortably seated, gazing languidly at their
mother, a very heavy fat sow, which sat, with what seemed
an expression of settled despair, on the sofa. In a fit of
wrath, Mr Seaforth seized the young pigs and tossed them
out of the window, whereupon the old one jumped down,
and half-walking, half-swimming, made her way to her
companions in the dining-room. The old gentleman now
ascended to the garret, where, from a small window, he
looked out upon the scene of devastation. His chief
anxiety was about the foundation of the house, which,
being made of a wooden framework, like almost all the
others in the colony, would certainly float if the water
rose much higher. His fears were better founded than the
house. As he looked up the river, which had by this
time overflowed all its banks and was spreading over the
plains, he saw a fresh burst of water coming down, which,
when it dashed against his dwelling, forced it about two
yards from its foundation. Suddenly he remembered that
there was a large anchor and chain in the kitchen, both
of which he had brought there one day, to serve as a sort

of anvil, when he wanted to do some blacksmith work.
Hastening down, he fastened one end of the chain to the
sofa, and cast the anchor out of the window. A few
minutes afterwards another rush of water struck the
building, which yielded to pressure, and swung slowly
down until the anchor arrested its further progress. This
was only for a few seconds, however. The chain was a
slight one. It snapped, and the house swept majestically
down the stream, while its terrified owner scrambled to
the roof, which he found already in possession of his favourite cat. Here he had a clear view of his situation.
The plains were converted into a lake, above whose surface
rose trees and houses, several of which, like his own, were
floating on the stream or stranded among shallows. Settlers were rowing about in boats and canoes in all
directions, but, although some of them noticed the poor
man sitting beside his cat on the house-top, they were
either too far off or had no time to render him assistance.

For two days nothing was heard of old Mr Seaforth.
Indeed, the settlers had too much to do in saving themselves and their families to think of others ; and it was
not until the third day that people began to inquire
about him. His son Peter had taken a canoe and made
diligent search in all directions, but although he found
the house sticking on a shallow point, neither his father
nor the cat were on, or in it. At last he was brought to
the island, on which nearly half the colony had collected,
by an Indian who had passed the house and brought him
away in his canoe, along with the old cat. Is he not a
wonderful man, to have come through so much in his old
age ? and he is still so active and hearty ! Mr Swan of
the mill is dead. He died of fever last week. Poor old

Mr Gordon is also gone. His end was very sad. About a month ago he ordered his horse and rode off, intending to visit Fort Garry. At the turn of the road, just above Grant's House, the horse suddenly swerved, and its rider was thrown to the ground. He did not live more than half an hour after it. Alas! how very sad to see a man, after escaping all the countless dangers of a long life in the woods, (and his, you know, was a very adventurous one,) thus cut violently down in his old age! O Charley, how little we know what is before us! How needful to have our peace made with God through Jesus Christ, so that we may be ready at any moment when our Father calls us away. There are many events of great interest that have occurred here since you left. You will be glad to hear that Jane Patterson is married to our excellent friend Mr Cameron, who has taken up a store near to us, and intends to run a boat to York Fort next summer. There has been another marriage here, which will cause you astonishment at least, if not pleasure. Old Mr Peters has married Marie Peltier! What *could* have possessed her to take such a husband? I cannot understand it. Just think of her, Charley, a girl of eighteen, with a husband of seventy-five!———

*　　*　　*　　*　　*　　*

At this point the writing, which was very close, and very small, terminated. Harry laid it down with a deep sigh; wishing much that Charley had thought it advisable to send him the second sheet also. As wishes and regrets on this point were equally unavailing, he endeavoured to continue it in imagination, and was soon as deeply absorbed in following Kate through the well-remembered scenes of Red River, as he had been, a short

time before, in roaming with her brother over the wide
prairies of the Saskatchewan. The increasing cold, however, soon warned him that the night was far spent. He
rose and went to the stove, but the fire had gone out, and
the almost irresistible frost of these regions was already
cooling everything in Bachelors' Hall down to the freez-
ing point. All his companions had put out their candles,
and were busy, doubtless, dreaming of the friends whose
letters had struck and re-awakened the long dormant
chords that used to echo to the tones and scenes of other
days. With a slight shiver, Harry returned to his apartment, and kneeled to thank God for protecting and pre-
serving his absent friends, and especially, for sending him
"good news from a far land." The letter with the
British post-marks on it was placed under his pillow.
It occupied his waking and sleeping thoughts that night,
and it was the first thing he thought of and re-read on
the following morning, and for many mornings afterwards. Only those can fully estimate the value of such
letters, who live in distant lands, where letters are few
—very, very few—and far between.

CHAPTER XXIII.

Changes; Harry and Hamilton find that variety is indeed charming;
the latter astonishes the former considerably.

THREE months passed away, but the snow still lay deep, and white, and undiminished around York Fort. Winter—cold, silent, unyielding winter—still drew its white mantle closely round the lonely dwelling of the fur-traders of the far north.

Icicles hung, as they had done for months before, from the eves of every house, from the tall black scaffold on which the great bell hung, and from the still taller erection that had been put up as an outlook for " *the ship* " in summer. At the present time, it commanded a bleak view of the frozen sea. Snow covered every house-top, and hung in ponderous masses from their edges, as if it were about to fall; but it never fell, it hung there in the same position day after day, unmelted, unchanged. Snow covered the whole land, and the frozen river, the swamps, the sea-beach and the sea itself, as far as the eye could reach, seemed like a pure white carpet. Snow lined the upper edge of every paling, filled up the key-hole of every door, embanked about half of every window, stuck in little knobs on the top of every picket, and clung in masses on every drooping branch of the pine-trees in the forest. Frost—sharp, biting frost—solidified, surrounded, and pervaded everything. Mercury was congealed by it; vapour was condensed by it; iron was cooled by it until it could scarcely be touched without (as the men expressed it) "burning" the fingers. The water-jugs in Bachelors' Hall and the water-buckets were frozen by it, nearly to the bottom; though there was a good stove there, and the Hall was not *usually* a cold place by any means. The breath of the inhabitants was congealed by it on the window-panes, until they had become coated with ice an inch thick. The breath of the men was rendered white and opaque by it, as they panted and hurried to and fro about their ordinary avocations; beating their gloved hands together, and stamping their well-wrapped-up feet on the hard beaten snow to keep them warm. Old Robin's nose seemed to be entirely shrivelled up into his face by it, as he drove his ox-cart to the river to fetch his daily supply of water. The only things that were not affected by it were the fires, which crackled and roared as if in laughter, and twisted and leapt as if in uncontrollable glee at the bare idea of John Frost acquiring, by any artifice whatever, the smallest possible influence over *them*. Three months had elapsed, but frost and snow, instead of abating, had gone on increasing and intensifying, deepening and extending its work, and riveting its chains. Winter—cold, silent, unyielding winter—still reigned at York Fort, as though it had made it a *sine qua non* of its existence at all that it should reign there for ever!

But although everything was thus wintry and cold, it was by no means cheerless or dreary. A bright sun shone in the blue heavens with an intenseness of brilliancy that was quite dazzling to the eyes, that elated the spirits, and caused man and beast to tread with a more elastic

step than usual. Although the sun looked down upon
the scene with an unclouded face, and found a mirror in
every icicle, and in every gem of hoarfrost with which the
objects of nature were loaded, there was, however, no
perceptible heat in his rays. They fell on the white earth
with all the brightness of midsummer, but they fell
powerless as moonbeams in the dead of winter.

On the frozen river, just in front of the gate of the
fort, a group of men and dogs were assembled. The dogs
were four in number, harnessed to a small flat sledge of
the slender kind used by Indians to drag their furs and
provisions over the snow. The group of men was composed of Mr Rogan, and the inmates of Bachelors' Hall,
one or two men who happened to be engaged there at the
time in cutting a new water-hole in the ice, and an
Indian, who, to judge from his carefully adjusted costume,
the snow-shoes on his feet, and the short whip in his
hand, was the driver of the sledge, and was about to start
on a journey. Harry Somerville and young Hamilton
were also wrapped up more carefully than usual.

"Good-bye, then, good-bye," said Mr Rogan, advancing
towards the Indian, who stood beside the leading dog,
ready to start. "Take care of our young friends; they've
not had much experience in travelling yet ; and don't over-
drive your dogs. Treat them well and they'll do more
work. They're like men in that respect." Mr Rogan
shook the Indian by the hand, and the latter immediately
flourished the whip and gave a shout, which the dogs no
sooner heard than they uttered a simultaneous yell, sprang
forward with a jerk, and scampered up the river, closely
followed by their dark-skinned driver.

"Now, lads, farewell," said the old gentlemen, turning

with a kindly smile to our two friends, who were shaking
hands for the last time with their comrades. " I'm sorry
you're going to leave us, my boys. You've done your
duty well while here, and I would willingly have kept you
a little longer with me, but our governor wills it otherwise. However, I trust that you'll be happy wherever
you may be sent. Don't forget to write to me.—God
bless you—farewell."

Mr Rogan shook them heartily by the hand, turned
short round, and walked slowly up to his house, with an
expression of sadness on his mild face, while Harry and
Hamilton, having once more waved farewell to their
friends, marched up the river side by side in silence.
They followed the track left by the dog-sledge, which
guided them with unerring certainty, although their
Indian leader and his team were out of sight in advance.

A week previous to this time, an Indian arrived from
the interior, bearing a letter from head-quarters, which
directed that Messrs Somerville and Hamilton should be
forthwith despatched on snow-shoes to Norway House.
As this establishment is about three hundred miles from
the sea-coast, the order involved a journey of nearly two
weeks' duration, through a country that was utterly
destitute of inhabitants. On receiving a command from
Mr Rogan to prepare for an early start, Harry retired precipitately to his own room, and there, after cutting
unheard-of capers, and giving vent to sudden incomprehensible shouts, all indicative of the highest state of
delight, he condescended to tell his companions of his
good fortune, and set about preparations without delay.
Hamilton, on the contrary, gave his usual quiet smile on
being informed of his destination, and, returning some-

what pensively to Bachelors' Hall, proceeded leisurely to make the necessary arrangements for departure. As the time drew on, however, a perpetual flush on his countenance, and an unusual brilliancy about his eye, shewed that he was not quite insensible to the pleasures of a change, and relished the idea more than he got credit for. The Indian who had brought the letter was ordered to hold himself in readiness to retrace his steps and conduct the young men through the woods to Norway House, where they were to await further orders. A few days later, the three travellers, as already related, set out on their journey.

After walking a mile up the river, they passed a point of land which shut out the fort from view. Here they paused to take a last look, and then pressed forward in silence, the thoughts of each being busy with mingled recollections of their late home, and anticipations of the future. After an hour's sharp walking they came in sight of the guide, and slackened their pace.

"Well, Hamilton," said Harry, throwing off his reverie with a deep sigh, "are you glad to leave York Fort, or sorry?"

"Glad, undoubtedly," replied Hamilton, "but sorry to part from our old companions there. I had no idea, Harry, that I loved them all so much; I feel as if I should be glad were the order for us to leave them countermanded even now."

"That's the very thought," said Harry, "that was passing through my own brain, when I spoke to you. Yet, somehow, I think I should be uncommonly sorry, after all, if we were really sent back. There's a queer contradiction, Hammy; we're sorry and happy at the same time! If I were the skipper, now, I would found a philosophical argument upon it."

"Which the skipper would carry on with untiring vigour," said Hamilton, smiling, "and afterwards make an entry of in his log. But I think, Harry, that to feel the emotion of sorrow and joy at the same time is not such a contradiction as it at first appears."

"Perhaps not," replied Harry; "but it seems very contradictory to *me*, and yet, it's an evident fact—for I'm *very* sorry to leave *them*, and I'm *very* happy to have you for my companion here."

"So am I, so am I," said the other, heartily. "I would rather travel with you, Harry, than with any of our late companions—although I like them all very much."

The two friends had grown, almost imperceptibly, in each other's esteem during their residence under the same roof, more than either of them would have believed possible. The gay, reckless hilarity of the one, did not at first accord with the quiet gravity, and, as his comrades styled it, *softness*, of the other. But character is frequently misjudged at first sight—and sometimes men, who, on a first acquaintance, have felt repelled from each other, have, on coming to know each other better, discovered traits and good qualities that, ere long, formed enduring bonds of sympathy, and have learned to love those whom at first they felt disposed to dislike or despise. Thus, Harry soon came to know that what he at first thought, and, along with his companions, called, softness in Hamilton, was in reality gentleness of disposition, and thorough good-nature, united in one who happened to be utterly unacquainted with the *knowing* ways of this peculiarly sharp and clever world ; while, in the course of time, new qualities shewed themselves in a quiet, unobtrusive way that won upon his affections and raised his esteem. On the other hand, Hamilton found that, although Harry was volatile, and possessed of an irresistible tendency to fun and mischief, he never by any chance gave way to anger, or allowed malice to enter into his practical jokes. Indeed, he often observed him restrain his natural tendencies when they were at all likely to give pain—though Harry never dreamed that such efforts were known to any one but himself. Besides this, Harry was peculiarly *unselfish*; and when a man is possessed of this inestimable disposition, he is, not *quite* but *very nearly*, perfect!

After another pause, during which the party had left the open river and directed their course through the woods, where the depth of the snow obliged them to tread in each other's footsteps, Harry resumed the conversation.

" You have not yet told me, by the bye, what old Mr Rogan said to you just before we started. Did he give you any hint as to where you might be sent to after reaching Norway House ? "

" No, he merely said he knew that clerks were wanted both for Mackenzie River and the Saskatchewan districts, but he did not know which I was destined for."

" Hum ! exactly what he said to me, with the slight addition that he strongly suspected that Mackenzie River would be my doom. Are you aware, Hammy, my boy, that the Saskatchewan district is a sort of terrestrial paradise, and Mackenzie River equivalent to Botany Bay ? "

"I have heard as much during our conversations in Bachelors' Hall, but —— Stop a bit, Harry, these snow

shoe lines of mine have got loosened with tearing through
this deep snow, and these shockingly thick bushes.
There—they are right now ; go on, I was going to say
that I don't —— oh!"

This last exclamation was elicited from Hamilton by a
sharp blow, caused by a branch which, catching on part
of Harry's dress, as he plodded on in front, suddenly re-
bounded and struck him across the face.   This is of common occurrence in travelling through the woods, especially
to those who, from inexperience, walk too closely on the
heels of their companions.

"What's wrong now, Hammy?" inquired his friend,
looking over his shoulder.

"Oh, nothing worth mentioning—rather a sharp blow
from a branch, that's all."

" Well, proceed ; you've interrupted yourself twice in
what you were going to say ;--perhaps it'll come out if
you try it a third time."

"I was merely going to say, that I don't much care
where I am sent to, so long as it is not to an outpost
where I shall be all alone."

"All very well, my friend ; but, seeing that outposts
are, in comparison with principal forts, about a hundred
to one, your chance of avoiding them is rather slight.
However, our youth and want of experience is in our
favour, as they like to send men who have seen some
service to outposts.   But I fear that, with such brilliant
characters as you and I, Hammy, youth will only be an
additional recommendation, and inexperience won't last
long.—Hallo ! what's going on yonder?"

Harry pointed as he spoke to an open spot in the
woods about a quarter of a mile in advance, where a

21

dark object was seen lying on the snow, writhing about,
now coiling into a lump, and anon extending itself like a
huge snake in agony.

As the two friends looked, a prolonged howl floated
towards them.

"Something wrong with the dogs, I declare!" cried
Harry.

"No doubt of it," replied his friend, hurrying forward,
as they saw their Indian guide rise from the ground and
flourish his whip energetically, while the howls rapidly
increased.

A few minutes brought them to the scene of action,
where they found the dogs engaged in a fight among
themselves; and the driver, in a state of vehement passion,
alternately belabouring and trying to separate them. Dogs
in these regions, like the dogs of all other regions, we suppose, are very much addicted to fighting ; a propensity
which becomes extremely unpleasant, if indulged while
the animals are in harness, as they then become peculiarly
savage, probably from their being unable, like an ill-
assorted pair in wedlock, to cut or break the ties that
bind them.   Moreover, they twist the traces into such
an ingeniously complicated mass, that it renders disen-
tanglement almost impossible, even after exhaustion has
reduced them to obedience.   Besides this, they are so
absorbed in worrying each other, that, for the time, they
are utterly regardless of their driver's lash or voice.
This naturally makes the driver angry ; and sometimes
irascible men practise shameful cruelties on the poor
dogs.   When the two friends came up, they found the
Indian glaring at the animals, as they fought and writhed
in the snow, with every lineament of his swarthy face

distorted with passion, and panting from his late exer
tions.   Suddenly he threw himself on the dogs again,
and lashed them furiously with the whip.   Finding
that this had no effect, he twined the lash round his hand,
and struck them violently over their heads and snouts
with the handle; then, falling down on his knees, he
caught the most savage of the animals by the throat, and
seizing its nose between his teeth, almost bit it off.   The
appalling yell that followed this cruel act seemed to
subdue the dogs, for they ceased to fight, and crouched,
whining, in the snow.

With a bound like a tiger, young Hamilton sprang
upon the guide, and, seizing him by the throat, hurled
him violently to the ground.   "Scoundrel!" he cried,
standing over the crestfallen Indian with flushed face and
flashing eyes, "how dare you thus treat the creatures of
God?"

The young man would have spoken more, but his
indignation was so fierce that it could not find vent in
words.   For a moment he raised his fist, as if he meditated dashing the Indian again to the ground as he
slowly arose; then, as if changing his mind, he seized him
by the back of the neck, thrust him towards the panting
dogs, and stood in silence over him with the whip grasped
firmly in his hand, while he disentangled the traces.

This accomplished, Hamilton ordered him, in a voice of
suppressed anger, to "go forward"—an order which the
cowed guide promptly obeyed—and, in a few minutes
more, the two friends were again alone.

"Hamilton, my boy," exclaimed Harry, who, up to
this moment, seemed to have been petrified, "you have
perfectly amazed me!   I'm utterly bewildered."

" Indeed, I fear that I have been very violent," said Hamilton, blushing deeply.

" Violent !" exclaimed his friend. " Why, man, I've completely mistaken your character. I, I —— "

" I hope not, Harry," said Hamilton, in a subdued tone ; " I hope not. Believe me, I am not naturally violent ; I should be very sorry were you to think so. Indeed, I never felt thus before, and, now that it is over, I am amazed at myself; but surely you'll admit that there was great provocation. Such terrible cruelty to ——— "

" My dear fellow, you quite misunderstand me. I'm amazed at your pluck, your energy. *Soft*, indeed ! we have been most egregiously mistaken. Provocation ! I just think you had ; my only sorrow is, that you didn't give him a little more."

" Come, come, Harry ; I see you would be as cruel to him, as he was to the poor dog. But let us press forward ; it is already growing dark, and we must not let the fellow out of sight a-head of us."

" *Allons donc*," cried Harry ; and, hastening their steps, they travelled silently and rapidly among the stems of the trees, while the shades of night gathered slowly round them.

That night, the three travellers encamped in the snow, under the shelter of a spreading pine. The encampment was formed almost exactly in a similar manner to that in which they had slept on the night of their exploits at North River. They talked less, however, than on that occasion, and slept more soundly. Before retiring to rest, and while Harry was extended, half-asleep and half-awake, on his green blanket, enjoying the delightful repose that follows a hard day's march and a good supper, Hamilton drew near to the Indian, who sat sullenly smoking, a little apart from the young men. Sitting down beside him, he administered a long rebuke, in a low, grave tone of voice. Like rebukes generally, it had the effect of making the visage of the Indian still more sullen. But the young man did not appear to notice this; he still continued to talk. As he went on, the look grew less and less sullen, until it faded entirely away, and was succeeded by the grave, quiet, respectful expression peculiar to the face of the North American Indian.

Day succeeded day, night followed night, and still found them plodding laboriously through the weary waste of snow, or encamping under the trees of the forest. The two friends went through all the varied stages of experience which are included in what is called "becoming used to the work," which is sometimes a modified meaning of the expression, "used up." They started with a degree of vigour that one would have thought no amount of hard work could possibly abate. They became aware of the melancholy fact, that fatigue unstrings the youngest and toughest sinews. They pressed on, however, from stern necessity, and found, to their delight, that young muscles recover their elasticity, even in the midst of severe exertion. They still pressed on, and discovered, to their dismay, that this recovery was only temporary, and that the second state of exhaustion was infinitely worse than the first. Still they pressed on, and raised blisters on their feet and toes, that caused them to limp wofully; then they learned that blisters break, and take a long time to heal, and are much worse to walk upon during the healing process than they are

at the commencement,—at which time they innocently
fancied that nothing could be more dreadful. Still they
pressed on, day after day, and found, to their satisfaction,
that such things can be endured and overcome,—that feet
and toes can become hard like leather, that muscles can
grow tough as India-rubber, and that spirits and energy
can attain to a pitch of endurance which nothing within
the compass of a day's march can by any possibility overcome. They found also, from experience, that their conversation changed, both in manner and subject, as they
progressed on their journey. At first they conversed frequently, and on various topics, chiefly on the probability
of their being sent to pleasant places, or the reverse. Then
they spoke less frequently, and growled occasionally, as
they advanced in the painful process of training. After
that, as they began to get hardy, they talked of the trees,
the snow, the ice, the tracks of wild animals they happened
to cross, and the objects of nature generally that came
under their observation. Then, as their muscles hardened,
and their sinews grew tough, and the day's march at
length became, first, a matter of indifference, and, ulti-
mately, an absolute pleasure, they chatted cheerfully on
any and every subject, or sang occasionally, when the
sun shone out, and cast an *appearance* of warmth across
their path. Thus onward they pressed, without halt or
stay, day after day, through wood and brake, over river
and lake, on ice and on snow, for miles and miles together,
through the great, uninhabited, frozen wilderness.

CHAPTER XXIV.

Hopes and fears; an unexpected meeting; philosophical talk between the
hunter and the parson.

On arriving at Norway House, Harry Somerville and his
friend Hamilton found that they were to remain at that
establishment during an indefinite period of time, until
it should please those in whose hands their ultimate destination lay, to direct them how and where to proceed.
This was an unlooked-for trial of their patience ; but,
after the first exclamation of disappointment, they made
up their minds, like wise men, to think no more about
it, but bide their time, and make the most of present
circumstances.

"You see," remarked Hamilton, as the two friends,
after having had an audience of the gentleman in charge
of the establishment, sauntered towards the rocks that
overhang the margin of Playgreen Lake, "you see, it is
of no use to fret about what we cannot possibly help.
Nobody within three hundred miles of us knows where
we are destined to spend next winter. Perhaps orders
may come in a couple of weeks, perhaps in a couple of
months, but they will certainly come at last. Anyhow,
it is of no use thinking about it, so we had better forget
it, and make the best of things as we find them."

"Ah!" exclaimed Harry, "your advice is, that we

should by all means be happy, and if we can't be happy
be as happy as we can. Is that it ?"

"Just so. That's it exactly."

"Ho ! But then, you see, Hammy, you're a philosopher,
and I'm not, and that makes all the difference. I'm not
given to anticipating evil, but I cannot help dreading
that they will send me to some lonely, swampy, out-of-
the-way hole, where there will be no society, no shooting,
no riding, no work even, to speak of,—nothing, in fact,
but the miserable satisfaction of being styled 'bourgeois'
by five or six men, wretched outcasts like myself."

"Come, Harry," cried Hamilton, "you are taking the
very worst view of it. There certainly are plenty of
such outposts in the country, but you know very well
that young fellows like you are seldom sent to such
places."

"I don't know that," interrupted Harry ; "there's
young M'Andrew ; he was sent to an outpost up the
Mackenzie his second year in the service, where he was
all but starved, and had to live for about two weeks on
boiled parchment. Then there's poor Forrester ; he was
shipped off to a place—the name of which I never could
remember—somewhere between the head waters of the
Athabasca Lake and the North Pole. To be sure, he
had good shooting, I'm told, but he had only four labouring men to enjoy it with ; and he has been there *ten*
years now, and he has more than once had to scrape the
rocks of that detestable stuff called *tripe de roche* to keep
himself alive. And then there's——"

"Very true," interrupted Hamilton ; "then there's
your friend Charles Kennedy, whom you so often talk
about, and many other young fellows we know, who have

been sent to the Saskatchewan, and to the Columbia,
and to Athabasca, and to a host of other capital
places, where they have enough of society—male society,
at least—and good sport."

The young men had climbed a rocky eminence, which
commanded a view of the lake on the one side, and the fort,
with its background of woods, on the other. Here they
sat down on a stone, and continued for some time to
admire the scene in silence.

"Yes," said Harry, resuming the thread of discourse,
"you are right; we have a good chance of seeing some
pleasant parts of the country. But suspense is not pleasant. Oh, man, if they would only send me up the
Saskatchewan river! I've set my heart upon going
there. I'm quite sure it's the very best place in the
whole country."

"You've told the truth that time, master," said a deep
voice behind them.

The young men turned quickly round. Close beside
them, and leaning composedly on a long Indian fowling-
piece, stood a tall, broad-shouldered, sun-burnt man,
apparently about forty years of age. He was dressed in
the usual leathern hunting coat, cloth leggins, fur cap,
mittens, and moccasins, that constitute the winter garb of
a hunter; and had a grave, firm, but good-humoured expression of countenance.

"You've told the truth that time, master," he repeated,
without moving from his place. "The Saskatchewan *is*,
to my mind, the best place in the whole country, and
havin' seen a considerable deal o' places in my time, I can
speak from experience."

"Indeed, friend," said Harry, "I'm glad to hear you

say so. Come, sit down beside us, and let's hear some
thing about it.

Thus invited, the hunter seated himself on a stone, and
laid his gun on the hollow of his left arm.

"First of all, friend," continued Harry, "do you
belong to the fort here?"

"No," replied the man, "I'm stayin' here just now, but
I don't belong to the place."

"Where do you come from, then; and what's your
name?"

"Why, I've comed d'rect from the Saskatchewan with
a packet o' letters. I'm payin' a visit to the missionary
village, yonder;" the hunter pointed, as he spoke, across
the lake; "and when the ice breaks up I shall get a canoe
and return again."

"And your name?"

"Why I've got four or five names. Somehow or other,
people have given me a nickname wherever I ha' chanced
to go. But my true name, and the one I hail by just
now, is Jacques Caradoc."

"Jacques Caradoc!" exclaimed Harry, starting with surprise. "You knew a Charley Kennedy in the Saskatchewan, did you?"

"That did I. As fine a lad as ever pulled a trigger."

"Give us your hand, friend," exclaimed Harry, springing forward and seizing the hunter's large, hard fist in
both hands. "Why, man, Charley is my dearest friend,
and I had a letter from him some time ago, in which he
speaks of you, and says you're one of the best fellows he
ever met."

"You don't say so," replied the hunter, returning
Harry's grasp warmly, while his eyes sparkled with plea

sure, and a quiet smile played at the corners of his mouth.

" Yes I do," said Harry, " and I'm very nearly as glad to meet with you, friend Jacques, as I would be to meet with him. But come. It's cold work talking here. Let's go to my room. There's a fire in the stove. Come along, Hammy," and taking his new friend by the arm, he hurried him along to his quarters in the fort.

Just as they were passing under the fort gate, a large mass of snow became detached from a house-top, and fell heavily at their feet, passing within an inch of Hamilton's nose. The young man started back with an exclamation, and became very red in the face.

"Hallo !" cried Harry, laughing, "got a fright, Hammy ? That went so close to your chin, that it almost saved you the trouble of shaving."

" Yes, I got a little fright from the suddenness of it," said Hamilton, quietly.

" What do you think of my friend there ? " said Harry to Jacques, in a low voice, pointing to Hamilton, who walked on in advance.

" I've not seen much of him, master," replied the hunter. " Had I been asked the same question about the same lad twenty years agone, I should ha' said he was soft, and perhaps chicken-hearted. But I've learned from experience to judge better than I used to do. I niver thinks o' formin' an opinion o' any one till I've seen them called to sudden action. It's astonishin' how some faint-hearted men will come to face a danger, and put on an awful look o' courage, if they only get warnin'—but take them by surprise ; that's the way to try them."

" Well, Jacques, that is the very reason why I ask

your opinion of Hamilton. He was pretty well taken by surprise that time, I think."

"True, master, but *that* kind o' start don't prove much. Hows'ever, I don't think he's easy upset. He does *look* uncommon soft, and his face grew red when the snow fell, but his eyebrow and his under lip shewed that it wasn't from fear."

During that afternoon and the greater part of that night the three friends continued in close conversation, Harry sitting in front of the stove, with his hands in his pockets, on a chair tilted as usual on its hind legs, and pouring out volleys of questions, which were pithily answered by the good-humoured, loquacious hunter, who sat behind the stove, resting his elbows on his knees, and smoking his much-loved pipe; while Hamilton reclined on Harry's bed, and listened with eager avidity to anecdotes and stories, which seemed, like the narrator's pipe, to be inexhaustible.

"Good night, Jacques, good night," said Harry, as the latter rose at last to depart, " I'm delighted to have had a talk with you. You must come back to-morrow. I want to hear more about your friend Redfeather. Where did you say you left him ?"

" In the Saskatchewan, master. He said that he would wait there, as he'd heer'd the missionary was comin' up to pay the Injins a visit."

" By the bye, you're going over to the missionary's place to-morrow, are you not ?"

" Yes, I am."

" Ah ! then, that'll do. I'll go over with you. How far off is it ?"

" Three miles, or thereabouts."

"Very good. Call in here as you pass, and my friend Hamilton and I will accompany you. Good night."

Jacques thrust his pipe into his bosom, held out his horny hand, and giving his young friends a hearty shake, turned and strode from the room.

On the following day, Jacques called, according to promise, and the three friends set off together to visit the Indian village. This missionary station was under the management of a Wesleyan clergyman, Pastor Conway by name, an excellent man, of about forty-five years of age, with an energetic mind and body, a bald head, a mild, expressive countenance, and a robust constitution. He was admirably qualified for his position, having a natural aptitude for every sort of work that man is usually called on to perform. His chief care was for the instruction of the Indians, whom he had induced to settle around him, in the great and all-important truths of Christianity. He invented an alphabet, and taught them to write and read their own language. He commenced the laborious task of translating the Scriptures into the Cree language; and, being an excellent musician, he instructed his converts to sing in parts the psalms and Wesleyan hymns, many of which are exceedingly beautiful. A school was also established, and a church built, under his superintendence, so that the natives assembled, in an orderly way, in a commodious sanctuary. every Sabbath-day, to worship God; while the children were instructed, not only in the Scriptures, and made familiar with the narrative of the humiliation and exaltation of our blessed Saviour, but were also taught the elementary branches of a secular education. But good Pastor Conway's energy did not stop here. Nature had

gifted him with that peculiar genius which is powerfully
expressed in the term, "*a jack-of-all-trades.*" He could
turn his hand to anything; and being, as we have said,
an energetic man, he *did* turn his hand to almost everything. If anything happened to get broken, the pastor
could either mend it himself, or direct how it was to be
done. If a house was to be built for a new family of
red men, who had never handled a saw or hammer in
their lives, and had lived up to that time in tents, the
pastor lent a hand to begin it, drew out the plan (not a
very complicated thing, certainly), set them fairly at
work, and kept his eye on it until it was finished. In
short, the worthy pastor was everything to everybody,
"that by all means he might gain some."

Under such management, the village flourished, as a
matter of course, although it did not increase very rapidly,
owing to the almost unconquerable aversion of North
Amercian Indians to take up a settled habitation.

It was to this little hamlet, then, that our three
friends directed their steps. On arriving, they found
Pastor Conway in a sort of workshop, giving directions to
an Indian, who stood with a soldering-iron in one hand,
and a sheet of tin in the other, which he was about to
apply to a curious-looking half-finished machine, that bore
some resemblance to a canoe.

"Ah, my friend Jacques!" he exclaimed, as the hunter
approached him, "the very man I wished to see; but I
beg pardon, gentlemen,—strangers, I perceive. You are
heartily welcome. It is seldom that I have the pleasure
of seeing new friends in my wild dwelling. Pray come
with me to my house."

Pastor Conway shook hands with Harry and Hamilton

with a degree of warmth that evinced the sincerity of his
words. The young men thanked him, and accepted the
invitation.

As they turned to quit the workshop, the pastor
observed Jacques' eye fixed, with a puzzled expression of
countenance, on his canoe.

" You have never seen anything like that before, I
dare say," said he, with a smile.

" No, sir ; I never did see such a queer machine afore."

" It is a tin canoe, with which I hope to pass through
many miles of country this spring, on my way to visit a
tribe of Northern Indians ; and it was about this very
thing that I wanted to see you, my friend."

Jacques made no reply, but cast a look savouring very
slightly of contempt on the unfinished canoe as they
turned and went away.

The pastor's dwelling stood at one end of the village,
a view of which it commanded from the back windows,
while those in front overlooked the lake. It was pleasantly situated, and pleasantly tenanted, for the pastor's
wife was a cheerful, active, little lady, like-minded with
himself, and delighted to receive and entertain strangers.
To her care Mr Conway consigned the young men, after
spending a short time in conversation with them ; and
then, requesting his wife to show them through the village,
he took Jacques by the arm, and sauntered out.

" Come with me, Jacques," he began, " I have somewhat to say to you. I had not time to broach the subject
when I met you at the Company's fort, and have been
anxious to see you ever since. You tell me that you
have met with my friend Redfeather ?"

" Yes, sir ; I spent a week or two with him last fall.

I found him stayin' with his tribe, and we started to come down here together."

"Ah! that is the very point," exclaimed the pastor, "that I wished to inquire about." I firmly believe that God has opened that Indian's eyes to see the truth; and I fully expected, from what he said when we last met, that he would have made up his mind to come and stay here."

"As to what the Almighty has done to him," said Jacques, in a reverential tone of voice, "I don't pretend to know; he did for sartin speak and act too in a way that I never seed an Injin do before;—but, about his comin' here, sir, you were quite right; he did mean to come, and I've no doubt will come yet."

"What prevented him coming with you, as you tell me he intended?" inquired the pastor.

"Well, you see, sir, he, and I, and his squaw, as I said, set off to come here together, but when we got the length o' Edmonton House, we heerd that you were comin' up to pay a visit to the tribe to which Redfeather belongs; and so seein' that it was o' no use to come down here-away just to turn about an' go up agin, he stopped there to wait for you, for he knew you would want him to interpret ——"

"Ay," interrupted the pastor, "that's true. I have two reasons for wishing to have him here. The primary one is, that he may get good to his immortal soul; and then, he understands English so well, that I want him to become my interpreter; for, although I *understand* the Cree language pretty well now, I find it exceedingly difficult to explain the doctrines of the Bible to my people in it. But pardon me. I interrupted you."

"I was only going to say," resumed Jacques, "that I made up my mind to stay with him; but they wanted a man to bring the winter packet here; so, as they pressed me very hard, an' I had nothin' particular to do, I 'greed and came; though I would rather ha' stopped, for Red-feather an' I ha' struck up a friendship togither,—a thing that I would niver ha' thought it poss'ble for me to do with a red Injin."

"And why not with a red Indian, friend?" inquired the pastor, while a shade of sadness passed over his mild features, as if unpleasant thoughts had been roused by the hunter's speech.

"Well, it's not easy to say why," rejoined the other. "I've no partic'lar objection to the redskins. There's only one man among them that I bears a grudge agin, and even that one I'd rayther avoid than otherwise."

"But you should *forgive* him, Jacques; the Bible tells us not only to bear our enemies no grudge, but to love them and to do them good."

The hunter's brow darkened. "That's impossible, sir," he said; "I couldn't do *him* a good turn if I was to try ever so hard. He may bless his stars that I don't want to do him mischief; but to *love him*, it's jist imposs'ble."

"With man it is impossible, but with God *all* things are possible," said the pastor, solemnly.

Jacques' naturally philosophic, though untutored mind, saw the force of this. He felt that God, who had formed his soul, his body, and the wonderfully complicated ma-chinery and objects of nature, which were patent to his observant and reflective mind wherever he went, must, of necessity, be equally able to alter, influence, and re-mould them all according to his will. Common sense was suf-

22

ficient to teach him this; and the bold hunter exhibited
no ordinary amount of common sense in admitting the fact
at once; although, in the case under discussion, (the loving
of his enemy), it seemed utterly impossible to his feelings
and experience. The frown, therefore, passed from his
brow, while he said respectfully, "What you say, sir, is
true; I believe, though I can't *feel* it. But I s'pose the
reason I niver felt much drawn to the redskins is, that
all the time I lived in the settlements, I was used to hear
them called and treated as thievin' dogs, an' when I com'd
among them I didn't see much to alter my opinion. Here
an' there I have found one or two honest Injins, an' Redfeather is as true as steel; but the most o' them are no
better than they should be. I s'pose I don't think much
o' them just because they *are* redskins."

"Ah, Jacques, you will excuse me if I say that there is
not much sense in *that* reason. An Indian cannot help
being a red man any more than you can help being a
white one, so that he ought not to be despised on that
account. Besides, God made him what he is, and to despise the *work* of God, or to undervalue it, is to despise
God himself. You may indeed despise, or rather, abhor,
the sins that red men are guilty of; but if you despise
them on this ground, you must much more despise white
men, for *they* are guilty of greater iniquities than Indians
are. They have more knowledge, and are therefore more
inexcusable when they sin; and any one who has travelled
much must be aware, that, in regard to general wickedness,
white men are at least quite as bad as Indians. Depend
upon it, Jacques, that there will be Indians found in
heaven at the last day as well as white men. God is no
respecter of persons."

"I niver thought much on that subject afore, sir," returned the hunter; "what you say seems reasonable enough. I'm sure an' sartin, any way, that if there's a redskin in heaven at all, Redfeather will be there, an' I only hope that I may be there too to keep him company."

"I hope so, my friend," said the pastor, earnestly, "I hope so too, with all my heart. And if you will accept of this little book, it will shew you how to get there."

The missionary drew a small, plainly-bound copy of the Bible from his pocket, as he spoke, and presented it to Jacques, who received it with a smile, and thanked him; saying, at the same time, that he "was not much up to book-larnin', but he would read it with pleasure."

"Now, Jacques," said the pastor, after a little farther conversation on the subject of the Bible, in which he endeavoured to impress upon him the absolute necessity of being acquainted with the blessed truths which it contains—"Now, Jacques, about my visit to the Indians. I intend, if the Almighty spares me, to embark in yon tin canoe that you found me engaged with, and, with six men to work it, proceed to the country of the Knisteneux Indians, visit their chief camp, and preach to them there as long as the weather will permit. When the season is pretty well advanced and winter threatens to cut off my retreat, I shall re-embark in my canoe and return home. By this means I hope to be able to sow the good seed of Christian truth in the hearts of men, who, as they will not come to this settlement, have no chance of being brought under the power of the gospel by any other means."

Jacques gave one of his quiet smiles on hearing this. "Right sir, right," he said, with some energy; "I have always thought, although I niver made bold to say it

before, that there was not enough o' this sort o' thing.
It has always seemed to me a kind o' madness (excuse my
plainness o' speech, sir) in you pastors, thinkin' to make
the redskins come an' settle round you like so many squaws,
and dig up an' grub at the ground, when its quite clear
that their natur' and the natur' o' things about them
meant them to be hunters. An' surely since the Almighty
made them hunters, He intended them to *be* hunters, an'
won't refuse to make them Christians on *that* account. A
redskin's natur' is a huntin' natur', an' nothin' on arth 'll
ever make it anything else."

"There is much truth in what you observe, friend,"
rejoined the pastor; "but you are not *altogether* right.
Their nature *may* be changed, although, certainly, nothing
on *earth* will change it. Look at that frozen lake." He
pointed to the wide field of thick snow-covered ice that
stretched out for miles like a sheet of white marble
before them. "Could anything on earth break up or
sink or melt that?"

"Nothin'," replied Jacques, laconically.

"But the warm beams of yon glorious sun can do it,"
continued the pastor, pointing upwards as he spoke, "and
do it effectually too; so that, although you can scarcely
observe the process, it nevertheless turns the hard, thick,
solid ice into limpid water at last. So is it in regard to
man. Nothing on earth can change his heart or alter his
nature; but our Saviour, who is called the Sun of righteousness, can. When he shines into a man's soul, it melts.
The old man becomes a little child—the wild savage a
Christian. But I agree with you in thinking that we have
not been sufficiently alive to the necessity of seeking to con
vert the Indians before trying to gather them round us

The one would follow as a natural consequence, I think, of the other; and it is owing to this conviction that I intend, as I have already said, to make a journey in spring to visit those who will not or cannot come to visit me; and now, what I want to ask is, whether you will agree to accompany me as steersman and guide on my expedition?"

The hunter slowly shook his head. "I'm afeerd not, sir; I have already promised to take charge of a canoe for the Company. I would much rather go with you, but I must keep my word."

"Certainly, Jacques, certainly, that settles the question, you cannot go with me—unless——" the pastor paused as if in thought for a moment—"unless you can persuade them to let you off."

"Well, sir, I can try," returned Jacques.

"Do, and I need not say how happy I shall be if you succeed. Good day, friend, good-bye;" so saying, the missionary shook hands with the hunter, and returned to his house, while Jacques wended his way to the village in search of Harry and Hamilton.

CHAPTER XXV.

Good news and romantic scenery ; bear-hunting and its results.

JACQUES failed in his attempt to break off his engagement
with the fur-traders.   The gentleman in charge of
Norway House, albeit a good-natured, estimable man,
was one who could not easily brook disappointment,
especially in matters that involved the interests of the
Hudson's Bay Company ; so Jacques was obliged to hold
to his compact, and the pastor had to search for another
guide.

Spring came, and with it the awakening (if we may
use the expression) of the country from the long, lethargic
sleep of winter. The sun burst forth with irresistible
power, and melted all before it. Ice and snow quickly
dissolved, and set free the waters of swamp and river,
lake and sea, to leap and sparkle in their new-found
liberty. Birds renewed their visits to the regions of the
north ; frogs, at last unfrozen, opened their leathern jaws
to croak and whistle in the marshes ; and men began their
preparations for a summer campaign.

At the commencement of the season an express arrived
with letters from head-quarters, which, among other
matters of importance, directed that Messrs Somerville
and Hamilton should be despatched forthwith to the
Saskatchewan district, where, on reaching Fort Pitt, they
were to place themselves at the disposal of the gentleman

in charge of the district. It need scarcely be added that
the young men were overjoyed on receiving this almost
unhoped-for intelligence, and that Harry expressed his
satisfaction in his usual hilarious manner, asserting somewhat profanely, in the excess of his glee, that the governor-
in-chief of Rupert's Land was a "regular brick." Hamilton
agreed to all his friend's remarks with a quiet smile,
accompanied by a slight chuckle, and a somewhat desperate attempt at a caper, which attempt, bordering as it
did on a region of buffoonery into which our quiet and
gentlemanly friend had never dared hitherto to venture,
proved an awkward and utter failure. He felt this and
blushed deeply.

It was further arranged and agreed upon that the
young men should accompany Jacques Caradoc in his
canoe. Having become sufficiently expert canoe-men to
handle their paddles well, they scouted the idea of taking
men with them, and resolved to launch boldly forth at
once as *bonâ-fide voyageurs.* To this arrangement,
Jacques, after one or two trials to test their skill, agreed;
and very shortly after the arrival of the express, the
trio set out on their voyage, amid the cheers and adieus
of the entire population of Norway House, who were
assembled on the end of the wooden wharf to witness their
departure, and with whom they had managed, during
their short residence at that place, to become special
favourites. A month later, the pastor of the Indian
village, having procured a trusty guide, embarked in his
tin canoe with a crew of six men, and followed in their
track.

In process of time, spring merged into summer,—a
season chiefly characterised, in those climes,

heat and innumerable clouds of mosquitoes, whose vicious and incessant attacks render life, for the time being, a burden. Our three *voyageurs*, meanwhile, ascended the Saskatchewan, penetrating deeper each day into the heart of the North American continent. On arriving at Fort Pitt, they were graciously permitted to rest for three days, after which they were forwarded to another district, where fresh efforts were being made to extend the fur trade into lands hitherto almost unvisited. This continuation of their travels was quite suited to the tastes and inclinations of Harry and Hamilton, and was hailed by them as an additional reason for self-gratulation. As for Jacques, he cared little to what part of the world he chanced to be sent. To hunt, to toil in rain and in sunshine, in heat and in cold, at the paddle or on the snowshoe, was his vocation, and it mattered little to the bold hunter whether he plied it upon the plains of the Saskatchewan, or among the woods of Athabasca. Besides, the companions of his travels were young, active, bold, adventurous; and, therefore, quite suited to his taste. Redfeather, too, his best and dearest friend, had been induced to return to his tribe for the purpose of mediating between some of the turbulent members of it, and the white men who had gone to settle among them, so that the prospect of again associating with his red friend was an additional element in his satisfaction. As Charley Kennedy was also in this district, the hope of seeing him once more was a subject of such unbounded delight to Harry Somerville, and so, sympathetically, to young Hamilton, that it was with difficulty they could realise the full amount of their good fortune, or give adequate expression to their feelings. It is therefore probable that

there never were three happier travellers than Jacques,
Harry, and Hamilton, as they shouldered their guns and
paddles, shook hands with the inmates of Fort Pitt, and,
with light steps and lighter hearts, launched their canoe,
turned their bronzed faces once more to the summer sun,
and dipped their paddles again in the rippling waters of
the Saskatchewan river.

As their bark was exceedingly small, and burthened
with but little lading, they resolved to abandon the usual
route, and penetrate the wilderness through a maze of
lakes and small rivers well known to their guide.   By
this arrangement they hoped to travel more speedily, and
avoid navigating a long sweep of the river by making a
number of portages ; while, at the same time, the change-
ful nature of the route was likely to render it more
interesting.   From the fact of its being seldom traversed,
it was also more likely that they should find a supply of
game for the journey.

Towards sunset, one fine day, about two weeks after
their departure from Fort Pitt, our *voyageurs* paddled
their canoe round a wooded point of land that jutted out
from, and partially concealed, the mouth of a large river,
down whose stream they had dropped leisurely during
the last three days, and swept out upon the bosom of a
large lake.   This was one of those sheets of water which
glitter in hundreds on the green bosom of America's
forests, and are so numerous and comparatively insignificant, as to be scarce distinguished by a name, unless
when they lie directly in the accustomed route of the fur-
traders.   But although, in comparison with the fresh-
water oceans of the Far West, this lake was unnoticed and
almost unknown, it would by no means have been

regarded in such a light had it been transported to the
plains of England. In regard to picturesque beauty, it
was perhaps unsurpassed. It might be about six miles
wide, and so long that the land at the further end of it
was faintly discernible on the horizon. Wooded hills,
sloping gently down to the water's edge—jutting pro-
montories, some rocky and barren, others more or less
covered with trees—deep bays, retreating in some places
into the dark recesses of a savage-looking gorge, in others
into a distant meadow-like plain, bordered with a stripe
of yellow sand—beautiful islands of various sizes, scattered
along the shores as if nestling there for security, or
standing barren and solitary in the centre of the lake,
like bulwarks of the wilderness, some covered with
luxuriant vegetation, others bald and grotesque in out-
line, and covered with gulls and other waterfowl,—this
was the scene that broke upon the view of the travellers
as they rounded the point, and, ceasing to paddle, gazed
upon it long and in deep silence, their hands raised to
shade their eyes from the sun's rays, which sparkled in
the water, and fell, here in bright spots and broken
patches, and there in yellow floods, upon the rocks, the
trees, the forest glades and plains around them.

"What a glorious scene!" murmured Hamilton,
almost unconsciously.

"A perfect paradise!" said Harry, with a long-drawn
sigh of satisfaction. "Why, Jacques, my friend, it's a
matter of wonder to me that you, a free man, without
relations or friends to curb you, or attract you to other
parts of the world, should go boating and canoeing all
over the country at the beck of the fur-traders, when you
might come and pitch your tent here for ever!"

" For ever ! " echoed Jacques.

" Well, I mean as long as you live in this world."

" Ah, master," rejoined the guide, in a sad tone of voice, " it's just because I have neither kith, nor kin, nor friends to draw me to any partic'lar spot on arth, that I don't care to settle down in this one, beautiful though it be."

" True, true," muttered Harry, " man's a gregarious animal, there's no doubt of that."

" Anon ?" exclaimed Jacques.

" I meant to say that man naturally loves company," replied Harry, smiling.

" An' yit I've seen some as didn't, master, though to be sure that was onnat'ral, and there's not many o' them, by good luck. Yes, man's fond o' seein' the face o' man."

" And woman too," interrupted Harry. " Eh ! Hamilton, what say you ?—

> 'O woman ! in our hours of ease,
> Uncertain, coy, and hard to please,
> When pain and anguish wring the brow,
> A ministering angel thou !'

Alas! Hammy, pain and anguish and everything else may wring our unfortunate brows here long enough before woman, 'lovely woman,' will come to our aid. What a rare sight it would be, now, to see even an ordinary house-maid or a cook out here ! It would be good for sore eyes. It seems to me a sort of horrible untruth to say that I've not seen a woman since I left Red River, and yet it's a frightful fact, for I don't count the copper-coloured nondescripts one meets with hereabouts to be women at all. I suppose they are, but they don't look like it."

" Don't be a goose, Harry," said Hamilton.

"Certainly not, my friend. If I were under the disagreeable necessity of being anything but what I am, I should rather be something that is not in the habit of being shot," replied the other, paddling with renewed vigour in order to get rid of some of the superabundant spirits that the beautiful scene and brilliant weather, acting on a young and ardent nature, had called forth.

"Some of these same redskins," remarked the guide, "are not such bad sort o' women, for all their ill looks. I've know'd more than one that was a first-rate wife, an' a good mother; though it's true they had little edication, beyond that o' the woods."

"No doubt of it," replied Harry, laughing gaily. "How shall I keep the canoe's head, Jacques?"

"Right away for the pint that lies jist between you an' the sun."

"Yes; I give them all credit for being excellent wives and mothers, after a fashion," resumed Harry; "I've no wish to asperse the character of the poor Indians; but you must know, Jacques, that they're very different from the women that I allude to, and of whom Scott sung. His heroines were of a *very* different stamp and colour!"

"Did *he* sing of niggers?" inquired Jacques, simply.

"Of niggers!" shouted Harry, looking over his shoulder at Hamilton, with a broad grin; "no, Jacques, not exactly of niggers ―― "

"Hist!" exclaimed the guide, with that peculiar subdued energy that at once indicates an unexpected discovery, and enjoins caution, while, at the same moment, by a deep, powerful back-stroke of his paddle, he suddenly checked the rapid motion of the canoe.

Harry and his friend glanced quickly over their shoulders with a look of surprise.

"What's in the wind now?" whispered the former.

"Stop paddling, masters, and look ahead at the rock yonder, jist under the tall cliff. There's a bear a-sittin' there, an' if we can only get to shore afore he sees us, we're sartin sure of him."

As the guide spoke, he slowly edged the canoe towards the shore, while the young men gazed with eager looks in the direction indicated, where they beheld what appeared to be the decayed stump of an old tree, or a mass of brown rock. While they strained their eyes to see it more clearly, the object altered it's form and position.

"So it is," they exclaimed, simultaneously, in a tone that was equivalent to the remark, "Now we believe, because we see it."

In a few seconds the bow of the canoe touched the land, so lightly as to be quite inaudible, and Harry, stepping gently over the side, drew it forward a couple of feet, while his companions disembarked.

"Now, Mister Harry," said the guide, as he slung a powder-horn and shot-belt over his shoulder, "we've no need to circumvent the beast, for he's circumvented hisself."

"How so?" inquired the other, drawing the shot from his fowling-piece, and substituting in its place a leaden bullet.

Jacques led the way through the somewhat thinly scattered underwood, as he replied, "You see, Mister Harry, the place where he's gone to sun hisself is jist at the foot o' a sheer precipice, which runs round ahead of him, and juts out into the water, so that he's got three ways to choose between. He must clamber up the precipice, which'll take him some time, I guess, if he can do it at all ; or he must take to the water, which he don't like, and won't do if he can help it ; or he must run out the way he went in, but as we shall go to meet him by the same road, he'll have to break our ranks before he gains the woods, an' *that* 'll be no easy job."

The party soon reached the narrow pass, between the lake and the near end of the cliff, where they advanced with greater caution, and, peeping over the low bushes, beheld bruin, a large brown fellow, sitting on his haunches, and rocking himself slowly to and fro, as he gazed abstractedly at the water. He was scarcely within good shot, but the cover was sufficiently thick to admit of a nearer approach.

" Now, Hamilton," said Harry, in a low whisper, " take the first shot. I killed the last one, so it's your turn this time."

Hamilton hesitated, but could make no reasonable objection to this, although his unselfish nature prompted him to let his friend have the first chance. However, Jacques decided the matter, by saying, in a tone that savoured strongly of command, although it was accompanied with a good-humoured smile—

" Go for'ard, young man; but you may as well put in the primin' first."

Poor Hamilton hastily rectified this oversight, with a deep blush, at the same time muttering that he never *would* make a hunter; and then advanced cautiously through the bushes, slowly followed at a short distance by his companions.

On reaching a bush within seventy yards of the bear,

Hamilton pushed the twigs aside with the muzzle of his gun; his eye flashed, and his courage mounted, as he gazed at the truly formidable animal before him, and he felt more of the hunter's spirit within him at that moment than he would have believed possible a few minutes before. Unfortunately, a hunter's spirit does not necessarily imply a hunter's eye or hand. Having with much care, and long time, brought his piece to bear exactly where he supposed the brute's heart should be, he observed that the gun was on half-cock, by nearly breaking the trigger in his convulsive efforts to fire. By the time that this error was rectified, bruin, who seemed to feel intuitively that some imminent danger threatened him, rose, and began to move about uneasily, which so alarmed the young hunter lest he should lose his shot, that he took a hasty aim, fired, and *missed*. Harry asserted afterwards that he even missed the cliff! On hearing the loud report, which rolled in echoes along the precipice, bruin started, and, looking round with an undecided air, saw Harry step quietly from the bushes, and fire, sending a ball into his flank. This decided him. With a fierce growl of pain, he scampered towards the water; then, changing his mind, he wheeled round, and dashed at the cliff, up which he scrambled with wonderful speed.

"Come, Mister Hamilton, load again; quick. I'll have to do the job myself, I fear," said Jacques, as he leaned quietly on his long gun, and, with a half-pitying smile, watched the young man, who madly essayed to recharge his piece more rapidly than it was possible for mortal man to do. Meanwhile, Harry had re-loaded and fired again; but, owing to the perturbation of his young spirits, and the frantic efforts of the bear to escape, he missed

Another moment, and the animal would actually have
reached the top, when Jacques hastily fired, and brought it
tumbling down the precipice.   Owing to the position of
the animal at the time he fired, the wound was not mortal;
and, foreseeing that bruin would now become the aggressor,
the hunter began rapidly to re-load, at the same time
retreating with his companions, who, in their excitement,
had forgotten to re-charge their pieces.   On reaching level ground, bruin rose, shook himself, gave a
yell of anger on beholding his enemies, and rushed at
them.

It was a fine sight to behold the bearing of Jacques at
this critical juncture.   Accustomed to bear-hunting from
his youth, and utterly indifferent to consequences when
danger became imminent, he saw at a glance the probabili-
ties of the case.   He knew exactly how long it would
take him to load his gun, and regulated his pace so as
not to interfere with that operation.   His features wore
their usual calm expression.   Every motion of his hands
was quick and sudden, yet not hurried, but performed in
a way that led the beholder irresistibly to imagine that
he could have done it even more rapidly if necessary.
On reaching a ledge of rock that overhung the lake a few
feet, he paused, and wheeled about,—click went the dog-
head, just as the bear rose to grapple with him,—another
moment, and a bullet passed through the brute's heart,
while the bold hunter sprang lightly on one side, to avoid
the dash of the falling animal.   As he did so, young
Hamilton, who had stood a little behind him with an uplifted axe, ready to finish the work should Jacques' fire
prove ineffective, received bruin in his arms, and tumbled
along with him over the rock, headlong into the water,

from which, however, he speedily arose unhurt, spluttering and coughing, and dragging the dead bear to the shore.

"Well done, Hammy," shouted Harry, indulging in a prolonged peal of laughter, when he ascertained that his friend's adventure had cost him nothing more than a ducking; "that was the most amicable, loving plunge I ever saw."

"Better a cold bath in the arms of a dead bear, than an embrace on dry land with a live one," retorted Hamilton, as he wrung the water out of his dripping garments.

"Most true, O sagacious diver! But the sooner we get a fire made the better; so come along."

While the two friends hastened up to the woods to kindle a fire, Jacques drew his hunting-knife, and, with doffed coat and upturned sleeves, was soon busily employed in divesting the bear of his natural garment. The carcase, being valueless in a country where game of a more palatable kind was plentiful, they left behind as a feast to the wolves. After this was accomplished, and the clothes dried, they re-embarked, and resumed their journey, plying the paddles energetically in silence, as their adventure had occasioned a considerable loss of time.

It was late, and the stars had looked down for a full hour into the profound depths of the now dark lake, ere the party reached the ground at the other side of the point, on which Jacques had resolved to encamp. Being somewhat wearied, they spent but little time in discussing supper, and partook of that meal with a degree of energy that implied a sense of duty as well as of pleasure. Shortly after, they were buried in repose, under the scanty shelter of their canoe.

23

CHAPTER XXVI.

An unexpected meeting, and an unexpected deer-hunt; arrival at the outpost disagreement with the natives; an enemy discovered, and a murder.

NEXT morning, they rose with the sun, and, therefore, also with the birds and beasts.

A wide traverse of the lake now lay before them. This they crossed in about two hours, during which time they paddled unremittingly, as the sky looked rather lowering, and they were well aware of the danger of being caught in a storm in such an egg-shell craft as an Indian canoe.

"We'll put in here now, Mister Harry," exclaimed Jacques, as the canoe entered the mouth of one of those small rivulets, which are called in Scotland, *burns*, and in America, *creeks;* "it's like that your appetite is sharpened after a spell like that. Keep her head a little more to the left—straight for the pint—so. It's likely we'll get some fish here if we set the net."

"I say, Jacques, is yon a cloud or a wreath of smoke above the trees in the creek?" inquired Harry, pointing with his paddle towards the object referred to.

"It's smoke, master; I've seed it for some time, and mayhap we'll find some Injins there who can give us news of the traders at Stoney-creek."

"And, pray, how far do you think we may now be from that place?" inquired Harry.

" Forty miles, more or less."

As he spoke, the canoe entered the shallow water of the creek, and began to ascend the current of the stream, which at its mouth was so sluggish as to be scarcely perceptible to the eye. Not so, however, to the arms. The light bark, which, while floating on the lake, had glided buoyantly forward as if it were itself consenting to the motion, had now become apparently imbued with a spirit of contradiction, bounding convulsively forward at each stroke of the paddles, and perceptibly losing speed at each interval. Directing their course towards a flat rock on the left bank of the stream, they ran the prow out of the water and leaped ashore. As they did so, the unexpected figure of a man issued from the bushes and sauntered towards the spot. Harry and Hamilton advanced to meet him, while Jacques remained to unload the canoe. The stranger was habited in the usual dress of a hunter, and carried a fowling-piece over his right shoulder. In general appearance, he looked like an Indian; but, though the face was burnt by exposure to a hue that nearly equalled the red skins of the natives, a strong dash of pink in it, and the mass of fair hair which encircled it, proved that, as Harry paradoxically expressed it, its owner was a *white* man. He was young, considerably above the middle height, and apparently athletic. His address and language, on approaching the young men, put the question of his being a *white* man beyond a doubt.

"Good morning, gentlemen," he began. "I presume that you are the party we have been expecting for some time past to reinforce our staff at Stoney-creek. Is it not so?"

To this query, young Somerville, who stood in ad-

vance of his friend, made no reply, but, stepping hastily
forward, laid a hand on each of the stranger's shoulders,
and gazed earnestly into his face; exclaiming as he did
so—

"Do my eyes deceive me? Is Charley Kennedy before me—or his ghost?"

"What! eh!" exclaimed the individual thus addressed,
returning Harry's gripe and stare with interest, "is it
possible! no—it cannot—Harry Somerville, my old, dear,
unexpected friend!"—and, pouring out broken sentences,
abrupt ejaculations, and incoherent questions, to which
neither vouchsafed replies, the two friends gazed at and
walked round each other, shook hands, partially embraced,
and committed sundry other extravagances, utterly unconscious of, or indifferent to the fact, that Hamilton was
gazing at them, open-mouthed, in a species of stupor, and
that Jacques was standing by, regarding them with a look
of mingled amusement and satisfaction. The discovery of
this latter personage was a source of renewed delight and
astonishment to Charley, who was so much upset by the
commotion of his spirits, in consequence of this, so to
speak, double shot, that he became rambling and incoherent in his speech, during the remainder of that day, and
gave vent to frequent and sudden bursts of smothered enthusiasm, in which it would appear, from the occasional
muttering of the names of Redfeather and Jacques, that
he not only felicitated himself on his own good fortune,
but also anticipated renewed pleasure in witnessing the
joyful meeting of these two worthies ere long. In fact,
this meeting did take place on the following day, when
Redfeather, returning from a successful hunt, with part of
a deer on his shoulders, entered Charley's tent, in which

the travellers had spent the previous day and night, and discovered the guide gravely discussing a venison steak before the fire.

It would be vain to attempt a description of all that the re-united friends said and did during the first twenty-four hours after their meeting;—how they talked of old times, as they lay extended round the fire, inside of Charley's tent, and recounted their adventures by flood and field since they last met;—how they sometimes diverged into questions of speculative philosophy, (as conversations *will* often diverge, whether we wish it or not), and broke short off to make sudden inquiries after old friends; —how this naturally led them to talk of new friends, and new scenes, until they began to forecast their eyes a little into the future; and how, on feeling that this was an uncongenial theme under present circumstances, they reverted again to the past, and, by a peculiar train of conversation, —to retrace which were utterly impossible,—they invariably arrived at *old* times again. Having in course of the evening pretty well exhausted their powers, both mental and physical, they went to sleep on it, and resumed the colloquial *mélange* in the morning.

"And now tell me, Charley, what you are doing in this uninhabited part of the world, so far from Stoney-creek," said Harry Somerville, as they assembled round the fire to breakfast.

"That is soon explained," replied Charley. "My good friend and superior, Mr Whyte, having got himself comfortably housed at Stoney-creek, thought it advisable to establish a sort of half outpost, half fishing-station about twenty miles below the new fort, and, believing (very justly) that my talents lay a good deal in the way of fishing and shooting, sent me to superintend it during the summer months. I am, therefore, at present monarch of that notable establishment, which is not yet dignified with a name. Hearing that there were plenty of deer about twenty miles below my palace, I resolved the other day to gratify my love of sport, and, at the same time, procure some venison for Stoney-creek; accordingly, I took Redfeather with me, and—here I am."

"Very good," said Harry; "and can you give us the least idea of what they are going to do with my friend Hamilton and me when they get us?"

"Can't say. One of you at any rate will be kept at the creek, to assist Mr Whyte; the other may, perhaps, be appointed to relieve me at the fishing for a time, while *I* am sent off to push the trade in other quarters, but I'm only guessing. I don't know anything definitely, for Mr Whyte is by no means communicative."

"An' please, master," put in Jacques, "when do you mean to let us off from this place? I guess the bourgeois won't be over pleased if we waste time here."

"We'll start this forenoon, Jacques. I and Redfeather shall go along with you, as I intended to take a run up to the creek about this time at any rate. Have you the skins and dried meat packed, Redfeather?"

To this the Indian replied in the affirmative, and the others having finished breakfast, the whole party rose to prepare for departure, and set about loading their canoes forthwith. An hour later they were again cleaving the waters of the lake, with this difference in arrangement, that Jacques was transferred to Redfeather's canoe, while Charley Kennedy took his place in the stern of that occupied by Harry and Hamilton.

The establishment of which our friend Charley pronounced himself absolute monarch, and at which they arrived in the course of the same afternoon, consisted of two small log-houses or huts, constructed in the rudest fashion, and without any attempt whatever at architectural embellishment. It was pleasantly situated on a small bay, whose northern extremity was sheltered from the arctic blast by a gentle rising ground clothed with wood. A miscellaneous collection of fishing apparatus lay scattered about in front of the buildings, and two men in a canoe completed the picture. The said two men and an Indian woman were the inhabitants of the place; the king himself, when present, and his prime minister, Redfeather, being the remainder of the population.

"Pleasant little kingdom that of yours, Charley," remarked Harry Somerville, as they passed the station.

"Very," was the laconic reply.

They had scarcely passed the place above a mile, when a canoe, containing a solitary Indian, was observed to shoot out from the shore and paddle hastily towards them. From this man they learned that a herd of deer was passing down towards the lake, and would be on its banks in a few minutes. He had been waiting their arrival when the canoes came in sight, and induced him to hurry out so as to give them warning. Having no time to loose, the whole party now paddled swiftly for the shore, and reached it just a few minutes before the branching antlers of the deer came in sight above the low bushes that skirted the wood. Harry Somerville embarked in the bow of the strange Indian's canoe, so as to lighten the other and enable all parties to have a fair chance.

After snuffing the breeze for a few seconds, the foremost animal took the water and commenced swimming towards the opposite shore of the lake, which, at this particular spot, was narrow. It was followed by seven others. After sufficient time was permitted to elapse, to render their being cut off, in an attempt to return, quite certain, the three canoes darted from the shelter of the overhanging bushes, and sprang lightly over the water in pursuit.

"Don't hurry, and strike sure," cried Jacques, to his young friends, as they came up with the terrified deer, that now swam for their lives.

"Ay, ay," was the reply.

In another moment, they shot in among the struggling group. Harry Somerville stood up, and seizing the Indian's spear, prepared to strike, while his companions directed their course towards others of the herd. A few seconds sufficed to bring him up with it. Leaning backwards a little, so as to give additional force to the blow, he struck the spear deep into the animal's back. With a convulsive struggle, it ceased to swim, its head slowly sank, and, in another second, it lay dead upon the water. Without waiting a moment, the Indian immediately directed the canoe towards another deer; while the remainder of the party, now considerately separated from each other, despatched the whole herd by means of axes and knives.

"Ha!" exclaimed Jacques, as they towed their booty to the shore, "that's a good stock o' meat, Mister Charles. It will help to furnish the larder for the winter pretty well."

"It was much wanted, Jacques; we've a good many mouths to feed, besides *treating* the Indians now and then. And this fellow, I think, will claim the most of

DEER-SPEARING IN THE FAR NORTH

Page 394

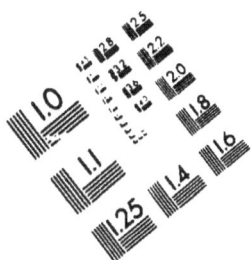

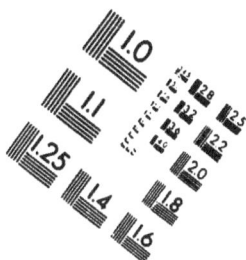

IMAGE EVALUATION
TEST TARGET (MT-3)

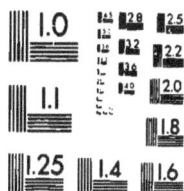

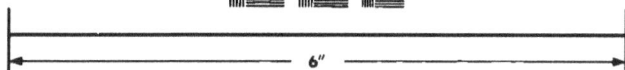

6"

Photographic
Sciences
Corporation

23 WEST MAIN STREET
WEBSTER, N.Y. 14580
(716) 872-4503

our hunt as his own. We should not have got the deer but for him."

"True, true, Mister Charles. They belong to the redskin by rights, that's sartin."

After this exploit, another night was passed under the trees; and at noon, on the day following, they ran their canoe alongside the wooden wharf, at Stoney-creek.

"Good day to you, gentlemen," said Mr Whyte to Harry and Hamilton as they landed; "I've been looking out for you these two weeks past. Glad you've come at last, however. Plenty to do, and no time to lose. You have dispatches, of course. Ah! that's right," (Harry drew a sealed packet from his bosom, and presented it with a bow) "that's right. I must peruse these at once. Mr Kennedy, you will shew these gentlemen their quarters. We dine in half an hour." So saying, Mr Whyte thrust the packet into his pocket, and, without further remark, strode towards his dwelling, while Charley, as instructed, led his friends to their new residence; not forgetting, however, to charge Redfeather to see to the comfortable lodgment of Jacques Caradoc.

"Now it strikes me," remarked Harry, as he sat down on the edge of Charley's bed, and thrust his hands doggedly down into his pockets, while Hamilton tucked up his sleeves and assaulted a washhand-basin, which stood on an unpainted wooden chair in a corner, "it strikes me that if *that's* his usual style of behaviour, old Whyte is a pleasure that we didn't anticipate."

"Don't judge from first impressions, they're often deceptive," spluttered Hamilton, pausing in his ablutions to look at his friend through a mass of soap-suds,—an act

which afterwards cost him a good deal of pain and a
copious flow of unbidden tears.

"Right," exclaimed Charley, with an approving nod to
Hamilton. "You must not judge him prematurely,
Harry. He's a good-hearted fellow at bottom; and if he
once takes a liking for you, he'll go through fire and
water to serve you, as I know from experience."

"Which means to say *three* things," replied the impla-
cable Harry—"first, that for all his good-heartedness *at
bottom*, he never shews any of it *at top*, and is, therefore,
like unto truth, which is said to lie at the bottom of a
well—so deep, in fact, that it is never got out, and so is of
use to nobody; secondly, that he is possessed of that
amount of affection which is common to all mankind, (to
a great extent, even to brutes)—which prompts a man to
be reasonably attentive to his friends; and, thirdly, that
you, Master Kennedy, enjoy the peculiar privilege of
being the friend of a two-legged polar bear!"

"Were I not certain that you jest," retorted Kennedy,
"I would compel you to apologise to me for insulting my
friend, you rascal! But see, here's the cook coming to
tell us that dinner waits. If you don't wish to see the
teeth of the polar bear, I'd advise you to be smart."

Thus admonished, Harry sprang up, plunged his hands
and face in the basin and dried them, broke Charley's
comb in attempting to pass it hastily through his hair,
used his fingers savagely as a substitute, and overtook his
companions just as they entered the mess-room.

The establishment of Stoney-creek was comprised within
two acres of ground. It consisted of eight or nine
houses—three of which, however, alone met the eye on
approaching by the lake. The "great" house, as it was

termed, on account of its relative proportion to the other buildings, was a small edifice, built substantially but roughly of unsquared logs, partially whitewashed, roofed with shingles, and boasting six small windows in front, with a large door between them. On its east side, and at right angles to it, was a similar edifice, but smaller, having two doors instead of one, and four windows instead of six. This was the trading-shop and provision-store. Opposite to this was a twin building which contained the furs and a variety of miscellaneous stores. Thus was formed three sides of a square, from the centre of which rose a tall flagstaff. The buildings behind those just described were smaller and insignificant—the principal one being the house appropriated to the men; the others were mere sheds and workshops. Luxuriant forests ascended the slopes that rose behind and encircled this oasis on all sides, excepting in front, where the clear waters of the lake sparkled like a blue mirror.

On the margin of this lake the new arrivals, left to enjoy themselves as they best might for a day or two, sauntered about and chatted to their hearts' content of things past, present, and future.

During these wanderings, Harry confessed that his opinion of Mr Whyte had somewhat changed; that he believed a good deal of the first bad impression was attributable to his cool, not to say impolite, reception of them: and that he thought things would go on much better with the Indians if he would only try to let some of his good qualities be seen through his exterior.

An expression of sadness passed over Charley's face as his friend said this.

"You are right in the last particular," he said, with a

sigh—"Mr Whyte is so rough and overbearing, that the Indians are beginning to dislike him. Some of the more clear-sighted among them see that a good deal of this lies in mere manner, and have penetration enough to observe that in all his dealings with them he is straightforward and liberal ; but there are a set of them who either don't see this, or are so indignant at the rough speeches he often makes, and the rough treatment he sometimes threatens, that they won't forgive him, but seem to be nursing their wrath. I sometimes wish he was sent to a district where the Indians and traders are, from habitual intercourse, more accustomed to each other's ways, and so less likely to quarrel."

"Have the Indians, then, used any open threats?" asked Harry.

"No, not exactly ; but, through an old man of the tribe, who is well affected towards us, I have learned that there is a party among them who seem bent on mischief."

"Then we may expect a row, some day or other. That's pleasant ! what think you, Hammy ?" said Harry, turning to his friend.

"I think that it would be anything but pleasant," he replied ; "and I sincerely hope that we shall not have occasion for a row."

"You're not afraid of a fight, are you, Hamilton ?" asked Charley.

The peculiarly bland smile with which Hamilton usually received any remark that savoured of banter, overspread his features as Charley spoke, but he merely replied—

"No, Charley, I'm not afraid."

" Do you know any of the Indians who are so anxious to vent their spleen on our worthy bourgeois?" asked Harry, as he seated himself on a rocky eminence, commanding a view of the richly-wooded slopes, dotted with huge masses of rock that had fallen from the beetling cliffs behind the creek.

" Yes, I do," replied Charley ; "and, by the way, one of them—the ringleader—is a man with whom you are acquainted,—at least by name. You've heard of an Indian called Misconna ?"

"What !" exclaimed Harry, with a look of surprise, " you don't mean the blackguard mentioned by Redfeather, long ago, when he told us his story on the shores of Lake Winipeg,—the man who killed poor Jacques' young wife ?"

" The same," replied Charley.

" And does Jacques know he is here ?"

" He does ; but Jacques is a strange, unaccountable mortal. You remember that, in the struggle described by Redfeather, the trapper and Misconna had neither of them seen each other, Redfeather having felled the latter before the former reached the scene of action,—a scene which, he has since told me, he witnessed at a distance, while rushing to the rescue of his wife,—so that Misconna is utterly ignorant of the fact that the husband of his victim is now so near him ; indeed, he does not know that she had a husband at all. On the other hand, although Jacques is aware that his bitterest enemy is within rifle-range of him at this moment, he does not know him by sight ; and this morning he came to me, begging that I would send Misconna on some expedition or other, just to keep him out of his way."

" And do you intend to do so ?"

" I shall do my best," replied Charley ; " but I cannot
get him out of the way till to-morrow, as there is to be a
gathering of Indians in the hall this very day, to have a
palaver with Mr Whyte about their grievances, and Misconna wouldn't miss that for a trifle ;—but Jacques won't
be likely to recognise him among so many ; and, if he
does, I rely with confidence on his powers of restraint and
forbearance. By the way," he continued, glancing upwards, " it is past noon, and the Indians will have begun
to assemble, so we had better hasten back, as we shall be
expected to help in keeping order."

So saying, he rose, and the young men returned to the
fort.   On reaching it, they found the hall crowded with
natives, who sat cross-legged around the walls, or stood in
groups conversing in low tones, and, to judge from the
expression of their dark eyes and lowering brows, they
were in extremely bad humour.   They became silent and
more respectful, however, in their demeanour when the
young men entered the apartment and walked up to the
fire-place, in which a small fire of wood burned on the
hearth, more as a convenient means of re-kindling the
pipes of the Indians when they went out, than as a means
of heating the place.   Jacques and Redfeather stood
leaning against the wall near to it, engaged in a whispered conversation.   Glancing round as he entered,
Charley observed Misconna sitting a little apart by himself, and apparently buried in deep thought.   He had
scarcely perceived him, and nodded to several of his particular friends among the crowd, when a side-door
opened, and Mr Whyte, with an angry expression on his
countenance, strode up to the fire-place, planted himself

before it, with his legs apart and his hands behind him,
while he silently surveyed the group.

"So," he began, "you have asked to speak with me:
well—here I am. What have you to say?"

Mr Whyte addressed the Indians in their native
tongue, having, during a long residence in the country,
learned to speak it as fluently as English.

For some moments there was silence. Then an old
chief—the same who had officiated at the feast described
in a former chapter—rose, and, standing forth into the
middle of the room, made a long and grave oration, in
which, besides a great deal that was bombastic, much
that was irrelevant, and more that was utterly fabulous
and nonsensical, he recounted the sorrows of himself and
his tribe, concluding with a request that the great chief
would take these things into consideration—the principal
" *things* " being, that they did not get anything in the
shape of gratuities, while it was notorious that the Indians in other districts did, and that they did not get
enough of goods in advance, on credit of their future
hunts.

Mr Whyte heard the old man to the end in silence;
then, without altering his position, he looked round on
the assembly with a frown, and said—"Now, listen to
me: I am a man of few words. I have told you over
and over again, and I now repeat it, that you shall get
no gratuities until you prove yourselves worthy of them;
I shall not increase your advances by so much as half an
inch of tobacco, till your last year's debts are scored off,
and you begin to shew more activity in hunting and less
disposition to grumble. Hitherto you have not brought
in anything like the quantity of furs that the capabilities

of the country led me to expect. You are lazy. Until
you become better hunters, you shall have no redress
from me."

As he finished, Mr Whyte made a step towards the
door by which he had entered, but was arrested by another chief, who requested to be heard. Resuming his
place and attitude, Mr Whyte listened with an expression
of dogged determination, while guttural grunts of unequivocal dissatisfaction issued from the throats of several of
the malcontents. The Indian proceeded to repeat a few
of the remarks made by his predecessor, but more con-
cisely, and wound up by explaining that the failure in
the hunts of the previous year was owing to the will of
the Great Manito, and not by any means on account of
the supposed laziness of himself or his tribe.

"That is false," said Mr Whyte; "you know it is not
true."

As this was said, a murmur of anger ran round the
apartment, which was interrupted by Misconna, who,
apparently unable to restrain his passion, sprang into
the middle of the room, and, confronting Mr Whyte,
made a short and pithy speech, accompanied by violent gesticulation, in which he insinuated that, if
redress was not granted, the white men would bitterly
repent it.

During his speech, the Indians had risen to their feet
and drawn closer together, while Jacques and the three
young men drew near their superior. Redfeather remained apart, motionless, and with his eyes fixed on the
ground.

"And, pray, what dog—what miserable thieving cur
are you, who dare to address me thus?" cried Mr Whyte,

as he strode, with flashing eyes, up to the enraged Indian.

Misconna clenched his teeth, and his fingers worked convulsively about the handle of his knife, as he exclaimed—"I am no dog. The palefaces are dogs. I am a great chief. My name is known among the braves of my tribe. It is Misconna ——"

As the name fell from his lips, Mr Whyte and Charley were suddenly dashed aside, and Jacques sprang towards the Indian, his face livid, his eyeballs almost bursting from their sockets, and his muscles rigid with passion. For an instant he regarded the savage intently as he shrank appalled before him—then his colossal fist fell like lightning, with the weight of a sledge-hammer, on Misconna's forehead, and drove him against the outer door, which, giving way before the violent shock, burst from its fastenings and hinges, and fell, along with the savage, with a loud crash to the ground.

For an instant every one stood aghast at this precipitate termination to the discussion, and then, springing forward in a body, with drawn knives, the Indians rushed upon the white men, who, in a close phalanx, with such weapons as came first to hand, stood to receive them. At this moment Redfeather stepped forward unarmed between the belligerents, and turning to the Indians, said—

"Listen! Redfeather does not take the part of his white friends against his comrades. You know that he never failed you in the war-path, and he would not fail you now if your cause were just. But the eyes of his comrades are shut. Redfeather knows what they do not know. The white hunter" (pointing to Jacques) "is a friend of Redfeather. He is a friend of the Knisteneux.

24

He did not strike because you disputed with his bourgeois; he struck because Misconna *is his mortal foe.* But
the story is long. Redfeather will tell it at the council
fire."

" He is right," exclaimed Jacques, who had recovered
his usual grave expression of countenance, "Redfeather is
right. I bear you no ill-will, Injins, and I shall explain
the thing myself at your council fire."

As Jacques spoke, the Indians sheathed their knives,
and stood with frowning brows, as if uncertain what to
do. The unexpected interference of their comrade in
arms, coupled with his address and that of Jacques, had
excited their curiosity. Perhaps the undaunted deport-
ment of their opponents, who stood ready for the en-
counter with a look of stern determination, contributed a
little to allay their resentment.

While the two parties stood thus confronting each
other, as if uncertain how to act, a loud report was heard
just outside the doorway. In another moment, Mr Whyte
fell heavily to the ground, shot through the heart.

CHAPTER XXVII.

The chase; the fight; retribution. Low spirits and good news.

THE tragical end of the consultation related in the last chapter, had the effect of immediately reconciling the disputants. With the exception of four or five of the most depraved and discontented among them, the Indians bore no particular ill-will to the unfortunate principal of Stoney-creek; and, although a good deal disappointed to find that he was a stern, unyielding trader, they had, in reality, no intention of coming to a serious rupture with him, much less of laying violent hands either upon master or men of the establishment.

When, therefore, they beheld Mr Whyte weltering in his blood at their feet, a sacrifice to the ungovernable passion of Misconna, who was by no means a favourite among his brethren. their temporary anger was instantly dissipated, and a feeling of deepest indignation roused in their bosoms against the miserable assassin who had perpetrated the base and cowardly murder. It was, therefore, with a yell of rage that several of the band, immediately after the victim fell, sprang into the woods in hot pursuit of him whom they now counted their enemy. They were joined by several men belonging to the fort, who had hastened to the scene of action on hearing that the people in the hall were likely to come to blows. Redfeather was the first who had bounded like a deer into the woods in pursuit of the fugitive. Those who remained assisted Charley and his friends to convey the body of Mr Whyte into an adjoining room, where they placed him on a bed. He was quite dead; the murderer's aim having been terribly true.

Finding that he was past all human aid, the young men returned to the hall, which they entered just as Redfeather glided quickly through the open doorway, and, approaching the group, stood in silence beside them, with his arms folded on his breast.

"You have something to tell, Redfeather," said Jacques, in a subdued tone, after regarding him a few seconds. "Is the scoundrel caught?"

"Misconna's foot is swift," replied the Indian, "and the wood is thick. It is wasting time to follow him through the bushes."

"What would you advise, then?" exclaimed Charley, in a hurried voice. "I see that you have some plan to propose."

"The wood is thick," answered Redfeather, "but the lake and the river are open. Let one party go by the lake, and one party by the river."

"That's it, that's it, Injin," interrupted Jacques, energetically, "yer wits are always jumpin'. By crossin' over to Duck River, we can start at a point five or six miles above the lower fall, an' as it's thereabouts he must cross, we'll be time enough to catch him. If he tries the lake, the other party'll fix him there; an' he'll be soon poked up if he tries to hide in the bush."

"Come, then, we'll all give chase at once," cried Charley, feeling a temporary relief in the prospect of energetic action. from the depressing effects of the calamity that had so suddenly befallen him in the loss of his chief and friend.

Little time was needed for preparation. Jacques, Charley, and Harry proceeded by the river; while Redfeather and Hamilton, with a couple of men, launched their canoe on the lake, and set off in pursuit.

Crossing the country for about a mile, Jacques led his party to the point on the Duck River to which he had previously referred. Here they found two canoes, into one of which the guide stepped with one of the men, a Canadian, who had accompanied them; while Harry and Charley embarked in the other. In a few minutes they were rapidly descending the stream.

" How do you mean to act, Jacques?" inquired Charley, as he paddled alongside of the guide's canoe. " Is it not likely that Misconna may have crossed the river already? In which case we shall have no chance of catching him."

" Niver fear," returned Jacques. " He must have longer legs than most men if he gets to the flat-rock fall before us, an' as that's the spot where he'll nat'rally cross the river, being the only straight line for the hills that escapes the bend o' the bay to the south o' Stoney-creek, we're pretty sartin to stop him there."

" True; but that being, as you say, the *natural* route, don't you think it likely he'll expect that it will be guarded, and avoid it accordingly?"

" He *would* do so, Mister Charles, if he thought we were *here*; but there are two reasons agin this. He thinks that he's got the start o' us, an' won't need to double by way o' deceivin' us; an' then he knows that the whole tribe is after him, and, consekintly, won't take

a long road, when there's a short one, if he can help it.
But here's the rock. Look out, Mr Charles. We'll have
to run the fall, which isn't very big just now, and then
hide in the bushes at the foot of it till the blackguard
shews himself. Keep well to the right, an' don't mind
the big rock ; the rush o' water takes you clear o' that
without trouble."

With this concluding piece of advice, he pointed to the
fall, which plunged over a ledge of rock about half a mile
ahead of them, and which was distinguishable by a small
column of white spray that rose out of it. As Charley
beheld it, his spirits rose, and forgetting, for a moment,
the circumstances which called him there, he cried out—

"I'll run it before you, Jacques. Hurrah! Give
way, Harry!" and, in spite of a remonstrance from the
guide, he shot the canoe ahead, gave vent to another
reckless shout, and flew, rather than glided, down the
stream. On seeing this, the guide held back, so as to give
him sufficient time to take the plunge ere he followed.
A few strokes brought Charley's canoe to the brink of
the fall, and Harry was just in the act of raising himself
in the bow to observe the position of the rocks, when a
shout was heard on the bank close beside them. Looking up, they beheld an Indian emerge from the forest, fit
an arrow to his bow, and discharge it at them. The
winged messenger was truly aimed, it whizzed through
the air and transfixed Harry Somerville's left shoulder
just at the moment they swept over the fall. The arrow
completely incapacitated Harry from using his arm, so
that the canoe, instead of being directed into the broad
current, took a sudden turn, dashed in among a mass of
broken rocks, between which the water foamed with

violence, and upset. Here the canoe stuck fast, while its owners stood up to their waists in the water, struggling to set it free,—an object which they were the more anxious to accomplish that its stern lay directly in the spot where Jacques would infallibly descend. The next instant their fears were realised. The second canoe glided over the cataract, dashed violently against the first, and upset, leaving Jacques and his man in a similar predicament. By their aid, however, the canoes were more easily righted, and embarking quickly they shot forth again, just as the Indian, who had been obliged to make a detour in order to get within range of their position, re-appeared on the banks above, and sent another shaft after them,—fortunately, however, without effect.

"This is unfortunate," muttered Jacques, as the party landed and endeavoured to wring some of the water from their dripping clothes, "an' the worst of it is that our guns are useless after sich a duckin', an' the varmint knows that, an' will be down on us in a twinklin'."

"But we are four to one," exclaimed Harry. "Surely we don't need to fear much from a single enemy."

"Humph!" ejaculated the guide, as he examined the lock of his gun. "You've had little to do with Injins, that's plain. You may be sure he's not alone, an' the reptile has a bow with arrows enough to send us all on a pretty long journey. But we've the trees to dodge behind. If I only had *one* dry charge!" and the disconcerted guide gave a look, half of perplexity, half of contempt, at the dripping gun.

"Never mind," cried Charley, "we have our paddles. But I forgot, Harry, in all this confusion, that you are

wounded, my poor fellow — we must have it examined
before doing anything farther."

" Oh ! it's nothing at all—a mere scratch, I think ; at
least I feel very little pain."

As he spoke the twang of a bow was heard, and an
arrow flew past Jacques' ear.

" Ah ! so soon !" exclaimed that worthy, with a look
of surprise, as if he had unexpectedly met with an old
friend. Stepping behind a tree, he motioned to his
friends to do likewise ; an example which they followed
somewhat hastily on beholding the Indian who had
wounded Harry step from the cover of the underwood
and deliberately let fly another arrow, which passed
through the hair of the Canadian they had brought with
them.

From the several trees behind which they had leaped
for shelter, they now perceived that the Indian with the
bow was Misconna, and that he was accompanied by
eight others, who appeared, however, to be totally unarmed ; having, probably, been obliged to leave their
weapons behind them, owing to the abruptness of their
flight. Seeing that the white men were unable to use
their guns, the Indians assembled in a group, and, from
the hasty and violent gesticulations of some of the party,
especially of Misconna, it was evident that a speedy
attack was intended.

Observing this, Jacques coolly left the shelter of his
tree, and, going up to Charley, exclaimed, " Now, Mister
Charles, I'm goin' to run away, so you'd better come
along with me."

" That I certainly will not ! Why, what do you
mean ?" inquired the other, in astonishment.

" I mean that these stupid redskins can't make up
their minds what to do, an', as I've no notion o' stoppin
here all day, I want to make them do what will suit us
best. You see, if they scatter through the wood and
atta.' us on all sides, they may give us a deal o' trouble,
and git away after all ; whereas, if we *run away*, they'll
bolt after us in a body, and then we can take them in
hand all at once, which 'll be more comfortable like, an'
easier to manage."

As Jacques spoke, they were joined by Harry and the
Canadian ; and, being observed by the Indians thus
grouped together, another arrow was sent among them.

" Now, follow me," said Jacques, turning round with
a loud howl, and running away. He was closely followed
by the others. As the guide had predicted, the Indians
no sooner observed this than they rushed after them in a
body, uttering horrible yells.

" Now, then ; stop here ; down with you."

Jacques instantly crouched behind a bush, while each
of the party did the same. In a moment the savages
came shouting up, supposing that the white men were
still running on in advance. As the foremost, a tall,
muscular fellow, with the agility of a panther, bounded
over the bush behind which Jacques was concealed, he
was met with a blow from the guide's fist, so powerfully
delivered into the pit of his stomach, that it sent him
violently back into the bush, where he lay insensible.
This event, of course, put a check upon the headlong pursuit of the others, who suddenly paused, like a
group of infuriated tigers, unexpectedly baulked of their
prey. The hesitation, however, was but for a moment.
Misconna, who was in advance, suddenly drew his bow

again, and let fly an arrow at Jacques, which the latter
dexterously avoided; and, while his antagonist lowered
his eyes for an instant to fit another arrow to the string,
the guide, making use of his paddle as a sort of javelin,
threw it with such force and precision that it struck
Misconna directly between the eyes, and felled him to the
earth.   In another instant, the two parties rushed upon
each other and a general *melée* ensued, in which the white
men, being greatly superior to their adversaries in the
use of their fists, soon proved themselves more than a
match for them all although inferior in numbers.   Charley's
first antagonist, making an abortive attempt to grapple
with him, received two rapid blows, one on the chest and
the other on the nose, which knocked him over the bank
into the river, while his conqueror sprang upon another
Indian.   Harry, having unfortunately selected the biggest
savage of the band, as his special property, rushed upon
him and dealt him a vigorous blow on the head with his
paddle.

The weapon, however, was made of light wood, and,
instead of felling him to the ground, broke into shivers.
Springing upon each other, they immediately engaged in
a fierce struggle, in which poor Harry learned, when too
late, that his wounded shoulder was almost powerless.
Meanwhile, the Canadian having been assaulted by three
Indians at once, floored one at the onset, and immediately
began an impromptu war-dance round the other two,
dealing them occasionally a kick or a blow, which would
speedily have rendered them *hors de combat*, had they not
succeeded in closing upon him, when all three fell heavily
to the ground.   Jacques and Charley having succeeded in
overcoming their respective opponents, immediately has-

tened to his rescue. In the mean time, Harry and his
foe had struggled to a considerable distance from the
others, gradually edging towards the river's bank. Feeling faint from his wound, the former at length sank
under the weight of his powerful antagonist, who endeavoured to thrust him over a kind of cliff, which they had
approached. He was on the point of accomplishing his
purpose, when Charley and his friends perceived Harry's
imminent danger, and rushed to the rescue. Quickly
though they ran, however, it seemed likely that they would
be too late. Harry's head already overhung the bank,
and the Indian was endeavouring to loosen the gripe of
the young man's hand from his throat, preparatory to
tossing him over, when a wild cry rang through the forest,
followed by the reports of a double-barrelled gun, fired in
quick succession. Immediately after, young Hamilton
bounded like a deer down the slope, seized the Indian by
the legs, and tossed him over the cliff, where he turned a
complete summersault in his descent, and fell with a
sounding splash into the water.

"Well done, cleverly done, lad!" cried Jacques, as he
and the rest of the party came up and crowded round
Harry, who lay in a state of partial stupor on the bank.

At this moment Redfeather hastily but silently approached; his broad chest was heaving heavily, and his
expanded nostrils quivering with the exertions he had
made to reach the scene of action in time to succour his
friends.

"Thank God," said Hamilton, softly, as he kneeled
beside Harry, and supported his head, while Charley
bathed his temples, "thank God that I have been in
time! Fortunately I was walking by the river consider-

ably in advance of Redfeather, who was bringing up the
canoe, when I heard the sounds of the fray, and hastened
to your aid."

At this moment, Harry opened his eyes, and, saying
faintly that he felt better, allowed himself to be raised to
a sitting posture, while his coat was removed and his
wound examined. It was found to be a deep flesh wound
in the shoulder, from which a fragment of the broken
arrow still protruded.

"It's a wonder to me, Mister Harry, how ye held on
to that big thief so long," muttered Jacques, as he drew
out the splinter and bandaged up the shoulder. Having
completed the surgical operation after a rough fashion,
they collected the defeated Indians. Those of them that
were able to walk, were bound together by the wrists and
marched off to the fort, under a guard which was
strengthened by the arrival of several of the fur-traders,
who had been in pursuit of the fugitives, and were
attracted to the spot by the shouts of the combatants.
Harry, and such of the party as were more or less
severely injured, were placed in canoes and conveyed to
Stoney-creek by the lake, into which Duck River runs at
the distance of about half a mile from the spot on which
the skirmish had taken place. Misconna was among the
latter.

On arriving at Stoney-creek, the canoe party found a
large assemblage of the natives awaiting them on the
wharf, and, no sooner did Misconna land, than they advanced to seize him.

"Keep back, friends," cried Jacques, who perceived
their intentions, and stepped hastily between them.
"Come here, lads," he continued, turning to his com-

panions, "surround Misconna. He is *our* prisoner, and must ha' fair justice done him, accordin' to white law."

They fell back in silence on observing the guide's determined manner, but, as they hurried the wretched culprit towards the house, one of the Indians pressed close upon their rear, and, before any one could prevent him, dashed his tomahawk into Misconna's brain. Seeing that the blow was mortal, the traders ceased to offer any further opposition, and the Indians rushing upon his body, bore it away amid shouts and yells of execration to their canoes, to one of which the body was fastened by a rope, and dragged through the water to a point of land that jutted out into the lake near at hand. Here they lighted a fire and burned it to ashes.

*   *   *   *   *

There seems to be a period in the history of every one, when the fair aspect of this world is darkened; when everything, whether past, present, or future, assumes a hue of the deepest gloom—a period when, for the first time, the sun, which has shone in the mental firmament with more or less brilliancy from childhood upwards, entirely disappears behind a cloud of thick darkness, and leaves the soul in a state of deep melancholy—a time when feelings somewhat akin to despair pervade us, as we begin gradually to look upon the past as a bright, happy vision, out of which we have at last awakened to view the sad realities of the present, and look forward with sinking hope to the future. Various are the causes which produce this, and diverse the effects of it on differently constituted minds; but there are few, we apprehend, who have not passed through the cloud in one or other of its phases, and who do not feel that this *first* period of

prolonged sorrow is darker, and heavier, and worse to
bear, than many of the more truly grievous afflictions
that sooner or later fall to the lot of most men.

Into a state of mind somewhat similar to that which
we have endeavoured to describe, our friend Charley Kennedy fell immediately after the events just narrated. The
sudden and awful death of his friend Mr Whyte fell upon
his young spirit, unaccustomed as he was to scenes of
bloodshed and violence, with overwhelming power. From
the depression, however, which naturally followed, he
would probably soon have rallied had not Harry Somerville's wound in the shoulder taken an unfavourable turn,
and obliged him to remain for many weeks in bed, under
the influence of a slow fever, so that Charley felt a desolation creeping over his soul, that no effort he was capable
of making could shake off. It is true, he found both
occupation and pleasure in attending upon his sick friend ;
but as Harry's illness rendered great quiet necessary,
and as Hamilton had been sent to take charge of the
fishing-station mentioned in a former chapter, Charley
was obliged to indulge his gloomy reveries in silence. To
add to his wretchedness, he received a letter from Kate
about a week after Mr Whyte's burial, telling him of the
death of his mother.

Meanwhile, Redfeather and Jacques,—both of whom, at
their young master's earnest solicitation, agreed to winter
at Stoney-creek,—cultivated each other's acquaintance
sedulously. There were no books of any kind at the outpost, excepting three Bibles—one belonging to Charley,
and one to Harry, the third being that which had been presented to Jacques by Mr Conway the missionary. This
single volume, however proved to be an ample library to

Jacques and his Indian friend. Neither of these sons of the forest were much accustomed to reading; and neither of them would have for a moment entertained the idea of taking to literature as a pastime; but Redfeather loved the Bible for the sake of the great truths which he discovered in its inspired pages, though much of what he read was to him mysterious and utterly incomprehensible. Jacques, on the other hand, read it, or listened to his friend, with that philosophic gravity of countenance, and earnestness of purpose, which he displayed in regard to everything; and deep, serious, and protracted were the discussions they plunged into, as, night after night, they sat on a log, with the Bible spread out before them, and read by the light of the blazing fire, in the men's house at Stoney-creek. Their intercourse, however, was brought to an abrupt conclusion by the unexpected arrival, one day, of Mr Conway, the missionary, in his tin canoe. This gentleman's appearance was most welcome to all parties. It was like a bright ray of sunshine to Charley, to meet with one who could fully sympathise with him in his present sorrowful frame of mind. It was an event of some consequence to Harry Somerville, inasmuch as it provided him with an amateur doctor, who really understood somewhat of his physical complaint, and was able to pour balm, at once literally and spiritually, into his wounds. It was an event productive of the liveliest satisfaction to Redfeather, who now felt assured that his tribe would have those mysteries explained, which he only imperfectly understood himself; and it was an event of much rejoicing to the Indians themselves, because their curiosity had been not a little roused by what they heard of the doings and sayings of the white missionary, who lived on the

borders of the great lake. The only person, perhaps.
on whom Mr Conway's arrival acted with other than a
pleasing influence, was Jacques Caradoc. This worthy,
although glad to meet with a man whom he felt inclined
both to love and respect, was by no means gratified to
find that his friend Redfeather had agreed to go with the
missionary on his visit to the Indian tribe, and thereafter
to accompany him to the settlement on Playgreen
Lake. But, with the stoicism that was natural to him,
Jacques submitted to circumstances which he could not
alter, and contented himself with assuring Redfeather
that if he lived till next spring, he would most certainly
" make tracks for the great lake," and settle down at the
missionary's station along with him. This promise was
made at the end of the wharf of Stoney-creek, the morning
on which Mr Conway and his party embarked in their
tin canoe,—the same tin canoe at which Jacques had curled
his nose contemptuously when he saw it in process of
being constructed, and at which he did not by any means
curl it the less contemptuously now that he saw it finished.
The little craft answered its purpose marvellously well,
however, and bounded lightly away under the vigorous
strokes of its crew, leaving Charley and Jacques on the
pier gazing wistfully after their friends, and listening sadly
to the echoes of their parting song, as it floated more and
more faintly over the lake.

Winter came ; but no ray of sunshine broke through
the dark cloud that hung over Stoney-creek. Harry
Somerville, instead of becoming better, grew worse and
worse every day, so that when Charley despatched the
winter packet, he represented the illness of his friend to
the powers at head-quarters as being of a nature that re

quired serious and immediate attention, and change of
scene. But the word *immediate* bears a slightly different
si_nification in the backwoods to what it does in the lands
of railroads and steamboats. The letter containing this
hint took many weeks to traverse the waste wilderness to
its destination—months passed before the reply was
written, and many weeks more elapsed ere its contents
were perused by Charley and his friend. When they did
read it, however, the dark cloud that had hung over them
so long burst at last—a ray of sunshine streamed down
brightly upon their hearts, and never forsook them again,
although it did lose a little of its brilliancy after the first
flash. It was on a rich, dewy, cheerful morning in early
spring when the packet arrived, and Charley led Harry,
who was slowly recovering his wonted health and spirits,
to their favourite rocky resting-place on the margin of the
lake. Here he placed the letter in his friend's hand, with
a smile of genuine delight. It ran as follows :—

My DEAR SIR,—Your letter, containing the account
of Mr Somerville's illness, has been forwarded to me; and
I am instructed to inform you that leave of absence, for a
short time, has been granted to him. I have had a conversation with the doctor here, who advises me to recommend that, if your friend has no other summer residence
in view, he should spend part of his time in Red River
settlement. In the event of his agreeing to this, I would
suggest that he should leave Stoney-creek with the first
brigade in spring, or by express canoe, if you think it
advisable.—I am, &c.

" Short but sweet, uncommonly sweet!" said Harry,
25

as a deep flush of joy crimsoned his pale cheeks, while his
own merry smile, that had been absent for many a weary
day, returned once more to its old haunt, and danced
round its accustomed dimples like a repentant wanderer
who has been long absent from, and has at last returned
to, his native home.

"Sweet, indeed!" echoed Charley. "But that's not all;
here's another lump of sugar for you." So saying, he
pulled a letter from his pocket, unfolded it slowly, spread
it out on his knee, and, looking up at his expectant
friend, winked.

"Go on, Charley; pray don't tantalise me."

"Tantalise you! My dear fellow, nothing is farther
from my thoughts. Listen to this paragraph in my dear
old father's letter:—

"'So, you see, my dear Charley, that we have managed
to get you appointed to the charge of Lower Fort Garry,
and as I hear that poor Harry Somerville is to get leave
of absence, you had better bring him along with you. I
need not add that my house is at his service as long as he
may wish to remain in it.'

"There! what think ye of that, my boy?" said
Charley, as he folded the letter, and returned it to his
pocket.

"I think," replied Harry, "that your father is a dear
old gentleman, and I hope that you'll only be half as good
when you come to his time of life; and I think I'm so
happy to-day, that I'll be able to walk without the
assistance of your arm to-morrow; and I think we had
better go back to the house now, for I feel, oddly enough,
as tired as if I had had a long walk. Ah! Charley,
my dear fellow, that letter will prove to be the best

doctor I have had yet.   But now tell me what you intend to do."

Charley assisted his friend to rise, and led him slowly back to the house, as he replied—

" Do, my boy ?   That's soon said.   I'll make things square and straight at Stoney-creek; I'll send for Hamilton, and make him interim commander-in-chief; I'll write two letters, one to the gentleman in charge of the district, telling him of my movements; the other (containing a screed of formal instructions) to the miserable mortal who shall succeed me here; I'll take the best canoe in our store, load it with provisions, put you carefully in the middle of it, stick Jacques in the bow, and myself in the stern, and start, two weeks hence, neck and crop, head over heels, through thick and thin, wet and dry, over portage, river, fall, and lake, for Red River settlement !"

CHAPTER XXVIII.

Old friends and scenes; coming events cast their shadows before

Mr KENNEDY, senior, was seated in his own comfortable arm-chair before the fire, in his own cheerful little parlour, in his own snug house, at Red River; with his own highly characteristic breakfast of buffalo-steaks, tea, and pemican before him, and his own beautiful, affectionate daughter Kate presiding over the tea-pot, and exercising unwarrantably despotic sway over a large gray cat, whose sole happiness seemed to consist in subjecting Mr Kennedy to perpetual annoyance, and whose main object in life was to catch its master and mistress off their guard, that it might go quietly to the table, the meat-safe, or the pantry, and there —deliberately—steal !

Kate had grown very much since we saw her last. She was quite a woman now, and well worthy of a minute description here; but we never could describe a woman to our own satisfaction.   We have frequently tried and failed; so we substitute, in place, the remarks of Kate's friends and acquaintances about her—a criterion on which to form a judgment, that is a pretty correct one, especially when the opinion pronounced happens to be favourable.   Her father said she was an angel, and the only joy of his life.   This latter expression, we may remark, was false; for Mr Kennedy frequently said to Kate, confidentially, that Charley was a great happiness to him ; and we are quite sure that the pipe had something to do with the felicity of his existence. But the old gentleman *said* that Kate was the *only* joy of his life, and that is all we have to do with at present. Several ill-tempered old ladies in the settlement said that Miss Kennedy was really a quiet modest girl;—testimony this (considering the source whence it came) that was quite conclusive. Then, old Mr Grant remarked to old Mr Kennedy, over a confidential pipe, that Kate was certainly, in his opinion, the most modest and the prettiest girl in Red River. Her old school companions called her a darling. Tom Whyte said "he never see'd nothink like her nowhere." The clerks spoke of her in terms too glowing to remember; and the last arrival among them, the youngest, with the slang of the "old country" fresh on his lips, called her a *stunner!* Even Mrs Grant got up one of her half-expressed remarks about her, which everybody would have supposed to be quizzical in its nature, were it not for the frequent occurrence of the terms "good girl," "innocent creature," which seemed to contradict that idea. There were also one or two hapless swains who *said* nothing, but what they *did* and *looked* was, in itself, unequivocal. They went quietly into a state of slow, drivelling imbecility whenever they happened to meet with Kate; looked as if they had become shockingly unwell, and were rather pleased than otherwise that their friends should think so, too; and, upon all and every occasion in which Kate was concerned, conducted themselves with an amount of insane stupidity (although sane enough at other times), that nothing could account for, save the idea that their admiration of her was inexpressible, and that *that* was the most effective way in which they could express it.

"Kate, my darling," said Mr Kennedy, as he finished the last mouthful of tea, "wouldn't it be capital to get another letter from Charley?"

"Yes, dear papa; it would, indeed! But I am quite sure that the next time we shall hear from him will be when he arrives here, and makes the house ring with his own dear voice."

"How so, girl?" said the old trader, with a smile. It may as well be remarked here that the above opening of conversation was by no means new. It was stereotyped now. Ever since Charley had been appointed to the management of Lower Fort Garry, his father had been so engrossed by the idea, and spoke of it to Kate so frequently, that he had got into a way of feeling as if the event so much desired would happen in a few days, although he knew quite well that it could not, in the course of ordinary or extra-ordinary circumstances, occur in less than several months. However, as time rolled on, he began regularly, every day or two, to ask Kate questions about Charley that she could not by any possibility answer, but which, he knew from experience, would lead her into a confabulation about his son, which helped a little to allay his impatience.

"Why, you see, father," she replied, "it is three months since we got his last, and you know there has been no opportunity of forwarding letters from Stoney-creek since it was despatched. Now, the next opportunity that occurs ——"

"Mee-now!" interrupted the cat, which had just finished two pats of fresh butter without being detected, and began, rather recklessly, to exult.

"Hang that cat!" cried the old gentleman, angrily.

"it'll be the death o' me yet;" and, seizing the first
thing that came to hand, which happened to be the loaf
of bread, discharged it with such violence, and with so
correct an aim, that it knocked, not only the cat, but
the tea-pot and sugar-bowl also, off the table.

"O dear papa!" exclaimed Kate.

"Really, my dear," cried Mr Kennedy, half-angry and
half-ashamed, "we must get rid of that brute immediately. It has scarcely been a week here, and it has done
more mischief already than a score of ordinary cats would
have done in a twelvemonth."

"But then, the mice, papa ——"

"Well, but—but—oh! hang the mice!"

"Yes; but how are we to catch them?" said Kate.

At this moment, the cook, who had heard the sound of
breaking crockery, and judged it expedient that he should
be present, opened the door.

"How now, rascal!" exclaimed his master, striding up
to him. "Did I ring for you? eh?"

"No, sir; but ——"

"But! eh! but! no more buts, you scoundrel, else
I'll ——"

The motion of Mr Kennedy's fist warned the cook to
make a precipitate retreat, which he did at the same
moment that the cat resolved to run for its life. This
caused them to meet in the doorway, and, making a compound entanglement with the mat, they both fell into the
passage with a loud crash. Mr Kennedy shut the door
gently, and returned to his chair, patting Kate on the
head as he passed.

"Now, darling, go on with what you were saying;
and don't mind the tea-pot—let it lie."

"Well," resumed Kate, with a smile, "I was saying that the next opportunity Charley can have will be by the brigade in spring, which we expect to arrive here, you know, a month hence, but we won't get a letter by that, as I feel convinced that he and Harry will come by it themselves."

"And the express canoe, Kate—the express canoe," said Mr Kennedy, with a contortion of the left side of his head that was intended for a wink,—"you know they got leave to come by express, Kate."

"Oh, as to the express, father, I don't expect them to come by that, as poor Harry Somerville has been so ill that they would never think of venturing to subject him to all the discomforts, not to mention the dangers, of a canoe voyage."

"I don't know that, lass—I don't know that," said Mr Kennedy, giving another contortion with his left cheek. "In fact, I shouldn't wonder if they arrived this very day, and it's well to be on the look-out, so I'm off to the banks of the river, Kate." Saying this, the old gentleman threw on an old fur cap with the peak all awry, thrust his left hand into his right glove, put on the other with the back to the front and the thumb in the middle finger, and bustled out of the house, muttering as he went— "Yes, its well to be on the look-out for him."

Mr Kennedy, however, was disappointed; Charley did not arrive that day, nor the next, nor the day after that. Nevertheless the old gentleman's faith each day remained as firm as on the day previous, that Charley would arrive on *that* day "for certain." About a week after this, Mr Kennedy put on his hat and gloves as usual, and saun-tered down to the banks of the river, where his persever-

FROM THE FAR NORTH.

ance was rewarded by the sight of a small canoe rapidly
approaching the landing-place. From the costume of
the three men who propelled it, the cut of the canoe
itself, the precision and energy of its movements, and
several other minute points about it, only apparent to
the accustomed eye of a nor'wester, he judged at
once that this was a new arrival, and not merely one
of the canoes belonging to the settlers, many of which
might be seen passing up and down the river. As they
drew near, he fixed his eyes eagerly upon them.

"Very odd," he exclaimed, while a shade of disappointment passed over his brow, "it ought to be him, but its
not like him—too big—different nose altogether—don't
know any of the three—humph!—well, he's *sure* to come
to-morrow, at all events." Having come to the conclusion
that it was not Charley's canoe, he wheeled sulkily round
and sauntered back towards his house, intending to solace
himself with a pipe. At that moment he heard a shout
behind him, and, ere he could well turn round to see
whence it came, a young man bounded up the bank and
seized him in his arms with a hug that threatened to
dislocate his ribs. The old gentleman's first impulse was
to bestow on his antagonist (for he verily believed him to
be such) one of those vigorous touches with his clenched
fist, which, in days of yore, used to bring some of his dis-
putes to a summary and effectual close; but his intention
changed when the youth spoke.

"Father, dear, dear father!" said Charley, as he loosened
his grasp, and, still holding him by both hands, looked
earnestly into his face with swimming eyes.

Old Mr Kennedy seemed to have lost his powers of
speech. He gazed at his son for a few seconds in silence,

then suddenly threw his arms around him and engaged
in a species of wrestle, which he intended for an embrace.

"O Charley, my boy!" he exclaimed, "you've come at
last—God bless you! let's look at you—quite changed—
six feet—no, not quite changed—the old nose—black as an
Indian. O Charley, my dear boy! I've been waiting for
you for months; why did you keep me so long? eh! Hang
it, where's my handkerchief?" At this last exclamation,
Mr Kennedy's feelings quite overcame him; his full
heart overflowed at his eyes, so that when he tried to look
at his son, Charley appeared partly magnified and partly
broken up into fragments. Fumbling in his pocket for
the missing handkerchief, which he did not find, he suddenly seized his fur cap, in a burst of exasperation, and
wiped his eyes with that. Immediately after, forgetting
that it *was* a cap, he thrust it into his pocket.

"Come, dear father," cried Charley, drawing the old
man's arm through his, "let us go home. Is Kate there?"

"Ay, ay," cried Mr Kennedy, waving his hand as
he was dragged away, and bestowing, quite unwittingly,
a back-handed slap on the cheek to Harry Somerville,
which nearly felled that youth to the ground. "Ay, ay!
Kate, to be sure, darling; yes, quite right, Charley; a pipe
—that's it my boy, let's have a pipe!" And thus, uttering
incoherent and broken sentences, he disappeared through
the doorway with his long lost and now recovered son.

Meanwhile Harry and Jacques continued to pace
quietly before the house, waiting patiently until the first
ebullition of feeling, at the meeting of Charley with his
father and sister, should be over. In a few minutes
Charley ran out.

"Hallo, Harry! come in, my boy; forgive my forget-
fulness, but ——"

"My dear fellow," interrupted Harry, "what nonsense
you are talking! Of course you forgot me, and everybody, and everything on earth just now; but have you
seen Kate? is ——"

"Yes, yes," cried Charley, as he pushed his friend
before him, and dragged Jacques after him into the
parlour. "Here's Harry, father, and Jacques; you've
heard of Jacques, Kate?"

"Harry, my dear boy," cried Mr Kennedy, seizing his
young friend by the hand, "how are you, lad? Better, I
hope."

At that moment Mr Kennedy's eye fell on Jacques,
who stood in the doorway, cap in hand, with the usual
quiet smile lighting up his countenance.

"What! Jacques! Jacques Caradoc!" he cried, in
astonishment.

"The same, sir; you an' I have know'd each other afore
now in the way o' trade," answered the hunter, as he
grasped his old bourgeois by the hand, and wrung it
warmly.

Mr Kennedy, senior, was so overwhelmed by the combination of exciting influences to which he was now
subjected, that he plunged his hand into his pocket for
the handkerchief again, and pulled out the fur hat instead, which he flung angrily at the cat; then, using the
sleeve of his coat as a substitute, he proceeded to put a
series of abrupt questions to Jacques and Charley simultaneously.

In the mean time, Harry went up to Kate and *stared*
at her. We do not mean to say that he was intentionally

rude to her. No! He went towards her intending
to shake hands, and renew acquaintance with his old
companion; but the moment he caught sight of her, he
was struck not only dumb, but motionless. The odd
part of it was that Kate, too, was affected in precisely
the same way, and both of them exclaimed mentally, "Can
it be possible?" Their lips, however, gave no utterance
to the question. At length Kate recollected herself, and
blushing deeply, held out her hand, as she said—

"Forgive me, Har—Mr Somerville, I was so surprised
at your altered appearance, I could scarcely believe that
my old friend stood before me."

Harry's cheeks crimsoned, as he seized her hand and
said—"Indeed, Ka—a—Miss—that is, in fact, I've been
very ill, and doubtless have changed somewhat; but the
very same thought struck me in regard to yourself, you
are so—so——"

Fortunately for Harry, who was gradually becoming
more and more confused, to the amusement of Charley,
who had closely observed the meeting of his friend and
sister, Mr Kennedy came up.

"Eh! what's that? What did you say *struck* you, Harry,
my lad?"

"*You* did, father, on his arrival," replied Charley, with
a broad grin, "and a very neat back-hander it was."

"Nonsense, Charley," interrupted Harry, with a laugh,
"I was just saying, sir, that Miss Kennedy is so changed
that I could hardly believe it to be herself."

"And I had just paid Mr Somerville the same compliment, papa," cried Kate, laughing and blushing simultaneously.

Mr Kennedy thrust his hands into his pockets, frowned

portentously as he looked from the to th ther, nd
said, slowly, "*Miss* Kennedy, *M* Somer ie!" then
turning to his son, remarked—" at's se ething new,
Charley, lad ; that girl is *Miss* Ken dy, and that youth
there is *Mr* Somerville!"

Charley laughed loudly at this sally, especially when
the old gentleman followed it up with a series of contor-
tions of the left cheek, meant for violent winking.

"Right, father, right, it won't do here. We don't
know anybody but Kate and Harry in this house."

Harry laughed in his own genuine style at this.

"Well, Kate be it, with all my heart," said he;
"but, really, at first she seemed so unlike the Kate of
former days, that I could not bring myself to call her
so."

"Humph!" said Mr Kennedy. "But come, boys,
with me to my smoking room, and let's have a talk over
a pipe, while Kate looks after dinner." Giving Charley
another squeeze of the hand, and Harry a pat on the
shoulder, the old gentleman put on his cap, (with the
peak behind) and led the way to his glass divan in the
garden.

It is perhaps unnecessary for us to say, that Kate Kennedy
and Harry Somerville had, within the last hour, fallen
deeply, hopelessly, utterly, irrevocably, and totally in
love with each other. They did not merely fall up to
the ears in love. To say that they fell *over* head and ears
in it would be, comparatively speaking, to say nothing.
In fact, they did not *fall* into it at all. They went
deliberately backwards, took a long race, sprang high
into the air, turned completely round, and went down
head first into the flood, descending to a depth utterly

beyond the power of any deep-sea-lead to fathom, or of any human mind adequately to appreciate. Up to that day, Kate had thought of Harry as the hilarious youth who used to take every opportunity he could of escaping from the counting-room and hastening to spend the afternoon in rambling through the woods with her and Charley. But the instant she saw him, a man—with a bright cheerful countenance, on which rough living and exposure to frequent peril had stamped unmistakable lines of energy and decision, and to which recent illness had imparted a captivating touch of sadness,—the moment she beheld this, and the undeniable scrap of whisker that graced his cheeks, and the slight *shade* that rested on his upper lip, her heart leapt violently into her throat, where it stuck hard and fast, like a stranded ship on a lee-shore.

In like manner, when Harry beheld his former friend, a woman—with beaming eyes and clustering ringlets, and—(there, we won't attempt it!)—in fact, surrounded by every nameless and nameable grace that makes woman exasperatingly delightful, his heart performed the same eccentric movement, and he felt that his fate was sealed, that he had been sucked into a rapid which was too strong even for his expert and powerful arm to contend against, and that he must drift with the current now, *nolens volens*, and run it as he best could.

When Kate retired to her sleeping apartment that night, she endeavoured to comport herself in her usual manner; but all her efforts failed. She sat down on her bed and remained motionless for half an hour, then she started and sighed deeply; then she smiled and opened her Bible, but forgot to read it; then she rose hastily sighed again, took off her gown, hung it up on a peg, and, returning to the dressing table, sat down on her best bonnet; then she cried a little, at which point the candle suddenly went out, so she gave a slight scream, and at last went to bed in the dark.

Three hours afterwards, Harry Somerville, who had been enjoying a cigar and a chat with Charley and his father, rose, and, bidding his friends good-night, retired to his chamber, where he flung himself down on a chair, thrust his hands into his pockets, stretched out his legs, gazed abstractedly before him, and exclaimed—"O Kate! my exquisite girl, you've floored me quite flat!"

As he continued to sit in silence, the gaze of affection gradually and slowly changed into a look of intense astonishment as he beheld the gray cat sitting comfortably on the table, and regarding him with a look of complacent interest, as if it thought Harry's style of addressing it was highly satisfactory—though rather unusual.

"Brute!" exclaimed Harry, springing from his seat, and darting towards it. But the cat was too well accustomed to old Mr Kennedy's sudden onsets to be easily taken by surprise. With a bound it reached the floor, and took shelter under the bed, whence it was not ejected until Harry, having first thrown his shoes, soap, clothes-brush, and razor-strop at it, besides two or three books, and several miscellaneous articles of toilet—at last opened the door (a thing, by the way, that people would do well always to remember before endeavouring to expel a cat from an impregnable position) and drew the bed into the middle of the room. Then, but not till then, it fled, with its back, its tail, its hair, its eyes—in short, its entire body, bristling in rampant indignation

Having dislodged the enemy, Harry re-placed the bed,
threw off his coat and waistcoat, untied his neckcloth,
sat down on his chair again, and fell into a reverie ; from
which, after half an hour, he started, clasped his hands,
stamped his foot, glared up at the ceiling, slapped his
thigh, and exclaimed, in the voice of a hero—"Yes, I'll
do it, or die !"

CHAPTER XXIX.

The first day at home; a gallop in the prairie, and its consequences.

NEXT morning, as the quartette were at breakfast, Mr Kennedy, senior, took occasion to propound to his son the plans he had laid down for them during the next week.

"In the first place, Charley, my boy," said he, as well as a large mouthful of buffalo steak and potato would permit, "you must drive up to the fort and report yourself; Harry and I will go with you, and, after we have paid our respects to old Grant, (another cup of tea, Kate, my darling,) you recollect *him*, Charley, don't you?"

"Yes, perfectly."

"Well, then, after we've been to see him, we'll drive down the river, and call on our friends at the mill. Then we'll look in on the Thomsons; and give a call, in passing, on old Neverin—he's always out, so he'll be pleased to hear we were there, and it won't detain us. Then ——"

"But, dear father, excuse my interrupting you, Harry and I are very anxious to spend our first day at home entirely with you and Kate. Don't you think it would be more pleasant? and then, to-morrow ——"

"Now, Charley, this is too bad of you," said Mr Kennedy, with a look of affected indignation; "no sooner have you come back, than you're at your old tricks, opposing and thwarting your father's wishes."

26

"Indeed, I do not wish to do so, father," replied Charley, with a smile; "but I thought that you would like my plan better yourself, and that it would afford us an opportunity of having a good, long, satisfactory talk about all that concerns us, past, present, and future."

"What a daring mind you have, Charley," said Harry, "to speak of cramming a *satisfactory* talk of the past, the present, and the future all into *one* day!"

"Harry will take another cup of tea, Kate," said Charley, with an arch smile, as he went on—

"Besides, father, Jacques tells me that he means to go off immediately, to visit a number of his old *voyageur* friends in the settlement, and I cannot part with him till we have had one more canter together over the prairies. I want to shew him to Kate, for he's a great original."

"Oh! that *will* be charming!" cried Kate. "I should like of all things to be introduced to the bold hunter;—another cup of tea, Mr S—Harry, I mean?"

Harry started on being thus unexpectedly addressed. "Yes, if you please—that is—thank you—no, my cup's full already, Kate!"

"Well, well," broke in Mr Kennedy, senior, "I see you're all leagued against me, so I give in. But I shall not accompany you on your ride, as my bones are a little stiffer than they used to be" (the old gentleman sighed heavily), "and riding far knocks me up;—but I've got business to attend to in my glass house which will occupy me till dinner-time."

"If the business you speak of," began Charley, "is not incompatible with a cigar, I shall be happy to ——

"Why, as to that, the business itself has special refe-

rence to tobacco, and, in fact, to nothing else ; so come
along, you young dog," and the old gentleman's cheek
went into violent convulsions as he rose, put on his cap,
with the peak very much over one eye, and went out in
company with the young men.

An hour afterwards, four horses stood saddled and
bridled in front of the house. Three belonged to Mr
Kennedy ; the fourth had been borrowed from a neighbour as a mount for Jacques Caraboe. In a few minutes
more, Harry lifted Kate into the saddle, and, having
arranged her dress with a deal of unnecessary care,
mounted his nag. At the same moment, Charley and
Jacques vaulted into their saddles, and the whole cavalcade galloped down the avenue that led to the prairie,
followed by the admiring gaze of Mr Kennedy, senior, who
stood in the doorway of his mansion, his hands in his vest
pockets, his head uncovered, and his happy visage smiling
through a cloud of smoke that issued from his lips. He
seemed the very personification of jovial good-humour, and
what one might suppose Cupid would become, were he permitted to grow old, dress recklessly, and take to smoking !

The prairies were bright that morning, and surpassingly
beautiful. The grass looked greener than usual, the dew-
drops more brilliant as they sparkled on leaf and blade
and branch in the rays of an unclouded sun. The turf
felt springy, and the horses, which were first-rate animals,
seemed to dance over it, scarce crushing the wildflowers
beneath their hoofs, as they galloped lightly on, imbued
with the same joyous feeling that filled the hearts of
their riders. The plains at this place were more picturesque than in other parts, their uniformity being broken
up by numerous clumps of small trees and wild shrub-

bery, intermingled with lakes and ponds, of all sizes,
which filled the hollows for miles around,—temporary
sheets of water these, formed by the melting snow, that
told of winter now past and gone.   Additional animation
and life was given to the scene by flocks of waterfowl,
whose busy cry and cackle in the water, or whirring
motion in the air, gave such an idea of joyousness in the
brute creation, as could not but strike a chord of sympathy in the heart of man, and create a feeling of grati-
tude to the Maker of man and beast.   Although brilliant
and warm, the sun, at least during the first part of their
ride, was by no means oppressive; so that the equestrians
stretched out at full gallop for many miles over the
prairie, round the lakes and through the bushes, ere their
steeds shewed the smallest symptoms of warmth.

During the ride, Kate took the lead, with Jacques on
her left and Harry on her right, while Charley brought
up the rear, and conversed in a loud key with all three.
At length Kate began to think it was just possible the
horses might be growing wearied with the slapping pace,
and checked her steed ; but this was not an easy matter,
as the horse seemed to hold quite a contrary opinion, and
shewed a desire, not only to continue, but to increase its
gallop,—a propensity that induced Harry to lend his aid
by grasping the rein, and compelling the animal to walk.

"That's a spirited horse, Kate," said Charley, as they
ambled along,—"have you had him long ?"

"No," replied Kate ; "our father purchased him just
a week before your arrival, thinking that you would
likely want a charger now and then.   I have only been
on him once before.   Would he make a good buffalo-
runner, Jacques ?"

"Yes, Miss, he would make an uncommon good runner," answered the hunter, as he regarded the animal with a critical glance,—"at least, if he don't shy at a gunshot."

"I never tried his nerves in that way," said Kate, with a smile; "perhaps he would shy at *that*: he has a good deal of spirit—oh, I do dislike a lazy horse, and I do delight in a spirited one!" Kate gave her horse a smart cut with the whip, half involuntarily, as she spoke. In a moment it reared almost perpendicularly, and then bounded forward—not, however, before Jacques' quick eye had observed the danger, and his ever-ready hand arrested its course.

"Have a care, Miss Kate," he said, in a warning voice, while he gazed in the face of the excited girl with a look of undisguised admiration. "It don't do to wallop a skittish beast like that."

"Never fear, Jacques," she replied, bending forward to pat her charger's arching neck,—"see, he is becoming quite gentle again."

"If he runs away, Kate, we won't be able to catch you again, for he's the best of the four, I think," said Harry, with an uneasy glance at the animal's flashing eye and expanded nostrils.

"Ay, its as well to keep the whip off him," said Jacques. "I know'd a young chap once in St Louis, who lost his sweetheart by usin' his whip too freely."

"Indeed," cried Kate with a merry laugh, as they emerged from one of the numerous thickets and rode out upon the open plain at a foot pace, "how was that Jacques? Pray tell us the story."

"As to that, there's little story about it," replied the

hunter. " You see, Tim Roughead took a'rter his name,
an was always doin' some mischief or other, which more
than once nigh cost him his life ; for the young trappers
that frequent St Louis are not fellows to stand too much
jokin', I can tell ye. Well, Tim fell in love with a gal
there, who had jilted about a dozen lads afore ; and, bein'
an oncommon handsom', strappin' fellow, she encouraged
him a good deal. But Tim had a suspicion that Louise
was rayther sweet on a young storekeeper's clerk there ;
so, bein' an off-hand sort o' critter, he went right up to
the gal, and says to her, says he, ' Come, Louise, its o' no
use humbuggin' with *me* any longer. If you like me, you
like me ; and if you don't like me, you don't. There's only
two ways about it. Now, jist say the word at once an' let's
have an end on't. If you agree, I'll squat with you in
whativer bit o' the States you like to name ; if not, I'll
bid you good-bye this blessed mornin', an' make tracks
right away for the Rocky Mountains afore sun-down.
Aye or no, lass ; which is't to be ?'

"Poor Louise was taken all aback by this, but she knew
well that Tim was a man who never threatened in jest,
an' moreover, she wasn't quite sure o' the young clerk ;
so she agreed, an' Tim went off to settle with her father
about the weddin'. Well, the day came, an' Tim, with
a lot o' his comrades, mounted their horses, and rode off to
the bride's house, which was a mile or two up the river out
of the town. Just as they were startin', Tim's horse gave a
plunge that well-nigh pitched him over its head, an' Tim
came down on him with a cut o' his heavy whip that
sounded like a pistol-shot. The beast was so mad at this
that it gave a kind o' squeal an' another plunge that
burst the girths. Tim brought the whip down on its

flank again, which made it shoot forward like an arrow
out of a bow, leavin' poor Tim on the ground. So slick
did it fly away, that it didn't even throw him on his back,
but let him fall sittin'-wise, saddle and all, plump on the
spot where he sprang from. Tim scratched his head an'
grinned like a half-worried rattlesnake, as his comrades
almost rolled off their saddles with laughin'. But it was
no laughin' job, for poor Tim's leg was doubled under him,
an' broken across at the thigh. It was long before he was
able to go about again, and when he did recover, he found
that Louise and the young clerk were spliced an' away to
Kentucky."

"So you see what are the probable consequences, Kate,
if you use your whip so obstreperously again," cried
Charley, pressing his horse into a canter.

Just at that moment a rabbit sprang from under a bush
and darted away before them. In an instant Harry Somerville gave a wild shout, and set off in pursuit. Whether
it was the cry, or the sudden flight of Harry's horse, we
cannot tell, but the next instant, Kate's charger performed
an indescribable flourish with its hind legs, laid back its ears,
took the bit between its teeth, and ran away. Jacques
was on its heels instantly, and, a few seconds afterwards,
Charley and Harry joined in the pursuit, but their
utmost efforts failed to do more than enable them to keep
their ground. Kate's horse was making for a dense
thicket, into which it became evident they must certainly plunge. Harry and her brother trembled when
they looked at it, and realised her danger ; even Jacques'
face shewed some symptoms of perturbation for a moment,
as he glanced before him in indecision. The expression

vanished, however, in a few seconds, and his cheerful
self-possessed look returned, as he cried out—

"Pull the left rein hard, Miss Kate; try to edge up the
slope."

Kate heard the advice, and, exerting all her strength,
succeeded in turning her horse a little to the left, which
caused him to ascend a gentle slope, at the top of which
part of the thicket lay. She was closely followed by
Harry and her brother, who urged their steeds madly
forward in the hope of catching her rein, while Jacques
diverged a little to the right. By this manœuvre, the
latter hoped to gain on the runaway, as the ground along
which he rode was comparatively level, with a short but
steep ascent at the end of it, while that along which Kate
flew like the wind was a regular ascent, that would prove
very trying to her horse. At the margin of the thicket grew
a row of high bushes, towards which they now galloped
with frightful speed. As Kate came up to this natural fence, she observed the trapper approaching on
the other side of it. Springing from his jaded steed,
without attempting to check its pace, he leaped over
the underwood like a stag, just as the young girl cleared
the bushes at a bound. Grasping the reins, and checking
the horse violently with one hand, he extended the other
to Kate, who leaped unhesitatingly into his arms. At
the same instant, Charley cleared the bushes, and pulled
sharply up; while Harry's horse, unable, owing to its
speed, to take the leap, came crashing through them, and
dashed his rider with stunning violence to the ground.

Fortunately no bones were broken, and a draught of
clear water, brought by Jacques from a neighbouring
pond, speedily restored Harry's shaken faculties.

"Now, Kate," said Charley, leading forward the horse which he had ridden, "I have changed saddles, as you see ; this horse will suit you better, and I'll take the shine out of your charger on the way home."

"Thank you, Charley," said Kate, with a smile, "I've quite recovered from my fright, if, indeed, it is worth calling by that name ; but I fear that Harry has ——"

"Oh! I'm all right," cried Harry, advancing as he spoke to assist Kate in mounting. "I am ashamed to think that my wild cry was the cause of all this."

In another minute they were again in their saddles, and, turning their faces homeward, they swept over the plain at a steady gallop, fearing lest their accident should be the means of making Mr Kennedy wait dinner for them. On arriving, they found the old gentleman engaged in an animated discussion with the cook about laying the table-cloth, which duty he had imposed on himself, in Kate's absence.

"Ah! Kate, my love," he cried, as they entered, "come here, lass, and mount guard. I've almost broke my heart in trying to convince that thick-headed goose that he can't set the table properly. Take it off my hands, like a good girl. Charley, my boy, you'll be pleased to hear that your old friend Redfeather is here."

"Redfeather, father!" exclaimed Charley, in surprise.

"Yes ; he and the parson, from the other end of Lake Winipeg, arrived an hour ago in a tin kettle, and are now on their way to the upper fort."

"That is, indeed, pleasant news ; but I suspect that it will give much greater pleasure to our friend Jacques, who, I believe, would be glad to lay down his life for him, simply to prove his affection."

" Well, well," said the old gentleman, knocking the
ashes out of his pipe, and refilling it so as to be ready for
an after-dinner smoke, " Redfeather has come, and the
parson's come, too, and I look upon it as quite miraculous
that they *have* come, considering the *thing* they came in.
What they've come for is more than I can tell, but I suppose it's connected with Church affairs.   Now, then,
Kate, what's come o' the dinner, Kate ?   Stir up that
grampus of a cook !   I half expect that he has boiled the
cat for dinner, in his wrath, for it has been badgering
him and me the whole morning.   Hallo, Harry, what's
wrong ?"

The last exclamation was in consequence of an expression of pain which crossed Harry's face for a moment.

" Nothing, nothing," replied Harry, " I've had a fall
from my horse, and bruised my arm a little.   But I'll
see to it after dinner."

" That you shall not," cried Mr Kennedy, energetically,
dragging his young friend into his bedroom.   " Off with
your coat, lad.   Let's see it at once.   Ay, ay," he continued, examining Harry's left arm, which was very much
discoloured, and swelled from the elbow to the shoulder,
" that's a severe thump, my boy.   But it's nothing to
speak of; only you'll have to submit to a sling for a day or
two."

" That's annoying, certainly, but I'm thankful it's no
worse," remarked Harry, as Mr Kennedy dressed the
arm after his own fashion, and then returned with him
to the dining-room

CHAPTER XXX.

Love. Old Mr Kennedy puts his foot in it.

ONE morning, about two weeks after Charley's arrival at
Red River, Harry Somerville found himself alone in Mr
Kennedy's parlour. The old gentleman himself had just
galloped away in the direction of the lower fort, to visit
Charley, who was now formally installed there. Kate
was busy in the kitchen giving directions about dinner,
and Jacques was away with Redfeather visiting his
numerous friends in the settlement; so that, for the first
time since his arrival, Harry found himself at the hour
of ten in the morning utterly lone, and with nothing very
definite to do. Of course, the two weeks that had elapsed
were not without their signs and symptoms, their minor
accidents and incidents, in regard to the subject that filled
his thoughts. Harry had fifty times been tossed alternately from the height of hope to the depth of despair,
from the extreme of felicity to the uttermost verge of
sorrow, and he began seriously to reflect, when he remembered his desperate resolution on the first night of
his arrival, that if he did not "do," he certainly would
"die." This was quite a mistake, however, on Harry's
part Nobody ever did *die* of unrequited love. Doubtless many people have hanged, drowned, and shot themselves because of it ; but, generally speaking, if the patient
can be kept from maltreating himself long enough, *time*

will prove to be an infallible remedy. O youthful reader! lay this to heart; but, pshaw! why do I waste ink on so hopeless a task? *Every* one, we suppose, resolves once in a way to *die* of love; so—die away, my young friends—only, make sure that you don't *kill* yourselves, and I've no fear of the result.

But to return. Kate, likewise, was similarly affected. She behaved like a perfect maniac—mentally, that is—and plunged herself, metaphorically, into such a succession of hot and cold baths, that it was quite a marvel how her spiritual constitution could stand it.

But we were wrong in saying that Harry was *alone* in the parlour. The gray cat was there. On a chair before the fire it sat, looking dishevelled and somewhat *blasé*, in consequence of the ill-treatment and worry to which it was continually subjected. After looking out of the window for a short time, Harry rose, and, sitting down on a chair beside the cat, patted its head,—a mark of attention it was evidently not averse to, but which it received, nevertheless, with marked suspicion, and some indications of being in a condition of armed neutrality. Just then the door opened and Kate entered.

" Excuse me, Harry, for leaving you alone," she said, " but I had to attend to several household matters. Do you feel inclined for a walk ?"

" I do, indeed," replied Harry ; " it is a charming day, and I am exceedingly anxious to see the bower that you have spoken to me about once or twice, and which Charley told me of long before I came here."

" Oh ! I shall take you to it, with pleasure," replied Kate ; " my dear father often goes there with me to smoke. If you will wait for two minutes, I'll put on my bonnet," and she hastened to prepare herself for the walk, leaving Harry to caress the cat, which he did so energetically, when he thought of its young mistress, that it instantly declared war and sprang from the chair with a remonstrative yell.

On their way down to the bower, which was situated in a picturesque, retired spot on the river's bank, about a mile below the house, Harry and Kate tried to converse on ordinary topics, but without success, and were at last almost reduced to silence. One subject alone filled their minds—all others were flat. Being sunk, as it were, in an ocean of love, they no sooner opened their lips to speak than the waters rushed in, as a natural consequence, and nearly choked them. Had they but opened their mouths wide and boldly, they would have been pleasantly drowned together; but as it was, they lacked the requisite courage, and were fain to content themselves with an occasional frantic struggle to the surface, where they gasped a few words of uninteresting air, and sank again instantly.

On arriving at the bower, however, and sitting down, Harry plucked up heart, and, heaving a deep sigh, said:—

"Kate, there is a subject about which I have long desired to speak to you ——"

Long as he had been desiring it, however, Kate thought it must have been nothing compared with the time that elapsed ere he said anything else; so she bent over a flower, which she held in her hand, and said, in a low voice—"Indeed, Harry; what is it?"

Harry was desperate now. His usually flexible tongue was still as stone, and dry as a bit of leather. He could no more give utterance to an intelligible idea, than he could change himself into Mr Kennedy's gray cat,—a change that he would not have been unwilling to make at that moment. At last he seized his companion's hand, and exclaimed, with a burst of emotion that quite startled her—

"Kate! Kate! O dearest Kate, I love you! I *adore* you! I ——"

At this point poor Harry's powers of speech again failed; so, being utterly unable to express another idea, he suddenly threw his arms round her, and pressed her fervently to his bosom.

Kate was taken quite aback by this summary method of coming to the point. Repulsing him energetically, she exclaimed, while she blushed crimson—

"Oh, Harry—Mr Somerville!"—— and burst into tears.

Poor Harry stood before her for a moment, his head hanging down, and a deep blush of shame on his face.

"Oh, Kate," said he, in a deep, tremulous voice, "forgive me! Do—do forgive me! I know not what I said. I scarce knew what I did" (here he seized her hand). "I know but one thing, Kate, and tell it you I *will*, if it should cost me my life. I love you, Kate, to distraction, and I wish you to be my wife. I have been rude—very rude. Can you forgive me, Kate?"

Now, this latter part of Harry's speech was particularly comical, the comicality of it lying in this—that, while he spoke, he drew Kate gradually towards him, and, at the very time when he gave utterance to the penitential remorse for his rudeness, Kate was enfolded in a much more vigorous embrace than at the first; and, what is more remarkable still, she laid her little head quietly on his shoulder, as if she had quite changed her mind in regard to what was and what was not rude, and rather enjoyed it than otherwise.

While the lovers stood in this interesting position, it became apparent to Harry's olfactory nerves that the atmosphere was impregnated with tobacco smoke. Looking hastily up, he beheld an apparition that tended somewhat to increase the confusion of his faculties.

In the opening of the bower stood Mr Kennedy, senior, in a state of inexpressible amazement. We say *inexpressible* advisedly, because the extreme pitch of feeling which Mr Kennedy experienced at what he beheld before him, cannot possibly be expressed by human visage. As far as the countenance of man could do it, however, we believe the old gentleman's came pretty near the mark on this occasion. His hands were in his coat-pockets, his body bent a little forward, his head and neck outstretched a little beyond it, his eyes almost starting from the sockets, and, certainly, the most prominent feature in his face; his teeth firmly clenched on his beloved pipe, and his lips expelling a multitude of little clouds so vigorously, that one might have taken him for a sort of self-acting intelligent steam-gun, that had resolved utterly to annihilate Kate and Harry at short range in the course of two minutes.

When Kate saw her father, she uttered a slight scream, covered her face with her hands, rushed from the bower, and disappeared in the wood.

"So, young gentleman," began Mr Kennedy, in a slow, deliberate tone of voice, while he removed the pipe from his mouth, clenched his fist, and confronted Harry, "you've been invited to my house as a guest, sir, and you seize the opportunity basely to insult my daughter!"

"Stay, stay, my dear sir," interrupted Harry, laying his hand on the old man's shoulder, and gazing earnestly into his face—"Oh! do not, even for a moment, imagine that I could be so base as to trifle with the affections of your daughter. I may have been presumptuous, hasty, foolish, mad, if you will, but not base. God forbid that I should treat her with disrespect, even in thought! I love her, Mr Kennedy, as I never loved before ; I have asked her to be my wife, and—she ——"

"Whew!" whistled old Mr Kennedy, replacing his pipe between his teeth, gazing abstractedly at the ground, and emitting clouds innumerable. After standing thus a few seconds, he turned his back slowly upon Harry, and smiled outrageously once or twice, winking at the same time, after his own fashion, at the river. Turning abruptly round, he regarded Harry with a look of affected dignity, and said—"Pray, sir, what my daughter say to your very peculiar proposal ?"

"She said ye—ah! that is—she didn't exactly *say* anything, but she—indeed I ——"

"Humph !" ejaculated the old gentleman, deepening his frown as he regarded his young friend through the smoke. "In short, she said nothing, I suppose, but led you to infer, perhaps, that she would have said Yes, if I hadn't interrupted you."

Harry blushed, and said nothing.

"Now, sir," continued Mr Kennedy, "don't you think that it would have been a polite piece of attention on your part to have asked *my* permission before you addressed my daughter on such a subject ? eh ?"

"Indeed," said Harry, "I acknowledge that I have been hasty, but I must disclaim the charge of disrespect

HARRY'S CONFESSION.

to you, sir; I had no intention whatever of broaching the subject to-day, but my feelings unhappily carried me away, and—and—in fact ——"

"Well, well, sir," interrupted Mr Kennedy, with a look of offended dignity, "your feelings ought to be kept more under control; but come, sir, to my house. I must talk further with you on this subject. I must read you a lesson, sir—a lesson, humph! that you won't forget in a hurry."

"But, my dear sir——" began Harry.

"No more, sir—no more at present," cried the old gentleman, smoking violently as he pointed to the foot-path that led to the house; "lead the way, sir, I'll follow."

The foot-path, although wide enough to allow Kate and Harry to walk beside each other, did not permit of two gentlemen doing so, conveniently,—a circumstance which proved a great relief to Mr Kennedy, inasmuch as it enabled him, while walking behind his companion, to wink convulsively, smoke furiously, and punch his own ribs severely, by way of opening a few safety-valves to his glee, without which there is no saying what might have happened. He was nearly caught in these eccentricities more than once, however, as Harry turned half round, with the intention of again attempting to exculpate himself,—attempts which were as often met by a sudden start, a fierce frown, a burst of smoke, and a command to "go on." On approaching the house, the track became a broad road—affording Mr Kennedy no excuse for walking in the rear, so that he was under the necessity of laying violent restraint on his feelings,—a restraint which, it was evident, could not last long. At that

7

moment, to his great relief, his eye suddenly fell on the gray cat, which happened to be reposing innocently on the door-step.

"*That's* it ! There's the whole cause of it at last!" cried Mr Kennedy, in a perfect paroxysm of excitement, flinging his pipe violently at the unoffending victim as he rushed towards it. The pipe missed the cat, but went with a sharp crash through the parlour window, at which Charley was seated, while his father darted through the doorway, along the passage, and into the kitchen. Here the cat, having first capsized a pyramid of pans and kettles in its consternation, took refuge in an absolutely unassailable position. Seeing this, Mr Kennedy violently discharged a pailful of water at the spot, strode rapidly to his own apartment, and locked himself in.

"Dear me, Harry, what's wrong ? My father seems unusually excited," said Charley, in some astonishment, as Harry entered the room and flung himself on a chair with a look of chagrin.

"It's difficult to say, Charley ; the fact is, I've asked your sister Kate to be my wife, and your father seems to have gone mad with indignation."

"Asked Kate to be your wife !" cried Charley, starting up, and regarding his friend with a look of amazement.

"Yes I have," replied Harry, with an air of offended dignity ; "I know very well that I am unworthy of her, but I see no reason why you and your father should take such pains to make me feel it."

"Unworthy of her, my dear fellow !" exclaimed Charley, grasping his hand and wringing it violently ; "no doubt you are, and so is everybody, but you shall have her for all that, my boy. But tell me, Harry, have you spoken to Kate herself?"

"Yes I have."

"And does she agree?"

. "Well, I think I may say she does."

"Have you told my father that she does?"

"Why, as to that," said Harry, with a perplexed smile, "he didn't need to be told, he made *himself* pretty well aware of the facts of the case."

"Ah! I'll soon settle *him*," cried Charley; "keep your mind easy, old fellow, I'll very soon bring him round." With this assurance, Charley gave his friend's hand another shake that nearly wrenched the arm from his shoulder, and hastened out of the room in search of his refractory father

CHAPTER XXXI.

The course of true love, curiously enough, runs smooth for once ; and the curtain
falls.

TIME rolled on, and with it the sunbeams of summer
went—the snowflakes of winter came. Needles of ice
began to shoot across the surface of Red River, and gradually narrowed its bed. Crystaline trees formed upon
the window panes. Icicles depended from the eves of
the houses. Snow fell in abundance on the plains;
liquid nature began rapidly to solidify, and, not many
weeks after the first frost made its appearance, everything was (as the settlers expressed it) "hard and fast."

Mr Kennedy, senior, was in his parlour, with his back
to a blazing wood fire that seemed large enough to roast
an ox whole. He was standing, moreover, in a semi-
picturesque attitude, with his right hand in his breeches
pocket and his left arm round Kate's waist. Kate was
dressed in a gown that rivalled the snow itself in whiteness. One little gold clasp shone in her bosom; it was
the only ornament she wore. Mr Kennedy, too, had
somewhat altered his style of costume. He wore a sky-
blue swallow-tailed coat, whose maker had flourished in
London half a century before. It had a velvet collar
about five inches deep; fitted uncommonly tight to the
figure, and had a pair of bright brass buttons, very close
together, situated half a foot above the wearer's natural

waist. Besides this, he had on a canary-coloured vest, and a pair of white duck trowsers, in the fob of which *evidently* reposed an immense gold watch of the olden time, with a bunch of seals that would have served very well as an anchor for a small boat. Although the dress was, on the whole, slightly comical, its owner—with his full, fat, broad figure—looked remarkably well in it nevertheless.

It was Kate's marriage-day, or, rather, marriage-evening, for the sun had set two hours ago, and the moon was now sailing in the frosty sky, its pale rays causing the whole country to shine with a clear, cold, silvery whiteness.

The old gentleman had been for some time gazing in silent admiration on the fair brow and clustering ringlets of his daughter, when it suddenly occurred to him that the company would arrive in half an hour, and there were several things still to be attended to.

"Hallo, Kate!" he exclaimed, with a start, "we're forgetting ourselves. The candles are yet to light, and lots of other things to do;" saying this, he began to bustle about the room in a state of considerable agitation.

"Oh! don't worry yourself, dear father," cried Kate, running after him and catching him by the hand. "Miss Cookumwell, and good Mrs Taddipopple, are arranging everything about tea and supper in the kitchen; and Tom Whyte has been kindly sent to us by Mr Grant, with orders to make himself generally useful, so *he* can light the candles in a few minutes, and you've nothing to do but to kiss me and receive the company." Kate pulled her father gently towards the fire again, and re-placed his arm round her waist.

"Receive company! Ah! Kate, my love, that's just what I know nothing about. If they'd let me receive them in my own way, I'd do it well enough; but that abominable Mrs Taddi — what's her name, has quite addled my brains and driven me distracted with trying to get me to understand what she calls *etiquette*."

Kate laughed, and said she didn't care *how* he received them, as she was quite sure that, whichever way he did it, he would do it pleasantly and well.

At that moment the door opened, and Tom Whyte entered. He was thinner, if possible, than he used to be, and considerably stiffer, and more upright.

"Please, sir," said he, with a motion that made you expect to hear his back creak, (it was intended for a bow) —"please, sir, can I do hanythink for yer?"

"Yes, Tom, you can," replied Mr Kennedy; "light these candles, my man, and then go to the stable and see that everything there is arranged for putting up the horses. It will be pretty full to-night, Tom, and will require some management; then, let me see—ah! yes, bring me my pipe, Tom, my big meerschaum, I'll sport that to-night in honour of you, Kate."

"Please, sir," began Tom, with a slightly disconcerted air, "I'm afeer'd sir, that—um ——"

"Well, Tom, what would you say? Go on."

"The pipe, sir," said Tom, growing still more disconcerted; "says I to cook, says I, 'Cook, wots been an' done it, d'ye think?' 'Dun know, Tom,' says he, 'but it's smashed, that's sartin. I think the gray cat ——'"

"What!" cried the old trader, in a voice of thunder, while a frown of the most portentous ferocity darkened his brow for an instant. It was only for an instant, how-

ever. Clearing his brow quickly, he said with a smile,
"But it's your wedding-day, Kate, my darling. It
won't do to blow up anybody to-day—not even the cat.
There, be off, Tom, and see to things. Look sharp! I
hear sleigh-bells already."

As he spoke, Tom vanished perpendicularly; Kate
hastened to her room, and the old gentleman himself
went to the front door to receive his guests.

The night was of that intensely calm and still character that invariably accompanies intense frost, so that
the merry jingle of the sleigh-bells that struck on Mr
Kennedy's listening ear, continued to sound, and grow
louder as they drew near, for a considerable time ere the
visitors arrived. Presently, the dull, soft tramp of horses'
hoofs was heard in the snow, and a well-known voice
shouted out lustily, "Now, then, Mactavish, keep to the
left. Doesn't the road take a turn there? Mind the
gap in the fence. That's old Kennedy's only fault.
He'd rather risk breaking his friends' necks, than mend
his fences!"

"All right, here we are," cried Mactavish, as, the
next instant, two sleighs emerged out of the avenue into
the moonlit space in front of the house, and dashed up
to the door amid an immense noise and clatter of bells,
harness, hoofs, snorting, and salutations.

"Ah! Grant, my dear fellow," cried Mr Kennedy,
springing to the sleigh and seizing his friend by the hand
as he dragged him out. "This is kind of you to come
early—and Mrs Grant, too—take care, my dear madam,
step clear of the laps—now, then—cleverly done" (as
Mrs Grant tumbled into his arms in a confused heap)—
"come along now—there's a capital fire in here—don't

mind the horses, Mactavish—follow us, my lad—Tom
Whyte will attend to them."

Uttering such disjointed remarks, Mr Kennedy led
Mrs Grant into the house, and made her over to Mrs
Taddipopple, who hurried her away to an inner apart-
ment, while Mr Kennedy conducted her spouse, along with
Mactavish and our friend the head clerk at Fort Garry,
into the parlour.

"Harry, my dear fellow, I wish you joy," cried Mr
Grant, as the former grasped his hand.   "Lucky dog
you are. Where's Kate? eh! Not visible yet, I suppose."

"No, not till the parson comes," interrupted Mr
Kennedy, convulsing his left cheek.   "Hallo, Charley,
where are you? Ah! bring the cigars, Charley. Sit
down, gentlemen ; make yourselves at home.   I say, Mrs
Taddi—Taddi—oh ! botheration—popple !—that's it—
your name, madam, *is* a puzzler—but—we'll need more
chairs I think.   Fetch one or two, like a dear !"

As he spoke, the jingle of bells was heard outside, and
Mr Kennedy rushed to the door again.

"Good evening, Mr Addison," said he, taking that
gentleman warmly by the hand as he resigned the reins
to Tom Whyte.   "I am delighted to see you, sir—look
after the minister's mare, Tom—glad to see you, my
dear sir—some of my friends have come already—this
way, Mr Addison."

The worthy clergyman responded to Mr Kennedy's
greeting in his own hearty manner, and followed him
into the parlour, where the guests now began to assemble
rapidly.

"Father," cried Charley, catching his sire by the arm,
" I've been looking for you everywhere, but you danc·

about like a will-o'-the-wisp. Do you know I've invited
my friends Jacques and Redfeather to come to-night, and
also Louis Peltier, the guide, with whom I made my first
trip. You recollect him, father?"

"Ay, that do I, lad, and happy shall I be to see three
such worthy men under my roof, as guests on this night."

"Yes, yes, I know that, father, but I don't see them
here. Have they come yet?"

"Can't say, boy. By the way, Pastor Conway is also
coming, so we'll have a meeting between an Episcopalian
and a Wesleyan. I sincerely trust that they won't fight!"
As he said this, the old gentleman grinned and threw his
cheek into convulsions — an expression which was
suddenly changed into one of confusion, when he observed that Mr Addison was standing close beside him,
and had heard the remark.

"Don't blush, my dear sir," said Mr Addison, with a
quiet smile, as he patted his friend on the shoulder.
"You have too much reason, I am sorry to say, for
expecting that clergymen of different denominations
should look coldly on each other. There is far too much
of this indifference and distrust among those who labour
in different parts of the Lord's vineyard. But I trust
you will find that my sympathies extend a little beyond
the circle of my own particular body. Indeed, Mr
Conway is a particular friend of mine; so I assure you
we won't fight."

"Right, right," cried Mr Kennedy, giving the clergyman an energetic grasp of the hand; "I like to hear you
speak that way. I must confess that I have been a good
deal surprised to observe, by what one reads in the old-
country newspapers, as well as by what one sees even

hereaway in the backwood settlements, how little interest
clergymen shew in the doings of those who don't happen
to belong to their own particular sect, just as if a soul
saved through the means of an Episcopalian was not of
as much value as one saved by a Wesleyan, or a Presbyterian, or a Dissenter; why, sir, it seems to me just as
mean-spirited and selfish, as if one of our chief factors
was so entirely taken up with the doings and success of
his own particular district, that he didn't care a gunflint
for any other district in the Company's service."

There was at least one man listening to these remarks,
whose naturally logical and liberal mind fully agreed with
them.   This was Jacques Caradoc, who had entered the
room a few minutes before, in company with his friend
Redfeather and Louis Peltier.

"Right, sir! That's fact, straight up and down," said
he, in an approving tone.

"Ha! Jacques, my good fellow, is that you? Redfeather,
my friend, how are you?" said Mr Kennedy, turning
round and grasping a hand of each. "Sit down there,
Louis, beside Mrs Taddi—eh?—ah!—popple. Mr Addison,
this is Jacques Caradoc, the best and stoutest hunter
between Hudson's Bay and Oregon."

Jacques smiled and bowed modestly, as Mr Addison
shook his hand. The worthy hunter did indeed, at that
moment, look as if he fully merited Mr Kennedy's
eulogium. Instead of endeavouring to ape the gentleman,
as many men in his rank of life would have been likely
to do on an occasion like this, Jacques had not altered his
costume a hairsbreadth from what it usually was, excepting
that some parts of it were quite new, and all of it fault-
lessly clean. He wore the usual capote, but it was his

best one, and had been washed for the occasion. The scarlet belt and blue leggins were also as bright in colour as if they had been put on for the first time, and the moccasins, which fitted closely to his well-formed feet, were of the cleanest and brightest yellow leather, ornamented, as usual, in front. The collar of his blue striped shirt was folded back a little more carefully than usual, exposing his sunburnt and muscular throat; in fact, he wanted nothing, save the hunting knife, the rifle, and the powder-horn, to constitute him a perfect specimen of a thorough backwoodsman.

Redfeather and Louis were similarly costumed, and a noble trio they looked, as they sat modestly in a corner, talking to each other in whispers, and endeavouring, as much as possible, to curtail their colossal proportions.

"Now, Harry," said Mr Kennedy, in a hoarse whisper, at the same time winking vehemently, "we're about ready, lad. Where's Kate? eh? shall we send for her?"

Harry blushed, and stammered out something that was wholly unintelligible, but which, nevertheless, seemed to afford infinite delight to the old gentleman, who chuckled and winked tremendously, gave his son-in-law a facetious poke in the ribs, and turning abruptly to Miss Cookumwell, said to that lady—"Now, Miss Cookumpopple, we're all ready. They seem to have had enough tea and trash; you'd better be looking after Kate, I think."

Miss Cookumwell smiled, rose, and left the room to obey; Mrs Taddipopple followed to help, and soon returned with Kate, whom they delivered up to her father at the door. Mr Kennedy led her to the upper end of the room—Harry Somerville stood by her side, as if by magic—Mr Addison dropped opportunely before

them, as if from the clouds; there was an extraordinary
and abrupt pause in the hum of conversation, and, ere
Kate was well aware of what was about to happen, she
felt herself suddenly embraced by her husband, from
whom she was thereafter violently torn, and all but
smothered by her sympathising friends.

Poor Kate! she had gone through the ceremony almost
mechanically—*recklessly*, we might be justified in saying;
for not having raised her eyes off the floor, from its commencement to its close, the man whom she accepted for
better or for worse might have been Jacques or Redfeather, for all that she knew.

Immediately after this, there was heard the sound of a
fiddle, and an old Canadian was led to the upper end of
the room, placed on a chair, and hoisted, by the powerful
arms of Jacques and Louis, upon a table. In this conspicuous position the old man seemed to be quite at his ease.
He spent a few minutes in bringing his instrument into
perfect tune; then, looking round with a mild patronising
glance to see that the dancers were ready, he suddenly
struck up a Scotch reel with an amount of energy, precision, and spirit that might have shot a pang of jealousy
through the heart of Neil Gow himself. The noise that
instantly commenced, and was kept up from that moment,
with but few intervals, during the whole evening, was of
a kind that is never heard in fashionable drawing-rooms.
Dancing, in the backwood settlements, *is* dancing. It is
not walking; it is not sailing; it is not undulating; it is
not sliding; no, it is *bonâ fide* dancing! It is the performance of intricate evolutions with the feet and legs that
makes one wink to look at. Performed in good time too,
and by people who look upon *all* their muscles as being

useful machines, not merely things of which a select few,
that cannot be dispensed with, are brought into daily
operation. Consequently the thing was done with an
amount of vigour that was conducive to the health of
performers, and productive of satisfaction to the eyes of
beholders. When the evening wore on apace, however,
and Jacques' modesty was so far overcome as to induce
him to engage in a reel, along with his friend Louis Pei-
tier and two bouncing young ladies, whose father had
driven them twenty miles over the plains that day in
order to attend the wedding of their dear friend and
former playmate, Kate—when these four stood up, we
say, and the fiddler played more energetically than ever,
and the stout backwoodsmen began to warm and grow
vigorous, until, in the midst of their tremendous leaps
and rapid but well-timed motions, they looked like very
giants amid their brethren, then it was that Harry, as he
felt Kate's little hand pressing his arm, and observed her
sparkling eyes gazing at the dancers in genuine admiration, began at last firmly to believe that the whole thing
was a dream ; and then it was that old Mr Kennedy
rejoiced to think that the house had been built under his
own special directions, and he knew that it could not, by
any possibility, be shaken to pieces.

And well might Harry imagine that he dreamed ; for,
besides the bewildering tendency of the almost too-good-
to-be-true fact that Kate was really Mrs Harry Somerville, the scene before him was a particularly odd and
perplexing mixture of widely different elements—suggestive of new and old associations. The company was
miscellaneous. There were retired old traders, whose
lives from boyhood had been spent in danger, solitude,

wild scenes and adventures, to which those of Robinson
Crusoe are mere child's-play. There were young girls, the
daughters of these men, who had received good educations
in the Red River academy, and a certain degree of polish
which education always gives—a very *different* polish, indeed, from that which the conventionalities and refinements
of the old world bestow, but not the less agreeable on that
account—nay, we might even venture to say, all the *more*
agreeable on that account. There were Red Indians and
clergymen; there were one or two ladies, of a doubtful
age, who had come out from the old country to live there,
having found it no easy matter, poor things, to live at
home; there were matrons, whose absolute silence on
every subject save "yes" or "no," shewed that they had
not been subjected to the refining influences of the
academy, but whose hearty smiles, and laughs of genuine
good-nature proved that the storing of the brain has,
after all, *very* little to do with the best and deepest
feelings of the heart. There were the tones of Scotch
reels sounding,—tones that brought Scotland vividly before
the very eyes; and there were Canadian hunters and half-
breed *voyageurs*, whose moccasins were more accustomed
to the turf of the woods than the boards of a drawing-
room, and whose speech and accents made Scotland
vanish away altogether from the memory. There were
old people and young folk; there were fat and lean, short
and long. There were songs too; ballads of England,
pathetic songs of Scotland, alternating with the French
ditties of Canada, and the sweet, inexpressibly plaintive
canoe-songs of the *voyageur*. There were strong contrasts
in dress also—some wore the home-spun trousers of the
settlement, a few the ornamented leggins of the hunter

Capotes were there—loose, flowing, and picturesque ; and
broad-cloth tail-coats were there, of the last century,
tight-fitting, angular, in a word, detestable ; verifying the
truth of the proverb that extremes meet—by shewing
that the *cut*, which all the wisdom of tailors and scientific
fops, after centuries of study, had laboriously wrought out
and foisted upon the poor civilised world as perfectly sublime, appeared, in the eyes of backwoodsmen and Indians,
utterly ridiculous. No wonder that Harry, under the
circumstances, became quietly insane, and went about
committing *nothing* but mistakes the whole evening. No
wonder that he emulated his father-in-law, in abusing the
gray cat, when he found it surreptitiously devouring part
of the supper in an adjoining room ; and no wonder that,
when he rushed about vainly in search of Mrs Taddipopple,
to acquaint her with the cat's wickedness, he at last, in
desperation, laid violent hands on Miss Cooknmwell, and
addressed that excellent lady by the name of Mrs Popple-
taddy.

Were we courageous enough to make the attempt, we
would endeavour to describe that joyful evening from
beginning to end. We would tell you how the company's
spirits rose higher and higher, as each individual became
more and more anxious to lend his or her aid in adding
to the general hilarity ; how old Mr Kennedy nearly
killed himself in his fruitless efforts to be everywhere,
speak to everybody, and do everything at once ; how
Charley danced till he could scarcely speak, and then
talked till he could hardly dance ; and how the fiddler,
instead of growing wearied, became gradually and conti-
nuously more powerful, until it seemed as if fifty fiddles
were playing at one and the same time. We would tell

you how Mr Addison drew more than ever to Mr Conway, and how the latter gentleman agreed to correspond
regularly with the former thenceforth, in order that their
interest in the great work each had in hand for the *same*
Master might be increased and kept up ; how, in a spirit
of recklessness (afterwards deeply repented of), a bashful
young man was induced to sing a song, which, in the
present mirthful state of the company, ought to have
been a humorous song, or a patriotic song, or a good,
loud, inspiriting song, or *anything*, in short, but what it
was—a slow, dull, sentimental song, about wasting gradually away in a sort of melancholy decay, on account of
disappointed love, or some such trash, which was a false
sentiment in itself, and certainly did not derive any
additional tinge of truthfulness from a thin, weak voice,
that was afflicted with chronic flatness, and *edged* all its
notes.   Were we courageous enough to go on, we would
further relate to you how, during supper, Mr Kennedy,
senior, tried to make a speech, and broke down amid up-
roarious applause ; how Mr Kennedy, junior, got up
thereafter,—being urged thereto by his father, who said,
with a convulsion of the cheek, " Get me out of the
scrape, Charley, my boy,"—and delivered an oration,
which did not display much power of concise elucidation,
but was replete, nevertheless, with consummate impudence ; how, during this point in the proceedings, the
gray cat made a last desperate effort to purloin a cold
chicken, which it had watched anxiously the whole evening, and was caught in the very act,—nearly strangled,
and flung out of the window, where it alighted in safety
on the snow, and fled—a wiser, and, we trust, a better
cat.   We would recount all this to you, reader, and a

great deal more besides ; but we fear to try your patience,
and we tremble violently, much more so, indeed, than
you will believe, at the bare idea of waxing prosy.

Suffice it to say, that the party separated at an early
hour—a good, sober, reasonable hour for such an occasion—somewhere before midnight. The horses were
harnessed, the ladies were packed in the sleighs with furs
so thick and plentiful as to defy the cold; the gentlemen
seized their reins, and cracked their whips--the horses
snorted, plunged, and dashed away over the white plains
in different directions, while the merry sleigh-bells
sounded fainter and fainter in the frosty air. In half
an hour, the stars twinkled down on the still, cold scene,
and threw a pale light on the now silent dwelling of the
old fur-trader.

*   *   *   *   *   *

Ere dropping the curtain over a picture in which we
have sought faithfully to portray the prominent features
of those wild regions that lie to the north of the Canadas,
and in which we have endeavoured to describe some of
the peculiarities of a class of men whose histories seldom
meet the public eye, we feel tempted to add a few more
touches to the sketch ; we would fain trace a little
farther the fortunes of one or two of the chief actors in
our book. But this must not be.

Snowflakes and sunbeams came and went as in days
gone by. Time rolled on, working many changes in its
course, and, among others, consigning Harry Somerville
to an important post in Red River colony, to the unutterable joy of Mr Kennedy, senior, and of Kate. After
much consideration and frequent consultation with Mr
Addison, Mr Conway resolved to make another journey to

28

preach the gospel of Jesus Christ to those Indian tribes that
inhabit the regions beyond Athabasca ; and being a man
of great energy, he determined not to await the opening
of the river navigation, but to undertake the first part of
his expedition on snow-shoes. Jacques agreed to go with
him as guide and hunter—Redfeather as interpreter.
It was a bright, cold morning when he set out, accompanied part of the way by Charley Kennedy and Harry
Somerville, whose hearts were heavy at the prospect of
parting with the two men who had guided and protected
them during their earliest experience of a *voyageur's*
life—when, with hearts full to overflowing with romantic
anticipations, they first dashed joyously into the almost
untrodden wilderness.

During their career in the woods together, the young
men and the two hunters had become warmly attached to
each other ; and, now that they were about to part—it
might be for years, perhaps for ever—a feeling of sadness
crept over them, which they could not shake off, and
which the promise given by Mr Conway to revisit Red
River on the following spring, served but slightly to
dispel.

On arriving at the spot where they intended to bid
their friends a last farewell, the two young men held out
their hands in silence. Jacques grasped them warmly.

"Mister Charles, Mister Harry," said he, in a deep,
earnest voice, "the Almighty has guided us in safety
for many a day when we travelled the woods together—
for which praised be His holy name ! May He guide
and bless you still, and bring us together in this world
again, if in His wisdom He see fit."

There was no answer, save a deeply-murmured

tribes that
sing a man
he opening
first part of
l to go with
interpreter.
out, accom-
; and Harry
: prospect of
and protected
a *voyageur's*
with romantic
to the almost

ier, the young
nly attached to
out to part—it
eling of sadness
shake off, and
to revisit Red
but slightly to

intended to bid
ng men held out
them warmly.
l he, in a deep,
led us in safety
woods together—
May He guide
her in this world

" Amen." In another moment, the travellers resumed their march. On reaching the summit of a slight eminence, where the prairies terminated and the woods began, they paused to wave a last adieu ; then Jacques, putting himself at the head of the little party, plunged into the forest, and led them away towards the snowy regions of the Far North.

BOOKS OF HISTORY AND BIOGRAPHY.

BY ROBERT MACKENZIE.

THE 19TH CENTURY. A History. Crown 8vo. 464 Pages. Price 7s. 6d.

Presenting in a handy form a History of the great events and movements of the present century, in our own country, throughout the British Empire, on the Continent of Europe, and in America.

BY W. F. COLLIER, LL.D.

HISTORY OF ENGLAND. To which is added a History of Our Colonial Empire. Crown 8vo, cloth extra. Price 7s. 6d.

BY THE REV. J. C. RYLE, D.D.

THE CHRISTIAN LEADERS OF THE LAST CEN-TURY; or, England a Hundred Years Ago. Crown 8vo, cloth. Price 7s. 6d.

THOMAS CHALMERS, D.D.: His Life and its Lessons. By the Rev. NORMAN L. WALKER, Author of "Robert Buchanan, an Ecclesiastical Biography." Post 8vo, cloth. Price 1s. 6d.

RECOLLECTIONS OF ALEXANDER DUFF, D.D., and of the Mission College which he Founded in Calcutta. By the Rev. LAL BEHARI DAY, Author of "Govinda Samanta;" Professor in Government College, Hooghly. Post 8vo, cloth. Price 3s. 6d.

THE STORY OF SIR DAVID WILKIE: His Life and Works. By ADAM L. SIMPSON, D.D., Derby. With Sixteen Engravings. Post 8vo, cloth extra. Price 2s.

SELF-TAUGHT MEN. A Series of Biographies. With Four Illustrations. Post 8vo, cloth. Price 2s. 6d.

STORIES OF THE LIVES OF NOBLE WOMEN. By W. H. DAVENPORT ADAMS. Post 8vo, cloth. Price 2s. 6d.

JANE TAYLOR: Her Life and Letters. By Mrs. H. C. KNIGHT, Author of "No Pains, No Gains," &c. Post 8vo, cloth. Price 2s.

HEROES OF THE DESERT. The Story of the Lives and Labours of MOFFAT and LIVINGSTONE. With Frontispiece and Vignette. By the Author of "Mary Powell." Post 8vo, cloth extra. Price 3s. 6d.

"ABOVE RUBIES;" or, Memorials of Christian Gentle-women. By Miss C. L. BRIGHTWELL. Post 8vo, cloth extra, gilt edges. Price 3s. 6d.

LIVING IN EARNEST: Lessons and Incidents from the Lives of the Great and Good. By JOSEPH JOHNSON. Post 8vo, cloth. Price 2s. 6d.

LIVING TO PURPOSE. A Book for Young Men. By JOSEPH JOHNSON. Post 8vo, cloth. Price 2s. 6d.

MEMORIALS OF EARLY GENIUS, AND REMARK-ABLE RECORDS OF ITS ACHIEVEMENTS. By the Author of "Success in Life." Post 8vo, cloth extra. Price 2s. 6d.

RECORDS OF NOBLE LIVES. By W. H. DAVENPORT ADAMS. Post 8vo, cloth. Price 2s. 6d.

T. NELSON AND SONS, LONDON, EDINBURGH AND NEW YORK.

BOOKS OF NATURAL HISTORY ILLUSTRATED.

JENNY AND THE INSECTS; or, Little Toilers and their Industries. With Twenty-six Illustrations by GIACOMELLI. Post 8vo, cloth extra, gilt edges. Price 3s. 6d.

TINY WORKERS; or, Man's Little Rivals in the Animal World. With Thirteen Engravings. Price 1s. 6d.

THE HISTORY OF THE ROBINS. By Mrs. TRIMMER. Illustrated with Sixteen Full-page Illustrations by GIACOMELLI, engraved by Rouget, Berveiller, Whymper, Sargent, &c. Post 8vo, gilt edges. Price 3s.

IN THE WOODS. By M. K. M., Author of "The Birds We See," &c. With Thirty-four Illustrations by GIACOMELLI. Post 8vo, cloth extra. Price 2s. 6d.

SEA BIRDS, AND THE LESSONS OF THEIR LIVES. By Mrs. STEM. With Twenty-four Engravings. Foolscap 8vo, cloth, gilt edges. Price 2s.

GREAT FISHERIES OF THE WORLD DESCRIBED AND ILLUSTRATED. With numerous Engravings. Post 8vo, cloth extra. Price 3s. 6d.

THE MONSTERS OF THE DEEP, AND CURIOSITIES OF OCEAN LIFE. A Book of Anecdotes, Traditions, and Legends. With upwards of Seventy Engravings. Post 8vo, cloth extra. Price 3s. 6d.

STORIES OF THE DOG, AND HIS COUSINS THE WOLF, THE JACKAL, AND THE HYENA. With Stories Illustrating their Place in the Animal World. By Mrs. HUGH MILLER. With Thirty-four Engravings. Foolscap 8vo, cloth. Price 1s. 6d.

STORIES OF THE CAT, AND HER COUSINS THE LION, THE TIGER, AND THE LEOPARD. With Stories Illustrating their Place in the Animal World. By Mrs. HUGH MILLER. With Twenty-nine Engravings. Foolscap 8vo, cloth. Price 1s. 6d.

TALKS WITH UNCLE RICHARD ABOUT WILD ANIMALS. By Mrs. GEORGE CUPPLES. With Seventy-five Illustrations. 18mo, cloth. Price 1s. 6d.

MAMMA'S STORIES ABOUT DOMESTIC PETS. By Mrs. GEORGE CUPPLES. With Fifty-six Illustrations. 18mo, cloth. Price 1s. 6d.

IN THE FOREST; or, Pictures of Life and Scenery in the Woods of Canada. A Tale. By Mrs. TRAILL, Author of "The Canadian Crusoes," &c. With Nineteen Engravings. Post 8vo, cloth. Price 2s. 6d.

THINGS IN THE FOREST. By MARY and ELIZABETH KIRBY. With Coloured Frontispiece, and Fifty Illustrations. Royal 18mo. cloth. Price 1s. 6d.

T. NELSON AND SONS, LONDON, EDINBURGH, AND NEW YORK.

BOOKS FOR BOYS.

BY W. H. G. KINGSTON.

IN THE EASTERN SEAS; or, The Regions of the Bird of Paradise. A Tale for Boys. With One Hundred and Eleven Illustrations. Crown 8vo, cloth, richly gilt. Price 6s.

IN THE WILDS OF AFRICA. With Sixty-six Illustrations. Crown 8vo, cloth, richly gilt. Price 6s.

ROUND THE WORLD. A Tale for Boys. With Fifty-two Engravings. Crown 8vo, cloth extra. Price 5s.

OLD JACK. A Sea Tale. With Sixty Engravings. Crown 8vo, cloth extra. Price 5s.

MY FIRST VOYAGE TO SOUTHERN SEAS. With Forty-two Engravings. Crown 8vo, cloth extra. Price 5s.

THE SOUTH SEA WHALER. A Story of the Loss of the *Champion*, and the Adventures of her Crew. With Thirty Engravings. Crown 8vo, cloth extra. Price 5s.

SAVED FROM THE SEA; or, The Loss of the " Viper," and the Adventures of her Crew in the Desert of Sahara. With Thirty-two Engravings. Crown 8vo, cloth extra. Price 5s.

THE YOUNG RAJAH. A Story of Indian Life and Adventure. With Forty-four Engravings. Crown 8vo, cloth. Price 5s.

THE WANDERERS; or, Adventures in the Wilds of Trinidad and up the Orinoco. With Thirty-one Engravings. Crown 8vo, cloth. Price 5s.

TWICE LOST. A Story of Shipwreck, and Adventure in the Wilds of Australia. With Forty-six Engravings. Crown 8vo, cloth. Price 5s.

THE YOUNG LLANERO. A Story of War and Wild Life in Venezuela. With Forty-four Engravings. Crown 8vo, cloth. Price 5s.

IN THE ROCKY MOUNTAINS. A Tale of Adventure. With Forty-one Engravings. Post 8vo, cloth. Price 3s. 6d.

IN NEW GRANADA; or, Heroes and Patriots. A Tale for Boys. With numerous Engravings. Post 8vo, cloth. Price 3s. 6d.

AFAR IN THE FOREST. A Tale of Settler Life in North America. With Forty-one Full-page Engravings. Post 8vo, cloth extra. Price 3s. 6d.

STORIES OF THE SAGACITY OF ANIMALS. With Sixty Illustrations by HARRISON WEIR. Post 8vo, cloth. Price 3s. 6d.

ILLUSTRATED EDITIONS.

THE LIFE AND STRANGE ADVENTURES OF ROBINSON CRUSOE, OF YORK, MARINER. Written by Himself. Carefully Reprinted from the Original Edition. With an Introductory Memoir of Daniel De Foe, a Memoir of Alexander Selkirk, an Account of Peter Serrano, and other Interesting Additions. Illustrated with upwards of Seventy Engravings by KEELEY HALSWELLE. With a Portrait of De Foe, a Map of Crusoe's Island, De Foe's Tomb, Facsimiles of Original Title-Pages, &c., &c. Crown 8vo, cloth extra. Price 3s. 6d.

THE SWISS FAMILY ROBINSON; or, Adventures of a Shipwrecked Family on a Desolate Island. *Unabridged.* With upwards of Three Hundred Engravings. Crown 8vo, cloth extra. Price 3s. 6d.

T. NELSON AND SONS, LONDON, EDINBURGH, AND NEW YORK.

BOOKS FOR BOYS.

TALES OF ADVENTURE AND ENTERPRISE.

BY R. M. BALLANTYNE.

HUDSON BAY; or, Everyday Life in the Wilds of North America. With Forty-six Engravings. Crown 8vo, cloth extra. Price 5s.

THE YOUNG FUR-TRADERS. A Tale of the Far North. With Illustrations. Post 8vo, cloth. Price 3s. 6d.

UNGAVA. A Tale of Esquimaux Land. With Illustrations. Post 8vo, cloth. Price 3s. 6d.

THE CORAL ISLAND. A Tale of the Pacific. With Illustrations. Post 8vo, cloth. Price 3s. 6d.

MARTIN RATTLER; or, A Boy's Adventures in the Forests of Brazil. With Illustrations. Post 8vo, cloth. Price 3s. 6d.

THE DOG CRUSOE AND HIS MASTER. A Tale of the Western Prairies. With Illustrations. Post 8vo, cloth. Price 3s. 6d.

THE GORILLA HUNTERS. A Tale of Western Africa. With Illustrations. Post 8vo, cloth. Price 3s. 6d.

THE WORLD OF ICE; or, Adventures in the Polar Regions. With Engravings. Post 8vo, cloth. Price 3s. 6d.

THE OCEAN AND ITS WONDERS. With Sixty Engravings. Post 8vo, cloth extra. Price 5s.

TALES FOR THE HOME CIRCLE.

LOOK AT THE BRIGHT SIDE. A Tale for the Young. By JOANNA H. MATTHEWS, Author of "Little Sunbeams." Post 8vo, cloth extra. Price 2s. 6d.

ISABEL'S SECRET. By the Author of "The Story of a Happy Little Girl." Foolscap 8vo, cloth. Price 3s.

THE STORY OF A HAPPY LITTLE GIRL. By the Author of "Isabel's Secret." Royal 18mo. Price 1s. 6d.

THE BASKET OF FLOWERS. A Tale for the Young. With Coloured Frontispiece and numerous Engravings. Royal 18mo. Price 1s. 6d.

"OUR FATHER WHICH ART IN HEAVEN." A Story Illustrative of the Lord's Prayer. By a CLERGYMAN'S WIDOW. With Coloured Frontispiece and Sixteen Engravings. Royal 18mo. Price 1s.

T. NELSON AND SONS, LONDON, EDINBURGH, AND NEW YORK.

TALES OF DOMESTIC LIFE.

THE GOLDEN CROWN SERIES OF BOOKS FOR THE YOUNG.

ADA AND GERTY; or, Hand in Hand Heavenward.
A Tale. By LOUISA M. GRAY. Post 8vo, cloth extra. Price 3s. 6d.

NELLY'S TEACHERS, AND WHAT THEY LEARNED.
A Tale for the Young. By KATE THORNE. Price 3s. 6d.

STEPPING HEAVENWARD. A Tale of Home Life. By the Author of "The Flower of the Family." Post 8vo, cloth. Price 2s. 6d.

BY THE SAME AUTHOR.

EVER HEAVENWARD; or, A Mother's Influence. Post 8vo, cloth. Price 2s. 6d.

THE FLOWER OF THE FAMILY. A Tale of Domestic Life. Post 8vo, cloth. Price 2s. 6d.

HERMAN; or, The Little Preacher; LITTLE THREADS; and THE STORY LIZZIE TOLD. With Four Illustrations Printed in Colours. Post 8vo, cloth extra. Price 2s. 6d.

WORKS BY THE REV. RICHARD NEWTON, D.D.

IN BIBLE LANDS. A Narrative of Travel in the East. With Sixty Engravings. Price 3s. 6d.

PEBBLES FROM THE BROOK. A Book for the Young. With Eighteen Full-page Illustrations. Price 2s.

THE KING'S HIGHWAY; or, Illustrations of the Commandments. With Numerous Engravings. Post 8vo. Price 2s.

NATURE'S WONDERS. With Fifty-three Engravings. Post 8vo, cloth extra. Price 2s. 6d.

THE GIANTS, AND HOW TO FIGHT THEM. By the Rev. RICHARD NEWTON, D.D. With Coloured Frontispiece and numerous Engravings. Royal 18mo. Price 1s.

NEW EDITIONS OF STANDARD WORKS.

JOSEPHUS THE WORKS OF FLAVIUS JOSEPHUS Translated by WHISTON. With Thirty-six Illustrations. 8vo. 4s. 6d.

BUNYAN'S PILGRIM'S PROGRESS. With Twenty-four Illustrations. Post 8vo, cloth. Price 2s.

ANNALS OF THE POOR. By the Rev. LEGH RICHMOND. Royal 18mo. Price 1s.

GAUSSEN'S WORLD'S BIRTHDAY. Illustrated. Foolscap 8vo. Price 2s. 6d.

FAVOURITE NARRATIVES FOR THE CHRISTIAN HOUSEHOLD. Containing: THE SHEPHERD OF SALISBURY PLAIN; THE DAIRYMAN'S DAUGHTER; THE YOUNG COTTAGER, &c. Post 8vo, cloth. Price 2s.

T. NELSON AND SONS, LONDON, EDINBURGH, AND NEW YORK.

NEW SERIES OF PRIZES AND PRESENTATION BOOKS.

THE EUPHRATES AND THE TIGRIS. A Narrative of Discovery and Adventure. With a Description of the Ruins of Babylon and Nineveh. With Eighteen Full-page Illustrations. Post 8vo, cloth extra. Price 2s.

MOUNT SINAI, PETRA, AND THE DESERT. Described and Illustrated. With Twenty-three Full-page Illustrations. Post 8vo, cloth extra. Price 2s.

THE JORDAN AND ITS VALLEY, AND THE DEAD SEA. By the Author of "The Mediterranean Illustrated." Forty-five Engravings. Price 2s.

THE STORY OF IDA PFEIFFER AND HER TRAVELS IN MANY LANDS. With Twenty-five Full-page Engravings. Post 8vo, cloth extra. Price 2s.

THE STORY OF THE LIFE AND TRAVELS OF ALEXANDER VON HUMBOLDT. With Twenty-seven Full-page Engravings. Post 8vo, cloth extra. Price 2s.

THE AMAZON AND ITS WONDERS. With Illustrations of Animal and Vegetable Life in the Amazonian Forest. With Twenty-six Full-page Engravings. Post 8vo, cloth extra. Price 2s.

IN THE FAR EAST. A Narrative of Exploration and Adventure in Cochin-China, Cambodia, Laos, and Siam. With Twenty-eight Full-page Engravings. Post 8vo, cloth extra. Price 2s.

GIBRALTAR AND ITS SIEGES. With a Description of its Natural Features. With Eighteen Full-page Illustrations. Post 8vo, cloth extra. Price 2s.

CALIFORNIA AND ITS WONDERS. By the Rev. John Todd, D.D. A New Edition, carefully revised and brought down to the present time. With Seventeen Full-page Illustrations. Price 2s.

TEMPERANCE TALES.

FIRST PRIZE TEMPERANCE TALE, 1879.

SOUGHT AND SAVED. A Tale. By Miss M. A. Paull, Author of "Tim's Troubles; or, Tried and True," "The Vivians of Woodiford," &c. With Six Engravings. Post 8vo, cloth extra. Price 3s. 6d.
  * To this Tale was awarded the FIRST PRIZE (£100) offered by the United Kingdom Band of Hope Union.

SECOND PRIZE TEMPERANCE TALE, 1879.

LIONEL FRANKLIN'S VICTORY. By E. Van Sommer. With Six Engravings. Post 8vo, cloth extra. Price 3s. 6d.
  * This Tale secured the SECOND PRIZE (£50).

FRANK OLDFIELD; or, Lost and Found. By the Rev. T. P. Wilson, M.A. With Five Engravings. Post 8vo, cloth. Price 3s. 6d.

TIM'S TROUBLES; or, Tried and True. By M. A. Paull. With Five Engravings. Post 8vo, cloth. Price 3s. 6d.

TRUE TO HIS COLOURS; or, The Life that Wears Best. By the Rev. T. P. Wilson, M.A., Vicar of Pavenham, Author of "Frank Oldfield; or, Lost and Found." Illustrated. Post 8vo, cloth. Price 3s. 6d.

T. NELSON AND SONS, LONDON, EDINBURGH, AND NEW YORK.

BOOKS OF PRECEPT AND EXAMPLE.

LIVES MADE SUBLIME BY FAITH AND WORKS.
By the Rev. Robert Steel, D.D., Author of "Doing Good," &c. Post 8vo, cloth. Price 2s. 6d.

DOING GOOD; or, The Christian in Walks of Usefulness.
Illustrated by Examples. By the Rev. Robert Steel, D.D. Post 8vo, cloth extra. Gilt edges. Price 3s. 6d.

WILLING HEARTS AND READY HANDS; or, The Labours and Triumphs of Earnest Women. By Joseph Johnson. Post 8vo, cloth extra. Price 3s. 6d.

THE THRESHOLD OF LIFE. A Book of Illustrations and Lessons for the Encouragement and Counsel of Youth. By W. H. Davenport Adams. With Six Engravings. Post 8vo, cloth. Price 2s. 6d.

SEED-TIME AND HARVEST; or, Sow Well and Reap Well. A Book for the Young. By the late Rev. W. K. Tweedie, D.D. Post 8vo, cloth. Price 2s. 6d.

SUCCESS IN LIFE. A Book for Young Men. Post 8vo, cloth extra. Price 3s.

THE BOY MAKES THE MAN. A Book of Example and Encouragement for Boys. With Coloured Frontispiece, and numerous Engravings. Royal 18mo, cloth. Price 1s. 6d.

STORIES OF NOBLE LIVES.
EACH WITH COLOURED FRONTISPIECE.
Royal 18mo, cloth. Price 1s.

STORY OF AUDUBON, the Naturalist.

STORY OF HOWARD, the Philanthropist.

STORY OF PALISSY, the Potter.

STORY OF JOHN SMEATON and the Eddystone Lighthouse.

STORY OF DR. SCORESBY, the Arctic Navigator.

STORY OF CYRUS FIELD, the Projector of the Atlantic Cable.

STORY OF BENVENUTO CELLINI, the Italian Goldsmith.

STORY OF SIR HUMPHREY DAVY and the Invention of the Safety Lamp.

STORY OF GALILEO, the Astronomer of Pisa.

STORY OF THE HERSCHELS.

STORY OF THE STEPHENSONS, Father and Son.

STORY OF SAMUEL BUDGETT, the Successful Merchant.

T. NELSON AND SONS, LONDON, EDINBURGH, AND NEW YORK.

TRAVEL AND RESEARCH IN BIBLE LANDS.

THE LAND AND THE BOOK; or, Biblical Illustrations Drawn from the Manners and Customs, the Scenes and Scenery of the Holy Land. By the Rev. W. M. Thomson, D.D. Crown 8vo, 718 pages. With Twelve Coloured Illustrations, and One Hundred and Twenty Woodcuts. Price 7s. 6d., cloth.

THE GIANT CITIES OF BASHAN, AND SYRIA'S HOLY PLACES. By Professor Porter, Author of "Murray's Handbook to Syria and Palestine." With Eight Beautiful Engravings. Post 8vo, cloth extra. Price 7s. 6d.

BOOKS OF VOYAGES, TRAVEL, AND ADVENTURE.

RECENT POLAR VOYAGES. A Record of Adventure and Discovery. From the Search after Franklin to the Voyage of the *Alert* and the *Discovery* (1875-76). With Sixty-two Engravings. Crown 8vo, cloth. Price 5s.

GREAT SHIPWRECKS. A Record of Perils and Disasters at Sea, 1544-1877. With as fine Engravings. Crown 8vo, cloth. Price 5s.

KANE'S ARCTIC EXPLORATIONS. The Second Grinnell Expedition in Search of Sir John Franklin. With Sixty Woodcuts. Crown 8vo, cloth extra. Price 5s.

WRECKED ON A REEF; or, Twenty Months in the Auckland Isles. A True Story of Shipwreck, Adventure, and Suffering. With 40 Illustrations. Post 8vo, cloth extra. Price 3s. 6d.

ON THE NILE. A Story of Family Travel and Adventure in the Land of Egypt. By Sarah K. Hunt. With Sixteen Engravings. Post 8vo, cloth extra. Price 3s.

ROUND THE WORLD. A Story of Travel compiled from the Narrative of Ida Pfeiffer. By D. Murray Smith. With Thirty-six Engravings. Post 8vo, cloth. Price 2s.

PICTURES OF TRAVEL IN FAR-OFF LANDS. A Companion to the Study of Geography. Central America. With Fifty Engravings. Post 8vo, cloth. Price 2s.

PICTURES OF TRAVEL IN FAR-OFF LANDS. South America. With Fifty Engravings. Post 8vo, cloth. Price 2s.

HOME AMID THE SNOW; or, Warm Hearts in Cold Regions. By Captain Charles Ede, R.N. With Twenty-eight Engravings. Royal 18mo, cloth. Price 1s. 6d.

THE FOREST, THE JUNGLE, AND THE PRAIRIE; or, Tales of Adventure and Enterprise in Pursuit of Wild Animals. With Numerous Engravings. Post 8vo, cloth. Price 2s. 6d.

SCENES WITH THE HUNTER AND THE TRAPPER IN MANY LANDS. Stories of Adventure with Wild Animals. With numerous Engravings. Post 8vo, cloth. Price 2s. 6d.

DR. KANE, THE ARCTIC HERO. A Narrative of his Adventures and Explorations in the Polar Regions. By M. Jones. With Thirty-five Engravings. Post 8vo, cloth. Price 2s.

THE CHILDREN ON THE PLAINS. A Story of Travel and Adventure in the Great Prairies of North America. By the Author of "The Babes in the Basket." With Sixteen Illustrations. Royal 18mo, cloth. Price 1s. 6d.

T. NELSON AND SONS, LONDON, EDINBURGH, AND NEW YORK.

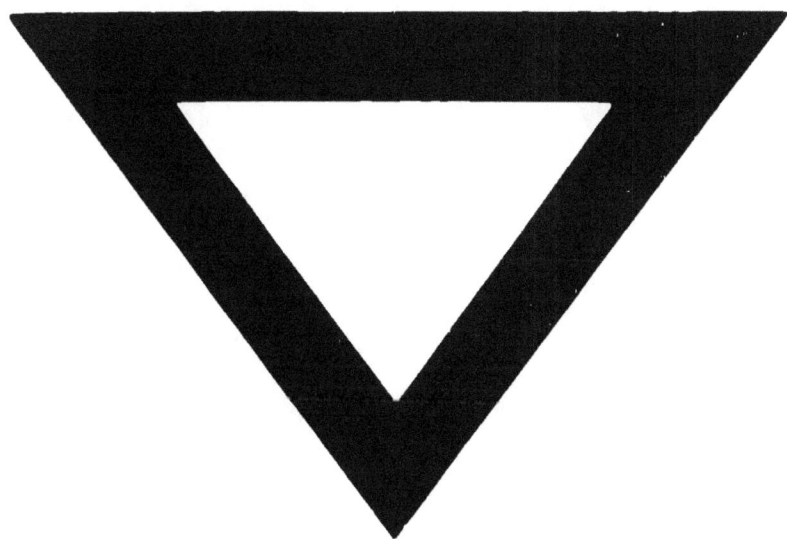

www.ingramcontent.com/pod-product-compliance
Lightning Source LLC
Chambersburg PA
CBHW031815270326
41932CB00008B/430